introduction to the fourth edition

This expanded and fully revised edition has been produced as a direct result of the changes in the BTEC National Award and the increasing importance of the GNVQ specifications. It is written specifically for the new BTEC National Diploma/Certificate 'Financial Resources' Core Module and for the 'Financial Resources' Unit of the GNVQ Level 3 Business specification.

Osborne Books has liaised closely with BTEC, NCVQ and with a number of Further Education Colleges to produce teaching material which suits the needs of the curriculum designers *and* the lecturers and teachers. Our thanks are due to those who have advised and answered our detailed questionnaires.

This new edition covers six areas:
* personal finance
* business finance
* financial statements of business, social and public sector organisations
* business planning and budgeting
* financial record keeping (including double-entry book-keeping)
* applying information technology to financial activities

Each section is designed to stand alone so that lecturers and teachers may use the material to support 'block' and integrated activities. Separate assignments have been retained throughout the book to reinforce the learning process. The sections are also designed to lead on to other option units such as 'Accounting Procedures' and 'Financial Planning and Control'. The section on book-keeping has been included as it is considered an appropriate element of any course in Finance, and is also a useful introduction to 'Accounting Procedures'.

Considerable emphasis has been placed in this new edtion of *Finance* on the use of Information Technology. At the end of the book there are separate chapters giving practical instructions on the use of computer accounting packages and spreadsheets. The use of spreadsheets is also integrated into the text and student activities elsewhere in the book.

Lastly, we would like to stress, as we have done in the past, that this text has been written by lecturers for lecturers, and is intended to be an essentially *practical* book. Osborne Books will always welcome your views, criticisms and suggestions.

Michael Fardon and David Cox
Worcester

Summer 1992

acknowledgements

The authors wish to thank Jean Cox for her invaluable assistance in the production of the text in its present form. They are also grateful to the following for their advice and expertise: John Colvin and Roger Petheram of Worcester College of Technology, Paul Russell of Birmingham City Council, the Cheltenham and Gloucester Building Society, the Department of Trade and Industry, Hereford and Worcester TEC, National Westminster Bank plc, the advisory staff at BTEC and NCVQ, and the numerous lecturers who answered questionnaires and discussed the new course specifications with the authors. Thanks are due to the following for permission to reproduce copyright material: Hereford and Worcester County Council, National Westminster Bank plc, The Royal Bank of Scotland plc.   Thanks are also due to the Sage Group plc who kindly allowed their software to be used in the practical illustration of computer accounting, and to Cathy Fardon for the cover design.

the authors

Michael Fardon, was born and educated in Worcester.   After completing academic studies at London University, he worked for Midland Bank plc, where he was involved in the areas of personal and small business finance as well as specialising in International Corporate Finance for a number of years. His publications include banking textbooks and other titles from Osborne Books. He currently writes and lectures on a freelance basis.

David Cox is a Senior Lecturer in the Management and Professional Studies Department at Worcester College of Technology. He worked for Midland Bank plc for a number of years, and has considerable teaching experience, having taught students over a wide range of levels. He is also a qualified accountant and the author of a number of accounting and banking textbooks. He is co-author with Michael Fardon of *Accounting* and *Business Record Keeping*, and author of *Business Accounts* published by Osborne Books.

contents

section five
financial record keeping

section six
applying information technology

index

introduction to assignments

Assignment work forms a major part of assessment. Although the emphasis is increasingly for integrated assignments, the nine 'Finance' assignments in this text have been included for two reasons: first they reinforce the learning process by developing the Common Skills, and secondly lecturers have asked for their inclusion. The assignments are ready for use, but as always, a certain amount of negotiation will have to take place between lecturer and students over issues such as group size, length of written work specified, time scale and resources which are available. Lecturers who have used the third edition of *Finance* should note that the former Assignments 'Southtown Supplies' and 'The Severn Social Club' appear here as Student Activities on pages 93 and 175.

section one
personal finance

In this section we look at the way in which an individual can manage his or her own finances. This is an important area of study because

- the ability to manage one's own financial resources involves the skill of self-development which forms part of your studies
- many of the principles relating to personal finance – such as borrowing and budgeting – also apply to business finance

In the next three chapters we will look at

- income – earnings and borrowings, and types of expenditure
- budgeting – planning on what you can afford to spend and when you can spend it
- personal taxation – how you are taxed and the type of documentation that you encounter when earning

1 Personal finance – income and expenditure

introduction

"Where shall I get the money to buy the things I need?
Can I borrow for what I want to buy?
How can I cope with all the bills when they come at once?
How much can I afford to spend on holiday?
Can I afford to go on holiday?"

Questions such as these are often asked by people who are concerned or worried about personal finance. What is required is a systematic way of evaluating one's financial resources and a method of managing those resources, in other words, *financial planning:*

Personal financial planning may be defined as a method of making the most efficient and sensible use of financial resources which are earned, saved and borrowed.

Personal financial planning involves the balancing of two variable factors

• income

• expenditure

If income exceeds expenditure, all is well. If expenditure exceeds income, problems arise.

In this chapter we will examine

• the various sources of income

• the choices that exist for expenditure

We will also look at how an individual can borrow to finance expenditure, and we will compare the cost of borrowing from different sources.

sources of personal finance

earnings

A part-time job is often the first experience a person will have of earning money. The job is likely to be paid by the hour, by commission, or by the number of items dealt with (piecework). Whatever the nature of the job, it provides a useful source of income in addition to any parental allowance. The extra money will make it necessary for the person earning to make a number of straightforward financial and personal decisions.

Take for example a student working during the holidays in the telephone answering department of a busy mail order firm. He or she will work, say, six hours a day during the week on a basic hourly rate. This provides extra cash which can be either spent or saved. The decision will not be difficult to make. A complication might arise, however, if the student is offered the option of a four hour shift on a Sunday at double the normal hourly rate. A number of questions will then need to be asked:

"Do I need the extra money?
What shall I do with the money? Save it or spend it?
Do I work the extra unsociable hours? Is it worth it? Will it spoil my social life?"

For anyone who works full-time, whether as a shop assistant or as a managing director, the same basic questions have to be answered. The following underlying principles will then apply:

* the harder the person is prepared to work, generally speaking, the more he or she earns
* the more the person earns, the more choices he or she has for spending or saving
* if a person works excessively hard, the greater the cost to health, social and family life
* the more the person earns, the more will be payable in tax (see Chapter 3, *Personal Taxation*)

Clearly, the individual needs to make a number of choices to dictate his or her lifestyle: it is up to the individual to decide.

savings

We have already mentioned that earnings can be saved. It should be mentioned that savings can be spent! It is a traditional viewpoint that if you want to buy something you should save up to buy it. Savings can therefore form a useful source of income. Savings should generally be used to purchase a specific item rather than be frittered away on day-to-day expenditure. As you will have gathered, personal finance involves making many decisions. When you want to buy an item you will be faced with two choices:

* buy now and use your savings - if the need for the item is urgent
* buy the item now and *borrow* for the purchase

You will see that the last option introduces another source of money: borrowing. This will be dealt with in detail in the next section. You should note now that deciding between using savings or borrowing for an item involves another factor: *interest*, the cost of money. As an exercise, investigate your local bank or building society and find out

* the level of interest rates **for** borrowing - ie what you have to pay to borrow
* the level of interest rates for saving - ie what you would receive on your savings

Borrowing rates are always higher than savings rates, so it follows that it is more expensive for you to borrow than to use your savings; in short, you *pay* more in interest than you would *lose* in interest on your savings if you used them to buy the item. This may be sufficient argument to make your decision for you!

borrowing

You may be fortunate enough to be able to borrow from a friend or a relative, in which case you may negotiate favourable terms such as a low interest rate (or *no* interest rate) and a long period in which to repay the money. More often than not, however, you will approach a financial institution or a retailer for finance. A wide range of commercial organisations offer finance to the individual:

- *banks:* overdrafts, personal loans, mortgages
- *building societies*: mortgages, personal loans, overdrafts
- *Finance Houses:* personal loans and hire purchase
- *credit card companies:* extended credit on credit cards
- *retail stores:* credit cards, hire purchase (through Finance Houses), credit terms

Students are strongly recommended to obtain leaflets from these organisations describing the various schemes on offer. These schemes will be explained in more detail later in the chapter (pages 8 to 12).

expenditure

Income can either be used for expenditure or for saving.

Expenditure is normally classed as either *capital* expenditure or as *revenue* expenditure, a distinction also used when dealing with business finance.

capital expenditure

If you buy a specific item for use in the long term (for example a car or a house), this is *capital expenditure*. Normally you would borrow for this type of expenditure by means of a loan with fixed repayments over a long period of time (for example by means of a personal loan, or a mortgage).

revenue expenditure

You buy many items which you will use up in the short term (food, travel, entertainment, giving to charity); this is *revenue expenditure*. At times of heavy spending you may need to borrow and repay in the short term (overdraft, credit card).

savings

return on your savings: interest received

Money under the mattress earns nothing. Money invested in a bank or a building society earns interest, representing the cost to you of being without your money for a period of time. You should maximise this return, as it represents future purchasing power.

Interest earned = Amount invested x $\frac{interest\ rate}{100}$ x period in years

the real rate of interest

The inflation rate is the percentage by which money loses its purchasing power over the period of a year. For example, if you have £100 at the beginning of the year and the inflation rate is 5%, you would need £105 at the end of the year in order to maintain the same purchasing power. Inflation can clearly erode the value of your savings. A *real interest rate* is the rate of return on your savings adjusted for inflation. It can be approximated by the following formula:

Real interest rate = Actual interest rate less inflation rate.

If the real interest rate is positive, your savings are maintaining their purchasing power; if it is negative, your savings are declining in real value and you may wish to spend the money instead.

motives for saving and investment

An individual normally saves or invests for one of two reasons:

- for a specific item, as already mentioned in this chapter
- for a 'rainy day', for the unforeseen event

In both cases it is in the individual's interest to find out the highest return, either in the form of interest paid or the capital growth of the investment scheme.

schemes paying interest

The financial services industry is always bringing out new schemes which pay interest and you are advised to investigate:

- bank deposit and savings account schemes
- building society accounts
- National Savings Ordinary and Investment Accounts and Income Bonds

When examining the interest paid on these schemes you will note that the interest rate payable may be quoted in a number of different ways, because of the income tax that is normally payable on interest received (see Chapter 3 for further details about income tax). The two common ways of referring to interest rates are:

- gross interest rate – interest rate *before* deduction of tax
- net interest rate – interest rate *after* deduction of tax

Bank and building society schemes normally deduct Income Tax before you receive the interest. If you are not liable to pay income tax you can arrange with the institution by filling in a form to receive interest gross (without deduction of tax). This is advisable if you are a full-time student not paying tax!

National Savings schemes, on the other hand, do not normally deduct the tax from the interest, and leave you to settle with the tax authorities the amount (if any) that you owe. Clearly, if you are a student and do not pay tax, the National Savings schemes are particularly attractive.

All the above schemes are suitable for money which will be deposited for a short time, or may be needed at short notice; they are said to be *liquid* deposits, and are quite unsuitable if you are looking for *capital growth*.

capital growth schemes

If you wish to invest your money for a long period of time you may well be looking for a scheme which will make your money grow in value over the years. Examples of this situation include parents investing money for their young children which the children can use when they leave home, and married couples saving for their retirement.

Many financial institutions and National Savings offer longer term investment opportunities. You should investigate the following:

- *stocks and shares* (available through banks and stockbrokers as direct investments or through Personal Equity Plan [PEP] schemes)
- *unit trusts* – investment in funds which invest in stocks and shares and other financial markets (available through banks and adverts in the financial press and investment magazines)
- *National Savings schemes* (information available at Post Offices)
- *endowment life assurance policies* (information from insurance brokers and the financial press)
- *Tax Exempt Special Savings Accounts (TESSAs)* available from banks and building societies, offering five year, tax free saving

Now examine the summary diagram (fig 1.1) on the next page.

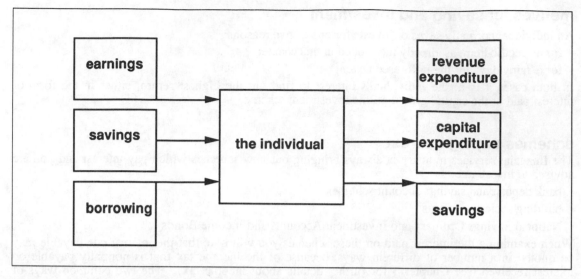

Fig 1.1   Personal finance – income and expenditure

borrowing

We will examine borrowing from financial institutions in terms of
- short-term borrowing (for up to 12 months) and
- long-term borrowing (for over 12 months)

First, however, it is necessary to establish a definition of *interest* and *APR*, and to explain the legal situation relating to borrowing by the under-18s.

interest: the cost of borrowing

Any commercial organisation lending money or granting credit (ie allowing you to repay what you owe over an extended period) will charge you for the use of the money by the addition of an *interest* amount to the sum that you repay. Any loan or credit therefore involves:
- the *principal* – the amount of the finance provided
- the *interest* – the added cost of providing that finance

The amount of interest is dependent on the prevailing *rate of interest*.

An interest rate is the amount of interest expressed as a percentage of the amount borrowed over a period of time, usually a year ('per annum', often abbreviated to 'p.a.').

The formula for calculating an interest amount from a given interest rate is as follows:

Interest = Amount borrowed x interest rate x period in years
100

For example, if you borrow £1,000 for a year at an interest rate of 10%, the calculation will be:

Interest = £1,000 x 10 x 1 = £100
100

Clearly, the higher the interest rate, the higher the cost of borrowing.

annual percentage rate (APR): the cost of borrowing

The Consumer Credit Act 1974 states that loans and credit (excluding house mortgages and overdrafts) up to £15,000 to individuals must be documented in the form of a *Regulated Agreement,* ie a loan or credit agreement which clearly sets out the terms of the finance granted, and which does not mislead the individual by using obscure language or, quite literally, small print.

The Consumer Credit Act also requires that the cost of borrowing must be clearly stated as an Annual Percentage Rate *(APR)* to enable the consumer to compare the cost of credit from different institutions.

Annual Percentage Rate (APR) is the total annual cost to the borrower in interest and fees, expressed as a percentage of the amount borrowed

It is important to note that *APR is not an interest rate.* The reason for this is that it also includes, as a cost, the fees which are sometimes payable when a consumer first signs a loan or credit agreement.

a legal note: borrowing by the under-18s

An important legal point is that under the Minors Contracts Act 1987, any person under the age of 18 (a 'minor') is not legally bound by contracts for money borrowed; these contracts are unenforceable, although in certain cases a minor could be taken to court to enforce return of the money, or goods bought with it. This is the reason why documents offering loans and credit often exclude applicants under the age of 18. If you are a minor and wish to borrow, your parents may need to sign a formal legal document, *a guarantee,* accepting liability for your debt, stating that they will repay the debt if you do not. If this document is signed, the institution can then rely on your parents if you do not repay the borrowing.

when is short term finance needed?

The need for finance can be over differing periods of time and for large or small amounts. We will first look at the needs for short term borrowing.

Borrowing for a short period of time may be needed
- in an emergency (if your car breaks down)
- at a time of heavy spending (Christmas)
- at the end of the month before your salary is received
- when money is needed but not available immediately (eg in a building society fixed term deposit)

The two most important sources of short term borrowing are a *bank overdraft* and the use of a *credit card.*

forms of short term borrowing

bank overdraft

An overdraft is borrowing on a bank account up to an agreed limit; interest is only charged on the amount borrowed.

Overdrafts are very useful for occasional or periodic borrowing on current account. Overdrafts for personal (as opposed to business) customers are charged at a rate of approximately 5% added to the bank's *Base Rate.* Base Rate is an advertised fixed rate, set and varied periodically by the major banks, who use it as a *base* for working out their interest rates for borrowers, who are charged an agreed percentage above Base Rate. *No-one ever borrows at Base Rate.* Overdraft interest is

normally calculated on a daily basis on the amount that is borrowed and charged to the borrower's current account quarterly (ie every three months). Some financial institutions also charge fixed fees, either an arrangement fee, or in some cases a fixed monthly or quarterly fee. Overdrafts may be arranged in a number of ways:
- an overdraft for a specific purpose (a holiday, a wedding, a purchase)
- as part of a special bank account package – some accounts have a 'built in' automatic overdraft

how to apply for an overdraft

Different types of overdraft are arranged in different ways. If you need a bank overdraft for a specific purpose, you should apply to your bank for an interview. If the bank is happy that you will be able to repay the borrowing, they will agree a *borrowing limit* on your current account, ie an amount up to which you can overdraw. You are then free to issue cheques as and when you wish, subject only to the agreed limit. An agreement letter setting out the terms of the overdraft will be drawn up and signed by the bank. If you open a bank account with a 'built in' overdraft limit, all you need to do is to complete the application form which will ask for a number of personal details to enable the bank to assess your creditworthiness (your ability to repay the credit). If you are allowed to open the account you will be authorised to overdraw the account to a specific limit.

credit cards

Credit cards are plastic cards issued by companies owned by the major banks, or by retail stores through these companies. Credit cards enable the holder to purchase goods and services and pay for them at a later date.

Cards issued by bank-owned companies include Visa and Access; these cards may be used to make purchases at numerous outlets including shops, garages, restaurants and theatres. Store cards enable the holder to make purchases only in that store or group of stores. A Habitat card, for example, may be used in Habitat, Mothercare, BHS and other stores owned by the Storehouse group.

A person uses a credit card to make purchases of goods over a period of time up to a total maximum amount, or credit limit. This limit is determined by the card company, and is often initially 10% of the cardholder's salary. The element of credit enters because the user does not have to pay straightaway. He or she will, in due course, be sent a monthly statement by the card company detailing all the purchases made, and asking for a payment to be made within 25 days. Payment may be made either by post, by means of a bank giro credit attached to the bottom of the statement, or by direct debit (automatic transfer) from the cardholder's bank account. Interest is normally charged on the card, and an annual fee is also usually payable. Credit cards are an easy and flexible way of obtaining credit: 'Buy now, pay later'.

how to apply for a credit card

Obtain from a bank or a store an application form similar to that illustrated in Fig. 1.2 on the opposite page. Complete the form and hand it to the appropriate bank or store. If the credit card company considers you creditworthy – it will judge this from details of your salary, status, and bank record on the form – you will be sent a card by post or asked to collect it from the bank or store.

personal loan

A personal loan is
- for a fixed amount (normally up to £10,000)
- over a fixed period (normally up to five years)
- at a fixed interest rate for the life of the loan
- repaid by fixed monthly instalments

The main characteristic of the personal loan is that the repayments are *fixed:* the borrower knows exactly *how much* he or she has to repay and *when*. To help the borrower, lending institutions usually provide repayment tables setting out the amount of the monthly instalments for loans of differing amounts and periods. On the opposite page (fig 1.2) is an illustration of an application form for a personal loan.

To National Westminster Bank PLC
Personal Loan Proposal
(Please complete all sections in **block capitals**)

	NYCHAVON	Branch

Surname	JONES
Surname	—
Address	102 ONSLOW GARDENS WOODBURY WORCS. Postcode WS2 8PZ

Mr/Mrs/Miss/Ms Forenames	ANNE CATHERINE
Mr/Mrs/Miss/Ms Forenames	—
Date of Birth/s	9 JULY 1957
Home Telephone Number	WOODBURY 691

Period at present address — **5** Years

Marital status — Married/Single/Other

Residential status — Owner/Tenant/With Parents/Other

If you own your residence give — Date of purchase **20.1.85** Cost £ **49,500**

Mortgage outstanding £ **29,500**

Occupation — **TEACHER**

Name and address of employer — **HEREFORD & WORCESTER COUNTY COUNCIL COUNTY HALL, SPETCHLEY ROAD WORCESTER**

Length of service with present employer — **12** Years **9** Months

If less than 3 years with present employer give time with previous employer — **—** Years **—** Months

Is your job pensionable? — Yes/No

Net Income (include overtime) after deduction of PAYE, National Insurance Stamps etc

	Monthly		Weekly	
	Self	Spouse	Self	Spouse
	£ 850	£ —	£ —	£ —

Is your salary paid direct to a bank? — Yes/No

Cheque Card held? — Yes/No

Give the name of Credit Cards held if any — ACCESS

Details of existing Bank Account(s)
(a) Type of account held — Current/Deposit/Other/None

(b) Bank/Branch where account maintained — NAT. WEST. Bank NYCHAVON Branch

(c) Period account maintained — 16 YEARS

The total cost of the transaction will be approximately — £ 6000

and the balance is to be found from — PERSONAL SAVINGS AT WESTMID BUILDING SOCIETY

Amount of loan required — £ 2,000

I/We require a loan for the purchase of (give brief details). — FORD FIESTA — NEW VEHICLE. (PRESENT VEHICLE NO LONGER SERVICEABLE)

Repayable by **36** monthly instalments

I/We require Personal Loan Protector Cover to apply to the first named person above (Delete if not required.)

I/We confirm that the above information is correct to the best of my/our knowledge and undertake to furnish the Bank if required, with evidence of expenditure.

Signature(s) of applicant(s) — *A. C. Jones*

Date **4 JULY 19-3**

For Bank use only	
PNL	
C/A	
S	
I/V	

Fig 1.2 A Personal Loan Application Form

how to apply for a personal loan

It is necessary to complete a Personal Loan application form (see fig. 1.2), obtainable, for example, from a bank or a building society. The form will ask for details such as occupation, salary, property owned (if any) and other credit commitments. These details will be processed ('credit-scored') by the lender's staff (or by computer) to decide whether or not you are suitable for the granting of a loan. You will be seen to be more creditworthy if you:

- own your house
- are in a stable job
- have a regular salary paid to the bank

You may or may not have an interview with a manager or other member of staff. You will be given a decision very rapidly (often the same day) so that you may, if successful, buy the item you want without delay. The agreement to lend will be documented in a formal Loan Agreement required by the Consumer Credit Act, and signed by both lender and borrower.

instalment credit: hire purchase (HP)

A Hire Purchase credit, like a Personal Loan, enables an individual to obtain consumer goods, and to repay the cost of the item over a period of time, normally up to five years.

The difference between a Personal Loan and an HP agreement is that with HP ownership of the goods does not pass to the borrower until repayment is complete.

A deposit is payable when the finance is arranged. If you fall behind with your repayments, but have paid off a third of the amount owed, the goods cannot be repossessed. Hire Purchase is usually offered by retail outlets who have an arrangement with a Finance Company to offer 'point of sale' credit.

how to apply for hire purchase

The purchaser applies for credit to the Finance House via the supplier of the goods, who also processes the paperwork. In this triangular relationship of purchaser, supplier and Finance House, the borrower rarely comes into contact with the lender.

Case Study: purchasing a video camera

Situation

You wish to buy a video camera and recorder to enable you to make home movies. You have no savings but think that you may be able to afford some money out of your income each month towards the machine. By shopping around you discover that the price for a reasonable set of equipment is £750. Where could you obtain finance, and what considerations would you bear in mind when arranging it?

Solution

Assuming that you will take out some form of fixed repayment finance rather than an overdraft, the following steps should be taken:

- estimate the amount you can afford to repay each month for repayments
- by comparing the APRs of bank, building society and shop HP schemes, find the lowest APR, the cheapest source of finance.
- examine the repayment tables provided and find out if you can realistically repay the £750 within three to five years.
- if you can afford the repayments, apply for the credit and get the agreement signed as soon as possible so that you can buy the item while the price still holds

long-term finance: mortgages

The personal finance we have looked at so far has been *unsecured*. The lending institutions have provided finance on the basis of the borrower's ability to repay, ie his or her *creditworthiness:* usually the fact that there is a salary or other funds to meet repayments. A borrower may also raise *long-term* finance (25 to 30 years), normally for the purchase of a house, by giving *security*, ie by giving the lender legal rights over his or her property by means of a *mortgage*.

A mortgage is a formal legal document signed by the borrower giving the lender legal rights over the property, including a power of sale if the borrower is unable to repay the loan

The word 'mortgage' is consequently used to describe a long-term loan which provides money for the purchase of a property. Mortgages are available from banks, building societies and specialist companies. People who borrow by means of a mortgage should appreciate the fact that if they fail to repay, the lender can sell the house and make the borrower homeless. There are three principal methods of repaying a mortgage loan: repayment mortgage, endowment mortgage and pension mortgage. The difference lies in the way in which the principal amount is repaid.

repayment mortgage
A fixed amount is borrowed at the outset: normally up to 90% of the purchase price of the house (often 95% for a first-time buyer). Repayments, which are monthly, are made up of two elements: the principal (fixed amount) and the interest on whatever principal remains to be repaid. The interest rate, set by the lending institutions, varies in line with interest rates in the economy, and so therefore does the amount of the monthly repayments. By the end of the loan (usually after 25 years) principal and interest have both been fully repaid; the house belongs to the borrower.

endowment mortgage
The loan will be treated in the same way as a repayment mortgage, except for the repayment of the principal amount borrowed. An *endowment life assurance policy* on the life of the borrower is taken out to repay the principal at the end of the loan. An endowment policy is a life assurance policy which will pay out a sum of money on a fixed date (in this case at the end of the loan) or on the death of the borrower, whichever occurs earlier. Assuming the borrower remains alive, which is hopefully the case, he or she will make monthly payments, normally in one amount, which cover *interest on the loan* and *premiums* to the Life Assurance Company. These mortgages have proved popular because the insurance policy often pays an added bonus when the loan is repaid (say after 25 years) which is an extra benefit for the borrower. The bonus comes out of the profits of the insurance company.

pension mortgage
A pension mortgage works in exactly the same way as an endowment mortgage, except that the loan is repaid in one amount at the end of the loan period from a lump sum payment from a *personal pension scheme* on the retirement of the borrower. The pension scheme will also, of course, provide pension payments for the rest of the borrower's life. During the period of the loan the borrower makes monthly repayments (attracting tax relief) covering interest and pension contributions.

other forms of mortgages
There are other types of mortgage which are forms of the repayment and endowment mortgages; these other types vary the way in which the money is repaid:
* a *fixed rate mortgage* offers a fixed rate of interest for an initial period, enabling the borrower to budget more easily because the repayments will not vary with other interest rates in the economy
* a *low start mortgage* is an endowment mortgage where the insurance premiums are set at a lower rate (or are waived entirely) for an initial period, often two years; the insurance premiums for the remaining period of the loan are set at a correspondingly higher rate
* a *low cost endowment mortgage*, on the other hand, saves the borrower money by calculating that part of the mortgage will be repaid out of the terminal bonus offered by the endowment policy

Case Study: the Jones family – raising a mortgage

Situation

Ben and Lou Jones are planning to buy a home of their own and are examining the options. They have building society savings of £5,000 between them. The husband, Ben, earns £12, 000 per year and Lou does part-time work bringing in £7,500 per year.

Lending institutions, such as banks and building societies, each have their own *two* formulas for calculating the maximum amount that can be borrowed. These formulas are commonly:

1. maximum amount of loan = 90% (or 95% for first-time buyers) of valuation of property

2. maximum amount of loan = 3 x the major wage-earner's salary plus the secondary salary <u>or</u> 2.25 x the combined salaries

The lending institution will only lend the *lower* of the two amounts calculated in 1. and 2.

The Jones couple have seen in a local development a flat on which they have set their hearts. The asking price is £55,000. They calculate the maximum amount they can borrow as follows on the formulas given them by their Building Society:

1. The building society will lend them a maximum of 95% of the valuation = £52,250.
2. The amount they can borrow based on the earnings formula is lower. They choose the 2.25 x combined income formula, as the other formula results in a figure of £43,500.

Ben Jones' salary	£12,000
Lou Jones' income	£7,500
combined income	£19,500
combined income x 2.25	£43,875

The maximum that they can borrow is therefore the *lower* of £52,250 and £43,875.

They clearly have a number of problems:
* If the flat costs £55,000 and they can only borrow £43,875, they need £11,125. They have only £5,000 saved. They will also have to pay other expenses including legal fees. They cannot, on the face of it, afford the flat.
* Repayments on a loan of £43,875 over 25 years would be approximately £450 per month. Can they afford this?
* When they have resolved the problem of which flat to buy, do they choose a repayment, endowment or pension mortgage?

Solution

It appears that the couple must either raise further finance, which may be difficult, or rethink their ideas.

Further sources of finance might include:
* a loan from the family with low interest and deferred repayment
* increased income from earnings – is the husband due for promotion or a rise – can the wife take a full-time or more remunerative job?

A more sensible solution, bearing in mind the likely additional cost of fitting out and running a new home would be to reconsider the situation:

- to find a cheaper flat in the same or similar development
- to find a secondhand flat of a similar type – the seller of the flat may be prepared to drop the price

In any event, the couple must work out how much they can afford to repay each month. Once a reasonable figure is established for a purchase price and the monthly repayment, the couple must approach one or a number of lending institutions to obtain quotations for repayment, endowment and pension mortgages. These institutions might include:

- the building society with which they have their savings
- banks (including foreign banks in the UK) and other building societies
- mortgage brokers and specialist companies offering endowment mortgages
- the company operating the development (if they want to buy a new flat) – such companies often enter into deals with building societies to offer attractive mortgage terms

The couple will then decide on the best terms, submit a formal written mortgage application and, if successful, receive an offer of finance. The lending institution will often help to arrange surveys, legal services and insurance. The whole transaction, from application to moving in, will often take six weeks or more.

Chapter Summary

❏ The sources of personal finance include earnings, savings and borrowing.

❏ Expenditure can be for
- revenue expenditure (short-term running expenses)
- capital expenditure(purchases which are intended to be retained for the long-term)
- savings and investments

❏ Personal borrowing involves an interest cost to the borrower measured in terms of an interest rate.

❏ The cost of personal borrowing schemes may be compared by examining the Annual Percentage Rate (APR).

❏ Forms of short term personal borrowing include:
- overdrafts
- credit cards

❏ Fixed repayment finance can take the form of instalment credit (up to 5 years) or mortgage finance (up to 25 years).

❏ Instalment credit includes personal loans and hire purchase.

❏ Mortgage finance includes repayment, endowment and pension mortgages.

In the next chapter we examine how an individual can plan personal spending in the form of a *budget*.

Student Activities

1.1   A friend, aged 18, wishes to borrow money to buy a stereo system costing £750, but she is confused by the references in publicity material from lending institutions to interest rates and 'APR'. Write down what you understand by the relationship between interest rates and APR, giving examples from publicity material for credit schemes. Would there by any further points to consider if your friend were aged 17?

1.2   You are changing jobs and find that instead of being paid weekly you are going on to a monthly payroll. As a result you will be very short of money during your first month in the new job. You estimate that you will need £100 to see you through. What sources of finance are available, and how would you apply for credit?

1.3   Calculate the interest you will pay if you borrow:

(a)   £1,250 @ 12% for 2 years
(b)   £1,650 @ 9% for 3 years
(c)   £1,000 @ 17% for 6 months
(d)   £22,000 @ 11% for 25 years

Suggest the types of items (eg a car, a house) which could be purchased by these borrowings.

1.4   **Subject for discussion**
Investigate the salaries earned by a solicitor, an accountant, a bank manager, a teacher, a clerical worker, an unskilled worker, all at the age of 35. Discuss in your group:

(a)   the reasons for the difference in salaries
(b)   the disadvantages of being highly paid
(c)   any evidence that the highly paid save more, or borrow less

Information for the above could be obtained from newspaper advertisements or from your local careers library.

1.5   Calculate how much you spent last month under two headings: 'revenue expenditure' and 'capital expenditure'. Analyse the sources of finance which enabled you to make this expenditure. If you are familiar with pie charts, construct two: one for revenue and capital expenditure and one showing the sources of finance.

1.6   You want to buy a dining room suite of furniture for £1,000 from a major retail store. Investigate the different types of finance that are available. Write down a description of each scheme, detailing its terms, the cost of borrowing and the likely repayments over three years. Recommend the scheme which you consider to be the best. Obtain an application form for the recommended scheme and complete it, assuming that you are 25, married, a house owner and working for the local authority.

1.7   If a building society will lend on mortgage up to 90% of the value of a house and works on the formula 3 x the major salary plus the whole of the second salary, what is the most expensive house the following couples can afford? Remember that the savings figure quoted will form the couple's 10% contribution in each case.

(a) Hugh and Anne, salaries £7,000 and £5,000, savings £3,000.

(b) Rodney and Jan, salaries £8,000 and £7,000, savings £5,000.

(c) William and Sue, salaries £17,000 and £6,000, savings £10,000.

(d) Mike and Anne, salaries £25,000 and £8,000, savings £5,000.

1.8   You work in the Westmidlands Building Society, 2 The Parade, Mereford, MR1 2FD, and receive the following letter from John Nuttall. Write a reply for signature by your branch manager, John Grant, explaining the three types of mortgage available, and your lending formula. (Assume you will lend 90% of the value of the house [95% to first-time buyers] and 3 x major salary + whole of second salary).

---

12 Magnolia Walk
Mereford
MR2 1FG

1 July 19-3

Dear Sir,

My wife and I have lived in a rented flat for the last
three years. We are now considering the possibility of
buying a property valued at £85,000. I earn £18,000 a
year and my wife earns £6,000 a year. I shall be
grateful if you would let me know how much we could
borrow, and also what is the difference between a
repayment, endowment and pension mortgage.

I look forward to hearing from you.

Yours faithfully,

J. Nuttall

John Nuttall

2 Personal finance – budgeting

introduction

People sometimes run into financial trouble because of factors beyond their control, such as redundancy and illness. These circumstances are distressing. Equally disturbing are two other frequent causes of financial problems: a lack of control over personal spending and a lack of forward planning by the individual or family. Mr Micawber, a character created by the English author Charles Dickens, had a famous saying:

Income greater than expenditure = happiness
Expenditure greater than income = misery

The misery referred to by Mr Micawber is often caused by
• deficiencies in personal accounting:
How much money do I have?
How much money have I spent?
• the inability to calculate for future needs:
How am I going to manage when all the bills arrive at once?
How am I going to pay the car tax and insurance after I have paid for the holiday I have just booked?

The solution is one of simple housekeeping and basic common sense:
• calculate your income
• calculate your expenses, both regular expenses and 'one-off' expenses such as a holiday or a car purchase
• calculate the difference between income and expenditure
• if there is a surplus it can be used for increased spending, or better, for saving
• if there is a deficit, you may need to borrow and you will certainly need to revise your pattern of spending
• monitor your income and expenditure from time-to-time to see if you are on target

This process – the forecast of future income and expenditure – is known as *budgeting,* and the calculation is known as a *budget.*

Look now at Fig. 2.1 on the opposite page. It sets out the items for which an 'average' family will have to budget. Compare your own expenditure with these items.

HOUSEHOLD AND PERSONAL EXPENDITURE

This summary sets out the items of household and personal spending undertaken by a typical household of four: two parents and two children of school age. The sections are set out in order of priority.

regular essential spending for the household
• mortgage payments/rent   • Council tax   • water bills   • gas bills
• fuel   (oil or coal)   • electricity   • telephone   • insurance (house, contents)
• food   • household maintenance and repairs   • TV licence   • schooling

regular essential expenses for members of the family
• travel   • car tax, insurance and maintenance   • life assurance   • personal loan and credit card repayments   • medical and dentist's fees   • basic clothing

less essential items of personal expenditure
• books, magazines and newspapers   • cinema, discos, entertainment
• drinks   • cigarettes • CD's, tapes, videos   • presents   • holidays
• fashion clothes   • hobbies and sports activities

SPENDING BY THE AVERAGE FAMILY

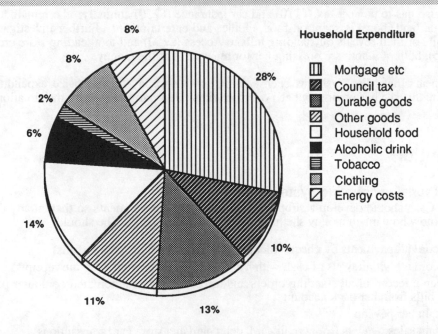

Household Expenditure

- Mortgage etc
- Council tax
- Durable goods
- Other goods
- Household food
- Alcoholic drink
- Tobacco
- Clothing
- Energy costs

8%
8%
2%
6%
14%
11%
13%
10%
28%

Source: Central Statistical Office Monthly Digest of Statistics (amended)

Fig 2.1 Household and personal expenditure

Case Study: Miss Florence Cash

Situation

Florence Cash has recently left home in rural Herefordshire where she has lived comfortably with her parents. She qualified as a bilingual secretary at the local Technical College, and has now moved to London, having been fortunate to obtain a job with a salary of £14,000 a year.

Miss Cash, however, has been in financial difficulties. She has just received another letter from her bank manager, this time asking her to return her combined cheque card/debit card and cheque book, and requesting that she restore her bank account to credit, the balance being £250 overdrawn. The bank is threatening legal action if she doesn't repay.

What has happened? From the pile of unopened bank statements to be found in her rented flat, it will be seen that she receives pay of £800 a month, but out of that she pays each month, on average:

• rent	£320
• electricity and gas bill (£25 each)	£50
• telephone	£20
• car (servicing, petrol)	£40
• TV and video rental (includes licence fee)	£20
• travel (season ticket)	£40
Total average monthly expenditure	£490

She also has to pay car tax (£110) and car insurance (£250) annually; the remainder of her income (and more) is spent on food, clothes and entertainment. Further investigation into her pile of mail reveals outstanding bills to Access (£250) and to a leading store credit card (£175), both of whom are pressing her for repayment of the money.

It appears that Miss Cash has been earning enough to pay for her basic expenditure, but despite this she has obviously been overspending. How can she remedy the situation?

Solution

a personal accounting system
Miss Cash should develop a simple system to record her payments so that, at any time, she will know how much money she has left in the bank to spend. She should:

- record all payments by cheque (details to be written on the counterfoils)
- record all withdrawals of cash with her cash card (she should keep the receipts)
- keep a record of all standing orders and direct debits, ie automated computer payments of bills from her bank account
- retain her payslip
- retain sales receipts from credit card, debit card and store card transactions

She might find a notebook or a personal organiser a useful means of recording some of these details.

the use of the bank statement to estimate spending power
When each monthly bank statement arrives she can estimate how much remains before the next pay day by carrying out some simple checks and calculations:

- checking the statement to make sure her salary has been received
- ticking off on the statement each item paid out, either against cheque counterfoils, debit card vouchers or against her own separate record of standing orders and direct debits
- deducting from the final statement balance any outstanding cheques written out but not yet deducted from the account
- deducting from the final statement balance any items to be paid before the next pay day (such as standing orders and direct debits)

The total of this calculation will give her the amount she will have available for food, clothes, entertainment and other expenses. The choice is hers entirely, but it would be sensible to allow enough money for food for the month before spending out on other items.

the use of budget planning to calculate future needs
Miss Cash will have to arrange an appointment with her bank manager: it is clear that they are going to have to work out between them how much she owes, how she is going to repay her borrowing, and how she is to continue to meet her commitments.

Her present borrowing is:

Bank overdraft	£250
Access card debt	£250
Store credit card debt	£175
Total borrowing	£675

The bank manager is sympathetic and will allow Miss Cash to repay the overdraft by an agreed amount each month. He also appreciates that she will repay the credit card debts over a period of time at £30 per month. Before reaching his decision the bank manager has asked her to complete a 'Budget Planner'. Most banks provide these forms free of charge for their customers. Fig 2.2 on the next page shows a typical 'Budget Planner' filled in with Miss Cash's details.

the budget planner: monthly expenditure schedule
Miss Cash has completed the Budget planner (Fig.2.2) with *monthly* figures for income and expenditure. Most of the figures already quoted relate to one month, but some adjustments have been necessary:

- the annual car tax (£110) and insurance (£250) payable in March – total £360 – are divided by 12 to give a monthly total of £30 (this is in addition to petrol/servicing costs of £40 per month)
- the cost of an annual holiday in August – £360 – is divided by 12 to give a monthly cost of £30

In addition she has budgeted for the following *monthly* payments:
- Access and store card debt payment of £30
- clothing and shoes £20
- housekeeping £120
- entertainment (going out with friends and boyfriend) £40

BUDGET PLANNER

monthly income

	£	£
earnings after tax	800	
partner's earnings after tax	-	
other income	-	
total monthly income		800

monthly expenditure

	£	£
mortgage/rent	320	
council tax	-	
house insurance	-	
life assurance	-	
water	-	
electricity	25	
gas	25	
telephone	20	
property maintenance	-	
car expenses (petrol/servicing)	40	
car tax & insurance	30	
TV (rental/licence fee)	20	
travel	40	
clothing	20	
housekeeping	120	
loans/HP/credit cards	30	
entertainment	40	
holidays	30	
savings	-	
total monthly expenditure		760
monthly surplus/(deficit)		40

IMPORTANT NOTE
Please enter monthly figures in the boxes above:
- to convert annual figures, divide by twelve
- to convert quarterly figures, divide by three
- to convert weekly figures, multiply by four

Fig 2.2 Budget Planner

personal cash flow forecast

Another exercise which Miss Cash can carry out is to complete a personal cash flow forecast, which she can show to the bank manager. A cash flow forecast – a financial statement used also by businesses and other organisations – sets out a month-by-month projection of

- cash received (salary in the case of Miss Cash)
- cash spent (monthly expenses and annual expenses *as they fall due*)

These figures, taken from the Budget Planner, are then related to the amount in the bank account at the beginning and the end of the month. The object of the exercise is to calculate the fluctuating balance of the bank account (shown on the bottom line of the forecast) over a period of time.   This will help Miss Cash to see that she can repay her borrowing and will enable the bank to see how much she needs to borrow on overdraft (£310 in this case)

The cash flow forecast set out below shows Miss Cash's projected bank balance over a twelve month period. Look at the format of the forecast and then read the notes below.

cash flow forecast name......*Florence Cash*......dates......*Jan–Dec 19–1*						
month:	Jan	Feb	Mar	Apl	May	Jun
income (A)	800	800	800	800	800	800
expenses: monthly	700	700	700	700	700	700
quarterly						
annual			360			
total expenses (B)	700	700	1,060	700	700	700
Bank balance at beginning of month	(250)	(150)	(50)	(310)	(210)	(110)
Add income (A) less expenses (B)	100	100	(260)	100	100	100
Bank balance at end of month	(150)	(50)	(310)	(210)	(110)	(10)
month:	Jul	Aug	Sep	Oct	Nov	Dec
income (A)	800	800	800	800	800	800
expenses: monthly	700	700	700	700	700	700
quarterly						
annual		360				
total expenses (B)	700	1,060	700	700	700	700
Bank balance at beginning of month	(10)	90	(170)	(70)	30	130
Add income (A) less expenses (B)	100	(260)	100	100	100	100
Bank balance at end of month	90	(170)	(70)	30	130	230

- the figures are taken from the Budget Planner; negative figures are shown in brackets
- income is £800 per month
- annual expenses are: March car tax and insurance £360, August holiday £360
- monthly expenses are £700; this figure is arrived at by deducting the *monthly* cost of the *annual* expenses from the total monthly expenses figure on the budget planner: £760 less £30 (car tax and insurance) less £30 (holiday) equals £700
- the monthly bank balance shows a maximum overdraft of £310 in March and a healthy balance of £230 in the bank at the end of December

cash flow forecasts and computer spreadsheets

how to complete a cash flow forecast

It is a simple matter to complete a cash flow forecast once all the appropriate figures have been calculated. The notes set out below are intended as a practical guide, and work from the top of the forecast downwards. The important point to remember is that income and expense items must be entered in the month in which they are received or paid.

1   complete the top of the form with the name of the person and the period covered by the forecast

2   start with income (shown as letter A) and enter the total monthly income for each of the twelve months

3   enter the monthly expenses figure on the first line of the expenses section (remember if you are working from a Budget Planner that you will need to deduct the monthly equivalents of items paid annually and quarterly from the total monthly expenses figure on the Budget Planner)

4   enter any amounts paid quarterly on the next line in the appropriate month column

5   enter any amounts paid annually on the next line in the appropriate month column

6   add up all the expenses for each month and enter the total figure at the bottom of the expenses section on the 'total expenses (B)' line

7   deduct 'total expenses (B)' from 'income (A)' for each month and enter the result on the line 'Add income (A) less expenses (B)'; if the figure is negative, enter it in brackets

8   enter the bank balance at the beginning of January in the January column on the line above the calculation you have just carried out in 7 above, add the figure calculated in 7 above and enter the result on the bottom line of the month column – this is the bank balance at the *end* of the month; remember that if the figure is negative (ie an overdraft) it should be shown in brackets

9   copy this figure into the line 'Bank balance at beginning of month' for February and repeat the process in 8 above using the February figures

10   repeat this process (8 and 9) for each month (using that month's figures) until the forecast is complete

11   check your figures: one useful check for accuracy is that the difference between the bank balance at the beginning and at the end should equal the difference between total income and total expenses for the period

using a computer spreadsheet

The important point to remember about a cash flow forecast is that it is only an *estimate* of future income and expenditure, and is subject to a number of variable factors. Suppose that Miss Cash in the Case Study gets a pay rise; suppose that she is made redundant; suppose that she decides to buy a flat and incurs more expenses than originally budgeted for. All these 'suppose' or 'what if' situations will cause the cash flow forecast to change and will necessitate lengthy recalculations. A computer spreadsheet – a calculation program explained fully in Chapter 31 - is exceptionally useful for cash flow forecasts. Any changes in income or expenditure can be entered into the computer and the recalculations will be performed automatically. You may already be familiar with the computer spreadsheet in your studies. If this is not the case you should read Chapter 31 at the end of this book before attempting to use a spreadsheet for a cash flow forecast.

For your guidance there are two illustrations on the next page:

•   a personal cash flow forecast on a spreadsheet, using the figures from Miss Cash in the Case Study; note that the first six months' figures only are shown here.

•   an illustration of the same spreadsheet file showing the *formulas* used; please check with your lecturer or computer manual for the formula commands, as computer spreadsheet programs differ from one another in this respect

Personal Cash flow Forecast on a spreadsheet
Miss Cash's projections (January – June)

	A	B	C	D	E	F	G
1	Cash Flow Forecast: Florence Cash						
2	Period: January – June 19-1						
3							
4		Jan	Feb	Mar	Apl	May	Jun
5		£	£	£	£	£	£
6	INCOME						
7	Earnings	800	800	800	800	800	800
8	Other income						
9	TOTAL INCOME (A)	800	800	800	800	800	800
10							
11	EXPENSES						
12	Monthly expenses	700	700	700	700	700	700
13	Quarterly expenses						
14	Annual expenses			360			
15	TOTAL EXPENSES (B)	700	700	1060	700	700	700
16	OPENING BANK	-250	-150	-50	-310	-210	-110
17	Cash flow (A) less (B)	100	100	-260	100	100	100
18	CLOSING BANK	-150	-50	-310	-210	-110	-10

Personal Cash flow Forecast on a spreadsheet
Formulas used for calculation (January – March)

	A	B	C	D
1	Cash Flow Forecast			
2	Period: month - month 19--			
3				
4		Jan	Feb	Mar
5		£	£	£
6	INCOME			
7	Earnings			
8	Other income			
9	TOTAL INCOME (A)	=Sum(B7:B8)	=Sum(C7:C8)	=Sum(D7:D8)
10				
11	EXPENSES			
12	Monthly expenses			
13	Quarterly expenses			
14	Annual expenses			
15	TOTAL EXPENSES (B)	=Sum(B12:B14)	=Sum(C12:C14)	=Sum(D12:D14)
16	OPENING BANK		=B18	=C18
17	Cash flow (A) less (B)	=B9-B15	=C9-C15	=D9-D15
18	CLOSING BANK	=B16+B17	=C16+C17	=D16+D17

Chapter Summary

❑ Budgeting for future income and expenditure is essential for individuals and families.

❑ The budgeting process involves
  • recording personal spending
  • reconciling the records with your bank statement
  • itemising personal spending on some form of Budget Planner schedule
  • preparing a cash flow forecast if you need to know how your bank balance is going to fluctuate during the year (using a spreadsheet if you have one)

❑ As the Case Study demonstrates, failure to plan can result in an individual running into severe problems even when all *necessary* expenditure can be met out of income.

❑ As we will see in later chapters, accounting control and budget planning are also important to the efficient functioning of business, Public Sector and social organisations.

In the next chapter we look at the deductions made from the earnings of an individual by way of Income Tax and National Insurance contributions.

 Student Activities

2.1   Examine the list of household and personal expenditure items illustrated in Fig. 2.1 on page 19. Compile a *monthly* expenditure estimate for an imaginary family of four, based on your own and your family's experience. Construct either two pie charts or a comparative table showing how the spending pattern corresponds with the national average set out in Fig. 2.1. Give reasons for any significant differences.

2.2   You are paid a salary of £500 on the 27th of each month. Your regular monthly outgoings by standing order and direct debit from your bank account (with dates) are:

1st   mortgage of £200.00, Council tax £30.00
2nd   season ticket £20.50, telephone £20.75
23rd   TV and video rental £20.50
25th   HP payment £32.23
28th   life insurance £12.12

On 22nd May you receive your monthly bank statement which shows a credit balance at 15th May of £155.71. You go through your records and find that the following items are not on the statement: 20th May, cash card withdrawal £30; 20th May, cheque issued to Sainsbury's for £35.93; 21st May, cheque issued to W.H. Smith for £41.50. You estimate that you will also need £50 to cover expenses before the receipt of your salary. How much money (if any) do you have available, and what are you going to do about your personal budgeting?

2.3   You have noticed that during the last year your bank charges have been high because you have from time-to-time gone overdrawn without realising it. You decide to draw up a Budget Planner and monthly cash flow forecast for the 12 months from January 19-8, so that you can see what is happening to your finances. If you have access to a computer spreadsheet program you are strongly advised to use it for the cash flow forecast and also possibly for the Budget Planner schedule. The details of your finances are:

- your bank balance at the beginning of the year is £250 overdrawn
- your net monthly income is £575

your outgoings are as follows:

- *monthly*   mortgage £170, Council tax £30, car £35, housekeeping £160

- *quarterly*   telephone £53, electricity £67 (both paid in March, June, September, December)

- *annual*   car tax and insurance £284 (February), holiday £500 (August), Christmas shopping £200 (December)

When you have drawn up the Budget Planner and the cash flow forecast

(a)   state whether or not you are living within your means, justifying your statement with figures

(b)   work out the effect on the Budget Planner and cash flow forecast of a pay rise to £650 a month or a drop in pay to £475 a month

(c)   how would you adjust your spending pattern to these situations?

2.4   You have qualified as a chartered accountant, you are married, with five children, and live in a comfortable detached house. Your *monthly* income and expenditure are as follows:

income	£	expenditure	£
net earnings	1590	mortgage	450
partner's part-time earnings	250	council tax	45
interest from savings account	25	house insurance	35
		life assurance	60
		water bill	40
		car servicing and petrol	60
		TV (rental and licence)	20
		clothing	50
		housekeeping	400
		HP and credit cards	165
		entertainment	60
		savings schemes	55

Your other additional outgoings are:

- *quarterly:*   £180 electricity and £150 telephone (paid March, June, September, December)
- *annually:*   £480 car tax and insurance (August) and £1,440 holiday (January)

(a)   You are to draw up (with the aid of a computer spreadsheet if available) a Budget Planner and a cash flow forecast for twelve months (use your own name and the current date)

(b)   State what you would do if your partner (wife or husband!) gave up work

3 Personal taxation

introduction

Income is often referred to in terms of 'wages' or 'salary'. Wages are normally paid weekly to employees in the areas of production and service. A salary is the payment to employees working in administration and management; it is usually paid monthly, and often direct into a bank or a building society account. If you earn either wages or a salary, you will look at your income in two ways:

1 You will be aware of the amount you earn before deductions, your *gross* earnings, when you say, for instance, 'I earn £10,000 a year'.

2 You will know how much you receive each week or month after your employer has made certain deductions, as this is the amount you have available for the budgeting process. This is your *net* income.

Income can also include investment income: interest from savings accounts and income (dividends) from shares. All forms of income may be liable to tax. In this chapter we will look in detail at the deductions of Income Tax and National Insurance. We will then examine the situation of an employee starting work for the first time and encountering unfamiliar forms and procedures.

deductions from gross pay

There are a number of deductions from gross pay, some compulsory and some voluntary:

compulsory deductions
Your employer will deduct the following as a matter of course:
* Income Tax – money paid to the Inland Revenue to fund Government spending
* National Insurance Contributions – money paid to the State to fund retirement pensions and sickness benefit

voluntary deductions
Your employer will deduct the following at your request:
* pension/superannuation scheme payments
* union subscriptions
* payments to charity (if your employer operates a charitable giving scheme)

It is the responsibility of your employer to account to the various bodies concerned for the amounts deducted from your gross pay.

taxation of income: the flow of funds

The following diagram shows
- *on the left* the various sources of income received by the individual
- *on the right* the deductions made from that income

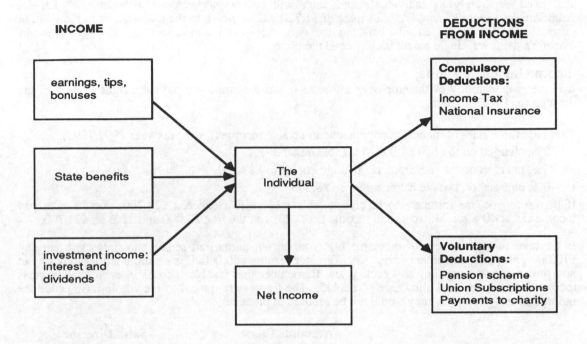

income tax

Income tax is a tax on income received by an individual.

'Income' for tax purposes includes pay, tips, bonuses, and benefits in kind (eg company car, cheap loans), pensions, most State benefits, and interest and dividends from investments.

If you are in employment the Income Tax on your pay is deducted by the employer from your gross pay by means of a scheme known as PAYE (Pay As You Earn). This scheme, as its title suggests, enables you to spread out your taxation evenly over the year instead of having to pay it in one amount.

taxable income: the Personal Allowance

Income which is liable to tax is known as taxable income.

Taxable income is calculated by deducting the personal allowance from gross income.

You do not, fortunately, have to pay tax on all your income. In order to help the lower paid, the Government gives a *Personal Allowance*, an amount which you can earn during the tax year (6 April – 5 April), on which no tax is paid at all. The personal allowance, which is announced by the Chancellor of the Exchequer in his annual budget, is normally increased in line with inflation each year, and is fixed for each tax year. The amount of the personal allowance varies, depending on factors such as whether you are single or married, or over a certain age.

The allowances fixed for the tax year from 6 April 1992 to 5 April 1993 include the following:
• personal allowance £3,445
• married couple's allowance £1,720

A single male or female may therefore earn up to £3,445 without deduction of tax . Married couples are taxed separately as individuals and each will receive a *personal* allowance of £3,445. Additionally a *married couple's allowance* of £1,720 will be given to the husband, or to the wife, or (after April 1993) split equally between the two. Additional allowances are also given to the over-65's, widows, single parent families and the blind.

income tax calculations
It is the responsibility of the employer to see to it that the employee pays the right amount of tax through the PAYE system.

There are three rates of income tax applicable to taxable income (for the tax year 1992/1993):
• 20%, charged on the first £2,000 of taxable income
• 25%, charged on the remaining taxable income *up to* £23,700
• 40%, charged on taxable income *above* £23,700

If therefore you are fortunate to receive taxable income that exceeds £23,700, you have to pay income tax at 40% *on the excess* and income tax at 20% on the first £2,000 and 25% on £21,700.

If we take two employees of the same organisation, an unmarried senior accounts clerk earning £10,000 gross p.a., and an unmarried sales director earning £30,000, it is a simple matter to work out how much income tax they pay each year. Remember that taxable income in each case is gross income less the personal allowance of £3,445. The figures are quoted to the whole £ (ie pence are ignored in this example – they would not be ignored in practice).

	Accounts Clerk	Sales Director
	£	£
Gross income	10,000	30,000
less personal allowance	3,445	3,445
Taxable income	6,555	26,555
Income tax @ 20%,	400	£2,000 @ 20% = 400
Income tax @ 25%,	1,139	£21,700 @ 25% = 5,425
Income tax @ 40%	nil	£2,855 @ 40% = 1,142
TOTAL INCOME TAX (to nearest £)	1,539	6,967

These tax calculations cannot, however, be taken in isolation, as the employer will also, as we will see, deduct National Insurance Contributions, and the Inland Revenue may make further adjustments by means of a *tax code*.

tax codes and allowances

additional allowances
The Inland Revenue, as well as granting the personal allowance, gives additional allowances against tax. For the person in employment they could include expenses incurred in employment, professional subscriptions, and clothing and specialist equipment used when working.

The allowance system works so that earnings spent on these items up to the amount of the appropriate allowance will not be subject to income tax.

calculation of the tax code

How does the employer know what allowances have been given to the employee and how much tax to deduct? How do the tax authorities make allowances, in practical terms, for clothing, equipment and subscriptions? The Inland Revenue gives each employee a *tax code,* a number which is used by the employer to calculate the taxable pay. The tax code incorporates *all* the tax allowances, including the personal allowance.

Typical allowances for an unmarried factory worker would be:

Personal allowance	£3,445
Allowance for work clothing	£50
Total allowances	£3,495

During the tax year the employee's tax code will be 349, the amount of the total allowances less the last digit. The code will be followed by a letter, the two most common of which are:

L = a code incorporating a single person's allowance
H = a code incorporating a married person's allowance

In the case of this factory worker the full code will be 349L.

When the Inland Revenue has allocated the tax code to the employee, the tax is, in principle, easy to calculate. Take, for example, the factory worker referred to above who earns, say, £8,000 a year.

Gross annual pay	£8,000
Less allowances (code 349L – see above)	£3,490
Taxable annual pay	£4,510
Tax payable on £4,510 = £2,000 @ 20% (£400)	
plus £2510 @ 25% (£627.50) =	£1,027.50

The employer's task of collecting the tax on a weekly or a monthly basis is less simple. What happens for instance if an unmarried employee starts work, for the first time, halfway through the tax year? No tax will be payable, unless the employee earns over £3,445, ie the personal allowance, in that year. How is the employer to know how much to deduct, and when? The Inland Revenue makes the calculation of tax on a *weekly or monthly* basis possible for the employer through the PAYE system.

PAYE: calculation of net pay

The Inland Revenue supplies the employer with tax tables and deduction sheets (P11) for working out an individual's net pay on a *weekly* (or monthly where appropriate) and *cumulative* basis. There are two sets of tables:
* the Free Pay tables
* the Taxable Pay tables

The *Free Pay Tables* have a page for each week and month, telling the employer for that particular week or month, depending on the tax code of the employee, how much income since the beginning of the tax year is *not* subject to tax. This figure is the *Free Pay* of the employee.

The *Taxable Pay Tables* tell the employer how much tax is payable on the employee's taxable income since the beginning of the year. Tax is worked out at 25% and adjustments made for the £2,000 taxable at 20% and any amounts attracting the 40% rate.

The employer must therefore keep the following cumulative (running) totals for each employee from the beginning of the tax year (or when the employee starts work with the employer in that tax year) on his deduction sheets:

(a)   The Total Gross Pay to date
(b)   The Total Free Pay to date (from the Free Pay Table)
(c)   The Total Taxable Pay to date, this is (a) minus (b)
(d)   The Total Tax due to date (from Taxable Pay Table)

To work out an employee's tax for the week, all the employer has to do is fill in the totals indicated above, and subtract *last week's* Total Tax due from this week's figure; the difference is this week's tax due, which is then recorded on the deduction sheet.

We do not at this stage of your studies need to examine all the mechanics of payroll. You should nevertheless be aware of the terminology used and also the fact that many businesses now use computer payroll packages to work out these complex calculations. Most packages will also print out a payslip and the means of payment (a cheque or a bank giro credit).

The employer collects Income Tax on behalf of the Inland Revenue by means of the PAYE scheme and so enables the employee to pay tax as he or she earns. This scheme also allows for flexibility. If an employee moves job, the previous employer will simply provide the new employer with the cumulative totals for pay and tax to date on a form P45, so that tax may be correctly calculated from the first pay date in the new job. In all cases the employer will, after the end of a tax year, give the employee a P60 form which will state the amount of gross pay, the tax paid and National Insurance Contributions.

National Insurance Contributions

The employer will also have to account for the employee's National Insurance contributions by deduction from gross pay. Payment of National Insurance enables the employee in time of need to claim benefits from the State such as retirement pension and sickness benefits. The amount contributed depends on earnings. The employer also makes a contribution. The contributions of both employer and employee are recorded on the P11 deduction sheet.

The amounts payable, for example, for an employee earning between £54.00 and £89.99 per week are: employee 2% on earnings up to £54 and 9% on earnings from £54 to £89.99, employer 4.6% of gross pay. *No* National Insurance is payable by the employee if earnings are less than £54.00 a week and *no* National Insurance Contributions are payable by the employee on any earnings *above* £405 a week.

The National Insurance 'not contracted-out' rates (which are commonly used) are set out below. Tables for the calculation of the rates are available from the Department of Social Security.

National Insurance Contributions (1992/1993)

Total weekly earnings	Employee	Employer
Under £54	Nil	Nil
£54 to £89.99	2% on earnings up to £54, plus 9% on earnings between £54 and £405	4.6%
£90 to £134.99		6.6%
£135 to £189.99		8.6%
£190 to £405		10.4%
£405 or more	2% on £54 and 9% on £351	10.4%

Case Study: Dora Penny starting work

Situation

Dora Penny is a newly qualified accountant who is starting work for the first time in the Treasury of the local authority. She has been given a contract by the Local Authority and will receive her salary direct into her bank account from the local County Council. Her personal situation is as follows:

- her annual gross salary is £14,400
- she receives the personal allowance of £3,445
- National Insurance is paid at the not contracted-out rate
- 6% of her gross salary is paid into a pension scheme
- she pays £40 subscription to her professional association each year (direct from her bank account)

What are the forms and procedures she is likely to encounter during her first few months at work?

Solution

- Her employer will give her a form P46 to sign; this is a declaration that she has not worked before or received unemployment benefit. Her employer will send this form when signed to the Inland Revenue to tell them that she has started work with them.

- Her employer will also give her a 'Coding Claim Form' to enable her to claim for additional allowances such as her £40 a year subscription to the professional association. Dora will have to send this herself to the local Inland Revenue office which will deal with her tax affairs.

Having worked for two months Dora has received her second payslip from her employers. This form is illustrated and explained on the next page.

From this point onwards it is unlikely that Dora will have any further problems or queries. All she will receive will be:

- monthly payslips from her employer
- an annual P60 from her employer setting out her total pay and deductions for the tax year
- an annual Notice of Coding from the Inland Revenue to advise code changes brought about by the annual personal allowance increase after the budget

She should check these documents, as the Inland Revenue and employers have been known to make mistakes with tax codes and payslips.

Dora Penny's payslip

$\mathcal{WCC}$ **Wyvern County Council**		**Pay Statement** May 1992	
	£		**£**
Pay	1200.00	Tax (Code 348L)	218.92
Overtime	0.00	N.I. Non-Contr Out	91.62
		Superannuation	72.00
TOTAL GROSS PAY	1200.00		
		TOTAL DEDUCTIONS	382.54
		NET PAY	817.46

CUMULATIVES		**EMPLOYEE DETAILS**
Taxable earnings	1818.50	
Tax to date	437.83	Miss D Penny
NI to date	183.24	Staff No 0178653425
Superannuation	144.00	NI No YT 77 77 01 A
		Tax Ref 792/W1
NET PAY	1634.93	Payment via BACS

notes

- the Net Pay box shows the amount received by Dora Penny in May
- the left hand side of the payslip (upper half) shows the gross amount earned in May
- the right hand side of the payslip (upper half) shows the income tax and National Insurance Contributions for May
- the superannuation payment is 6% of Dora's gross salary
- the tax code shown (348L) is calculated as follows:

single person's allowance	£3,445
professional subscription	£40
total allowances	£3,485

- the final digit of 3485 is removed and the letter 'L' added to give a code of 348L
- the 'cumulatives' section sets out for Dora the running totals of taxable earnings and deductions in the current tax year
- Dora's staff number, National Insurance number and reference number from the local tax office and means of payment are shown in the Employee Details section
- figures for Income Tax and National Insurance can be taken from calculation tables, but are most likely to be produced by a computer payroll package

Chapter Summary

❏ Personal taxation is often seen as a problem area associated with complex form filling.

❏ Once the basic principles have been grasped – the assessment for tax, the allowance system and its administration through PAYE – personal taxation should present few problems, either when you have to pay tax, or if you work in an office and have to calculate deductions from wages and salaries.

❏ So far we have looked at *personal* taxation. It should be noted that any individual in *business,* as a sole trader or partner, is equally liable to Income Tax, but directly liable, ie tax is generally payable in lump sums rather than through PAYE. Limited companies, on the other hand, are liable to pay Corporation Tax on their profits.

In the next section of the book we turn to the subject of *business* finance.

 ## Student Activities

3.1 A fellow student has started a holiday job earning £90 per week. He only expects to work 12 weeks during the year and has no other income. He says that his employer has deducted tax amd National Insurance Contributions from his earnings for the first two weeks, and he does not think that this is right. Advise him accordingly.

3.2 Using the tax rates and personal allowances quoted in the chapter, and ignoring National Insurance and other deductions, work out the monthly pay received by the following, after tax:

- Henry Eliot, unmarried, earning £5,500 a year
- Charles Kingsley, married, earning £12,000 a year
- Francis Bacon, married, earning £27,000 a year
- Rebecca Mills, unmarried, earning £6,000 a year
- Michael Idas, unmarried, earning £40,000 a year
- Andrew Brown, married, earning £29,000 a year
- Christopher Williams, unmarried, earning £19,000 a year

Note: assume that if the employee is married that he *or she* has the married couple's allowance.

3.3 You are a wages clerk working for Saxon Burgers, a fast food store. Obtain a set of Tax Tables and work out the net weekly pay (ignoring National Insurance) for Jane Willis (who is single and works irregular hours) for the first eight weeks of the tax year. Jane's gross weekly wages are as follows:

Week 1	£159.00
Week 2	£152.00
Week 3	£158.50
Week 4	£153.25
Week 5	£158.90
Week 7	£152.35
Week 8	£161.50

Assignment 1
Personal financial planning : Adam Smith

LEARNING OUTCOMES COVERED:
Personal finance: personal budgeting, use of Budget Planner, cash flow forecast,
spreadsheets, raising short-term and long-term finance, decision-making

SITUATION

Adam Smith, aged 21, has left the Polytechnic in Rowcester where he has been studying for a degree in Business Studies. He has obtained a management trainee post with Brentfield plc, a fast growing household products retailing company which offers a wide variety of goods, including food, D-I-Y products and garden accessories. Adam will be based in Greenham, a new town. He has a starting salary of £15,000 gross per annum, and will be paid monthly, at the end of the month. He starts work on 1st January 19-4.

At present he lives at home in Rowcester and will initially stay at Greenham during the week, Brentfield paying his travel and accommodation expenses. In three months' time they will cease to pay his keep, and he will have to fend for himself. He is an ambitious individual and has a number of plans:

*   to buy, with the help of a mortgage, a new fully-furnished town house (Greenham, being a new town, has a number of low cost housing developments, with units starting at £45,000)
*   to buy a car, with the help of a personal loan or on HP, to enable him to travel home at weekends and to take friends out

His present financial situation is as follows:

*   he has building society savings of £15,000, largely from a legacy
*   he has lived at home, and has had to pay only £10 a week from part-time earnings for his keep

He discusses his plans with his parents, who point out that he will soon be incurring a great deal of expenditure, including:

*   *household expenditure:* mortgage, Council tax, telephone, electricity, TV, housekeeping (food, repairs)
*   *car expenditure*: repayments on loan/HP, tax, insurance, servicing, petrol
*   *personal expenditure:* clothing, entertainment, holidays

His parents have generously offered to provide him with all the necessary basic household items (such as linen and pots and pans) to enable him to set up home.

Adam realises that he will have first to calculate his income, and then plan his expenditure.

STUDENT TASKS

You are to assume the role of Adam Smith (or Alice Smith if you prefer) and undertake the following tasks. You are to write an individual assignment answer, but may work in groups to gather and process the information.

1. ***Calculate the net monthly pay Adam will receive by drawing a mock-up of his payslip***
    Assume that he has the basic personal allowance and pays National Insurance. His pension is non-contributory, ie his employer pays. He intends to join the Union, which charges £7.50 a month for its subscription; this will be deducted by his employer.

2. Calculate the monthly cost of living in Greenham

Assume that Adam will live in a small town house, runs a small car and allows for personal expenditure. A Budget Planner form should be used in this exercise. Note: *pencil in* the total monthly expenditure for the time being (this will have to be amended after Task 3 has been completed). Alternatively the Budget Planner could be set up on a computer spreadsheet, which will allow for future changes to the figures. Note that the costs of borrowing for a house and a car should be ignored at this stage – they will be investigated in the next Task.

3. Calculate the cost of borrowing for the house and car

The differences between the totals arrived at in Tasks 1 and 2 will give the amount available each month for repayment of any borrowing. This will enable Adam to decide whether or not he can afford either a house or a car (or both), and if he can, what price brackets he will be looking at. You should look at personal loan and mortgage application forms and repayment tables; these are normally available from banks and building societies, who will also advise on the proportion of the purchase price of the house or car which can be borrowed (normally 95% of the house price for a first-time buyer, and up to 100% of the cost of the car). When the monthly repayment figures have been decided upon, they can be entered into the Budget Planner (or spreadsheet) used in Task 2, and then the total monthly expenditure can be calculated. If there is a monthly surplus, all is well; if there is a deficit, you will need to carry out the next task.

4. Deciding on the alternatives

Note: this task should only be completed if Adam decides not to go ahead with the mortage and/or the car loan.

If Adam finds that he has a monthly deficit on the Budget Planner, he will have to make alternative plans. These might include renting a flat, buying an 'old banger' or a motor bike. The decision will be one of personal choice. Write down the final decision and the reasons for the action taken. You will need to amend the Budget Planner (or spreadsheet file) accordingly in preparation for Task 5.

5. Cash flow forecast for the first year

Adam has access to a computer with a spreadsheet program, so he decides to draw up a cash flow forecast for his bank account for the first twelve months in his new job and and changed circumstances.

You are to draw up a suitable spreadsheet file using the following figures:

- the monthly income and expenditure from the Budget Planner (or spreadsheet) – but remember that any annual payments such as car tax and insurance should be entered in the month in which they are incurred – this may require an adjustment to the monthly expenditure figure
- an opening bank balance of £250
- any loan raised (normally paid into the bank account) and payment made for a car (these will go through in the same month)

The house purchase money, fees etc. are passed through the building society where Adam has his savings, so they can be ignored for the purposes of the cash flow forecast.

You are to set down in writing the answers to the following questions:

What does the spreadsheet tell you about Adam's financial position?
Will he need to take any further action about his his expected income and expenditure?

Note: if a computer spreadsheet program is not available, the cash flow forecast should be drawn up by hand and the calculations performed manually.

Assignment 2
Personal Taxation : an information leaflet

LEARNING OUTCOMES COVERED:
Personal finance: payment of wages, deductions from wages, tax calculations,
payslips and other documents

SITUATION

You are a wages clerk in a medium-sized engineering firm, Technocomponents Limited. In preparation for an intake of new employees joining the firm in September, your supervisor has allocated to you the task of preparing an explanatory leaflet containing details of how wages will be paid, and what deductions will be made. The reason for this leaflet is that normally when new employees join the firm, the accounts department is overwhelmed with small queries such as:

"How can my wages be paid to my bank account?"

"How do I pay tax?"

"How much tax do I have to pay, and when?"

"How do I know that I am paying the right amount of tax?"

"Who pays my National Insurance?"

"Do I get a pension, and who pays for it?"

"Do I pay my Union subscription through you?"

"Can I give money to charity through you?"

Your supervisor hopes that a suitable leaflet will save the accounts department a great deal of time. Technocomponents Limited, which operates on the PAYE system, has a computerised payroll producing bank giro credits which the firm passes through the bank clearing system. Some employees are still paid in cash; in their case the pay details and payslip are processed on the computer, and a wage packet is then made up manually. The company also runs a pension scheme which takes 5% of employees' gross pay, and has an arrangement with the Union to deduct the subscription of £36 p.a.

STUDENT TASKS

1.   Individually, you are to design a leaflet for new employees to explain:

   • how wages can be paid into a bank account, or in cash

   • what 'personal allowances' are

   • how taxable pay and tax is calculated by using the personal allowance – give examples

   • how income tax and National Insurance are deducted by the employer using the PAYE scheme, (a mock-up of a wage slip would be useful here)

   • what a Notice of Coding is, and where it comes from

   • what a P60 is, and where it comes from

   • the situation regarding pension and Union payments

   • what to do if the payslip or Notice of Coding seem to be incorrect

2.   Divide into groups of three or four and give a talk entitled 'Your Tax and You' to the rest of the class, who will play the role of new employees. Your lecturer will be able to help with visual aids such as charts and overhead projector slides. The material for the talk will be based on the leaflets produced by the members of the group.

section two
business finance

In this section we look at the financing of business. In the next three chapters we examine

- *the different types of business organisation*
- *how to start up in business*
- *the resources a business needs in order to be able to operate*
- *the sources of finance – capital and borrowing*
- *the balance sheet of a business*
- *types of bank finance*
- *other sources of finance: financial institutions and the Government*
- *financial services*
- *the cost of finance*

We conclude the section with an Assignment 'Tudor Catering' which develops these themes in a business start-up exercise.

4 Financial resources – starting a business

introduction

Individuals, businesses and other organisations need *financial resources*. These may be described as:

- *items that the individual, business or other organisation owns* - money in the bank, a car, property – all items which enable the individual or organisation to function

- *the sources of finance* which can be called upon to enable the individual, business or other organisation to obtain the car and the property, for example bank loans, family loans and private savings

As you can see, financial resources concern money – where it comes from and how it can be used.

In this chapter we will start by describing the different types of business organisation, their goals, and how they function in the economy. We will then look more specifically at how an individual starts up a business, and will examine the financial choices he or she faces and the decisions that have to be made. A number of questions will need to be answered:

- what sort of business will it be?
- where can advice be obtained?
- what legal form will the business take – sole trader, partnership or limited company?

types of business organisation

If you walk down your local main street you will see evidence of a wide variety of business organisations in operation: bus services, telephones, the Post Office, shops, banks, newspaper sellers and even the market research lady with a clipboard who always detains you with detailed questions when you are in a hurry to get somewhere else.

In this chapter we will be dealing with the specific situation of someone starting up in business. It is essential first, however, to obtain a *perspective* of the wide variety of businesses we have just mentioned, and appreciate their *goals* and *objectives*.

public sector and private sector organisations

public sector   *Public sector organisations* are owned directly or indirectly by central or local government. They are not all businesses as such, although the trends for business goals such as profit and efficiency are becoming more dominant. Examples of public sector organisations include the National Health Service, the Post Office, and probably your local Sports and Leisure Centre.

private sector   *Private sector organisations* are owned by private individuals in the form of companies, partnerships, and sole trader businesses.   Examples include well known names such as Marks and Spencer and W H Smith.

types of industry

The term 'industry' is loosely applied to a variety of businesses, some produce goods, some sell goods, others provide services. Industry is normally classified under the following sector headings:

primary   Primary industry produce the raw materials used by other businesses. Examples include oil, gas, mining, agriculture and fishing

manufacturing   Manufacturing industry processes the raw materials into finished products. Examples include the aircraft industries, electronics and pharmaceuticals.

service   Service industries do not produce manufactured items but provide services such as transport, financial services (banking and insurance), and tourism.

You will be aware from the newspapers and TV and what you see around you that the UK primary and manufacturing industries are in decline, while some businesses in the service sector are holding their own. If you are considering starting your own business, you should consider carefully which sector you are entering.

goals of business organisations

Most people go into business to make money. The *profit* motive remains the most important goal of any business organisation.   There are, however, other goals.   Generally speaking the larger the organisation, the more developed are the objectives. Examine any large company and you will find that, as well as the profit motive, it has very specific policies related to

- improving the environment by way of 'green' initiatives
- benefiting society by sponsorship of sport and the Arts
- political allegiance – large companies often pay large sums of money to political parties

We will now turn to the questions asked by a person setting up a new business in any of the sectors described above.

starting up – what sort of business?

People who start up in business normally do so for one of a number of possible reasons. They may be out of a job and want to 'get going' again, they may be in a job and thoroughly bored with it, or they may be 'self-starters' who have great ambitions. Whatever the situation the most important factor to be borne in mind is the *type* of business chosen. If you are making this choice you should take account of

experience   You should chose a trade with which you are familiar, either through a previous job, or through an interest – restoring classic cars, for example.

the market Size up the *market* for the product or service you have in mind, and preferably fill a gap in that market. Too many businesses fail – 'nice little shops' for instance – because the demand for the product is low or the number of existing businesses selling similar products is high.

your personality Size up *yourself* to see if you are suited to running a business. Are you hardworking, healthy, determined, willing to work long hours with few holidays, a risk-taker and able to communicate with people? If you are, you will probably survive and succeed in business, but if you have doubts, you are better off in paid employment.

where can you get advice?

You cannot be expected to know everything. The decisions, procedures and paperwork involved in starting a business can often assume nightmare proportions if you do not seek proper advice. There are a number of sources of information: some of them are free, and some of them will cost you money.

the professionals You will probably need to take professional advice from a solicitor or an accountant, or possibly from both. The accountant will help you establish your accounting system and advise on taxation and setting up a system for paying the wages. The solicitor will help by advising on the legal aspects of your business – the form of the business, employment of staff, maintenance of premises. Solicitors and accountants charge for their services, and you should be prepared for this! It may be useful to establish links with an accountant at this early stage because you will need one later on to help with the books, financial statements and tax calculations for the business. The major banks, too, offer specialist advice to new businesses; some may charge for the service, a fact you should establish before approaching a bank.

TECs *Training and Enterprise Councils (TECs)* are government sponsored independent regional bodies – there are over eighty in number - which provide training and advice to all types of business. They run the *Enterprise Allowance*, a scheme which provides financial assistance and training to selected unemployed people who want to start their own business.

Enterprise Agencies Most cities and large towns run *Enterprise Agencies* which offer small businesses free advice, run training schemes and introduce businesses to sources of finance such as the Local Authority.

If you want advice you should be prepared to go and 'shop around'. You will be able to find a solicitor or accountant in the 'Yellow Pages', but best of all is a recommendation from someone you know who already has dealings with a good solicitor or accountant. You will find the telephone numbers of TECs and Enterprise Agencies in the local phone book and at the Job Centre.

Whatever you do, you must seek advice. Even the most elementary point can be overlooked if a business is established without proper care and consultation. There are some horror stories about businesses that have failed because they did not know of the need to register for VAT (ie they should have added VAT to the prices of the goods they sold). When the VAT authorities (HM Customs and Excise) eventually caught up with them some time later, they were faced with bills for VAT which bankrupted them. Ignorance of the law is no excuse!

what form of business?

You will have to ask yourself a number of important questions when starting a business:

What legal form will my business take: sole trader, partnership or limited company?

We will look at all three types of business formation – sole trader, partnership and limited company – and examine the advantages and disadvantages of each.

sole trader

A sole trader is an individual trading in his or her name, or under a suitable trading name.

If you set up in business, you may do so for a number of reasons: redundancy, dissatisfaction with your present job, or developing a hobby or interest into a business. The majority of people setting up in this way do so on their own. If you decide to do so, you become a *sole trader*. You can use your own name, or adopt a trading name. You do not have to register a trading name, but you may find yourself in court if you use someone else's name or a name connected with royalty. You cannot, for instance open a shop and call it 'Marks and Spencer' or 'Royal Designs'.

There are a number of *advantages* of being a sole trader:

* freedom – you are your own boss
* simplicity – there is less form-filling than there is, for instance, for limited companies, and the book-keeping should be less complex
* savings on fees – there are none of the legal costs of drawing up partnership agreements or limited company documentation

There are also *disadvantages*:

* risk – you are on your own, with no-one to share the responsibilities of running the business
* time – you will need to work long hours to meet tight deadlines
* expertise – you may have limited skills in areas such as finance and marketing

You must also bear in mind the following *financial* considerations:

* capital – do you have sufficient money to start the business?
* tax – as a self-employed person you will have to pay Income Tax and National Insurance
* providing security to a lender – if you borrow for setting up in business you will probably have to pledge valuable assets (such as your home) or obtain the guarantee of someone you know
* liability for debt – you will be solely liable for all debts of the business; if the business fails you will have to repay all its debts, and may have to sell your personal assets; you may be taken to Court and be made bankrupt if you cannot do so

The accounting statements of sole traders are studied in detail in Chapter 7.

It is clear that setting up in business as a sole trader involves total commitment in terms of your capital, your time, your home, and the risk involved. If you are starting your business with other people or need to raise substantial capital, you may consider establishing a partnership or a limited company. The question is, which form of business is the better in your circumstances?

partnership

A partnership is a group of individuals working together in business with a view to making a profit.

A *partnership* is simple to establish and involves two or more people running a business together. The partners *are* the business. Examples of partnerships include groups of doctors, dentists, accountants, and solicitors.

A partnership – often known as a 'firm' – can either trade in the name of the partners, or under a suitable trading name. For example if M Smith & G Jones set up a glazing business, they could call themselves 'Smith and Jones & Co.' or adopt a more catchy name such as 'Classy Glass Merchants'. You should note that the '& Co.' does *not* mean that the partnership is a limited company.

A partnership does not have to be registered anywhere but it is often advisable for partners to have a partnership agreement drawn up by a solicitor. This will state what money is being invested by each partner, how profits are split, and what will happen if there is a dispute. It is an unfortunate fact that partners can argue, and if you are entering into a partnership you will have to make sure that you can get on with and trust your co-partners – they will be spending your money and running up business debts for which you will be liable!

The accounting statements of partnerships are covered in detail in Chapter 12.

limited company

A limited company is a separate legal body, owned by shareholders, run by directors.

A *limited company* is quite different from a sole trader in that it has a legal identity separate from its owners. The owners – the shareholders – are not personally liable for the business debts (the company's debts) but can be made so if they are asked by a lender to provide security (eg their homes) or give a guarantee (an undertaking to pay up if the company fails to repay its debts).

A company is managed by directors appointed by the shareholders (also known as members). In the case of many small companies the shareholders *are* the directors. A company must be registered at a central office known as Companies House. An annual return and financial statement must be sent each year to Companies House by the company. The rules for running the company must be set out in a set of documents known as the 'Memorandum and Articles of Association' which must also be sent to Companies House. As you will see there is much paperwork and 'red tape' involved in establishing and running a limited company.

It should be noted that a limited company can be referred to as either

* a *private limited company* (abbreviated to *Ltd*), or
* a *public limited company* (abbreviated to *plc*)

Most small or medium-sized businesses which decide to incorporate (form a company) become private limited companies. If, however, they are larger, with a share capital of over £50,000, they can become public limited companies. A plc *can* be quoted on the Stock Market, but not all take this step.

The accounting statements of limited companies are studied in detail in Chapter 13.

financing of business organisations

If you are starting a business, the type of business you choose – sole trader, partnership, limited company – will partly depend on the *financial needs* of the business. The question you should ask yourself is:

Do I have sufficient financial resources (savings and possible bank borrowing) to finance the business? Or will I have to involve partners or other people who can invest in the business?

In the next chapter we will look in detail at how to *calculate* the financial needs of a business. In this chapter we will confine ourselves to looking at the likely sources of finance and for what purposes the money will be required.

sole trader

sources A sole trader has to rely heavily on his or her own resources to finance the business. Sources of finance include

- savings
- sale of possessions, eg selling a house and buying a smaller one
- possible redundancy payments
- loans from family and friends
- loans from external sources – banks, Government agencies
- hire purchase
- profits from the business

needs A sole trader will use the money for two main purposes when starting or expanding a business

- *long-term* purchases such as premises, vehicles and equipment
- *short-term* requirements such as buying stock, paying bills, paying wages

Sole traders generally rely on their own financial resources and bank borrowing. Partnerships and limited companies on the other hand have more sources of finance that they can call upon. They need these further financial resources because their businesses are generally on a larger scale.

partnership

sources Partnerships can normally raise more money than sole trader businesses because there are more individuals who can contribute money to the enterprise. Further sources of finance for partnerships therefore include

- contributions from partners active in the business
- contributions from partners who are *not* active in the business; these partners are normally referred to as 'sleeping partners' – they provide the money, share in the profits, and let the other partners get on with running the business!

needs The financial needs of a partnership are largely the same as those of a sole trader business, but usually on a larger scale:

- *long-term* purchases such as premises, vehicles and equipment
- *short-term* requirements such as buying stock, paying bills, paying wages

limited company

sources
Limited companies are the largest form of business enterprise. The larger they are the more they rely on investment from individuals. Finance is provided by individuals buying *shares* in the company. The way the investment is made will depend on the size of the company:

- *small private limited company* – the shareholders may well be the directors who run the company
- *medium-sized private limited company* – the shares may be sold to outside companies or investors looking for a good return on their money
- *large public limited companies* – the shares may be sold to the public, eg British Telecom

Limited companies will, of course, still rely on other forms of external financing such as bank loans, hire purchase and loans from other companies.

needs
Limited companies, like sole traders and partnerships need finance for long-term and short-term purposes. They may also need finance for the acquisition of other companies and businesses.

The Case Study which follows looks at a small business wishing to expand. It highlights the advantages and disadvantages of partnerships and limited companies, and looks at the sources of and needs for finance.

Case Study: Output Services – partnership or limited company?

Situation

James Curry has been running a computer bureau as a sole trader for two years. His business, 'Output Systems', has involved managing the accounts and payroll for a number of local firms on his computer. He has worked from home and made a substantial profit in the first two years. He realises however that he must diversify to develop the business and he has suggested to Joe Harvey, a friend of his, that they join forces. Joe Harvey's interest is also in computers and he has been specialising in producing promotional literature for local firms and organising mailshots for them under the name 'Intermail Services'. Joe has agreed that they could pool their resources and offer a useful package of computer services, trading under the name of 'Output Services'. They seek professional advice from a solicitor and an accountant as to whether they should form a trading partnership or a limited company. They also ask about the financial aspects of their proposals.

the solicitor's advice

liability

If they form a *partnership,* they are both individually and collectively responsible for all he debts of the partnership. If they form a *limited company* it is a separate legal entity, responsible for its own debts. They will become directors, ie employees of the company, and not strictly speaking liable for its debts, but . . .

security

If a partnership borrows from the bank, the partners will invariably have to offer a mortgage of their homes as security. If they become directors of a company and the company borrows, the directors may be asked to guarantee the borrowing and support the guarantee with a mortgage over their homes – ie the position of personal liability with respect to *security* is little changed whether they are partners or directors.

documentation

A *partnership* is often (not always) formalised in a written Partnership Agreement which the solicitor can draw up for them. The formation and registration of a *limited company* require much more documentation (including the Memorandum and Articles of Association) and are therefore more expensive in terms of legal fees. Running a limited company also involves more paperwork such as maintaining the minutes of meetings, filing accounts and annual returns.

The solicitor suggests that on the face of it a partnership would be the cheaper and simpler alternative, subject to their being able to get on with each other (the Partnership Agreement could cover cases of disputes) and also subject to the tax position, a subject with which the accountant can help them.

the accountant's advice

taxation

Partners are liable for personal Income Tax on profits divided between them and also liable for National Insurance Contributions. A limited company is subject to Corporation Tax on its profits and the directors are additionally liable on their salaries for Income Tax and National Insurance Contributions (which are also payable by the company).

audit and accounts

A partnership is not required to have its accounts audited, but a company's accounts must, by law, be audited and sent each year to Companies House where they are available for public inspection, although smaller companies can submit abridged accounts. The accountant's fees for a limited company will generally be higher than for a partnership.

raising of finance

It is often easier for a limited company to raise funds as there are generally individuals and companies ready to take shares in a small company as a form of investment. The accountant points out that this form of investment is more readily available to larger companies. This form of finance is not available to partnerships which rely more heavily on the introduction of money (capital) by the partners.

Solution

James and Joe decide that, as they work well together, they will choose the simpler and cheaper option of forming a partnership. They will ask the solicitor to draw up a Partnership Agreement for them and the accountant to advise on book-keeping, taxation and the payment of wages. They bear in mind that, if the business expands further, they may in the future form a limited company, but only if their personal tax bills justify the action (ie if they are paying tax at higher rates), and if they need to raise further finance from ouside investors who want to buy shares in the proposed company.

other organisations – financial resources

So far in this chapter we have dealt with the financing of businesses. It must be appreciated that other organisations own assets and require financing. Set out below is a summary of the financial resources of some of the other organisations we will be examining or referring to elsewhere in this book. The details given are typical only – organisations will vary enormously in the way they are established and run.

organisation	items owned	sources of finance
Local Authorities	buildings, vehicles, materials	local taxes, government grants, investors
clubs	buildings, equipment, materials	members' subscriptions, grants
charities	buildings and equipment	donations, fund raising efforts
the family	house, car and belongings	HP, loans, mortgage

You will probably wonder why the family – already dealt with in the first section of this book – has been included as an organisation. It is the most common social organisation in existence, and the principles of financial resourcing are as crucial to the family as they are to the business.

Chapter Summary

❏ An individual setting up in business needs to consider carefully the chosen type of business and examine critically the motives for starting the enterprise.

❏ The sources of advice for setting up a new business include banks, accountants, solicitors, TEC's and Enterprise Agencies.

❏ An individual setting up in business can operate either as a sole trader, or join forces with others to form a partnership, or set up a limited company.

❏ A partnership is simpler and less expensive to establish than a limited company, but the directors of a limited company have limited liability, unlike the partners of a firm who are each fully liable for the total debt of a partnership.

❏ The decision on the form of business will depend in part on the financial resources which are available and the financial resources which are needed.

❏ Partnerships and limited companies provide more scope for raising external finance than a sole trader business, whereas all types of business rely on bank borrowing as a financial resource.

In the next chapter we will look at the way in which a business sets out its sources and uses of finance in the form of a financial statement known as a *balance sheet*.

Student Activities

4.1 Assume that you have been in business as a sole trader for many years. You get talking to a friend in a pub; he says that he is thoroughly fed up with his present job as a wages clerk in a large organisation. He wants to set up his own business as a sole trader photographer. He asks "What does it take to set up on your own? What sort of a person do you have to be?" What would be your reply?

4.2 You meet the same friend (see Activity 4.1) a week later, and he has decided to go ahead with his plan to become a sole trader photographer. He says he is familiar with all there is to know about photography, but he is not so sure about running a business. To what sources of advice would you direct him? How could they help him?

4.3 You are the Enterprise Officer in the local TEC (Training and Enterprise Council) and have an interview with Tina Marchant in an hour's time. She is considering opening a maternity clothes and babywear shop called 'Great Expectations' in one of Stourminster's fashionable shopping arcades. She wants to be a sole trader. What sources of finance are available to her, and what will she need to spend her money on in the first month of trading? Prepare some notes to help you in the interview. (You do not need to provide detailed financial projections.)

4.4 Choose two different areas of business in your local Yellow Pages, for example cellular radio suppliers and TV repairers, and identify (where possible) what proportion of each are

- sole traders
- partnerships
- limited companies

Illustrate your findings by means of pie charts. Is there any difference in the proportional breakdown of different business types? If there is, explain the reasons for your findings.

4.5 John Simpson and Helen Jones are interested in setting up in business jointly to operate river cruises under the business name of 'Sabrina Cruises'. They have £30,000 between them to invest and need a further £25,000 to buy and equip their first boat. They are not sure whether to form a partnership or a limited company. You are the Enterprise Officer working in the local TEC. Set out your advice to them in the form of a letter. Make it as simple as possible, and avoid legal or financial jargon. (You can invent names/addresses/dates).

4.6 Helen Jones telephones you back the following week to say that she and John Simpson have still not sorted out their ideas about partnerships and limited companies. She adds that she has an uncle who is willing to invest £25,000 in their business (see Activity 4.5); he is not sure whether he will be a 'sleeping partner' or a shareholder. He is very firm on the point that he does not want to be liable for the business debts!

Investigate the matter and let Helen Jones know the outcome. (This could be an interview situation or a staged telephone call).

4.7 Draw up a list of the organisations with which you have contact or to which you belong – eg employer, college, transport service, shops, clubs. Draw up columns setting out:

- what types of organisation they are
- their sources of finance
- what they own

5 Assets, capital and liabilities

introduction

In the last chapter we saw that financial resources involve

- items that a business owns
- the sources of finance which enable the business to obtain those items

In this chapter we look more closely at how an organisation – a sole trader business in this case – balances these requirements in money terms in the form of a financial statement known as a *balance sheet*.

We shall look at types of expenditure – *capital expenditure* (buying items for long-term use in the business), and *revenue expenditure* (short-term items and running expenses), and introduce some accounting terminology.

Although in this chapter we will look at a sole trader business, it must be remembered that the same financial principles apply to *all* organisations: businesses, clubs and associations, local authorities, and so on. We will examine the financial statements of these bodies in detail later in the book (see Chapters 7 to 17).

Case Study: starting a business

Situation
You are setting up a fashion clothes shop as a sole trader business. Forget for the time being where the money is coming from (assume finance has been arranged).

1. What are your expenses going to be in the first month of trading? Write down all the expenses you are likely to incur for the business (ignore your personal expenses). Write down the *type* of expenses; it is not essential to write down actual figures, although you may do so if you wish.

2. Look critically at the types of expense involved and try to arrange these expenses into categories. What is the money going towards? Are you getting anything tangible as a result?

solution

Your list may include some of the following items and categories:

items bought (long-term)	items bought (short-term)	running expenses
premises	stock of clothes	rent for shop (if not bought)
shop fittings	stationery	business rates
delivery van	cash for the till	wages
		insurance
		electricity/gas/telephone/water
		petrol for van
		postage costs
		coffee for visitors

What conclusions can be drawn from this exercise? First, it is evident that it is very *expensive* to start in business, and the costing out of the enterprise is essential. We will return to this later in the chapter.

What do the categories of expense represent?

assets

The first two columns (from the left) show items bought which can be *used* in the business: for example premises, delivery van, stocks of clothes. These are known as *assets*.

assets are items owned

As we will see on the next page, assets can be categorised into *long-term* assets and *short-term* (current) assets. All organisations require assets. Examine the assets required by the three very different types of business set out below.

an insurance broker
- premises
- fittings (desks, reception area)
- equipment (telephones/fax, typewriter/word processor)
- office materials (stationery)
- a float of cash for use in the office
- money in the bank to pay the bills

a minicab service
- a car, licensed and equipped for carrying passengers
- a mobile phone
- a float of cash
- money in the bank to pay the bills

a manufacturing workshop
- premises
- machinery (lathes, tools)
- equipment (computer, typewriter)
- a delivery van
- materials
- a float of cash
- money in the bank to pay the bills

fixed and current assets

If you examine the assets described in the examples above and in the student activity you will see that they can be subdivided into two categories: fixed (long-term) assets and current (short-term) assets:

fixed assets   *Fixed assets are long-term assets* which the business intends to keep for use in the business. They include:
- premises
- vehicles
- machinery and equipment

current assets   *Current assets* are items used in the everyday running of the business, and not intended to be held for any length of time. They include:
- materials and stock
- money in the bank
- cash held

All of these items – current assets – will be changing from day-to-day in the normal course of trading.

A less obvious form of current asset not mentioned so far is money owed to the business by its customers and clients. This is an asset because it is a debt 'owned' by the business and will hopefully be paid and turned into money. In business such debts owed are known by the general term *debtors*.

assets and running expenses:
capital expenditure and revenue expenditure

If you refer to the answer to the student activity at the top of the previous page, you will see that the column on the right shows *running expenses:* the money is spent and you do not own anything as a result. You do however see a *benefit:* services such as street lighting and waste disposal from the local authority (for rates paid), staffing for the shop (wages paid), and so on. The distinction between spending money on assets and on running expenses should be borne clearly in mind.

It is now possible to define two different types of expenditure: *capital expenditure* and *revenue expenditure*.

capital expenditure   is expenditure on fixed (long-term) assets such as premises, vehicles, and equipment

revenue expenditure   is expenditure on current (short-term) assets such as stock and materials, and expenditure on running expenses

You may rightly ask why the distinction is important. There are two basic reasons:

information   The owner of the business and outside bodies such as banks, accountants and purchasers (if you are selling the business) will want to know what the business is worth and what financial resources are represented in the fixed assets of the business.

taxation   Businesses are taxed on their profits. They are allowed to set off most revenue expenses against tax, ie *these expenses are deducted from the profit figure which is used to calculate the tax bill*. So the lower the eventual profit figure, the lower the tax bill. Businesses can, generally speaking, only set off a proportion of their capital expenditure against tax. So if you buy a new fixed asset such as a van you cannot reduce your taxable profit by the full cost of that van in the year of purchase.

Two important questions to be considered when planning your expenditure are

> *How much is it all going to cost?*

> *Where is the money coming from?*

In the next chapter (and also in Chapter 22) we will see how this planning process is formalised in a document known as a Business Plan. First, however, we will examine the main sources of finance for the business – *capital* (money provided by the owner or owners) and *liabilities* (money borrowed from outside sources) – and see how these relate to the assets in a financial statement known as the *balance sheet*.

financing your assets - capital and liabilities

capital

capital is money introduced into the business by its owner(s)

Depending on the form of business involved, capital comprises:

- money introduced by the sole trader into his or her own business
- funds introduced by the partners into a partnership
- money paid by the shareholders of a limited company for shares in the company

Looked at another way, *capital is money owed to the owner by the business*.

liabilities

a liability is an amount owed to an outside source

Finance provided by outside sources includes

- bank loans and overdrafts
- loans from business associates, family and friends
- credit provided by organisations which supply you with goods or services, asking for payment at a later date. These are known as *creditors*. In effect they are providing you with a temporary loan, because you can make use of the money you owe them for the time being.

Just as assets are classified under the two headings of *fixed* (long-term) and *current* (short-term), so liabilities are subdivided according to how quickly the money has to be repaid:

long-term liabilities   Amounts owed to outside bodies which are repayable over a period *longer than a year*, eg fixed bank loans, commercial mortgages.

current liabilities   Amounts owing which are repayable within a year, eg bank overdraft (strictly speaking repayable on demand), and *creditors*, the amounts owing to suppliers of goods and services.

In the next section we will see how the two financial aspects of the business – items owned and the sources of finance – are balanced in a financial statement known as a *balance sheet*.

financing your assets – the balance sheet

the balance sheet equation

We have seen that the assets of a business (or any organisation) are financed by liabilities and capital:

Assets (items owned) = Capital (owner's investment) + Liabilities (amounts owed to outsiders)

This equation could be expressed in numerical terms as

Assets (£100,000) = Capital (£60,000) + Liabilities (£40,000)

If you wanted to work out the amount of capital of the business (ie what it is worth to the owner) in relation to to the assets and liabilities, you could rewrite the equation as

Assets (£100,000) - Liabilities (£40,000) = Capital (the owner's investment) of £60,000

The calculation of *Assets - Liabilities* is known as the *Net Assets* of the business, and this always equals the *Capital* (what the business is worth to the owner). The equation can be rewritten as:

Net Assets (here Assets of £100,000 less Liabilities of £40,000) = Capital (£60,000)

This equation forms the basis of the *balance sheet*, an important financial statement. The balance sheet is so called because it shows what a business or organisation owns and owes at any given date. The layout is normally vertical in form, with the figures set out in columns The total of the top section, the *net assets*, balances numerically with the bottom section, the *capital*. Note that the net assets distinguish between fixed assets (£80,000), long-term liabilities (£40,000) and *current* assets and liabilities. Note also that it is the *difference* between current assets and current liabilities (£20,000) which is used in the calculation.

Fixed Assets	**£80,000**
plus	*plus*
Current Assets *less* Current Liabilities	**£20,000**
	equals
	£100,000
less	*less*
Long Term Liabilities	**£40,000**
equals	*equals*
NET ASSETS	£60,000
FINANCED BY	*equals*
CAPITAL	£60,000

Now look carefully at the specimen balance sheet of Broadgreen Stores, a corner shop, and read the notes set out below:

BALANCE SHEET OF BROADGREEN STORES
AS AT 31 DECEMBER 1992

	£	£	£
Fixed Assets			
Premises			100,000
Equipment			30,000
Vehicles			21,500
			151,500
Current Assets			
Stock		36,300	
Debtors		3,850	
Cash in till		125	
		40,275	
Less Current Liabilities			
Creditors	15,516		
Bank overdraft	851		
		16,367	
Working Capital			23,908
			175,408
Less Long-term Liabilities			
Bank long-term loan			33,000
NET ASSETS			142,408
FINANCED BY			
CAPITAL			
Owner's capital			142,408

Although the construction and format of the balance sheet will be explained in full in Chapter 7, you should note the following at this stage:

- the balance sheet is given a name and a date
- the top section represents *Assets less Liabilities,* known as *Net Assets;* the bottom section is the *Capital*, the owner's investment – they balance numerically: £142,408 in this case
- the figures are set out in vertical columns
- for the sake of clarity some columns which carry out arithmetical calculations are inset *to the left* and the totals carried to the next *right*-hand column
- a new term – *working capital* – is introduced: this is simply the short-term position of the business (current assets less current liabilities) which shows how much money the business has to meet its immediate debts – here the figure is £23,908

Chapter Summary

❑ An individual setting up in business will spend money on
  • assets – items owned by the business
  • running expenses

❑ Assets can be
  • *fixed assets* – long term assets which the business intends to keep for an extended period
  • *current assets* – short term assets which are used in the everyday running of the business
  Debtors – classed as a current asset – are the people who owe the business money

❑ Expenditure can be classed as
  • *capital expenditure* – expenditure on fixed assets
  • *revenue expenditure*– expenditure on current assets and running expenses

❑ Assets can be financed by
  • *capital* – money introduced by the owner(s) of the busainess
  • *liabilities* – amounts owed to outside sources

❑ Liabilities can be
  • *long-term liabilities*– debts repayable over a period longer than a year
  • *current liabilities* – amounts repayable within a year
  Creditors – classed as a current liability – are the people to whom the business owes money

❑ A balance sheet is a financial statement used by businesses and other organisations showing how net assets (total assets less total liabilities) are financed by capital.   The equation is

assets less liabilities (ie net assets) = capital

In the next chapter we will look in detail at how organisations are financed from external sources such as bank lending and hire purchase.

 Student Activities

5.1 You are setting up in business as a sole trader courier, delivering messages, documents and small packages. You are adopting the trading name of 'Prestolink'. You intend to buy a motorbike for yourself, and work from home where you have a telephone. What sort of expenditure are you likely to incur in setting up this business? You should set out your requirements in terms of:

(a) fixed assets

(b) current assets

(c) running expenses

Try to estimate the costs as accurately as possible.

5.2 You are studying finance at college and have been asked by a friend who is setting up in business about certain terms he has come across in a book and which he does not really understand. These terms are:

(a) fixed and current assets

(b) capital and revenue expenditure

(c) capital and liabilities

(d) debtors and creditors

He adds that he is particularly confused by why capital is not an asset – he says that money is an asset, and capital is money put in by the owner. He says that he cannot see why a debtor is an asset – it is not an item owned 'which he can put in the back of his van,' it is a debt.

You are to set out brief notes explaining items (a) to (d) , and sorting out his muddled ideas.

5.3 You work as an Accounts Manager for Loveday & Loveday, accountants at 12 The High Street, Upton-on-Stour, WR5 6TF. Two of your clients, Fred Noakes and Alice Pereira, want to start up individual small businesses, Fred as a wine merchant and Alice working from home as a jewellery manufacturer. They provide you with financial details of the assets they need to purchase, and the money which they have available. They ask you if they will need any further finance. You are to draw up balance sheets, showing the bank finance which you think they may need (the type of finance is indicated by the question marks in the columns below). You should also draft covering letters briefly setting out your recommendations. Fred lives at 12 Church Walk, Upton-on-Stour, WR5 3LK, and Alice at 'The Nook', Welland Lane, Upton-on-Stour, WR5 6JH. Use your own name and today's date.

Financial details	Fred	Alice
	£	£
Premises	55,000	-
Vehicle	8,000	7,500
Equipment	1,000	1,000
Stocks	2,500	7,000
Cash	500	500
Capital available	25,000	9,000
Loan from family	30,000	-
Long-term loan from bank	?	-
Overdraft from bank	-	?

5.4 You are working as an assistant at the local TEC (Training and Enterprise Council). You are helping with a seminar 'Accounting for the Small Business.' Three sole trader businesses have produced at your request some financial details and have asked you to draw up balance sheets as at today's date. None of them knows what their 'capital' figure is. The businesses and their figures are as follows:

Rob's Minicab Service
Vehicle £8,500, cash-in-hand £100, money in the bank £900, creditors £500.

Cathy and Sarah's Flower Basket (a florists shop)
Premises £75,000, vehicle £5,000, shop fittings £5,000, stock £7,000, debtors £5,000, cash £275, creditors £2,175, bank overdraft £3,100.

Tom & Ben's Bistro
Premises £150,000, vehicle £9,000, wine bar fittings £10,000, stock £4,400, debtors £5,600, cash £278, creditors £3,510, bank overdraft £4,900, bank long-term loan £75,000.

6 Financing a business

introduction

In the last chapter we saw that individuals and organisations often need to fund their operations by means of *external finance* – which appears on the balance sheet as a *liability*.   In this chapter we will look at:

* the *types* of external finance available
* the *sources* of external finance
* the *costs* of external finance

We will also look at the different types of *financial services* available to organisations from the banks and other financial institutions.

We will examine by means of a Case Study how a business assesses its need for external finance and financial services when it is starting up, and also when it is expanding.

applying for external finance

how much external finance ?

There are a number of situations where external finance may be needed. These include

* starting up a new business
* buying a business
* expanding an existing business

Some people do not like relying on external finance. One sometimes hears the old-fashioned notion that there is something *wrong* with borrowing. It must be stressed that *sensible* borrowing is essential to business growth. Without outside finance many good ideas would never have got off the ground. What, however, is *sensible* borrowing? A provider of external finance – such as a bank – will need reassuring about the owner's commitment to the business, and will not want to lend more than the owner is contributing. The lender will ask the potential borrower:

What percentage of the total finance needed by the business are you putting in yourself?

If you are putting in less than 50%, is it possible for you to raise more from your private sources?

If you are borrowing from us, can you show how you can repay that borrowing?

If the business is a *new* one, the provider of finance will rarely lend more than half of the start-up cost, unless it will be repaid quickly. If the owner puts in less than 50%, a lender may quite rightly ask the question: "whose business is it?" If the finance is needed for expanding an *existing* business, the lender will not normally want to see outside borrowing (including the new borrowing) exceed the capital of the owner(s).

the Business Plan

It is normal, if you are applying to an outside body for finance – a bank for example – to prepare a written plan, normally referred to as a *Business Plan*. This sets out your product, expertise, market, your pricing policy and, most important of all, your *financial* requirements – ie how much you want to borrow. The Business Plan will be dealt with in detail in Chapter 22 following our explanation in intervening chapters of how differing business organisations prepare and finalise their accounts including their balance sheets), projections of which normally appear in the Business Plan.

It is sufficient for the purposes of this chapter to note that the borrowing requirements of a business are calculated by means of a *cash flow forecast* (also known as a *cash budget*) used by the business to forecast expected 'cash in' and expected 'cash out' on a monthly basis. If there is a cash shortfall, particularly in the early months of operations when substantial costs are incurred, then this difference is the amount of external finance required by the business. If you want to investigate Business Plans further at this stage, most banks provide helpful advice and literature about how to compile a Business Plan, and you are well advised to ask your local branch for assistance.

matching the finance to the assets

As you will have seen from the balance sheet in the previous chapter, it is customary to categorise both assets and liabilities into their expected life span: short-term and long-term. Lenders will normally want to match the period of any lending to the expected life of the asset financed. There are *three* generally accepted timescales for finance, although you may find definitions which will vary from these:

short-term	1 to 2 years	short-term requirements, eg stock
medium-term	3 to 10 years	purchase of fixed assets, eg machinery
long-term	11 to 25 years	purchase of land and premises

As you will see, the longer the life of the asset purchased, the longer the loan that will be made available. A lender will obviously be unwilling to lend money over 25 years to finance an ice cream salesman for his summer stocks, but will provide funds over that period to enable a company to purchase a factory unit. In short, the period for repayment of the finance should *match* the expected life of the asset. The next section examines the different *types* of finance available to businesses, and the *sources* of that finance.

bank finance

We will now consider the various types and sources of finance. It should be noted that some of the sources listed here only provide finance to limited companies: this will be made clear in the text. The banks are the largest providers of finance to *all* types of businesses. Forms of lending vary from bank to bank, and you should make your own investigations into the timespans of individual bank facilities. A bank will be able to arrange, by itself, or through specialised companies which it owns:

- overdraft
- short and medium-term loans ('business loans')
- commercial mortgage
- leasing for equipment purchase
- factoring services
- venture capital

Before looking at each of these forms of financing in turn, it is important to appreciate how *interest rates* are set, and also what *security* is required for lending.

interest rates

The cost of borrowing usually involves two separate expenses:

* an *arrangement fee* – charged when the finance is arranged, and in some cases when it is renewed
* *interest* – a specific charge calculated as a percentage of the amount borrowed

Banks generally set their interest rates at a set percentage (which varies according to the risk element in the lending) *above* the prevailing Base Rate. Base Rate is an advertised fixed rate, set and varied periodically by the major banks, who use it as a *base* for working out interest rates for borrowers. No-one ever borrows at Base Rate. Base Rate is varied in line with interest rates in the economy. In this respect business borrowing differs from most *personal* borrowing – eg a car loan – which is charged at a *fixed* rate expressed in terms of an APR (Annual Percentage Rate) which the law requires be quoted to the borrower.

Interest is normally charged to the bank account of the borrower on a monthly or quarterly basis.

security for lending

Lending to businesses is seen by the financial institutions as being risky, because statistically businesses become bankrupt more often than do personal borrowers. Whereas a bank may lend £2,000 to a private individual for a new kitchen and not require any security cover, business borrowers will nearly always be asked to provide some security. Security can be in the form of:

* a *mortgage* – a legal document which the borrower signs stating in effect that, if the finance is not repaid, the lender can sell whatever is being 'mortgaged' . The items mortgaged can include the house of the borrower (the most common form of security) or investments with a market value, such as stocks and shares and insurance policies
* a *guarantee* – a legal document signed by an individual (the 'guarantor') stating that, if the borrower fails to repay when asked to, then the guarantor will pay up; limited companies are often guaranteed by their directors in this way

Security for business borrowing is normally

sole trader	a mortgage over the home or any marketable investments
partnership	a mortgage over the homes or any marketable investments belonging to the partners
limited company	a mortgage over the assets of the company (this document is known as a 'debenture' or a 'fixed and floating charge') and/or the guarantees of the directors

types of bank finance

overdraft   An overdraft is short-term borrowing on bank current account. It is relatively cheap: the banks charge typically 4% to 6% over Base Rate for a new business, 2.5% to 5% over Base Rate for an existing business. Interest is normally charged quarterly, but you only pay interest on what you actually borrow. A 'limit' up to which you can borrow will be granted by the bank, and reviewed annually, when it can be increased, decreased or renewed at the same level. A renewal fee is payable for this service.

business loan
This is a fixed medium-term loan, typically for between 3 and 10 years, to cover the purchase of capital items such as machinery or equipment. Interest is normally 2% to 3% over base rate, and repayments are by instalments. Sometimes repayment of principal (the full amount borrowed) can be postponed during the first two years of the loan (a 'repayment holiday') when only interest payments are made.

commercial mortgage
If you are buying premises for your business you can arrange to borrow long-term by means of a commercial mortgage, typically up to 80% of the value of the property, repayable over a period of up to 25 years. Your premises will be taken as security for the loan: if the business fails, the premises will be sold.

other forms of finance arranged through bank-owned companies

Finance Houses, specialist companies owned in the main by the major banks, offer alternative ways of obtaining assets:

hire purchase (HP)
An HP agreement from a finance house enables a business to acquire an asset on the payment of a deposit and to pay back the cost plus interest over a set period, at the end of which ownership of the asset passes to the borrower. Hire purchase is often used to finance vehicles and machinery.

leasing
Leasing arrangements are also provided by finance houses. With a leasing agreement, the business has use of assets bought by the finance house, and the business pays a regular 'rental' payment, normally over a lease period of two to seven years. Ownership of the goods never passes to the business. A common form of lease is a *pay back lease* or *finance lease* in which the business will pay back the cost of the item plus finance costs over the period of the lease. Clearly a lease is not a loan, but it can substantially reduce a business' financial requirements when it needs to make a capital purchase. Computer equipment and fleets of company cars are often leased.

factoring
Many banks also provide *factoring services* through specialist factoring companies. A business may have valuable financial resources tied up because its customers owe it money and have not yet paid. A factoring company will effectively 'buy' these debts by providing a number of services:

- it will lend up to 80% of outstanding customer debts
- it will deal with all the paperwork of collecting customer debts
- it will insure against non-payment of debts

Factoring *frees* money due to the business and allows the business to use it in its general operations and expansion plans. It is therefore a valuable source of short-term finance.

finance for limited companies: venture capital

Many banks own *merchant banks,* specialist banks which offer advice and financial assistance to limited companies. This financial assistance takes the form of loans and *venture capital*. Ownership of a limited company is in the form of shares, known as equity capital, held by the investors. Merchant banks may view such companies as ripe for investment and will inject money either in the form of loans or by the purchase of shares, or both. In return, they may expect an element of control over the company and will possibly insist on having a director on the board of the company. A merchant bank considering investing in a limited company will look for a business with a good profit record, strong management and a viable product range.

The funds introduced by the merchant bank could be used for:

- financing an expansion or launching a new product
- acquisition of another company
- the management of the company 'buying out' control of the company
- financing the employees 'buying out' control of the company

Other financial institutions active in the venture capital market include:

- *Investors in Industry Group plc (3i)*, a company offering 5 to 20 year loans and requiring share capital in the borrowing company.
- *venture capital companies,* non-banking commercial organisations which attract money from private investors and re-invest in limited companies. Their financial assistance includes loans and investment in share capital. They often require a substantial element of control over the borrowing company.

financial assistance from the Government

The Government offers considerable assistance in the way of grants, subsidies and training. These are made available directly and indirectly to new and established businesses.

The Department of Trade and Industry (DTI) 'Enterprise Initiative'
The DTI has divided the UK into two types of area (illustrated in the map on the next page):

- *assisted* areas (development, intermediate and urban programme areas)
- *non-assisted areas* (the rest of the country)

The following schemes are currently available:

Assisted Areas
- Regional Selective Assistance (discretionary grants for companies creating new jobs)
- Regional Enterprise Grants for firms with under 25 employees (Development Areas only)
- Consultancy grants: two-thirds of the cost of approved business consultancy

Non-Assisted Areas
- Consultancy grants: half of the cost of approved business consultancy

other assistance for all areas
- 'Managing into the 90's' Programme: information and advice on the management of product design, quality manufacture, purchasing and sales
- Research and Technology Initiative: training sessions and grants towards research projects

The Rural Development Commission
The Rural Development Commission provides businesses in rural areas with free advice and technical support. In development areas (see above) loans and grants are available.

Inner City 'Task Forces'
Task Forces are advisory bodies which operate in Inner City areas. They provide advice, training and financial assistance for new and growing businesses. The Task Force Development Funds (TFDFs) provide last resort loans and grants through the Local Enterprise Agencies.

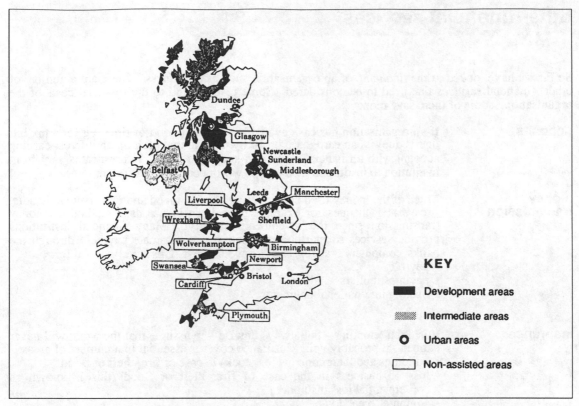

Fig 6.1 The DTI Enterprise Initiative: the Assisted Areas

The Department of Employment: Loan Guarantee Scheme

The government offers a guarantee for 70% (85% for certain Inner City 'Task Force' Areas) of a bank medium-term loan (2 to 7 years) up to £100,000. This security enables banks and other financial institutions to lend money for projects which would be too risky by normal criteria. Borrowing under this scheme is not cheap because a premium of 2.5% p.a. is charged to the borrower on the guaranteed amount of the loan. The scheme has been very successful, however, and has enabled many businesses to expand, Waterstones Bookshops in its early days, for example.

Training and Enterprise Councils (TECs) – Enterprise Allowance Scheme

The Enterprise Allowance scheme is run by the local TECs (Training and Enterprise Councils) and provides financial assistance and training to selected previously unemployed people wanting to set up a *new* business. The schemes are tailor-made by each local TEC. An applicant would typically:

- have been unemployed for six weeks
- be able to contribute £1,000 (from savings, or bank overdraft, or loan)
- attend an introductory training course
- write (with help provided by the TEC) a Business Plan which has to be approved by the TEC

If *accepted* by the local TEC the applicant would

- be paid a regular living wage for a year
- be given a free place on a 'Business Skills Seminar'
- be able to take advantage of advisory services and other training courses provided by the local TEC

other financial services

So far we have looked at the *financing* of an organisation such as a business. There are a number of other financial *services* that need to be considered. Some of them add to the financial costs of the organisation, some of them save money.

deposits

If an organisation has cash available for any period of time (eg for a tax bill that is due) it can earn extra profit by placing that cash on an interest-earning account with a financial institution such as a bank. Interest rates vary from institution to institution, and so it is worth comparing different rates.

money transmission

Much of the money used nowadays is old-fashioned and expensive to handle – cash and cheques for example have been in use as a method of money transmission since the seventeenth century!   Many financial institutions provide services so that an organisation can automate payment through the banks' computers systems, and so save money. This is very useful for:
• payroll
• paying suppliers
• making international payments

insurance

It is often tempting – but always unwise – to assume that the worst will never happen - it probably will!   Insurance cover is essential in a number of areas:
• buildings and their contents (eg stock) in case of fire, theft or flood
• loss of business in the case of fire, theft or flood (this is known as consequential loss insurance)
• computer breakdown
• your customer suing you because of a faulty product or service
• your customer suing you because of an accident on your premises

Insurance cover can also be arranged for employees of an organisation or for sole traders
• 'key person' insurance will pay compensation if a 'key' director or partner in a business dies or suffers some disability
• 'income protection' cover will compensate the self-employed person in cases of injury or illness

pensions

A working person will have to retire some day, and the provision for a suitable pension plan (in addition to the state pension) should not be overlooked, either by the employer or the employee. A pension plan is a form of savings scheme which provides a lump sum and/or annual payments on retirement.   The pension – which is normally organised by a specialised financial institution – can be contributed by
• an employer paying for the pension of its employee (possibly with additional contributions by the employee)
• a self-employed person paying into a specific pension plan
• an employer – such as a limited company contributing towards a specific pension plan for its directors

The person or organisation which contributes towards the pension plan is allowed to set the contributions, up to defined limits, against tax. In other words the individual or organisation which makes the contributions does not have to pay tax on the money invested – a major advantage. Some businesses borrow money against the pension scheme, or use the pension scheme money to buy premises and then rent the premises from the pension scheme.

the cost of bank finance

It is essential when carrying out financial planning that the *cost* of finance is considered.   As we saw earlier in the chapter, bank finance involves two types of charge – fees and interest:

fees   *arrangement fees* are charged when the finance is arranged

renewal fees are charged when the finance is renewed (eg every year for an overdraft)

security fees are charged when security is taken to cover the borrowing

interest   Interest – the basic cost of borrowing – is charged monthly or quarterly. For example, if a business borrows £100,000 to purchase fixed assets, and the interest rate is 16% p.a., the business will have to pay

$$£100,000 \quad x \quad \frac{16}{100} = \quad £16,000 \text{ interest per year}$$

The charges made by the banks vary from bank to bank, but most institutions now publish their business tariff in booklet form, available from the branches. A person starting up a business would be well advised to 'shop around' for the best deal. Some banks offer special terms for new business start-ups; these are well worth investigating. The table set out below shows some *typical* charges for bank facilities of £50,000. It must be remembered that interest rates will vary as base rate changes, and more risky customers will be charged higher rates than less risky customers. The figures set out below are for general guidance only.

typical cost of bank finance of £50,000 (assuming a base rate of 10%)		
type of finance	**interest payable**	**fees payable**
overdraft of £50,000 for day-to-day needs (working capital)	Base Rate + 4% 10% + 4% = 14% amount = £7,000 p.a.	arrangement fee of 1.25% of amount = £625 renewal fee of 0.75% of amount = £375 security fee = £500
business loan or **commercial mortgage** of £50,000 for purchase of fixed assets	Base Rate + 3% 10% + 3% = 13% amount = £6,500 p.a.	arrangement fee of 1.25% of amount = £625 no renewal fee security fee = £500

conclusions

You will see from the table that the interest costs for an overdraft appear higher, but in fact they will probably be lower, because for an overdraft *you are only charged interest for what you borrow on a day-to-day basis*.   As the balance of the account fluctuates from being overdrawn to being in credit, your interest charge will be calculated accordingly. The balances on a business loan and commercial mortgage on the other hand remain fairly constant, at a high level, and interest will be charged on the full amount.   This is the reason why the overdraft is often referred to as the cheapest form of borrowing.

The fees payable on the different types of bank finance do not differ significantly. In the long run the overdraft will incur more fees because, unlike a business loan or commercial mortgage, it is usually renewed on a yearly basis, and an additional renewal fee will then become payable.

Case Study:
Capability Landscapes – financing a business

Situation 1 – raising the finance

James Brown is a qualified landscape gardener who has been working for a large firm of gardening contractors for five years. His aim has been to gain experience of the trade so that he can eventually set up on his own as an independent landscape gardener. He has chosen the name 'Capability Landscapes' for his business. James intends to work from home, so he will not need premises. He will however need a pickup truck and equipment, including a lawnmower and cultivator. He has saved hard and has accumulated £5,000 in a building society account. In addition, his uncle has promised to lend him £5,000 over five years to help him get established. His uncle has also promised to guarantee any borrowing from the bank.

The question is, how much is it all going to cost, and will James need to borrow?

James is not experienced in financial matters, so he contacts his local Business Promotion Centre which puts him in touch with an accountant who specialises in helping small businesses.

Solution

The accountant asks him to set out on paper what items he will need for the business, and how much they are likely to cost – these items will be his *assets*. His accountant asks him to distinguish between items which he will need permanently in the business – *fixed assets* – and items which he will on a day-to-day basis – *current assets*. James produces the following figures:

	£	£
fixed assets required		
pickup truck, secondhand	8,000	
lawnmower and cultivator	900	
gardening tools	350	
total of fixed assets		9,250
current assets required		
initial stock of plants and seed	1,500	
fertilisers	150	
cash in hand	100	
total of current assets		1,750
TOTAL ASSETS REQUIRED		11,000

The accountant then asks James to look at how much finance he has available. He asks him to distinguish between *capital* (the amount he is putting in himself) and *liabilities* (any borrowing from other sources). James produces the following figures:

	£
capital	
building society savings	5,000
liabilities	
loan (long-term) from uncle	5,000
TOTAL FINANCE AVAILABLE	10,000

how much finance is needed?

The accountant points out that James needs finance of £1,000 on the basis of his calculations: he needs £11,000 of assets and has only £10,000 available.

The accountant recommends that James approaches his bank for an overdraft of £1,000, which can be guaranteed by his uncle. He says that an overdraft is the best solution because it is short-term (for financing short-term assets) and it is also the cheapest form of borrowing.

The accountant promises to draw up this proposal in a formal *Business Plan* for submission to the bank. The plan will include the projected balance sheet set out below. This shows clearly what assets are required and *how they are to be financed*.

BALANCE SHEET OF JAMES BROWN TRADING AS CAPABILITY LANDSCAPES
(PROJECTED AS AT 31 DECEMBER 19-5)

	£	£
Fixed Assets		
Vehicle		8,000
Equipment		900
Gardening tools		350
		9,250
Current Assets		
Gardening stock	1,500	
Fertilisers	150	
Cash	100	
	1,750	
Less Current Liabilities		
Bank overdraft	1,000	
Working Capital		750
		10,000
Less Long-term Liabilities		
Long-term loan from uncle		5,000
NET ASSETS		5,000
FINANCED BY		
Capital		
Owner's capital		5,000

---

the Business Plan

It must be appreciated that the projected balance sheet will form only part of the Business Plan. The document will also include a description of the business, the qualifications and experience of the owner and another important financial projection, the cash flow forecast, mentioned earlier in this chapter (page 59), and dealt with in depth in Chapter 22.

the interview with the bank

James and his accountant are interviewed by the bank manager who has been sent a copy of the Business Plan in advance. He readily agrees to James' request for finance. The bank manager hands him a booklet setting out the bank charges and terms for operating the account. He states that James will be charged as follows

overdraft interest	base rate (say 10%) + 5% = 15%
arrangement fee	£50
security fee (for the uncle's guarantee)	£100

James calculates that his interest cost for the first year - assuming that he will utilise the overdraft to the full will be £1,000 x 15%   = £150. His first year's finance costs will therefore be

interest	£150
arrangement fee	£50
security fee	£100
TOTAL COST	£300

Situation 2 – making the most of financial services

James Brown has been trading successfully for three years. His business has expanded rapidly and his annual fee income is now £350,000. His balance sheet as at the end of the third year is illustrated below.

BALANCE SHEET OF JAMES BROWN TRADING AS CAPABILITY LANDSCAPES
(END OF YEAR 3)

	£	£
Fixed Assets		
Vehicles		15,000
Equipment		2,500
Gardening tools		500
		18,000
Current Assets		
Gardening stock and chemicals	5,000	
Debtors	50,000	
Cash in till	200	
	55,200	
Less Current Liabilities		
Bank overdraft	10,000	
Working Capital		45,200
NET ASSETS		63,200
FINANCED BY		
Capital		
Owner's capital (including profits)		63,200

The balance sheet shows that he has now built up a capital (his investment plus profits for the three years) of £63,200. His bank overdraft has been increased to £10,000 to cover his day-to-day trading requirements, he has bought another truck and some equipment, and his uncle's loan has been repaid.

the problems

He employs ten people, rents a small workshop and yard and has to hire his equipment from a local machine hire firm. He is feeling the need to expand and reorganise his business. He again approaches his accountant who helps him to analyse his needs:

premises	he wants to buy a workshop and yard for £75,000
equipment	he wants to acquire more machinery at a cost of £50,000
debt chasing	he is finding it increasingly difficult to collect money he is owed by his customers – his debtors owe him a total of £50,000

His basic problem is not having the cash to be able to invest – it is all tied up in amounts due to him from debtors. He is also rather ambitious in his spending plans: he wants to buy premises for £75,000 and equipment for £50,000 – a total of £125,000 and approximately twice his own capital of £63,200. No lender would be willing to lend more than James Brown's own capital of £63,200. The bank is already lending £10,000 on overdraft.

Solution

His accountant and bank manager suggest:

factoring	the bank's factoring company will manage his debtors, lending him 80% of the £50,000 owing, thus releasing £40,000 which he can use in the business straightaway
commercial mortgage	the bank will lend him £40,000 for his new premises against a mortgage of the property; he will contribute the remaining £35,000
leasing	the bank's leasing company will buy the equipment he needs and lease it to him for a monthly rental

how much will it cost?

James will need to ensure that his business can afford these financial costs:

factoring	• an annual charge of 2% of the annual total of debts collected, here 2% x £350,000 = £7,000, <u>plus</u> • interest on amounts borrowed, say an annual average of £40,000 at base rate (10%) + 4% = 14% = £5,600
commercial mortgage	• interest at Base Rate (10%) + 3% = 13%; the annual cost will be £40,000 x 13% = £5,200, plus any repayments • arrangement fee 1.25% x £40,000 = £500 • security fee = £350
leasing	monthly rental payments to cover the financial cost of the lease, say twice the capital value of the assets (2 x £50,000) spread over 5 years (60 months): $\dfrac{£100,000}{60 \text{ months}}$ = £1,666 per month or £20,000 per year

other financial services

The bank manager also mentions a range of financial services which the bank can offer:

insurance   Will the premises, equipment and stock be adequately insured? Is James adequately insured – what protection exists if he dies or is disabled?

pensions   Does James have a suitable pension plan? As a self-employed man he is able to contribute to a plan and save tax.

Chapter Summary

❑ External finance is normally required for business start-ups, business purchase and business expansion.

❑ When applying for external finance you should prepare a full Business Plan which sets out your product or service, your market, your financial details and your financial needs (see also Chapter 22 for a full description of the Business Plan).

❑ The most common source of finance is the banks. They can offer overdrafts, business loans and commercial mortgages, usually against security put down by the borrower or other individuals.

❑ The banks also provide financial assistance through their finance houses (HP and leasing), factoring companies and merchant banks (venture capital funding).

❑ The Government also provides financial assistance and advice through the Department of Trade and Industry's 'Enterprise Initiative', the Loan Guarantee Scheme and the TECs' Enterprise Allowance

❑ The banks also provide other financial services such as deposit-taking, money transmission, insurance and pension plans.

❑ Banks charge the borrower for the provision of finance, both in the form of fees and also in interest charges. This expense should be budgeted for by the borrower.

 ## Student Activities

6.1   You work in the lending department of the National Bank plc,124 High Street, Stourminster, WR1 2JF and receive a number of enquiries during the week from customers wanting finance. What form of finance would you recommend in the situations set out below? In each case write a letter to the customer explaining:

• the type of finance appropriate to the situation
• how the finance will be repaid
• the likely cost to the customer in terms of interest and fees
• the bank's likely security requirements

When writing the letters use your own name, the title of Lending Officer, and today's date.   You are not required to investigate whether the bank will or will not lend – your task is to explain the type of finance available.

Your bank's fee and interest tariff for existing businesses is:

Overdraft: interest 4% over base rate, arrangement fee 1.25% (minimum £75)

Business Loan: interest 3% over base rate, arrangement fee 1.25% (minimum £100)

Commercial Mortgage: interest 3% over base rate, arrangement fee 1.5% (minimum £150)

Security fee (average): limited companies £350, other borrowers £250

(a) Tony Page of 47 Rydale Villas, Stourminster, WR4 5TY, a sole trader builder, is expanding his business. He has got all that he wants in the way of vehicles and equipment, but he needs more money – £5,000 he reckons – to buy building materials and to deal with day-to-day trading requirements. Mr Page owns his house in Rydale Villas.

(b) Beattie Gold of "Glendale", Mill Street, Stourminster, WR4 5TH, runs a successful and profitable catering business as a sole trader. She owns a bakery and shop in town; they are worth £125,000. She wants to expand by installing more ovens and modernising the bakery; the cost will be £25,000.

(c) Barbourne Sofware Supplies Limited is a mail-order computer software supplier operating from a small warehouse which it owns (Unit 1B Severnside Industrial Estate, Stourminster, WR2 5TF). The business is expanding rapidly and the company wants to purchase an adjacent warehouse (Unit 1A) which has recently become vacant following a bankruptcy. The price of the unit is £175,000, and the company will additionally need to purchase more equipment costing £12,500.

(d) Jim Steinitz of The Hop Kiln, Rushworth Common, Rushworth, WR7 7CS, has formed a company (British Vintage Limited) to export British Wine to the USA and EC countries. He needs to raise £100,000. He realises that his venture is risky, and mentions that he has heard that the Government sometimes guarantees bank borrowing.

6.2 You work as an adviser in the local Enterprise Agency. In the course of a working day you encounter a number of queries relating to financial problems and the raising of finance. Write down how you would deal with the problems set out below. In each case:

• identify the problem
• recommend a particular scheme which would solve the problem
• state where the scheme is made available, and whom the client should approach in the first instance

(a) Brian Richards was made redundant six months ago, and has since then been drawing Unemployment Benefit. He has £2,000 redundancy money left, and wishes to start up in business restoring antique furniture, a hobby he has practised for some time. He knows there is a market for his work, as he can sell to the local antique shops, making a good profit.

(b) Neeta Patel runs a clothing manufacturing business which sold more than £500,000 worth of goods last year. One problem she finds is that her customers are increasingly unwilling to pay up on time. As a result she is always short of money in the bank and cannot always pay *her* suppliers when she wants to.

(c) William Moss runs a computer consultancy service. He owns a number of computers which he bought eighteen months ago, but now finds that they are out-of-date. He is wary of buying new computers: in the first place he cannot afford them, in the second place they get out-of-date very quickly, and he does not want to be left with expensive obsolete equipment in a couple of years' time.

(d) Orchard Fruits Limited makes jam from fruit purchased in the local fruit growing area. It has recently been approached with the opportunity of buying Eveshore Fruiterers Limited, a major fruit growing company. The directors of Eveshore Fruiterers are retiring and want to sell their profitable company for £750,000. Orchard Fruits Limited are very interested in the proposed purchase as it will enable them to grow their own fruit. Their directors, however, are unable to raise the necessary capital for buying Evershore Fruiterers Limited.

Assignment 3
Business finance : Tudor Catering

SITUATION

Jenny Day and Kate Melbury both work full-time in an insurance office in Melchester. They both have an interest in catering, and in their spare time they have been cooking and selling their products to pubs, hotels and restaurants in the area. Their operations have been independent, and as such they have been 'sole traders'. They have operated from home, baking at the weekends and in the evenings, stocking their freezers, and supplying their customers on demand. Recently both Jenny and Kate have experienced a considerable increase in demand for their products and they reckon that the point has been reached where they can safely give up their jobs and set up in business together as 'Tudor Catering'. They have the added security that their husbands are in full-time employment, and can support them while they start their new venture. They know that they can trade as a partnership or as a limited company, but they have a number of points that need resolving before they can make up their minds:

1.   What is the difference between a partnership and a limited company? How do you set them up?

2.   Where are they going to get the necessary finance for their business? They will need four additional freezers at £400 each, a delivery van (which they can obtain second-hand for £7,500), and an initial stock of food costing £1,250.

3.   They have between them savings of £2,000, and their respective husbands will invest £2,500 each as long-term loans

4.   Will they need to borrow from the bank? Will they need a separate bank account?

They clearly need professional advice. They consult their bank manager and, on his recommendation, a solicitor, an accountant and also, for general advice, the local Enterprise Agency.

STUDENT TASKS

1.   Divide into groups of approximately three students. You will take the role of advisers to the business. Between you (ideally individually) draft a series of letters, having first undertaken the necessary research. The letters should be addressed to Mrs. Jenny Day, Willow Cottage, Greenwood Regis, Wiltshire GR1 9TN. The letters required are as follows:

A letter from the solicitor, Mr D Sykes, explaining the difference between a partnership and a limited company, and outlining the formalities that are required when forming each type of business entity.

A letter from the accountant, Mrs S Harris, setting out in *basic* terms the difference between taxation of a partnership and taxation of a limited company. You are to assume that Jenny and Kate are basic rate taxpayers, and are likely to remain so after the formation of the business.

A letter from the bank manager, Mr D Guest, setting out the different types of finance available for different types of asset, the cost of the finance, the likely security requirements, other bank services available, and the formalities that will have to be complied with when a business account is opened.

2.   In your groups from Task 1 you now take the role of an advisory panel from the local Enterprise Agency. You read and discuss the letters with the two businesswomen, who could be 'played' by your lecturer(s), and plan out how the business will operate.

3.   Write a short formal report from the Enterprise Agency, addressed to Jenny and Kate. The report will include a recommendation for the formation of a partnership *or* a limited company. It should cover:

•   a comparison of a partnership and a limited company in terms of costs and the liability of the owners

•   the sources of finance (savings, husbands' loans and bank finance) and how they should be used

section three
financial statements

In this section we look at the financial statements produced by a wide range of organisations:
- *sole trader businesses*
- *partnerships*
- *limited companies*
- *clubs and associations*
- *local authorities*

The financial statements examined include
- *trading and profit and loss account*
- *balance sheet*
- *cashflow statement*
- *income and expenditure account*

In each case we will explain
- *how the statement is set out*
- *how it is arrived at*
- *the concepts which underly the way it is presented*
- *the people who are interested in it*
- *how it can be interpreted*

7 Basic financial statements – final accounts

introduction

For most businesses, the basic financial statements, or final accounts, that are produced at the end of each financial year comprise:

- trading account
- profit and loss account
- balance sheet

You will already be familiar with the balance sheet if you have read Chapter 5. Each of these financial statements can be produced more often than once a year in order to give information to the owner(s) on how the business is progressing. However, it is customary to produce annual accounts for the benefit of the Inland Revenue, bank manager, and other interested parties. Limited companies also have a legal responsibility to report to their shareholders each year (see Chapter 13). The financial statements of non-trading organisations (such as clubs and societies) and Local Authorities are considered separately in Chapters 16 and 17 respectively.

In this chapter we will explain how final accounts can be produced from the trial balance (figures extracted from the accounting records) of a sole trader business.

final accounts and the trial balance

In a subject such as Finance we are not concerned with the detail of recording day-to-day transactions in the accounting records: this is the task of the book-keeper. Instead we are concerned with using the figures produced by the book-keeper to prepare financial statements which can then be of benefit to the management of the business. The book-keeper's role is to record day-to-day transactions by means of handwritten or computer systems. Every so often, the book-keeper will prove the accuracy of the work by extracting a trial balance of all the accounts in the books. In the example on the next page the book-keeper of John Smith, a sole trader business, has extracted the figures from the accounts for the trial balance.

Trial Balance of John Smith as at 31 December 19-1

	Dr. £	Cr. £
Stock at 1 January 19-1	12,500	
Purchases	105,000	
Sales		155,000
Salaries	23,500	
Heating and lighting	6,200	
Rent and rates	5,800	
Sundry expenses	500	
Premises	100,000	
Machinery	20,000	
Debtors	15,500	
Bank	450	
Cash	50	
Capital		75,000
Drawings	7,000	
Loan from bank		50,000
Creditors		16,500
	296,500	296,500

Note: Stock at 31 December 19-1 was valued at £10,500.

The trial balance will be produced more often than once a year in order to 'prove' the arithmetical accuracy of the transactions recorded by the book-keeper. It will also be produced at the end of a financial year (as is the above trial balance) in order that the year-end financial statements can be prepared. What the trial balance tells us is the balance of each accounting record kept by the business; it lists the balances into accounts with debit balances (the left-hand column), and accounts with credit balances (the right-hand column). Note that the columns are headed with 'Dr' and 'Cr' which are abbreviations for 'debit' and 'credit' respectively.

debit balances

These comprise *assets* of the business, and *expenses* representing totals of purchases made or the cost of benefits received for the year to date. Thus the debit (left-hand) money column indicates that this business has made purchases of goods at a cost of £105,000 during the year. While salaries is an expense it has been spent on a benefit: the business has gained the use of workers' time at a cost of £23,500. The balances for premises, machinery, stock, debtors, cash and bank indicate, in money terms, an asset of the business. The debtors' figure includes the individual balances of all the firm's debtors, ie those customers who owe money to the firm.

credit balances

These comprise *liabilities* of the business, and *income* amounts, including the total of sales for the year to date. For example, the sales figure shows the total amount of goods that has been sold by the business during the year. The figures for capital, loan from the bank and the creditors shows the amount of the liability at the trial balance date. The creditors figure includes all the individual balances of the business' creditors, ie those suppliers to whom the business owes money.

treatment of stock

You will see that the trial balance includes the stock value at the start of the year, while the end-of-year valuation is noted after the trial balance. For the purposes of financial accounting, the stock of goods for resale is valued by the business (and often verified by the auditor) at the end of each financial year, and the valuation is entered into the book-keeping system.

We will now present the final accounts in *vertical format,* ie in columnar form. The alternative layout – *horizontal format* – is looked at later in this chapter.

trading account and profit and loss account

trading account
The main activity of a trading organisation is to buy goods at one price and then to sell the same goods at a higher price. The difference between the two prices represents a profit known as *gross profit*.   Instead of calculating the gross profit on each item bought and sold, the accounting system stores up the totals of all transactions during the year in *purchases account* and *sales account*. Note that purchases account and sales account only record the buying and selling of the goods in which the business trades: the purchase of an item for use in the business is capital expenditure and is recorded in the balance sheet (see later in this chapter).

At the end of the business' financial year, which can end at any date – it does not have to be a calendar year – the totals of purchases and sales accounts are used to form the basis of a *trading account*. However, it is also necessary to take account of the stock of goods for resale which is held by most businesses at the beginning of the financial year, and at the year-end.   A trading account is illustrated below, combined, as it normally is, with a profit and loss account

profit and loss account
In this account are listed the various running expenses (or *revenue expenditure*) of the business. The total of running expenses is deducted from gross profit to give *net profit* for the year. The layout of the trading account and the profit and loss account usually combines the two accounts in the following form, in this case the accounts of the sole trader John Smith:

TRADING AND PROFIT AND LOSS ACCOUNT
OF JOHN SMITH FOR THE YEAR ENDED 31 DECEMBER 19-1

	£	£
Sales		155,000
Opening stock (1 January 19-1)	12,500	
Purchases	105,000	
	117,500	
Less Closing stock (31 December 19-1)	10,500	
Cost of Goods Sold		107,000
Gross profit		48,000
Less:		
Salaries	23,500	
Heating and lighting	6,200	
Rent and rates	5,800	
Sundry expenses	500	
		36,000
Net profit		12,000

Note the following:
* The trading account forms the first half of the account, as far as gross profit, while the profit and loss account is the second half of the account.
* Stock is valued by the business, and often verified by the auditor, at the end of each financial year. This figure forms the closing stock for that year and, also, the opening stock for the following financial year. Techniques of stock valuation are discussed in Chapter 11.
* The figure for *cost of goods sold* (often known as the *cost of sales*) represents the cost to the business of the goods which have been sold in the financial year. Cost of goods sold is opening stock, plus purchases, minus closing stock.
* The various running expenses shown in the profit and loss section can be listed to suit the needs of a particular business: the headings used here are for illustrative purposes only.
* Net profit belongs to the owner(s) of the business.

balance sheet

In Chapter 5 we introduced the format of the balance sheet to illustrate the sources and uses of business finance. We will now explain it from the accounting point of view. A balance sheet is a different type of financial statement from the trading profit and loss account. The latter shows two types of profit – gross profit and net profit respectively – *for the financial year* (or such other time period as may be chosen by the business). A balance sheet, on the other hand, shows the state of the business *at one moment in time*. It lists the *assets* (amounts owned by the business) and the *liabilities* and *capital* (amounts owed by the business) at a particular date. John Smith's balance sheet is shown below.

BALANCE SHEET OF JOHN SMITH AS AT 31 DECEMBER 19-1

	£	£
Fixed Assets		
Premises		100,000
Machinery		20,000
		120,000
Current Assets		
Stock	10,500	
Debtors	15,500	
Bank	450	
Cash	50	
	26,500	
Less Current Liabilities		
Creditors	16,500	
Working Capital*		10,000
		130,000
Less Long-term Liabilities		
Loan from bank		50,000
NET ASSETS		80,000
FINANCED BY		
Capital		
Opening capital		75,000
Add net profit		12,000
		87,000
Less drawings		7,000
		80,000

* Working capital (see Chapter 14) = current assets, less current liabilities.

Note the following:

fixed assets

Fixed assets comprise the long-term items owned by a business which are not bought with the intention of early resale, eg premises, machinery, motor vehicles, office equipment, fixtures and fittings, etc. When a business buys new fixed assets, such expenditure is called *capital expenditure,* in contrast to *revenue expenditure* which is the running cost of the business charged to profit and loss account.

current assets

Current assets comprise short-term assets which change regularly, eg stocks, debtors (amounts owed to the business by customers), bank balances and cash. Each one of these items will alter as the business trades, eg stocks will be sold, or more will be bought; debtors will make payment to the business, or sales on credit will be made; the cash and bank balances will alter with the flow of money paid into the bank account, or as withdrawals are made.

By tradition, assets are listed starting with the most permanent, ie premises, and working through to the most liquid, ie nearest to cash: either cash itself, or the balance at the bank.

current liabilities

These are liabilities which are due for repayment *within twelve months* of the date of the balance sheet, eg creditors (amounts owed by the business to suppliers), and bank overdraft (which is technically repayable on demand, unlike a bank loan which is negotiated for a particular time period).

long-term liabilities

Such liabilities are where repayment is due *in more than one year* from the date of the balance sheet; they are often described as 'bank loan', 'medium-term loan' or 'long-term loan'.

net assets

This shows the net amount of assets used by the business, ie fixed and current assets, less current liabilities. The net assets are financed by the owner(s) of the business, in the form of capital, and by means of loans, such as bank loans. The total of the net assets therefore equals the total of the 'Financed by' section, ie the balance sheet 'balances'.

capital

Capital is the owner(s) investment, and is a liability of a business, ie it is what the business owes the owner. It is important to realise that the assets and liabilities of a business are treated separately from the *personal* assets and liabilities of the owner(s) of the business. For example, if a group of people decided to set up in business they would each agree to put in a certain amount of capital to start the business. As individuals they regard their capital as an investment, ie an asset which may, at some time, be repaid to them. From the point of view of the business, the capital is a liability, because it is owed back to the owner(s). In practice, it is unlikely to be repaid, for then the business would cease to operate.

To the owner(s)' capital is added net profit for the year, while *drawings*, the amount withdrawn by the owner(s) during the year, is deducted. (Note: drawings must *not* be included amongst the expenses in the profit and loss account.) This calculation leaves a closing capital at the balance sheet date which balances with (agrees with) the net assets figure.

significance of the balance sheet

The balance sheet shows the assets used by the business and how they have been financed. The concept may be expressed as a formula:

Fixed assets
+ Working capital
- Long-term liabilities
= Net assets
= Capital

Thus it can be seen that the vertical presentation balance sheet agrees the figure for net assets (£80,000, in the example), with capital. An alternative style of balance sheet – the horizontal presentation – is shown on page 80.

preparation of final accounts from a trial balance

The trial balance contains the basic figures necessary to prepare the final accounts and is a suitable summary from which to prepare the final accounts. The information needed for the preparation of each of the final accounts needs to be picked out from the trial balance; you will find the following guidelines helpful:

* go through the trial balance and write against the items the final account in which each appears
* 'tick' each figure as it is used – each item from the trial balance appears in the final accounts *once only*
* the year-end (closing) stock figure is not listed in the trial balance, but is shown as a note; the closing stock appears *twice* in the final accounts – firstly in the trading account, and secondly in the balance sheet (as a current asset).

If this routine is followed with the trial balance of John Smith, it will then appear as shown in the illustration below:

Trial Balance of John Smith as at 31 December 19-1

	Dr. £	Cr. £			
Stock at 1 January 19-1	12,500		T		✓
Purchases	105,000		T		✓
Sales		155,000	T		✓
Salaries	23,500		P & L	(expense)	✓
Heating and lighting	6,200		P & L	(expense)	✓
Rent and rates	5,800		P & L	(expense)	✓
Sundry expenses	500		P & L	(expense)	✓
Premises	100,000		BS	(fixed asset)	✓
Machinery	20,000		BS	(fixed asset)	✓
Debtors	15,500		BS	(current asset)	✓
Bank	450		BS	(current asset)	✓
Cash	50		BS	(current asset)	✓
Capital		75,000	BS	(capital)	✓
Drawings	7,000		BS	(capital)	✓
Loan from bank		50,000	BS	(long-term liability)	✓
Creditors		16,500	BS	(current liability)	✓
	296,500	296,500			

Stock at 31 December 19-1 was valued at £10,500. $\begin{cases} T \\ BS \end{cases}$ (current asset) ✓ ✓

Note: T = trading account; P & L = profit and loss account; BS = balance sheet

vertical and horizontal presentations of final accounts

So far we have used the *vertical presentation* for setting out the final accounts of a business, ie we started at the top of the page and worked downwards in a narrative style. An alternative method is the *horizontal presentation*, where each of the financial statements has a definite left and right-hand side. The set of final accounts presented earlier would appear, in horizontal style, as follows:

TRADING ACCOUNT OF JOHN SMITH FOR THE YEAR ENDED 31 DECEMBER 19-1

	£		£
Opening stock (1 January 19-1)	12,500	Sales	155,000
Purchases	105.000		
	117,500		
Less Closing stock			
(31 December 19-1)	10.500		
Cost of Goods Sold	107,000		
Gross Profit	48.000		
	155,000		155,000

PROFIT AND LOSS ACCOUNT OF JOHN SMITH
FOR THE YEAR ENDED 31 DECEMBER 19-1

	£		£
Salaries	23,500	Gross profit	48,000
Heating and lighting	6,200		
Rent and rates	5,800		
Sundry expenses	500		
	36,000		
Net profit	12.000		
	48,000		48,000

BALANCE SHEET OF JOHN SMITH AS AT 31 DECEMBER 19-1

	£	£		£
Fixed Assets			**Capital**	
Premises		100,000	Opening capital	75,000
Machinery		20.000	Add net profit	12.000
		120 000		87,000
			Less drawings	7.000
Current Assets				80,000
Stock	10,500		**Long-term Liabilities**	
Debtors	15,500		Loan from bank	50,000
Bank	450			
Cash	50		**Current Liabilities**	
		26.500	Creditors	16.500
		146,500		146,500

In your studies you will see both forms of presentation from time-to-time in the accounts of different businesses and organisations. It should be noted, however, that the vertical format is more common, and will be used as the standard format in this book. As you will readily appreciate, both use the same information and, after a while, you are soon able to 'read' either version.

Chapter Summary

❑ The final accounts of a business comprise:
  • *trading account,* which shows gross profit
  • *profit and loss account,* which shows net profit
  • *balance sheet,* which shows the assets and liabilities of the business at the year-end

❑ The starting-point for the preparation of final accounts is the book-keeper's trial balance.

❑ Each item from the trial balance is entered into the final accounts once only.

❑ The closing stock is entered in the final accounts in two places: in the trading account and in the balalnce sheet.

❑ Final accounts can be presented in either a vertical or a horizontal format.

There is more material to cover in connection with final accounts, and the next few chapters (numbers 8 to 11) give further detail. The final accounts can also be analysed and interpreted (see Chapter 14) to give the user of the accounts information about the financial state of the business. In addition, the more specialist final accounts of partnerships and limited companies are covered in Chapters 12 and 13 respectively.

 Student Activities

You are training as a Chartered Accountant and, as part of your work, you are required to draft the final accounts of a number of clients. During the month you deal with six businesses.

7.1 Prepare a trading and profit and loss account for 'Speedoprint' for the year ended 31 December 19-8 from the following information:

	£
Opening stock	10,500
Closing stock	9,000
Purchases	52,500
Sales	75,250
Selling expenses	4,750
Administration expenses	7,850
Sundry expenses	1,750

7.2 Your next client is Parisien Perfumerie. Prepare a balance sheet as at 31 December 19-8 from the following information, using headings for fixed assets, current assets, current liabilities, long-term liabilities and capital:

	£
Capital at start of year	25,000
Premises	31,000
Stock at end of year	5,450

Cash	70
Vehicles	4,850
Net profit for year	6,430
Creditors	3,280
Debtors	4,655
Office equipment	2,200
Medium term loan from bank	19,500
Bank balance	2,110
Drawings for year	3,875

7.3   The following trial balance has been extracted by the book-keeper of John Adams at 31 December 19-8:

	£(Dr)	£(Cr)
Stock at 1 January 19-8	14,350	
Purchases	114,472	
Sales		259,688
Rates	13,718	
Heating and lighting	12,540	
Wages and salaries	42,614	
Motor vehicle expenses	5,817	
Advertising	6,341	
Premises	75,000	
Office equipment	33,000	
Motor vehicles	21,500	
Debtors	23,854	
Bank	1,235	
Cash	125	
Capital at 1 January 19-8		62,500
Drawings	12,358	
Loan from bank		35,000
Creditors		19,736
	376,924	376,924

Stock at 31 December 19-8 was valued at £16,280.

You are to prepare the trading and profit and loss account of John Adams for the year ended 31 December 19-8, together with his balance sheet at that date.

7.4   The following trial balance has been extracted by the book-keeper of Clare Lewis at 31 December 19-8:

	£(Dr)	£(Cr)
Debtors	18,600	
Creditors		13,350
Bank overdraft		4,610
Capital at 1 January 19-8		25,250
Sales		144,810
Purchases	96,318	
Stock at 1 January 19-8	16,010	
Salaries	18,465	
Heating and lighting	1,820	
Rent and rates	5,647	
Motor vehicles	9,820	
Office equipment	5,500	
Sundry expenses	845	
Motor vehicle expenses	1,684	
Drawings	13,311	
	188,020	188,020

Stock at 31 December 19-8 was valued at £13,735.

You are to prepare the trading and profit and loss accounts of Clare Lewis for the year ended 31 December 19-8, together with her balance sheet at that date.

7.5 The trial balance of Alan Harris, who runs a bookshop, has been prepared by his book-keeper at 31 December 19-8, as follows:

	Dr. £	Cr. £
Capital		25,000
Premises	35,000	
Fixtures and fittings	1,000	
Motor vehicle	2,500	
Purchases	50,000	
Sales		85,500
Vehicle expenses	850	
Stock at 1 January 19-8	5,000	
General expenses	800	
Rates	1,200	
Debtors	1,350	
Creditors		7,550
Assistants' wages	9,550	
Bank	2,100	
Cash	600	
Drawings	8,100	
	118,050	118,050

Stock at 31 December 19-8 was valued at £8,100.

You are to prepare the trading and profit and loss accounts of Alan Harris for the year ended 31 December 19-8, together with his balance sheet at that date.

7.6 Your last client is 'The Village Stores'. The trial balance at 31 December 19-8 is as follows:

	Dr. £	Cr. £
Premises	45,000	
Shop fittings	5,000	
Stock at 1 January 19-8	4,350	
Debtors	870	
Creditors		2,860
Motor vehicle	3,500	
Rates	1,750	
Heating and lighting	840	
Telephone	260	
General expenses	795	
Repairs	220	
Purchases	33,850	
Sales		41,730
Bank overdraft		2,840
Cash	65	
Loan from bank		25,000
Drawings	5,930	
Capital		30,000
	102,430	102,430

Stock at 31 December 19-8 was valued at £5,120

You are to prepare the trading and profit and loss account of The Village Stores for the year ended 31 December 19-8, together with a balance sheet at that date.

8 Accruals and prepayments

introduction

In the last chapter, we prepared the basic financial statements – trading and profit and loss account, and balance sheet – from the trial balance. It often happens that a number of adjustments need to be made to the trial balance figures so that the financial statements show a more accurate view of the state of the business. This and the next two chapters, are concerned with a number of such adjustments. This chapter is concerned with the accrual and prepayment of expenses; it also deals with returned goods, and discount allowed and received.

final accounts: Heather Lewis

To illustrate the effect of adjustments on the final accounts we shall, in this and the next two chapters, be referring to the following set of accounts of Heather Lewis, who owns an antiques shop:

TRADING AND PROFIT AND LOSS ACCOUNT
OF HEATHER LEWISFOR THE YEAR ENDED 31 DECEMBER 19-5

	£	£
Sales		60,000
Opening stock	5,000	
Purchases	40,000	
	45,000	
Less Closing stock	6,000	
Cost of Goods sold		39,000
Gross profit		21,000
Less:		
Rent and rates	4,000	
Salaries	10,000	
Electricity	1,000	
Sundry expenses	1,000	
		16,000
Net profit		5,000

BALANCE SHEET OF HEATHER LEWIS AS AT 31 DECEMBER 19-5

	£	£
Fixed Assets		
Fixtures and fittings		2,000
Delivery van		4,000
		6,000
Current Assets		
Stock	6,000	
Debtors	2,000	
Bank	500	
	8,500	
Less Current Liabilities		
Creditors	3,000	
Working Capital		5,500
NET ASSETS		11,500
FINANCED BY		
Capital		
Opening capital		10,000
Add net profit		5,000
		15,000
Less drawings		3,500
		11,500

accrual of expenses

In the profit and loss accounts that have been prepared so far we have taken the trial balance figure for each expense and listed it in the profit and loss account. The book-keeper records the expenses as they take place and this means that, when an expense has been paid, it will be entered in the accounting system.

For example, the trial balance of Heather Lewis would have shown a debit balance of £1,000 for electricity. However, Heather tells us that, on 1 January 19-6, i.e. on the first day of her new financial year, she received an electricity bill for £250 covering the period of the last quarter of 19-5. An adjustment needs to be made in her final accounts for 19-5 to record this *accrued expense*.

Accruals of expenses are money amounts which are due but unpaid at the financial year-end.

Accrued amounts must be:

• added to the expense from the trial balance before showing it in the profit and loss account
• added to current liabilities in the year-end balance sheet

In the above example, therefore, the total cost of £1,250 for electricity will be shown in profit and loss account, while £250 will be shown as a separate current liability 'electricity accrued £250' in the year-end balance sheet.

The reason for dealing with accruals in this way is to ensure that the profit and loss account records the cost that has been *incurred* for the year, instead of only the amount that has been *paid*. The year-end balance sheet shows a liability for the amount that is due, but unpaid.

prepayment of expenses

A prepayment is a money amount which is paid in advance.

A prepayment, therefore, is the opposite of an accrual: with a prepayment of expenses, some part of the expense has been paid in advance.

For example, Heather Lewis tells you that the figure for rent and rates amounting to £4,000 includes the rent on the shop for January 19-6, amounting to £200. An adjustment must, therefore, be made in her final accounts for 19-5 to take note of this *prepaid expense*. The amount of the prepayment will be:

• deducted from the expense before showing it in profit and loss account
• added to current assets in the year-end balance sheet

In the above example, therefore, the cost of rent and rates will be shown in the profit and loss account as £3,800, while £200 will be shown as a separate current asset (coming after debtors, but before bank and cash balances) 'rent prepaid £200' in the year-end balance sheet.

Case Study : accruals and prepayments – Heather Lewis

Situation

We must now show the effect of the two adjustments in the final accounts of Heather Lewis. We are taking note of the following items at 31 December 19-5:

• heating and lighting expenses accrued of £250
• rent prepaid £200

Solution

TRADING AND PROFIT AND LOSS ACCOUNT
OF HEATHER LEWIS FOR THE YEAR ENDED 31 DECEMBER 19-5

	£	£
Sales		60,000
Opening stock	5,000	
Purchases	40,000	
	45,000	
Less Closing stock	6,000	
Cost of Goods sold		39,000
Gross profit		21,000
Less:		
Rent and rates £4,000 - £200	3,800	
Salaries	10,000	
Electricity £1,000 + £250	1,250	
Sundry expenses	1,000	
		16,050
Net profit		4,950

Note: the calculations for accruals and prepayments are shown here for illustrative purposes only; they would not normally appear in the final accounts.

BALANCE SHEET OF HEATHER LEWIS AS AT 31 DECEMBER 19-5

	£	£	£
Fixed Assets			
Fixtures and fittings			2,000
Delivery van			4,000
			6,000
Current Assets			
Stock		6,000	
Debtors		2,000	
Rent prepaid		200	
Bank		500	
		8,700	
Less: Current Liabilities			
Creditors	3,000		
Electricity accrued	250		
		3,250	
Working Capital			5,450
NET ASSETS			11,450
FINANCED BY			
Capital			
Opening capital			10,000
Add net profit			4,950
			14,950
Less drawings			3,500
			11,450

notes:
- The effect of taking note of accruals and prepayments is to alter the net profit. Thus:

	£
Net profit (before adjustments)	5,000
Add rent prepaid	200
	5,200
Less electricity accrued	250
Net profit (after adjustments)	4,950

- A third money column has been used in the balance sheet to list the two current liabilities; the amounts are sub-totalled in the middle column when the sub-total can be deducted from the amount of current assets to give the working capital figure.

income and expenditure accounting

The reason for making adjustments for accruals and prepayments is to ensure that the profit and loss account shows the correct amount of the expense for the financial year, ie what should have been paid, instead of what has actually been paid. By recording what should have been paid we are adopting the principle of *income and expenditure accounting:* the expenses due for the year are related to the income that is due. If we simply used the trial balance figures, which show the payment amounts, we would be following the principle of *receipts and payments accounting,* ie comparing money coming in, with money going out.

The principle of income and expenditure accounting is applied in the same way to purchases and sales figures, although no adjustment is needed because of the way in which these two are handled in the accounting records. For purchases of goods for resale, the amount is normally entered in the accounts when the supplier's invoice is received, although the agreement to buy will be contained in the legal contract which exists between buyer and seller. Thus, from an accounting viewpoint, it is receipt of the supplier's invoice that causes an accounting entry to be made; the subsequent payment is handled as a different accounting transaction. Therefore a business could have bought goods, not paid for any of them, but will have a purchases figure to enter into the trading account – however, the creditors will soon be wanting their payment.

Sales are recorded when the invoice for the goods is sent, rather than when payment is made; thus applying the principle of income and expenditure accounting. Likewise, a business could have made a large amount of sales, which will be entered in the trading account, but may not yet have received any payments.

The way in which accounts are adjusted to take note of accruals and prepayments is formally recognised in the accruals (or matching) concept, which is discussed in more detail in Chapter 11.

Case Study: accruals and prepayments

Situation

How would you deal with each of the following situations in the profit and loss account, and balance sheet of a business at the financial year-end of 31 December 19-1?

- Rental payable on a photocopier is £100 per month; at the end of December eleven payments have been made, while the payment due in December is made during the first few days of January 19-2.
- Property insurance paid amounting to £500 covers the period from 1 January 19-1 to 31 March 19-2.
- The trial balance shows heating and lighting costs to be £725; in early January 19-2 a gas bill is received for £145 covering the quarter ended 31 December 19-1.

Solution

- Photocopier rental is recorded in the profit and loss account as £1,200; in the balance sheet, show a current liability of accrued expense for £100.
- Insurance is recorded in the profit and loss account as £400; a prepayment of £100 is shown as a current asset in the balance sheet.
- Heating and lighting in the profit and loss account £870; a current liability of £145 for the accrued expense.

sales returns and purchases returns

We must now consider the aspect of returned goods, which affects the trading account. A trial balance may include amounts for sales returns and purchases returns, as well as figures for purchases and sales.

Sales returns (also known as returns inwards) represent goods which have been sold by the business and then, for whatever reason, have been returned. The logical step is to deduct these items from the sales figure. This is done in the trading account when it is prepared.

Purchases returns (or returns outwards) occur when a business returns unsatisfactory purchases to the supplier. Here the logical step is to deduct the figure from purchases in the trading account.

At the end of a business' financial year, the total amount of each returns account for the year is deducted from the purchases or sales account (as appropriate) in the trading account.

Case Study: sales returns and purchases returns

Situation

Bill Bowen's business has the following figures in the trial balance at 31 December 19-7:

Trial Balance (extract) of Bill Bowen
as at 31 December 19-7

	Dr.	Cr.
	£	£
Stock at 1 January 19-7	7,500	
Purchases	65,000	
Sales		113,000
Sales returnss	500	
Purchases returns		1,000
etc.		

At 31 December 19-7 the closing stock is valued at £10,000.

Prepare the trading account for the year ended 31 December 19-7.

Solution

TRADING ACCOUNT OF BILL BOWEN
FOR THE YEAR ENDED 31 DECEMBER 19-7

	£	£	£
Sales			113,000
Less Sales returns			500
Net sales			112,500
Opening stock (1 January 19-7)		7,500	
Purchases	65,000		
Less Purchases returns	1,000		
Net purchases		64,000	
		71,500	
Less Closing stock (31 December 19-7)		10,000	
Cost of Goods Sold			61,500
Gross profit			51,000

Note that sales returns is deducted from sales giving a figure of £112,500 for net sales; similarly purchases returns is deducted from purchases to give a figure of £64,000 for net purchases.

discount allowed and discount received

A further topic to cover in this chapter is to see how cash discounts (*not* trade discount) *allowed* and *received* appear in the trial balance and in the financial statements. A cash discount is often offered by a supplier to encourage prompt settlement by the buyer. The distinction between discounts allowed and received is:

discount allowed – the amount of cash discount given by a business to encourage its debtors to pay promptly

discount received – the amount of cash discount taken by a business when it settles with its creditors promptly

The trial balance will have a figure for each account, with discount allowed on the *debit* side (as an expense), and discount received on the *credit* side (as income). At the end of a financial year the totals of these two accounts are entered in the profit and loss account, with discount allowed shown as an *expense,* and discount received as *income* which is added to the gross profit.

Case Study: discount allowed and discount received

Situation

Bill Bowen's business (see previous Case Study) has the following figures in the trial balance at 31 December 19-7:

**Trial Balance (extract) of Bill Bowen
as at 31 December 19-7**

	Dr.	Cr.
	£	£
Discount allowed	1,250	
Discount received		1,000
Expenses (various)	32,500	
etc.		

Prepare the profit and loss account for the year ended 31 December 19-7, starting with the gross profit (see previous Case Problem) of £51,000.

Solution

**PROFIT AND LOSS ACCOUNT OF BILL BOWEN
FOR THE YEAR ENDED 31 DECEMBER 19-7**

	£	£
Gross profit (see previous Case Study)		51,000
Add Discount received		1,000
		52,000
Less:		
Discount allowed	1,250	
Expenses (various)	32,500	
		33,750
Net profit		18,250

Chapter Summary

❑ Final accounts are prepared on the income and expenditure basis, rather than the receipts and payments basis.

❑ An adjustment is made at the end of the financial year in respect of accruals and prepayments.

❑ In the final accounts, accrued expenses are added to the expense from the trial balance and shown as a current liability in the balance sheet

❑ Prepaid expenses are deducted from the expense from the trial balance and shown as a current asset in the balance sheet

❑ Adjustments also need to be made in the business accounts for:
  • sales returns and purchases returns
  • discount allowed and discount received

These adjustment made at the end of a financial year are carried out in order to present the financial statements more accurately. The next chapter continues this theme by considering depreciation of fixed assets.

 Student Activities

8.1 Explain how the following would be dealt with in the profit and loss account, and balance sheet of a business with a financial year-end of 31 December 19-2.

(a) Wages and salaries paid to 31 December 19-2 amount to £55,640. However, at that date, £1,120 is owing: this amount is paid on 4 January 19-3.

(b) Business rates totalling £3,565 have been paid to cover the period 1 January 19-2 to 31 March 19-3.

(c) A computer is rented at a cost of £150 per month. The rental for January 19-2 was paid in December 19-1 and is included in the total payments during 19-1 which amount to £1,950.

8.2 You work for Don Smith who runs a wholesale stationery business. The book-keeper has extracted the following trial balance at 31 December 19-4:

	Dr. £	Cr. £
Debtors	24,325	
Creditors		19,684
Capital		30,000
Bank		1,083
Rent and rates	10,862	
Electricity	2,054	
Telephone	1,695	
Salaries	55,891	
Motor vehicles	22,250	
Office equipment	7,500	
Motor vehicle expenses	10,855	
Drawings	15,275	
Discount allowed	478	
Discount received		591
Purchases	138,960	
Sales		257,258
Stock at 1 January 19-4	18,471	
	308,616	308,616

You are to prepare the trading and profit and loss account of Don Smith for the year ended 31 December 19-4, together with his balance sheet at that date, taking into account the following:

- stock at 31 December 19-4 was valued at £14,075
- at 31 December 19-4 rates are prepaid £250
- at 31 December 19-4 electricity owing £110
- at 31 December 19-4 salaries are owing £365

8.3 The following trial balance has been extracted by the book-keeper of John Barclay at 30 June 19-6:

	Dr. £	Cr. £
Sales		864,321
Purchases	600,128	
Sales returns	2,746	
Purchases returns		3,894
Office expenses	33,947	
Salaries	122,611	
Motor vehicle expenses	36,894	
Discounts allowed	3,187	
Discounts received		4,951
Debtors and creditors	74,328	63,416
Stock at 1 July 19-5	63,084	
Motor vehicles	83,500	
Office equipment	23,250	
Land and buildings	100,000	
Bank loan		75,000
Bank	1,197	
Capital		155,000
Drawings	21,710	
	1,166,582	1,166,582

Notes at 30 June 19-6:
- stock was valued at £66,941
- motor vehicle expenses owing £1,250
- office expenses prepaid £346

You are to prepare the trading and profit and loss account of John Barclay for the year ended 30 June 19-6, together with his balance sheet at that date.

8.4. You work as book-keeper to Cindy Hayward who runs a delicatessen shop. You have produced the following trial balance at the end of the financial year on 30 June 19-5:

	Dr. £	Cr. £
Capital		20,932
Purchases	148,500	
Sales		210,900
Repairs to buildings	848	
Delivery van	5,000	
Van expenses	1,540	
Land and buildings	85,000	
Loan from bank		50,000
Bank balance	540	
Shop fittings	2,560	
Wages and salaries	30,280	
Discounts allowed	135	
Discounts received		1,319
Rates and insurance	2,690	
Debtors	3,175	
Creditors		8,295
Heating and lighting	3,164	
General expenses	2,170	
Sales returns	855	
Purchases returns		1,221
Stock at 1 July 19-4	6,210	
	292,667	292,667

Notes at 30 June 19-5:
• stock was valued at £7,515 • rates prepaid £255 • wages owing £560 • van expenses owing £85

You are to prepare the trading and profit and loss account of Cindy Hayward for the year ended 30 June 19-5, together with her balance sheet at that date.

8.5 You work in the accounts department of Southtown Supplies, a wholesaling business. At 31 December 19-3, the end of the financial year, the book-keeper extracts the following list of balances:

	£
Stock at 1 January 19-3	70,000
Purchases	280,000
Sales	420,000
Sales returns	6,000
Purchases returns	4,500
Discount received	750
Discount allowed	500
Heating and lighting	13,750
Salaries	35,600
Post and packing	1,400
Premises	120,000
Fixtures and fittings	45,000
Debtors	55,000
Creditors	47,000
Bank	5,000
Capital	195,000
Drawings	35,000

You are to
(a) prepare a trial balance as at 31 December 19-3
(b) prepare the year-end trading and profit and loss account and balance sheet, taking into account:
• closing stock of £60,000 • electricity owing at year-end £350 • salaries of £400 prepaid

9 Depreciation of fixed assets

introduction

Fixed assets, for example machinery and vehicles, reduce in value as time goes by, largely as a result of wear and tear. While we are concerned in this chapter with depreciation of fixed assets owned by businesses, the same principles apply to items that are owned by other types of organisations, and also by individuals. You may be thinking of buying a car in the next year or so, and people will be quick to tell you that you are spending your money on a 'depreciating asset'.

Depreciation is the estimate of the amount of the loss in value of fixed assets over an estimated time period.

To provide an accurate picture of a business we need to adjust the profit and loss account by showing the year's depreciation of fixed assets as an expense: in this way net profit is reduced. At the same time the value of the fixed assets shown in the balance sheet must be reduced to reflect the amount that they have depreciated. The reason for making these adjustments for depreciation is because the business has had the use of the assets during the year. Compare this with a business that chooses to rent a machine, instead of buying. Here rental payments to the hire company would be recorded in profit and loss account. On the same basis, a business that buys a machine must include the estimated fall in value in profit and loss account, so that a more accurate profit figure is shown. In the balance sheet, fixed assets are reduced in value to indicate their approximate 'true' value.

You might be wondering if buildings need to be depreciated - such assets would seem to rise in value rather than fall. However, buildings do 'wear out' over time and need to be knocked down and replaced. Land and buildings are sometimes increased in value from time-to-time, ie a revaluation takes place, and this is recorded in the accounts.

methods of calculating depreciation

There are several different ways in which we can allow for the fall in value of fixed assets. All of these are *estimates,* and it is only when the asset is sold that we will know the accuracy of the estimate (see also later in this chapter).

The two most common methods of calculating depreciation are:
* straight-line method
* reducing balance method (also called the diminishing balance method)

straight-line method

A fixed percentage is written off the *original cost* of the asset as the depreciation amount each year. For example, a machine costs £2,000 and it is decided to depreciate it at twenty per cent each year by the straight-line method. The depreciation amount for *each year* is:

£2,000 x 20% = £400 per year

The depreciation percentage will be decided by an individual business on the basis of how long it considers the asset will last. Different classes of fixed assets are often depreciated at different rates, ie motor vehicles can be depreciated at a different rate from office equipment, and so on.

An alternative method of calculating straight-line depreciation (taking into account the asset's estimated value on resale) is:

cost of asset - estimated residual sale proceeds
  number of years' expected use of asset

For example, a computer system is purchased for £2,000 and will be sold after three years' use for an estimated amount of £500. The straight-line depreciation amount is:

£2,000 - £500 = *£500 per year*
  3 years

reducing balance method

With this method, each year a fixed percentage is written off the *reduced balance,* ie after deducting the previous years' depreciation amount from the cost of the asset. For example, a car is purchased for £12,000 and it is decided to depreciate it by twenty-five per cent each year using the reducing balance method. The depreciation amounts for the first three years of ownership are:

Original cost	£12,000
Year 1 depreciation: 25% of £12,000	£3,000
Value at end of year 1	£9,000
Year 2 depreciation: 25% of £9,000	£2,250
Value at end of year 2	£6,750
Year 3 depreciation: 25% of £6,750	£1,687
Value at end of year 3	£5,063
	and so on

Case Study: comparison of straight-line and reducing balance methods

Situation

You work as a clerk for West-Mid Computers Limited, a company selling micro computers throughout the West Midlands. The company accountant asks you to investigate and compare straight-line and reducing balance methods of depreciating the company's office furniture and fittings. These have recently been purchased at a cost of £5,500 and are expected to be replaced in five years' time; it is expected that they will have a resale value at the end of this time of approximately £500. The company accountant, in particular, would like you to suggest appropriate rates (to the nearest 5 per cent) for each depreciation method, and to make comparisons between the two.

Solution

Furniture and fittings costing £5,500, to be depreciated to approximately £500 (expected sale value) in five years' time.

	Straight-line £1,000 per year £	Reducing balance *40% £
Original cost	5,500	5,500
Year 1 depreciation	1,000	2,200
Value at end of year 1	4,500	3,300
Year 2 depreciation	1,000	1,320
Value at end of year 2	3,500	1,980
Year 3 depreciation	1,000	792
Value at end of year 3	2,500	1,188
Year 4 depreciation	1,000	475
Value at end of year 4	1,500	713
Year 5 depreciation	1,000	285
Value at end of year 5	500	428

*reducing balance depreciation percentage found by trial and error

The year-by-year depreciation amounts from the Case Study are shown on the following bar chart:

Depreciation amounts using the straight-line and reducing balance methods

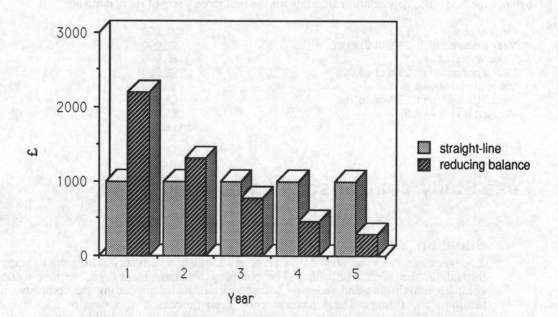

For comparisons between the two methods of depreciation, see the next section.

comparisons of depreciation methods

straight-line

- Same money amount each year

- Lower depreciation percentage required to achieve same residual value

- Best for use with fixed assets likely to be kept for the whole of their expected lives, eg machinery, office equipment, fixtures and fittings

reducing balance

- Different money amounts each year: more than straight-line in early years, less in later years

- Higher depreciation percentage required to achieve same residual value — but can never reach a nil value

- Best for use with fixed assets which depreciate more in early years and which are not to be kept for whole of expected lives, eg vehicles

depreciation and final accounts

profit and loss account
The depreciation amount calculated for each class of asset is listed amongst the other expenses as a *provision for depreciation* for that particular class of asset.

balance sheet
Each class of fixed asset should be shown at cost price, less total *depreciation to date* (ie this year's depreciation, plus depreciation from previous years if any). The resulting figure is the net book value of the fixed asset.

The usual way of setting these out in a balance sheet (using figures for a machine costing £2,000 and being depreciated at twenty percent each year by the straight-line method) is:

Balance sheet (extract) .... as at 31 December 19-1

	£ Cost	£ Dep'n to date	£ Net
Fixed Assets			
Machinery	2,000	400	1,600
Vehicles, etc	x	x	x
	x	x	x

Balance sheet (extract) .... as at 31 December 19-2

	£ Cost	£ Dep'n to date	£ Net
Fixed Assets			
Machinery	2,000	800	1,200
Vehicles, etc	x	x	x
	x	x	x

Notice, from the above, how depreciation to date increases with the addition of each further year's depreciation. At the same time, the net figure reduces – it is this net figure (or *net book value*) which is added to the other fixed assets to give a sub-total for this section of the balance sheet.

Case Study: Heather Lewis

Situation

We will now look to the final accounts of Heather Lewis referred to in the previous chapter. The final accounts of Heather, which were adjusted for accruals and prepayments, are shown on pages 86 and 87. Heather tells you that the fixed assets, being fixtures and fittings, and delivery van, will need replacing in a few year's time. After discussions, it is decided to depreciate fixtures and fittings by 20 per cent each year, using the straight-line method, and the delivery van by 30 per cent each year using the reducing balance method.

Solution

The depreciation amounts for this year will be:

fixtures and fittings	£2,000 x 20%	=	£400
delivery van	£4,000 x 30%	=	£1,200

These amounts will be shown as expenses in her profit and loss account, and will be deducted from the cost price of the appropriate fixed asset in the balance sheet. Thus her final accounts will appear as shown below and on the next page (the trading account is not affected by depreciation adjustments and therefore it is not shown).

TRADING AND PROFIT AND LOSS ACCOUNT (EXTRACT)
OF HEATHER LEWIS FOR THE YEAR ENDED 31 DECEMBER 19-5

	£	£
Gross profit		21,000
Less:		
Rent and rates	3,800	
Salaries	10,000	
Electricity	1,250	
Sundry expenses	1,000	
Provision for depreciation -		
fixtures and fittings	400	
delivery van	1,200	
		17,650
Net profit		3,350

BALANCE SHEET OF HEATHER LEWIS AS AT 31 DECEMBER 19-5

	£ Cost	£ Dep'n to date	£ Net
Fixed Assets			
Fixtures and fittings	2,000	400	1,600
Delivery van	4,000	1,200	2,800
	6,000	1,600	4,400
Current Assets			
Stock		6,000	
Debtors		2,000	
Rent prepaid		200	
Bank		500	
		8,700	
Less Current Liabilities			
Creditors	3,000		
Electricity accrued	250		
		3,250	
Working Capital			5,450
NET ASSETS			9,850
FINANCED BY:			
Capital			
Opening capital			10,000
Add Net profit			3,350
			13,500
Less Drawings			3,350
			9,850

notes:
- As this is the first year that she has made a provision for depreciation, the amount shown in the balance sheet is the same as that shown in the profit and loss account. Next year, the situation will be different. For example, for fixtures and fittings, the amount shown in the profit and loss account will still be £400, ie 20% of cost, but the balance sheet will show:

	Cost	Dep'n to date	Net
Fixtures and fittings	2,000	800	1,200

- The effect of creating a provision for depreciation in her 19-5 accounts has been to reduce the net profit by £1,600 to £3,350.

Case Study: depreciation and the trial balance

Situation
Usually the trial balance will distinguish between the cost of an asset and the depreciation already charged for that particular class of asset. In this example an extract of the trial balance of James Wilson as at 30 June 19-2 provided the following figures:

	Dr £	Cr £
Fixed assets at cost:		
Buildings	100,000	
Vehicles	30,000	
Machinery	25,000	
Provision for depreciation:		
Buildings		10,000
Vehicles		12,000
Machinery		10,000

In the profit and loss account for the year ended 30 June 19-2, depreciation is calculated as:

Buildings   £2,000
Vehicles   £6,000
Machinery   £5,000

Show the profit and loss account for the year assuming that gross profit is £76,000 and that other expenses for the year total £52,000. Show the fixed asset section of the balance sheet of James Wilson as at 30 June 19-2.

Solution

TRADING AND PROFIT AND LOSS ACCOUNT (EXTRACT)
OF JAMES WILSON FOR THE YEAR ENDED 30 JUNE 19-2

	£	£
Gross profit		76,000
Less:		
Expenses	52,000	
Provision for depreciation -		
buildings	2,000	
vehicles	6,000	
machinery	5,000	
		65,000
Net profit		11,000

BALANCE SHEET (EXTRACT) OF JAMES WILSON
AS AT 30 JUNE 19-2

	£ Cost	£ Dep'n to date	£ Net
Fixed Assets			
Buildings	100,000	12,000	88,000
Vehicles	30,000	18,000	12,000
Machinery	25,000	15,000	10,000
	155,000	45,000	110,000

Here, the middle column depreciation amounts are calculated by adding the trial balance provision for depreciation (previous years) to the profit and loss depreciation for 19-2.

depreciation: a non-cash expense

It is very important to realise that depreciation is a *non-cash expense*. Unlike the other expenses that we have come across in the profit and loss account, no cheque is written out to pay for depreciation. While rent and rates, salaries and telephone all have to be paid for by cheque (or in cash), depreciation causes no outflow of money. You will be able to understand this on a personal level by considering any fixed assets that you own, e.g. car, cycle, home computer, etc.; such assets are depreciating, but there is no immediate effect on your bank or cash balance. However, when the asset comes to be sold, you will receive rather less than was originally paid for it. Nevertheless, it is correct, in the final accounts of a business, to show in the profit and loss account an allowance for depreciation, because the business has had the use of the asset and needs to record a fall in value to present a more accurate picture of its financial state.

Often in business we need to know how much cash, or *funds*, has been generated from the trading activities during the year. ('Trading activities' in this context means the main activities of the business). The calculation is:

FUNDS GENERATED FROM TRADING = NET PROFIT + DEPRECIATION

For example, refer to the business of James Wilson above. Funds generated from the trading activities for the year ended 30 June 19-2 are:

£11,000 + £2,000 + £6,000 + £5,000 = £24,000.

Thus, as a result of the year's trading, the bank account has benefited by £24,000. However, it is likely that most of this increase will have been used up in a number of ways, eg to buy more fixed assets, for owner's drawings, to buy more stock, to allow debtors longer to pay, or to reduce the time the business takes to pay its creditors. So, it is highly unlikely that the year-end balance of the bank account will have increased by anything like the funds generated from trading.

sale of fixed assets

When a fixed asset is sold it is necessary to make a comparison between

(1) the original cost of the asset, and

(2) sale proceeds + depreciation provided over the life of the asset.

If *(1) is greater than (2)* there has been an *underprovision of depreciation* on the particular asset. The amount necessary to bring the total up to the original cost of the asset is shown as an expense in profit and loss account as 'underprovision of depreciation'. For example, a machine originally cost £5,000; it is depreciated for four years at ten per cent straight-line depreciation, and is then sold for £2,500. The comparison is:

(1) £5,000
(2) £2,500 + £2,000 (ie £500 x 4 years) = £4,500.

An extra £500 must, therefore, be charged to profit and loss account, along with the other expenses, for underprovision of depreciation (often described more simply as 'loss on sale').

The effect of this is that net profit for the year will be reduced by £500. The estimate of depreciation over the years for this machine was slightly understated, but this is no reflection on the financial management of the business.

If *(2) is greater than (1)* there has been an *overprovision of depreciation,* and the excess amount must be credited (added) to profit and loss account in the year of sale. For example, a car was purchased for £10,000; depreciation to date totals £6,000 and the car has been sold for £5,000. The comparison is:

(1) £10,000
(2) £5,000 + £6,000 = £11,000.

The £1,000, which represents an overprovision of depreciation (or 'profit on sale'), is added to profit and loss account in the income section.

Chapter Summary

❏ Depreciation is an estimate, in money terms, of the fall in value of fixed assets.

❏ Two common methods of calculating depreciation are the straight-line method and the reducing balance method.

❏ The depreciation amount for each class of fixed asset is included amongst the expenses in profit and loss account, while the value of the asset, as shown in the balance sheet, is reduced by the same amount.

❏ Depreciation is a non-cash expense.

❏ Net profit is reduced by the amount of depreciation charged.

❏ When an asset is sold it is necessary to make an adjustment in respect of any underprovision or overprovision of depreciation during the life of the asset.

In the next chapter we look at another expense to be shown in profit and loss account: bad debts, and provision for bad debts.

 Student Activities

9.1 A friend of yours has recently started in business; knowing that you are studying Finance, she seeks your assistance. She has just bought a machine at a cost of £1,000 and asks you to advise on depreciation methods. The machine is expected to last for five years after which it will be valueless. She tells you that, if there is a choice of depreciation methods, she would like to use the one "that gives the larger net profit in the early years because the business could make good use of the extra cash". Advise your friend.

9.2 On 1 January 19-1, Martin Jackson bought a car for £12,000. In his financial statements, which have a year-end of 31 December, he has been depreciating it at 25 per cent per annum using the reducing balance method. On 31 December 19-3 he sells the car for £5,500 (cheque received).

You are to show:
(a) The depreciation amounts shown in his profit and loss accounts for 19-1, 19-2 and 19-3
(b) How the asset would have been shown in his balance sheets at 31 December 19-1 and 19-2
(c) How the profit or loss on sale will be shown in his profit and loss account for 19-3

9.3 The following list of balances has been extracted from the books of J Henson at 31 December 19-4:

	£
Purchases	71,600
Sales	122,000
Stock at 1 January 19-4	6,250
Stock at 31 December 19-4	8,500

Vehicle running expenses	1,480
Rent and business rates	5,650
Office expenses	2,220
Discount received	285
Wages and salaries	18,950
Office equipment	10,000
Depreciation on office equipment for 19-4	1,000
Vehicle	12,000
Depreciation on vehicle for 19-4	3,000
Debtors	5,225
Creditors	4,910
Capital	20,000
Drawings for the year	13,095
Cash at bank	725

You are to prepare J Henson's trading and profit and loss account for the year ended 31 December 19-4, together with a balance sheet as at that date.

9.4   The following trial balance has been extracted by the book-keeper of Hazel Harris at 31 December 19-4:

	Dr £	Cr £
Bank loan		75,000
Capital		125,000
Purchases and sales	465,000	614,000
Building repairs	8,480	
Motor vehicle at cost	12,000	
Provision for depreciation on motor vehicles		2,400
Motor expenses	2,680	
Land and buildings at cost	100,000	
Bank overdraft		2,000
Furniture and fittings at cost	25,000	
Provision for depreciation on furniture and fittings		2,500
Wages and salaries	86,060	
Discounts	10,610	8,140
Drawings	24,000	
Rates and insurance	6,070	
Debtors and creditors	52,130	41,850
General expenses	15,860	
Stock at 1 January 19-4	63,000	
	870,890	870,890

Notes at 31 December 19-4:
* stock was valued at £88,000
* wages and salaries outstanding: £3,180
* rates and insurance paid in advance: £450
* depreciate the motor vehicle at 20 per cent using the straight-line method
* depreciate furniture and fittings at 10 per cent using the straight-line method

As accountant to Miss Harris, you are to prepare her trading and profit and loss account for the year ended 31 December 19-4, together with her balance sheet at that date.

9.5   Martin Hough, sole owner of Juicyburger, a fast food shop, operating from leased premises in the town, is suspicious of his accountant, Mr S Harris, whom he claims doesn't really understand the food business. On the telephone he asks Mr Harris why depreciation is charged on a rigid formula, as surely no-one really knows how much his equipment is worth, and in fact he might not get anything for it. Draft a reply to Mr Hough from Mr Harris explaining the importance of depreciation and its application to financial statements, together with its effect on Mr Hough's tax bill.

9.6   Cindy Smith owns an engineering supplies business, and the following trial balance has been extracted by her book-keeper at 30 June 19-3:

	Dr £	Cr £
Capital		38,825
Stock at 1 July 19-2	18,050	
Purchases	74,280	
Sales		149,410
Discounts	3,210	1,140
Rent and rates	7,280	
Returns	1,645	875
Cash	820	
Bank		13,300
Debtors and creditors	14,375	9,315
Wages and salaries	43,895	
General expenses	2,515	
Motor vehicles at cost	25,000	
Provision for depreciation on motor vehicles		6,250
Fixtures and fittings at cost	10,000	
Provision for depreciation on fixtures and fittings		3,000
Motor vehicle expenses	6,725	
Drawings	14,320	
	222,115	222,115

notes at 30 June 19-3:
* stock was valued at £20,145
* general expenses owing £175
* rates prepaid £95
* depreciate motor vehicles at 25 per cent per annum, using the reducing balance method
* depreciate fixtures and fittings at 10 per cent per annum, using the straight-line method

As accountant to Cindy Smith, you are to prepare her trading and profit and loss account for the year ended 30 June 19-3, together with her balance sheet at that date.

10 Bad debts and provision for bad debts

introduction

Most businesses selling their goods to other businesses do not receive payment immediately. Instead they often have to allow a period of credit and, until the payment is received, they have a current asset of *debtors*. Unfortunately, it is likely that not all debtors will eventually settle the amount they owe – some debts will become *bad debts*.

Let us consider Heather Lewis' business (introduced in the Case Studies in the previous chapters) that has debtors of £2,000. This total will, most probably, be made up of a number of smaller debtors' accounts. At any one time a few of these accounts will be bad, and therefore the amount due is uncollectable: these are *bad debts,* and they need to be written off, ie the business will give up trying to collect the debt and will accept the loss. At the same time there are likely to be some debtors' accounts which, although they are not yet bad, may be giving some concern as to their ability to pay: a *provision for bad debts* needs to be made in respect of these. The one thing that Heather, with debtors of £2,000, cannot do is to show this debtors amount as a current asset in the balance sheet: to do so would be to imply to the reader of the balance sheet that the full £2,000 is collectable. Instead this *gross* debtors' figure might be reduced in two stages:

- three debtors' accounts with balances totalling £100 are to be written off as bad
- a general provision for bad debts is to be made amounting, in this case, to five per cent of remaining debtors

Thus the debtors figure becomes:

Gross debtors	2,000
Less: bad debts written off	100
	1,900
Less: provision for bad debts,	
*five per cent in this example	95
Net debtors (recorded in balance sheet)	1,805

* The amount of the provision for bad debts will vary from business to business depending on past experience.

bad debts

As already noted, bad debts are written off when they become uncollectable. This means that all reasonable efforts to recover the amount owing have been exhausted, ie statements and letters have been sent to the debtor requesting payment, and legal action, where appropriate, or the threat of legal action has failed to obtain payment.

In writing off a debtor's account as bad, the business is bearing the cost of the amount due. The debtor's account is closed and the amount (or amounts, where a number of accounts are dealt with in this way) is deducted from profit and loss account as an expense. At the same time, the gross debtors figure is reduced by the amount being written off. Therefore, when writing off bad debts:

• deduct the total amount being written off from profit and loss account as an expense, describing the amount as *bad debts written off*

• if the bad debts figure is not already shown in the trial balance, reduce the debtors figure for the balance sheet: there is no need to show the deduction, just the reduced figure (before making any provision for bad debts – see below)

provision for bad debts

This is different from writing off a bad debt because there is the possibility – not the certainty – of future bad debts. The debtors figure is reduced either by totalling the balances of the accounts that may not pay or, more likely, by applying a percentage to the total figure for debtors. The percentage chosen will be based on past experience and will vary from business to business.

The money amount chosen as a provision for bad debts is deducted as an expense from profit and loss account (described as *provision for bad debts,* and kept separate from bad debts written off). At the same time the amount of the provision must be deducted from the debtors figure in the balance sheet, and the net amount of debtors is included in the current assets of the business. Therefore, to create a provision for bad debts:

• deduct the amount of the provision for bad debts as an expense to profit and loss account

• deduct the amount of the provision from the debtors figure in the balance sheet, after first writing off bad debts. Show the deduction in the balance sheet (see the example below)

Case Study: Heather Lewis

Situation

Refer back to the set of final accounts for Heather Lewis shown on pages 98 and 99. These have already been adjusted for accruals and prepayments, and depreciation. Heather now tells you to make the adjustments referred to earlier in this chapter, ie of the total debtors of £2,000, there are two debtors totalling £100 to be written off, and a general provision for bad debts should be made at 5 per cent of debtors to allow for possible future bad debts. How will the financial statements be affected by these adjustments?

Solution

Gross debtors	£2,000
Less bad debts written off	£100
	£1,900
Less provision for bad debts at 5 per cent	£95
Net debtors	£1,805

Her final accounts (except for trading account, which is unaffected) appear on the next page.

PROFIT AND LOSS ACCOUNT (EXTRACT)
OF HEATHER LEWIS FOR THE YEAR ENDED 31 DECEMBER 19-5

	£	£
Gross Profit		21,000
Less:		
Rent and rates	3,800	
Salaries	10,000	
Electricity	1,250	
Sundry expenses	1,000	
Provision for depreciation -		
fixtures and fittings	400	
delivery van	1,200	
Bad debts written off	100	
Provision for bad debts	95	
		17,845
Net Profit		3,155

BALANCE SHEET OF HEATHER LEWIS AS AT 31 DECEMBER 19-5

	£ cost	£ depreciation to date	£ net
Fixed Assets			
Fixtures and fittings	2,000	400	1,600
Delivery van	4,000	1,200	2,800
	6,000	1,600	4,400
Current Assets			
Stock		6,000	
Debtors	1,900		
Less provision for bad debts	95		
		1,805	
Rent prepaid		200	
Bank		500	
		8,505	
Less Current Liabilities			
Creditors	3,000		
Heating and lighting accrued	250		
		3,250	
Working Capital			5,255
NET ASSETS			9,655
FINANCED BY			
Capital			
Opening capital			10,000
Add net profit			3,155
			13,155
Less drawings			3,500
			9,655

Notes:

• This is now a much more accurate set of financial statements than those prepared on the first occasion (on pages 84 and 85). This is because adjustments have been made for accruals and prepayments, depreciation, bad debts written off, and provision for bad debts.

• Net profit has been reduced because two further costs in connection with bad debts written off and provision for bad debts have been deducted from profit and loss account.

increases/decreases in provision for bad debts

Having once created a provision for bad debts, the amount of the provision must be reviewed at the end of each subsequent financial year. The level of debtors is likely to be different at the end of each year as the business expands or contracts; if provision for bad debts is a fixed percentage of debtors, the amount of the provision will also need altering. A more radical change will be if the business decides to increase or decrease the *blanket* percentage of debtors it estimates may go bad, eg an increase from five per cent to ten per cent. Whatever the cause, the amount required as provision for bad debts will alter and it is *the amount of the change* that must be entered in profit and loss account; the *new total* is recorded in the balance sheet.

Case Study: Heather Lewis – provision for bad debts

Situation one

At 31 December 19-5, the balance sheet of Heather Lewis shows debtors of £1,900, and a 5 per cent provision for bad debts of £95. Let us assume that, twelve months later, debtors are £3,000 (after bad debts have been written off). Heather decides that the figure of 5 per cent of debtors is to be retained as a provision for bad debts. How will this be recorded in her financial statements for 19-6?

Solution

The provision for bad debts must now be £3,000 x 5% = £150. As the existing provision is £95, only the *difference* of £55 is charged to profit and loss account as an expense. It is described as an *increase in provision for bad debts*. The new figure of £150 is deducted *in full* from debtors in the balance sheet:

BALANCE SHEET (EXTRACT) OF HEATHER LEWIS AS AT 31 DECEMBER 19-6

	£	£
Current Assets		
Debtors	3,000	
Less provision for bad debts	150	
		2,850

Situation two

In the above example the provision for bad debts increased by £55 over the previous amount. In the following year, debtors (after allowing for bad debts) have fallen to £2,500. How will this be recorded in her financial statements for 19-7?

Solution

Now the provision for bad debts will need reducing to £125 (5% of £2,500). This is achieved by crediting to (adding to) profit and loss account the difference of £25, described as a *reduction in provision for bad debts*. The figure will be added to gross profit in the profit and loss account and will be recorded in the right hand column below gross profit. The balance sheet will show:

BALANCE SHEET (EXTRACT) OF HEATHER LEWIS AS AT 31 DECEMBER 19-7

	£	£
Current Assets		
Debtors	2,500	
Less provision for bad debts	125	
		2,375

The above Case Study shows that to change an existing provision for bad debts it is necessary to:

* charge as an expense to profit and loss account the amount of the increase, or credit (add to) profit and loss account the amount of the decrease in provision for bad debts; in both cases we are only concerned, in profit and loss account, with the *amount of the change*

* deduct the amount of the *total* provision, ie existing provision plus increase or less decrease, from debtors in the balance sheet

Chapter Summary

❏ Bad debts and the creation of a provision (or the increase in an existing provision) have the effect of reducing net profit. They represent costs which businesses that only sell goods for cash avoid. Many businesses, though, have to sell their goods on credit and they should take steps to minimise the possibility of bad debts.

❏ In the balance sheet the net figure for debtors included in current assets should give an indication of the *true* amount the business can expect to collect from its debtors.

❏ In adjusting the profit and loss account and balance sheet to take note of *bad debts written off* and *provision for bad debts* we are presenting more accurate financial statements.

Having looked at some specific methods of adjusting accounts to take note of accruals and prepayments, depreciation, and bad debts, the next chapter considers the basic framework within which financial statements are prepared.

 Student Activities

10.1   You are an accounts clerk for Waterston Plant Hire. At 31 December 19-2, the end of its financial year, the business has gross debtors of £20,210. The owner decides to:

(a) write off, as bad debts, the accounts of:

P. Ross	£55
J. Ball	£105
L. Jones	£50

(b) make a provision for bad debts of $2\frac{1}{2}$ per cent of debtors (after writing off the above bad debts)

You are to show how these transactions will be recorded in the financial statements at the end of the financial year.

10.2   Ross Engineering Ltd has an existing provision for bad debts of £300, based on 5 per cent of debtors. After writing off bad debts, the amounts of debtors at the end of the next two financial years are found to be:

30 June 19-2	£8,000
30 June 19-3	£7,000

The company continues to keep the provision for bad debts equal to 5 per cent of debtors.

As accountant to Ross Engineering Ltd, you are to show how the amount of the provision for bad debts will be adjusted at the end of the financial years ended 30 June 19-2 and 30 June 19-3, and how it will be recorded in the appropriate financial statements.

10.3   The following trial balance has been extracted by the book-keeper of P Sanders, who runs an import/export business, at 31 December 19-6:

	Dr £	Cr £
Purchases and sales	51 225	81 762
Returns	186	254
Stock at 1 January 19-6	6 031	
Discounts	324	438
Motor expenses	1 086	
Wages and salaries	20 379	
Electricity	876	
Telephone	1 241	
Rent and rates	4 565	
Sundry expenses	732	
Bad debts written off	219	
Debtors and creditors	1 040	972
Bank	3 501	
Cash	21	
Motor vehicles at cost	15 000	
Provision for depreciation on motor vehicles		3 000
Office equipment at cost	10 000	
Provision for depreciation on office equipment		5 000
Capital		33 000
Drawings	8 000	
	124 426	124 426

Notes at 31 December 19-6:

- stock was valued at £8 210
- electricity owing £102
- rent prepaid £251
- depreciate motor vehicles at 20 per cent and office equipment at 10 per cent per annum, using the straight-line method
- create a provision for bad debts of 5 per cent of debtors

As accountant to P Sanders, you are to prepare the trading and profit and loss account for the year ended 31 December 19-6, together with a balance sheet at that date.

10.4 The book-keeper of James Jenkins, who owns a patisserie and coffee lounge, has extracted the following trial balance at 30 June 19-2:

	Dr £	Cr £
Capital		32 175
Drawings	19 050	
Purchases and sales	105 240	168 432
Stock at 1 July 19-1	9 427	
Debtors and creditors	3 840	10 786
Returns	975	1 237
Discounts	127	643
Wages and salaries	30 841	
Motor vehicle expenses	1 021	
Rent and rates	8 796	
Heating and lighting	1 840	
Telephone	355	
General expenses	1 752	
Bad debts written off	85	
Motor vehicle at cost	8 000	
Provision for depreciation on motor vehicle		3 500
Shop fittings at cost	6 000	
Provision for depreciation on shop fittings		2 000
Provision for bad debts		150
Cash	155	
Bank	21 419	
	218 923	218 923

Notes at 30 June 19-2:

- stock was valued at £11 517
- motor vehicle expenses owing £55
- rent prepaid £275
- depreciate the motor vehicle at 25 per cent per annum, using the reducing balance method
- depreciate shop fittings at 10 per cent per annum, using the straight-line method
- the provision for bad debts is to be equal to 2.5 per cent of debtors

As accountant to James Jenkins, you are to prepare his trading and profit and loss account for the year ended 30 June 19-2, together with his balance sheet at that date.

11 Accounting concepts and stock valuation

introduction

In the preparation of financial statements (or final accounts) there are a number of basic rules that are followed. These rules, or *accounting concepts* as they are known, form a framework within which the financial statements of all organisations are constructed. By following the same concepts, broad comparisons can then be made between the financial results of different organisations.

two basic accounting concepts

There are two concepts so basic that they are followed in all circumstances:
* business entity concept
* money measurement concept

business entity concept

This refers to the fact that financial statements show the activities of one particular entity, ie business, local authority, society, etc, and do not include the activities of those who play a part in managing the organisation. For example, John Smith lives in a large house and owns a shoe shop. The financial statements of his shoe shop will not include any mention of his house, because the house is his personal asset and has nothing to do with the business entity. His wife, Jane Smith, is the treasurer of a local society which has a bank account with the National Bank, at the same branch of which she maintains her personal bank account. In producing the financial statements of the society (see also Chapter 16), no mention will be made of her own bank balance, only that of the society. The reason is that the two are separate entities.

money measurement concept

This means that, in finance, all items have to be expressed in the common denominator of money, eg the balance sheet of a farmer cannot measure his assets as being 50 cows, 200 sheep, etc; everything must be expressed in money. Only by using money can items be added together to give, for example, a net profit, or a balance sheet total. However, the money measurement concept does mean that a financial statement is only able to record items which can be expressed in terms of money. A business with an efficient management, and good labour relations will appear to have the same value as one that is overstaffed and has poor labour relations. Only in the longer term, with different levels of profit and balance sheet structure, will the differences between the two become apparent.

Another disadvantage of the money measurement concept is the effect of inflation on prices. For example, a business achieved sales of £100,000 this year, and hopes for £105,000 next year. Is this an improvement? The answer is that if inflation is greater than 5 per cent per annum, there has been no improvement at all and, in real terms, sales are reduced; if inflation is below 5 per cent, sales have increased in real terms.

Case Studies: for discussion

1. Profits last year were £10,000; this year they are £10,250. Has the business improved?

2. Two businesses each have fixed assets at cost of £100,000 in their balance sheets. One business bought the assets three years ago, while the other business bought them last week. What are the problems of comparison?

3. The owner of a business has a firm's car; her husband, a teacher, owns his own car. Which car will be shown on the business balance sheet? Would it make any difference if the husband was also a partner in the business?

4. A district nurse uses her own car for visiting patients and is reimbursed for petrol and other running expenses so incurred by the District Health Authority. Is the car an asset of the DHA?

further accounting concepts

The concepts we have considered so far are fundamental to all final accounts. Four further accounting concepts should also be applied:

*   going concern
*   accruals
*   consistency
*   prudence

going concern concept

This presumes that the business to which the final accounts relate will continue to trade in the foreseeable future. The trading and profit and loss account and balance sheet are prepared on the basis that there is no intention to reduce significantly the size of the business or to liquidate the business. If the business was not a going concern, assets would have very different values, and the balance sheet would be affected considerably. For example, a large, purpose-built factory has considerable value to a going concern business but, if the factory had to be sold, it is likely to have a limited use for other industries, and therefore will have a lower market value. The latter case is the opposite of the going concern concept and would be described as a *gone concern*. Also, in a gone concern situation, extra depreciation would need to be charged as an expense to profit and loss account to allow for the reduced value of fixed assets.

accruals (or matching) concept

This means that expenses and revenues must be matched so that they concern the same goods and the same time period. We have already put this concept into practice in Chapter 8, where expenses and revenues were adjusted to take note of prepayments and accruals. The trading and profit and loss account should always show the amounts of the expense that should have been incurred, ie the expenditure for the year, whether or not it has been paid. This is the principle of income and expenditure accounting, rather than using receipts and payments as and when they fall due. Further examples of the accruals concept are debtors, creditors, provision for depreciation, and the opening and closing stock adjustments in the trading account.

consistency concept

This requires that, when a business adopts particular accounting methods, it should continue to use such methods consistently. For example, a business that decides to make a provision for depreciation on machinery at ten per cent per annum, using the straight-line method, should continue to use that percentage and method for future final accounts for this asset. Of course, having once chosen a particular method, a business is entitled to make changes provided there are good reasons for so doing, and a note to the final accounts would explain what has happened. By applying the consistency concept, direct comparison between the final accounts of different years can be made. Another example of the use of the consistency concept is stock valuation (see later in this chapter).

prudence concept

This concept, also known as conservatism in accounting, requires that final accounts should always, where there is any doubt, report a conservative figure for profit or the valuation of assets. To this end, profits are not to be anticipated and should only be recognised when it is reasonably certain that they will be realised; at the same time all known liabilities should be provided for. A good example of the prudence concept is where a provision is made for bad debts (see Chapter 10) – the debtors have not yet gone bad, but it is expected, from experience, that a certain percentage will eventually need to be written off as bad debts. The valuation of stock (see later in this chapter) also follows the prudence concept. 'Anticipate no profit, but anticipate all losses' is a summary of the concept which, in its application, prevents an over-optimistic presentation of a business through the final accounts.

Note: These concepts apply equally to the final accounts of sole traders, partnerships and limited companies. In the case of limited companies the concepts are given legal force in the Companies Act 1985 (as amended by the Companies Act 1989), and a company which does not apply them will receive a qualified audit report from its auditors.

accounting standards

Over the last twenty-five years, a number of accounting standards have been produced to provide the rules, or framework, of accounting. The intention has been to reduce the variety of alternative accounting treatments. At present the rules of accounting are represented by:
- Statements of Standard Accounting Practice
- Financial Reporting Standards

Statements of Standard Accounting Practice – or SSAPs, as they are more usually known – are issued by the Accounting Standards Board. This Board requires accountants to observe the applicable accounting standards, and to disclose and explain significant departures from the standards. Twenty-five SSAPs have been issued, although some have been withdrawn or superseded. It is likely that, in the near future, a number of SSAPs will be withdrawn and replaced by Financial Reporting Standards (see below) as part of an attempt to reduce the number of permissible accounting treatments.

We have just looked at the four accounting concepts, above. These are detailed in SSAP 2, which is entitled 'Disclosure of accounting policies'. These concepts apply to all final accounts and, in the case of limited companies, are given legal force by the Companies Act.

In Chapter 9, when dealing with depreciation, we have already covered the main requirements of SSAP 12 'Accounting for depreciation'. Later in this chapter, we shall look at aspects of SSAP 9 'Stocks and long-term contracts'.

Financial Reporting Standards (FRSs). The Accounting Standards Board is currently undertaking a major review of accounting standards to ensure that standards are consistent and that there are few options allowed in the preparation of final accounts. Chapter 15, 'Cashflow Statements' is based on FRS 1.

valuation of stock

The control and valuation of stock is an important aspect in the efficient management of a business. Manual or computer records are used to show the amount of stock held and its value at any time during the year. However, at the end of the financial year it is essential for a business to make a physical *stock-take* for use in the final accounts. This involves stock control personnel going into the stores, the shop, or the warehouse and counting each item. The counted stock for each type of stock held is then valued as follows:

number of items held x stock valuation per item = stock value

The value of stock at the beginning and end of the financial year is used in the trading account to calculate the figure for cost of goods sold. Therefore, the stock value has an effect on the gross and net profit for the year.

Stock is valued at either:
- what it cost the business to buy the stock, or
- if the goods are old, deteriorated or have gone out of fashion, and their selling price is *less* than the original purchase price, then they will be valued at this selling price (less any costs of selling and distribution).

This stock valuation is often described as being *at the lower of cost and net realisable value*. This valuation is taken from SSAP 9 and applies the prudence concept . It is illustrated as follows:

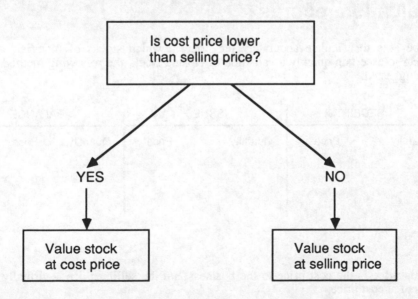

The difficulty in stock valuation is in finding out the cost price of stock – this is not easy when quantities of a particular stock item are continually being bought in – often at different prices – and then sold. Some businesses will have stock in a number of different forms, eg a manufacturing business (see Chapter 18) will have stocks of raw materials, work-in-progress and finished goods.

different methods used in stock valuation

Firms use different methods to calculate the cost price of stock. Three commonly used methods are:

- *FIFO (first in, first out)* This method assumes that the first stocks acquired are the first to be sold or used, so that the valuation of stock on hand at any time consists of the most recently acquired stock.

- *LIFO (last in, first out)* Here it is assumed that the last stocks acquired are the first to be sold or used, so that the stock on hand is made up of earlier purchases.

- *AVCO (average cost)* Here the average cost of items held at the beginning of the year is calculated; as new stocks are bought a new average cost is calculated (based on a weighted average, using the number of units bought as the weighting).

The use of a particular method does not necessarily correspond with the method of physical distribution adopted in a firm's stores. For example, in a car factory one starter motor of type X is the same as another, and no-one will be concerned if the storekeeper issues one from the last batch received, even if the FIFO system has been adopted. However, perishable goods are always physically handled on the basis of first in, first out, even if the accounting stock records use another method.

Having chosen a suitable stock valuation method, a business will continue to use that method unless there are good reasons for making the change. This is in line with the *consistency concept* of accounting.

stock valuation records

In order to be able to calculate accurately the price at which stocks of materials are issued to production, and to ascertain quickly a valuation of closing stock, the following method of recording stock data is suggested:

DATE	RECEIPTS		ISSUES		BALANCE		
19..	Quantity	Price	Quantity	Price*	Quantity	Price	Total

*Note that this price is the cost price to the business, *not* the selling price – virtually all stock records are kept at cost price.

Case Study: stock records

In order to show how the stock records would appear under FIFO, LIFO and AVCO, the following data has been used for each:

19-1
January Opening stock of 40 units at a cost of £3.00 each
February Bought 20 units at a cost of £3.60 each
March Sold 36 units for £6 each
April Bought 20 units at a cost of £3.75 each
May Sold 25 units for £6 each

FIFO

Date	Receipts			Issues			Balance			
19-1	Quantity		Price	Quantity		Price	Quantity		Price	Total
January	Balance b/d						40	x	£3.00 =	£120.00
February	20	@	£3.60				40	x	£3.00 =	£120.00
							20	x	£3.60 =	£72.00
							60			£192.00
March				36	@	£3.00	4	x	£3.00 =	£12.00
							20	x	£3.60 =	£72.00
							24			£84.00
April	20	@	£3.75				4	x	£3.00 =	£12.00
							20	x	£3.60 =	£72.00
							20	x	£3.75 =	£75.00
							44			£159.00
May				4	@	£3.00				
				20	@	£3.60				
				1	@	£3.75	19	x	£3.75 =	£71.25

LIFO

Date	Receipts			Issues			Balance			
19-1	Quantity		Price	Quantity		Price	Quantity		Price	Total
January	Balance b/d						40	x	£3.00 =	£120.00
February	20	@	£3.60				40	x	£3.00 =	£120.00
							20	x	£3.60 =	£72.00
							60			£192.00
March				20	@	£3.60				
				16	@	£3.00	24	x	£3.00 =	£72.00
April	20	@	£3.75				24	x	£3.00 =	£72.00
							20	x	£3.75 =	£75.00
							44			£147.00
May				20	@	£3.75				
				5	@	£3.00	19	x	£3.00 =	£57.00

AVCO

Date	Receipts		Issues		Balance		
19-1	Quantity	Price	Quantity	Price	Quantity	Price	Total
January	Balance b/d				40	x £3.00 =	£120.00
February	20 @	£3.60			40 20 60	x £3.00 = x £3.60 = x £3.20 =	£120.00 £72.00 £192.00
March			36 @	£3.20	24	x £3.20 =	£76.80
April	20 @	£3.75			24 20 44	x £3.20 = x £3.75 = x £3.45 =	£76.80 £75.00 £151.80
May			25 @	£3.45	19	x £3.45 =	£65.55

The closing stock valuations at the end of May under each method show cost prices of:
FIFO   £71.25
LIFO   £57.00
AVCO   £65.55

There is quite a difference, and this has come about because different stock methods have been used.

effect on profit

In the example above, the selling price was £6 per unit. The effect on gross profit of using different stock valuations is shown in the following trading accounts:

	FIFO £	LIFO £	AVCO £
Sales: 61 units at £6	366.00	366.00	366.00
Opening stock: 40 units at £3	120.00	120.00	120.00
Purchases: 20 units at £3.60 } 20 units at £3.75 }	147.00	147.00	147.00
	267.00	267.00	267.00
Less Closing stock: 19 units	71.25	57.00	65.55
Cost of Goods Sold	195.75	210.00	201.45
Gross profit	170.25	156.00	164.55
	366.00	366.00	366.00

In times of rising prices, FIFO produces the highest profit, LIFO the lowest, and AVCO between the other two. However, over the life of a business, total profit is the same in total, whichever method is chosen: the profit is allocated to different years depending on which method is used.

advantages and disadvantages to a business of FIFO, LIFO and AVCO

FIFO (first in, first out)

Advantages:
- realistic, ie it assumes that goods are issued in order of receipt
- it is easy to calculate
- stock valuation comprises actual prices at which items have been bought
- the closing stock valuation is close to the most recent prices

Disadvantages:
- prices at which goods are issued are not necessarily the latest prices
- in times of rising prices, profits will be higher than with other methods (resulting in more tax to pay)

LIFO (last in, first out)

Advantages:
- goods are issued at the latest prices
- it is easy to calculate

Disadvantages:
- illogical, ie it assumes goods are issued in reverse order from that in which they are received
- the closing stock valuation is not usually at most recent prices
- when stocks are being run down, issues will 'dip into' old stock at out-of-date prices

AVCO (average cost)

Advantages:
- over a number of accounting periods reported profits are smoothed, ie both high and low profits are avoided
- fluctuations in purchase price are evened out so that issues do not vary greatly
- logical, ie it assumes that identical units, even when purchased at different times, have the same value
- closing stock valuation is close to current market values (in times of rising prices, it will be below current market values)

Disadvantages:
- difficult to calculate, and calculations may be to several decimal places
- issues and stock valuation are usually at prices which never existed
- issues may not be at current prices and, in times of rising prices, will be below current prices

The important point to remember is that a business must adopt a *consistent* stock valuation policy, ie it should choose one method of finding the cost price, and not change it without good reason. FIFO and AVCO are more commonly used than LIFO; in particular, LIFO usually results in a stock valuation for the final accounts which bears little relationship to recent costs.

categories of stock

Statement of Standard Accounting Practice No 9 requires that, in calculating the lower of cost and net realisable value, note should be taken of
- separate items of stock, or
- groups of similar items

This means that the stock valuation 'rule' must be applied to each separate item of stock, or each group or category of similar stocks. The *total* cost cannot be compared with the *total* net realisable value. For example, a decorator's shop has two main categories of stock, paints and wallpapers; they are valued as follows:

	Cost £	Net realisable value £
Paints	2,500	2,300
Wallpapers	5,000	7,500
	7,500	9,800

The correct stock valuation is £7,300, which takes the lower of cost and net realisable value for each *group* of stock, ie

	£
Paints (at net realisable value)	2,300
Wallpapers (at cost)	5,000
	7,300

Note that this valuation is the lowest possible choice, so indicating that stock valuation follows the prudence concept of accounting.

Chapter Summary

❑ The two basic accounting concepts of business entity and money measurement always apply to the preparation of final accounts.

❑ In order to improve the usefulness of final accounts the four concepts of going concern, accruals, consistency and prudence should also be applied.

❑ The usual valuation for stock is *at the lower of cost and net realisable value* (SSAP 9).

❑ Common methods of accounting for stock include:
- FIFO (first in, first out)
- LIFO (last in, first out)
- AVCO (average cost, based on a weighted average)

❑ Having chosen one stock valuation method, a business should apply it consistently.

So far in this book we have concerned ourselves principally with the final accounts of sole trader businesses.   In the next two chapters we will look at the specialist financial statements of partnerships (Chapter 12), and limited companies (Chapter 13).

Student Activities

11.1 A discussion is taking place between Wendy Abrahams, a sole trader, who owns a furniture shop, and her husband, John, who solely owns an engineering business. The following points are made:

(a) John says that, having depreciated his firm's machinery last year on the reducing balance method, for this year he intends to use the straight-line method. By doing this he says that he will deduct less depreciation from profit and loss account, so his net profit will be higher and his bank manager will be impressed. He says he might revert back to the reducing balance method next year.

(b) At the end of her financial year, Wendy comments that the stock of her shop had cost £10,000. She says that, as she normally adds 50 per cent to cost price to give the selling price, she intends to put a value of £15,000 for stock in the trading account and balance sheet.

(c) John's car is owned by his business but he keeps referring to it as *my car*. Wendy reminds him that it does not belong to him, but to the firm. He replies that of course it belongs to him and, furthermore, if the firm went bankrupt, he would be able to keep the car.

(d) On the last day of her financial year, Wendy sold a large order of furniture, totalling £3,000, to a local hotel. The furniture was invoiced and delivered from stock that day, before year-end stocktaking commenced. The payment was received early in the new financial year and Wendy now asks John if she will be able to put this sale through the accounts for the new year, instead of the old, but without altering the figures for purchases and closing stock for the old year.

(e) John says that his accountant talks of preparing his accounts on a going concern basis. John asks Wendy if she knows of any other basis that can be used, and which it is usual to follow.

You are to take each of the points and state the correct accounting treatment, referring to appropriate accounting concepts.

11.2 A business buys twenty units of a product in January at a cost of £3 each; it buys ten more in February at £3.50 each, and ten in April at £4 each. Eight units are sold in March, and sixteen are sold in May. Calculate the value of closing stock at the end of May using:

(a) FIFO, (b) AVCO, (c) LIFO.

(Where appropriate, work to two decimal places.)

11.3 Tradeparts Ltd is a company which imports electrical parts for cars and sells in bulk to garage groups and car accessory shops. The stock record card for December 19-6 for a particular type of starter motor shows the following:

Opening stock	1 December	40 units @ £33 each
Receipts	4 December	50 units @ £36 each
	12 December	80 units @ £40 each
Sales	8 December	70 units
	21 December	50 units

As clerk in the accounts department of Tradeparts Ltd, you are to calculate the value of the closing stock at 31 December 19-6 using:

(a) first in, first out (FIFO) method
(b) last in, first out (LIFO) method
(c) average cost (AVCO) method

If the selling price for each unit at 31 December 19-6 is found to be (firstly) £60, or (secondly) £30, would your closing stock valuations alter?

11.4   XY Ltd is a wholesaling business which trades in two items of stock, 'X' and 'Y'. At the end of six months' trading, the stock record cards show the following:

X				Y		
19-1	Receipts (Units)	Sales (Units)		19-1	Receipts (Units)	Sales (Units)
Jan	100 @ £4.00			Jan	200 @ £10.00	
Feb		80		Feb	100 @ £8.50	
Mar	140 @ £6.00			Mar		240
Apr	100 @ £3.80			Apr	100 @ £11.50	
May		140		May	140 @ £10.00	
Jun	80 @ £5.00			Jun		100

As an accounts clerk, working for XY Ltd., you are to:

•   Using (a) the first in, first out (FIFO), (b) the last in, first out (LIFO), and the average cost (AVCO) methods, calculate the cost price of the closing stock for X and Y held on 30 June 19-1.

•   Prepare three trading accounts, each for the six months ended 30 June 19-1, for item X, assuming that the selling price has been £10 per unit. The first trading account will use for FIFO stock valuation for the closing stock, the second will use the LIFO stock valuation, the third will use the AVCO stock valuation (in all cases there was no opening stock).

•   Prepare three trading accounts, on the same basis, for stock item Y, assuming that the selling price has been £20 per unit.

•   Write a memorandum to the managing director of XY Ltd in response to his request that you are to implement the stock valuation method *that gives the larger profit*.

Assignment 4
Year-end Accounts: Tom Blake

LEARNING OUTCOMES COVERED:
Preparation of final accounts, adjustments to final accounts, accounting concepts, stock valuation

SITUATION

You are a junior clerk at Ticket & Runne, (address: Victoria Chambers, Ransome Walk, Rowcester, RW1 2EJ) a firm of chartered accountants. The firm has a wide range of clients for whom it prepares year-end accounts and provides financial advice. The following year-end trial balance has been received from the book-keeper of Tom Blake, a printer and stationer (address T Blake, Rapido Print, 7 High Street, Rowcester RW1 1LG):

TRIAL BALANCE AS AT 31 DECEMBER 19-1

	Dr. £	Cr. £
Debtors and creditors	34,600	20,900
Delivery van at cost	7,000	
Provision for depreciation on delivery van		1,400
Fixtures and fittings at cost	12,800	
Provision for depreciation on fixtures and fittings		2,560
Purchases and sales	94,500	166,100
Sales returns and purchases returns	7,600	4,100
Salaries	29,600	
Bank	7,500	
Cash	700	
Bad debts written off	1,900	
Rates and insurance	2,700	
Electricity	3,960	
Premises	60,000	
Drawings	18,200	
Sundry expenses	1,200	
Stock at 1 January 19-1	19,800	
Capital at 1 January 19-1		107,000
	302,060	302,060

Subsequent discussions with the book-keeper reveal that at 31 December 19-1:

* The closing stock had the following values:
    selling price £31,750
    cost price £20,500

* £250 of the rates for next year has been paid in advance

* £150 was owing for electricity

* The delivery van is being depreciated at 20 per cent per annum using the reducing balance method

* Fixtures and fittings are being depreciated using the straight-line method at 10 per cent per annum

* Past experience shows that 2 per cent of debtors are likely to become bad debts; you agree to create a provision to allow for this

STUDENT TASKS

1. Using the information above, prepare financial statements for Tom Blake covering the year to 31 December 19-1.

2. Draft an accompanying letter for signature by David Ticket of Ticket & Runne, Chartered Accountants, explaining the adjustments you have made to the trial balance figures, giving the reasons for so doing. The date of the letter is 26 January 19-2.

3. Draft a further letter for signature by the same partner, in answer to the following letter received:

Rapido Print
7 High Street
Rowcester
RW1 1LG

Tel 0805 672165 Fax 0805 672563
Vat Reg 652 7655 161

D Ticket FCCA
Ticket & Runne
Victoria Chambers
Ransome Walk
Rowcester RW1 2EJ

2 February 19-2

Dear Mr Ticket

Final Accounts 19-1

Thank you for your letter of 26 January and the enclosed financial statements and explanations of the adjustments made.

I still have some questions which I hope you will be able to answer:

1. There seems to be no allowance on the balance sheet for my loyal workforce nor for the excellent reputation of my business.

2. You state in the Trading and Profit and Loss Account and Balance Sheet that the closing stock is £20,500. We reckon, according to our latest sales catalogue that this stock is worth £31,750. Does this not mean that our business is being undervalued?

I shall be grateful if you could let me know the reasons for these apparent discrepancies. I shall be on holiday from tomorrow, so would you please reply in writing.

Yours sincerely

Tom Blake

Thomas Blake
Proprietor

12 Financial statements – partnerships

introduction

In Chapter 7 we considered the basic financial statements of business organisations. These statements consist of trading and profit and loss account, and balance sheet. They are produced usually at the end of each financial year and report the gross profit and net profit for the year, together with the assets and liabilities at the year-end. Until now we have considered only the financial statements of a sole trader, ie one person in business; in this chapter we will see how they are presented where two or more people own a business in the form of a partnership, an entity which we have already considered briefly in Chapter 4.

the Partnership Act 1890

The Partnership Act of 1890 defines a partnership as:

the relation which subsists between persons carrying on a business in common with a view of profit

A partnership normally consists of two to twenty partners, although some professional firms may exceed this limit. Common examples of partnerships are solicitors, dentists, and doctors. As the definition states, a partnership is a group of people working together; they contribute capital and expect to make and share a profit.

accounting requirements of the Partnership Act, 1890

The Partnership Act sets out the following accounting rules:
* profits and losses are to be shared equally between the partners
* no partner is entitled to a salary
* partners are not entitled to receive interest on their capital
* interest is not to be charged on partners' drawings (the amount they have taken out of the business)
* when a partner contributes more capital than agreed, he or she is entitled to receive interest at five per cent per annum on the excess

These rules *must* be followed unless the partners agree amongst themselves, by means of a written *partnership agreement,* to follow different accounting rules. In particular, a partnership agreement will often cover the following:
* division of profits or losses between partners
* partners' salaries
* whether interest is to be paid on capital, and at what rate
* whether interest is to be charged on partners' drawings, and at what rate

financial statements of a partnership

A partnership prepares the same type of financial statements as a sole-trader business:
- trading and profit and loss account
- balance sheet

One main difference is that, immediately after the profit and loss account, follows an *appropriation section* (see below). This shows how the net profit from profit and loss account is divided between the partners. A second difference is that the capital section of the balance sheet needs to be presented in such a way as to show the capital account of each partner separately. Partners usually have a current account (not to be confused with a bank current account), and this must also be stated on the balance sheet (see below). Apart from these differences, the other financial statements are presented in *exactly* the same way as for a sole trader.

appropriation of profits

As mentioned above, the appropriation section (often described as the appropriation account) follows the profit and loss account and shows how net profit has been divided amongst the partners.

For example, Able, Baker and Cox are partners sharing profits and losses equally; their profit and loss account for the current year shows a net profit of £30,000. The appropriation of profits appears as:

	£
Net profit	30,000
Appropriation of profits	
Able	10,000
Baker	10,000
Cox	10,000
	30,000

The appropriation of profits above is very simple. A more complex appropriation would show a salary paid to a partner (*not* to be shown in profit and loss account), interest allowed on partners' capital, and interest charged on partners' drawings.

An example of an appropriation account for the partnership of Davis and Eady is as follows:

	£	£
Net profit		25,000
Add interest charged on partners' drawings:		
Davis	1,000	
Eady	1,500	
		2,500
		27,500
Less appropriation of profits		
Salary: Eady		9,000
Interest allowed on partners' capitals:		
Davis	2,500	
Eady	1,000	
		3,500
		15,000
Share of remaining profits:		
Davis (60%)	9,000	
Eady (40%)	6,000	
		15,000
		15,500

Note that all of the available profit, after allowing for any salary, and interest charged and allowed, is shared amongst the partners, in the ratio in which they share profits and losses.

Case Study: Fox and Gun in partnership

Situation

Fox and Gun are in partnership with capital contributions of £20,000 and £15,000 respectively. The partnership agreement states that:

- Gun is to be paid a salary of £8,000 each year
- interest is allowed on partners' capital accounts at eight per cent per year
- interest is to be charged on drawings at five per cent
- remaining profits are to be shared by Fox and Gun in the ratio of 3:2 respectively

For the financial year which ended on 31 March 19-5, the profit and loss account shows a net profit of £21,000. During the year Fox made drawings of £9,000, Gun made drawings of £12,000. Show how the profits will be appropriated.

Solution

	£	£
Net profit		21,000
Add interest charged on partners' drawings:		
Fox	450	
Gun	600	
		1,050
		22,050
Less appropriation of profits		
Salary: Gun		8,000
Interest allowed on partners' capitals:		
Fox	1,600	
Gun	1,200	
		2,800
		11,250
Share of remaining profits:		
Fox (60%)	6,750	
Gun (40%)	4,500	
		11,250
		11,250

capital accounts and current accounts

Most partnerships keep a capital account and a current account for each partner. The capital account is *fixed,* and only alters if a permanent increase or decrease in capital contributed by the partner takes place. The current account is *fluctuating* and it is to this account that:

- share of profits is credited; share of losses is debited
- salary (if any) is credited
- interest allowed on partners' capital is credited
- drawings are debited
- interest charged on partners' drawings is debited

Thus, the current account is treated as a *working* account, while capital account remains fixed, except for capital introduced or withdrawn.

The current accounts for the partnership of Fox and Gun (see Case Study above) appear as follows – the opening balances on the partners' current accounts are Fox £1,000 credit, Gun £200 credit.

Dr.			**Partners' Current Accounts**			Cr.

	Fox £	Gun £			Fox £	Gun £
19-4/-5			19-4/-5			
31 Mar. Drawings for year	9,000	12,000	1 Apr. Balances b/d	1,000	200	
31 Mar. Interest on drawings	450	600	Salary	–	8,000	
31 Mar. Balance c/d	–	1,300	31 Mar. Interest on capital	1,600	1,200	
			31 Mar. Share of profits	6,750	4,500	
			31 Mar. Balance c/d	100	-	
	9,450	13,900		9,450	13,900	
19-5/-6			19-5/-6			
1 Apr. Balance b/d	100	–	1 Apr. Balance b/d	–	1,300	

Note that Fox has drawn more out of the current account than the balance of the account; accordingly, at the end of the year, Fox has a debit balance on the account with the partnership. By contrast, Gun has a credit balance of £1,300 on current account.

The balance sheet must show the year-end balances on each partner's capital and current account. However, it is usual to show the transactions that have taken place on each account in summary form, in the same way that, in a sole-trader's balance sheet, net profit is added, and drawings are deducted.

The following is an example layout for the capital and current accounts of the partnership of Fox and Gun (see Case Study above) as they will be shown in the balance sheet (the other sections of the balance sheet are not shown):

BALANCE SHEET (EXTRACT) OF FOX AND GUN AS AT 31 MARCH 19-5

	£	£	£
Capital Accounts			
Fox		20,000	
Gun		15,000	
			35,000
Current Accounts	FOX	GUN	
Opening balance	1,000	200	
Add: salary	–	8,000	
interest on capital	1,600	1,200	
share of profit	6,750	4,500	
	9,350	13,900	
Less: drawings	9,000	12,000	
interest on drawings	450	600	
	(100)	1,300	
			1,200
			36,200

Note that the other sections of the balance sheet, ie fixed assets, current assets, current liabilities, and long-term liabilities, are presented in the same way as for a sole-trader.

Chapter Summary

❑   A partnership is formed when two or more (usually up to a maximum of twenty) people set up in business.

❑   The Partnership Act, 1890, states certain accounting rules, principally that profits and losses must be shared equally.

❑   Many partnerships *over-ride* the accounting rules of the Act by creating a partnership agreement.

❑   In partnership accounting, an appropriation section follows profit and loss account to show the division of profits or losses between partners.

❑   The usual way to account for partners' capital is to maintain a fixed capital account for each partner. This is complemented by a fluctuating current account which is used as a *working* account for share of profits, drawings, etc.

The next chapter continues the theme of more specialist financial statements by looking at the year-end accounts of limited companies.

 Student Activities

You are a trainee accountant working in the local office of Anderson, Kerr, Price and Co., an international firm of Chartered Accountants. You have reached the point in your training when you are dealing with partnership accounts and today you have to work on the year-end accounts of four clients.

12.1   Box and Cox are in partnership running an electrical shop. On 30 June 19-5 their capital accounts, which have not changed during the previous 12 months, are: Box £30,000; Cox £20,000.

Their deed of partnership provides that:

• Cox is to receive a salary of £10,000 pa for managing the business
• each partner is to be credited with interest on capital at 8 per cent per annum
• profits or losses are to be shared equally
• interest is charged on drawings at 5 per cent on the total amount drawn in each year

On 1 July 19-4 Box's current account showed a debit balance of £120 and Cox's a credit balance of £150. During the year ended 30 June 19-5, their drawings were: Box £7,000 and Cox £13,000. Profits for the year ended 30 June 19-5 were £24,000 before appropriation.

You are to show the appropriation of profits for the year ended 30 June 19-5, together with the partners' capital and current accounts as they would appear in the balance sheet at 30 June 19-5.

Write a letter to the partners (The Electric Shop, 11 Green Street, Barchester, BR1 5AQ) enclosing the figures produced and explaining what they show. You know that each partner owns a large house and, yesterday, on the telephone, Box expressed his concern to you that these assets should not, under any circumstances, feature in the partnership accounts: give appropriate advice to Box and Cox in your letter.

12.2 Booth and Webster are partners in a wholesale stationery business. They share profits and losses in the ratio of 3:2. The following trial balance was extracted by their book-keeper at 30 June 19-5:

		Dr £	Cr £
Current accounts:	Booth		200
	Webster		100
Capital accounts:	Booth		27,800
	Webster		13,900
Drawings:	Booth	6,800	
	Webster	4,400	
Furniture and fittings at cost		1,700	
Provision for depreciation on furniture and fittings			340
Stock at 1 July 19-4		21,000	
Debtors and creditors		16,328	12,750
Purchases and sales		152,000	206,000
Freehold property at cost		68,500	
Wages and salaries		25,454	
Rates		300	
General expenses		9,832	
Bank		2,408	
Discounts		4,154	1,630
Rents received			156
Bank loan			50,000
		312,876	312,876

Notes at 30 June 19-5:

- stock is valued at £23,500
- wages and salaries outstanding: £304
- rates paid in advance: £60
- rent received includes £12 for July 19-5
- depreciation on furniture and fittings to be provided at 10% per annum on cost
- interest on capital is to be allowed at 5% per annum
- no interest is charged on drawings

You are to prepare the trading and profit and loss accounts (including appropriation account) of Booth and Webster for the year ended 30 June 19-5, together with a balance sheet at that date.

12.3   Anne Adams and Jenny Beeson are partners in an electrical supplies shop called 'A & B Electrics'. They share profits and losses equally.   The following trial balance was extracted by their book-keeper at 30 June 19-5:

		Dr £	Cr £
Capital accounts:	A. Adams		30,000
	J. Beeson		20,000
Current accounts:	A. Adams		780
	J. Beeson		920
Drawings:	A. Adams	16,000	
	J. Beeson	10,000	
Stock at 1 July 19-4		26,550	
Purchases and sales		185,290	250,140
Returns		1,360	850
Rent and rates		8,420	
Wages and salaries		16,290	
Motor vehicle expenses		2,470	
General expenses		6,210	
Motor vehicles at cost		12,000	
Fixtures and fittings at cost		4,000	
Provision for depreciation: motor vehicles			3,000
fixtures and fittings			800
Debtors and creditors		6,850	12,360
Bank		22,009	
Cash		1,376	
Bad debts written off		175	
Provision for bad debts			150
		319,000	319,000

Notes at 30 June 19-5:
- stock is valued at £27,750
- rates paid in advance £250
- wages and salaries owing £320
- provision for bad debts to be equal to 2 per cent debtors
- depreciation on fixtures and fittings to be provided at 10% per annum on cost using the straight-line method
- depreciation on motor vehicles to be provided at 25% per annum using the reducing balance method
- interest on capital is to be allowed at 8% per annum
- interest on drawings is to be charged at 5% per annum

You are to prepare the trading and profit and loss accounts (including appropriation section) of A & B Electrics for the year ended 30 June 19-5, together with a balance sheet at that date.

13 Financial statements – limited companies

introduction

In Chapter 4 we considered the different types of business entity – the sole trader, the partnership, the limited company - and examined the legal formation and the liability of the owner(s) in each case.

A limited company is a separate legal body, owned by shareholders and run by directors

The limited company is often chosen as the business entity for a number of reasons, which include:

- Liability of members (ie the shareholders, and directors who are shareholders) is *strictly limited* and their personal assets, unless pledged as security to a lender, are not available to the company's creditors.

- An expanding sole trader or partnership aiming to raise more finance by way of capital, may do so by incorporating into a company, enabling it to issue shares to the owner(s), family, business associates, and Venture Capital Companies. This small or medium-sized company is often referred to as a 'private company'.

- A larger company (with share capital over £50,000) may become a 'public limited company' (plc), and may raise finance from the public by means of a listing on the Stock Exchange, or a related market, although not all plcs do so.

Our studies require us to examine the year-end financial statements of limited companies. These statements broadly follow the layout of those prepared for sole-traders and partnerships. The Companies Act 1985 (amended by the Companies Act 1989) stipulates that certain annual financial statements must be filed with the Registrar of Companies and copies have to be sent to each shareholder. Such 'published accounts', as they are known, will not be discussed in this chapter: it may be that you will study these in detail as part of later accounting courses. Nevertheless, you should take the opportunity of obtaining and studying a set of such 'published accounts'.

In this chapter we will concentrate on the basic form of company year-end financial statements. Before we examine these statements in detail we will first look at the principal way a company raises finance: shares. There are different types of shares which appear in the company balance sheet as a capital item.

types of shares issued by limited companies

A clause contained in the Memorandum of Association (the document setting out the powers and objects of a company) states the share capital of that company and its division into shares of a fixed amount. This is known as the *authorised share capital,* ie the share capital that the company is allowed to issue. The authorised share capital may not be the same as the amount that the company has actually issued – this is known as the *issued share capital.* The latter can never exceed the former: if a company which has issued the full extent of its authorised share capital wishes to make an increase, it must first pass the appropriate resolution at a general meeting of the shareholders.

The authorised and issued share capital may be divided into a number of classes or types of share, the principal of which are *ordinary shares* and *preference shares.* Each share has a nominal or face value which is entered in the accounts. Shares may be issued with nominal values of 5p, 10p, 25p, 50p or £1, or indeed for any amount. Thus a company with an authorised share capital of £100,000 might state in its Memorandum of Association that this is divided up into:

100,000 ordinary shares of 50p each	£50,000
50,000 seven per cent preference shares of £1 each	£50,000
	£100,000

The nominal value of a share often bears little relationship to its true value. It is easy to find out the value of shares in a public limited company – if they are quoted on the Stock Exchange, the price may well be listed in the *Financial Times.* Shareholders receive *dividends* on their shares, being a distribution of a part of the company's earnings for a year or half-year. The dividend paid half-way through a financial year is known as an *interim dividend,* while that paid at the end of a year is a *final dividend.*

ordinary (equity) shares

These are the most commonly issued class of share. They take a share of the profits available for distribution after allowance has been made for all expenses of the business, including loan interest, taxation, and after preference dividends (if any). When a company makes large profits, it will have the ability to pay higher dividends to the ordinary shareholders; when profits are low or losses are made, the ordinary shareholders may receive a smaller or even no dividend. Companies rarely pay out all of their profits in the form of dividends; most retain some profits as reserves. These can always be used to enable a dividend to be paid in a year when the company makes little or no profit, always assuming that the company has sufficient cash in the bank to make the payment. Ordinary shareholders, in the event of the company ceasing to trade or 'winding up', will be the last to receive any repayment of their investment: other creditors will have to be paid off first.

preference shares

Such shares. which are less common, usually carry a fixed rate of dividend – 7% for example, based on the nominal share value – which, as their name suggests, is paid in preference to the ordinary shareholders; but it is only paid if the company makes profits. In the event of the winding up of the company, the 'preference' will also extend to repayment of capital before the ordinary shareholders.

Preference shares may be non-cumulative or cumulative:

- *non-cumulative* – if insufficient profits are made during a certain year to pay the preference dividend and the shares are designated as non-cumulative, then there is no provision for 'catching up' with missed dividends in future years

- *cumulative* – if the dividend on these is not paid in one year, it accumulates and will be paid in the future. In this way missing dividends will always be paid provided that the company makes sufficient profits in the future.

All preference shares are cumulative unless otherwise stated.

loans and debentures

In addition to money provided by shareholders, who are the owners of the company, further funds can be obtained by borrowing in the form of loans or debentures, for example, from a bank. The term 'debenture' usually refers to a formal certificate issued by a company acknowledging that a sum of money is owing to a specified person. Interest is normally payable on debentures; this must be paid, just like other business expense, whether a company makes profits or not. As loan and debenture interest is a business expense, this is charged to the profit and loss account along with all other expenses. In the event of the winding-up of the company, loan and debenture-holders would be repaid before any shareholders. Often debentures are *secured*, being backed by assets of the company pledged as security. A secured bank debenture is often referred to as a 'fixed and floating charge'. In the event of the winding up of the company, the assets would be sold and used to repay the debenture-holders before other creditors such as the company's suppliers.

limited companies: trading and profit and loss account

A limited company uses the same type of year-end financial statements as a sole trader or partnership. However, there are two items commonly found in the profit and loss account of a limited company that are not found in those of other business entities:

- **Directors' remuneration** ie amounts paid to directors. As directors are employed by the company, their *pay* appears amongst the expenses of the company.

- **Debenture and loan interest** as already noted, when debentures are issued and loans are raised by companies, the interest is shown as an expense in the profit and loss account.

In a similar way to a partnership, a limited company follows the profit and loss account with an *appropriation section* (often described as an appropriation account) to show how the net profit has been divided amongst the owners of the business – the shareholders. Here is an example of a simple appropriation account:

	£
Net profit for year	100,000
Less corporation tax	25,000
Profit after taxation	75,000
Less proposed ordinary dividend	50,000
Retained profit for year	25,000
Add balance of retained profits at beginning of year	35,000
Balance of retained profits at end of year	60,000

notes:

- The company has recorded a net profit of £100,000 in its profit and loss account – this is brought into the appropriation section.
- Corporation tax – the tax that a company has to pay on its profits, is shown in the appropriation account.
- The company proposes to distribute £50,000 to the ordinary shareholders as a dividend. This will be paid in the early part of the next financial year.

- Added to net profit is a balance of £35,000. This represents profits of the company from previous years that are undistributed, ie they have not been paid to the shareholders in the form of dividends. Unlike a sole trader or partnership, where all profits are added to owner's capital, a company will rarely distribute all its profits. You will note that this appropriation account shows a balance of retained profits at the year-end of £60,000. Such retained profits form a *revenue reserve* of the company. It is usual for a company to keep back some part of its profits in the form of reserves, to help the company build for the future.

- It should be noted that reserves are *not* a cash fund to be used whenever the company needs money, but are in fact represented by assets shown on the balance sheet. These assets may, or may not be realisable. The reserves recognise the fact that the assets belong to the shareholders (via the company).

- Besides the balance of retained profits – sometimes described as profit and loss account balance – companies often have several different revenue reserve accounts, eg general reserve or, for a specific purpose, reserve for the replacement of machinery. Transfers to or from these revenue reserve accounts are made in the appropriation section of the profit and loss account.

A more comprehensive appropriation account is shown below.

**APPROPRIATION ACCOUNT OF ORION LTD
FOR THE YEAR ENDED 31 DECEMBER 19-4**

	£	£
Net profit for year before taxation		43,000
Less corporation tax		<u>15,000</u>
Profit for year after taxation		28,000
Less: interim dividends paid		
ordinary shares	5,000	
preference shares	2,000	
final dividends proposed		
ordinary shares	10,000	
preference shares	<u>2,000</u>	
		<u>19,000</u>
		9,000
Less transfer to general reserve		<u>5,000</u>
Retained profit for year		4,000
Add balance of retained profits at beginning of year		<u>16,000</u>
Balance of retained profits at end of year		20,000

limited companies: balance sheet

The *balance sheet* of a limited company follows the same layout as that of a sole trader and a partnership but the capital section is more complex because of the different classes of shares that may be issued, and the various reserves.

Fig. 13.1 on the next page shows the balance sheet of Orion Ltd. as an example.

BALANCE SHEET OF ORION LTD AS AT 31 DECEMBER 19-4

Fixed Assets	Cost	Dep'n to date	Net
	£	£	£
Freehold land and buildings	180,000	20,000	160,000
Machinery	280,000	110,000	170,000
Fixtures and fittings	100,000	25,000	75,000
	560,000	155,000	405,000

Current Assets			
Stock		50,000	
Debtors		38,000	
Bank		22,000	
Cash		2,000	
		112,000	

Less Current Liabilities			
Creditors	30,000		
Proposed dividends	12,000		
Corporation tax	15,000		
		57,000	

Working Capital			55,000
			460,000
Less long-term Liabilities			
12% debentures			60,000
NET ASSETS			400,000

FINANCED BY		
Authorised Share Capital		
100,000 10% preference shares of £1 each		100,000
600,000 ordinary shares of £1 each		600,000
		700,000

Issued Share Capital		
40,000 10% preference shares of £1 each, fully paid		40,000
300,000 ordinary shares of £1 each, fully paid		300,000
		340,000

Capital Reserve		
Share premium account		10,000

Revenue Reserves		
General reserve*	30,000	
Profit and loss account	20,000	
		50,000
SHAREHOLDERS' FUNDS		400,000

* including transfer of £5,000 (see appropriation account on page 135)

Fig. 13.1   An example of a limited company balance sheet

A word of explanation about some of the items appearing in company balance sheets is appropriate at this point.

fixed assets

Like other balance sheets, this section comprises those items that do not change daily and are likely to be retained for use in the business for some time to come. It is usual for fixed assets, with the possible exception of freehold land, to be depreciated over a period of time or with use. The headings used for fixed assets in a balance sheet should read: *cost, depreciation to date* and *net* (see Fig. 13.1).

current assets

The usual current assets will be included, ie stocks, debtors, balance at bank, and cash in hand.

current liabilities

As with the balance sheets of sole traders and partnerships, this section contains those liabilities that are normally due to be paid within twelve months from the date of the balance sheet, eg creditors, bank overdraft. For limited companies, this section also contains the amount of proposed dividends and the amount of corporation tax to be paid within the next twelve months. Both of these amounts are also included in the appropriation account.

long-term liabilities

These are generally considered to be liabilities that are due to be repaid more than twelve months from the date of the balance sheet, eg loans and debentures.

authorised share capital

As already explained, this is the share capital of the company and its division into shares of a fixed amount as authorised by the company's Memorandum of Association. It is included on the balance sheet 'for information', but is not added into the balance sheet total, as it may not be the same amount as the issued share capital.

issued share capital

Here are detailed the classes and number of shares that have been issued. As stated earlier the issued share capital cannot exceed the amount authorised. In the balance sheet of Orion Ltd., the shares are described as being *fully paid,* meaning that the company has received the full amount of the value of each share from the shareholders. Sometimes shares will be *partly paid*, eg ordinary shares of £1, but 75p paid. This means that the company can make a *call* on the shareholders to pay the additional 25p to make the shares fully paid. Companies often issue partly paid shares and then make calls at certain times: for example, a company that is issuing shares to raise the finance for a new factory may wish to receive the proceeds of issue at different stages of the building and equipment of the factory. For the purpose of entering the amount of issued share capital in the balance sheet, always multiply the number of shares by the amount paid on them, eg 100,000 ordinary shares of £1 each, 75p paid = £75,000 (the other £25,000 will be called by the company at a later date).

capital reserves

A capital reserve is created as a result of a non-trading profit. Examples are:

* *Revaluation reserve*. This occurs when a fixed asset, most probably property, is revalued in the balance sheet. The amount of the revaluation is placed in a revaluation reserve where it increases the value of the shareholders' investment in the company. Note, however, that this is purely a 'book' adjustment, no cash has changed hands and the reserve cannot be used to fund the payment of dividends.

- *Share premium account*. An established company may well issue additional shares to the public at a higher amount than the nominal value. For example, Orion Ltd (Fig. 13.1) may seek finance for further expansion by issuing additional ordinary shares. Although the shares have a nominal value of £1 each, because Orion is a well-established company, the shares are issued at £1.50 each. Of this amount, £1 is recorded in the issued share capital section, and the extra 50p is the share premium.

A capital reserve cannot be used to fund the payment of dividends: one of its few uses is the issue of bonus (or 'free') shares.

revenue reserves

The reserves from profits are the amounts which the directors of the company have retained in the business. Examples of revenue reserves include *general reserve, profit and loss account,* and more specific reserves such as *debenture redemption reserve.*

shareholders' funds

This total represents the stake of the shareholders in the company. It comprises share capital (ordinary and preference shares), plus reserves (capital and revenue reserves).

Chapter Summary

❑ A limited company, unlike a sole trader or a partnership, has a separate legal entity from its owners.

❑ A company is regulated by the Companies Act 1985 (as amended by the Companies Act 1989), and is owned by shareholders and managed by directors.

❑ A limited company may be either a public limited company or a private limited company.

❑ The main types of shares issued by companies are ordinary shares and preference shares.

❑ Borrowings in the form of loans and debentures are a further source of finance.

❑ The year-end accounts of a company include an appropriation section, which follows the profit and loss account.

❑ The balance sheet of a limited company is similar to that of sole traders and partnerships, but the shareholders' funds section reflects the ownership of the company by its shareholders:
  – a statement of the authorised and issued share capital
  – details of capital reserves and revenue reserves

In the next chapter we turn to the *interpretation* of financial statements: the way in which they are read and assessed by a variety of different parties including lenders and investors.

✍️ Student Activities

13.1   (a)   Broadheath Ltd, a music publishing company, has an authorised share capital of £500,000 divided into 100,000 8 per cent preference shares of £1 each and 400,000 ordinary shares of £1 each. All the preference shares are issued and fully paid; 200,000 ordinary shares are issued and fully paid.

On 31 December 19-2 the company's reserves were £60,000; current liabilities £35,000; current assets £125,500; fixed assets (at cost) £350,000 and provisions for depreciation on fixed assets £80,500.

Prepare a summarised balance sheet as at 31 December 19-2 to display this information.

(b)   Explain to a potential shareholder the difference between ordinary shares and preference shares.

13.2   Rupert Ltd, a company selling cars, has retained profits of £5,000 on 1 January 19-7. The net profit for 19-7 amounts to £10,000. It is decided to create a general reserve of £2,000, and dividends are proposed as follows:

6% preference share dividend, the company having issued £20,000 of preference share capital

10% ordinary share dividend on issued share capital of £30,000

As accountant to Rupert Ltd, show the appropriation section of the profit and loss account for the year ended 31 December 19-7. Explain to one of the directors, Sid Smith, who does not understand finance, what you have done in the appropriation account. In particular, he wants to know why the transfer to general reserve has been made: as he comments, "it seems to me as though we have got another bank account and, surely, it would be better to pay off our existing overdraft with this money".

13.3   Mason Motors Limited is a second-hand car business. The following information is available for the year ended 31 December 19-1:
- balance of retained profits from previous years stands at £100,000
- net profit for the year was £75,000
- it has been agreed that a transfer to a general reserve of £20,000 is to be made
- corporation tax of £20,050 is to be paid on the year's profit
- it has been agreed that a dividend of 10% is to be paid on the issued share capital of £100,000

You are to:
(a)   Set out the appropriation account for Mason Motors Limited for the year ended 31 December 19-1.
(b)   One of the directors of the company asks if the £20,000 being transferred to general reserve could be used to rebuild the garage forecourt. How would you reply?

13.4   You are a trainee accountant working for Rossiter and Rossiter, a local firm of Chartered Accountants. The senior partner, Mrs Rossiter, hands you the following trial balance at 31 December 19-2, of Sidbury Trading Co. Ltd, a local stationery supplies firm:

	Dr £	Cr £
Share capital		240,000
Freehold land and buildings at cost	142,000	
Motor vans at cost	55,000	
Provision for depreciation on motor vans at 1 January 19-2		21,800
Purchases and sales	189,273	297,462
Rent and rates	4,000	
General expenses	9,741	
Wages and salaries	34,689	
Bad debts written off	948	
Provision for doubtful debts at 1 January 19-2		1,076
Directors' salaries	25,000	
Debtors and creditors	26,482	16,974
Retained profit at 1 January 19-2		18,397
Stock at 1 January 19-2	42,618	
Bank	65,958	
	595,709	595,709

You are given the following additional information:

- the authorized share capital is 300,000 ordinary shares of £1 each; all the shares which have been issued are fully paid

- wages and salaries outstanding at 31 December 19-2 amounted to £354

- the provision for doubtful debts is to be increased by £124

- stock at 31 December 19-2 is valued at £47,288

- rent and rates amounting to £400 were paid in advance at 31 December 19-2

- it is proposed to pay a dividend of £8,000 for 19-2

- depreciation on motor vans is to be charged at the rate of 20 per cent per annum on cost

You are to prepare appropriate final accounts for the year 19-2, together with a balance sheet at 31 December 19-2.

13.5 Another client of Rossiter and Rossiter, Chartered Accountants, is Playfair Ltd, a wholesaler of children's toys. The company has an authorised share capital of 50,000 ordinary shares of £1 each and 10,000 8% preference shares of £1 each. At 31 December 19-2, the following trial balance was extracted:

	Dr £	Cr £
Ordinary share capital		50,000
8% preference share capital		8,000
Plant and machinery at cost	34,000	
Motor vehicles at cost	16,000	
Debtors and creditors	34,980	17,870
Bank	14,505	
10% debentures		9,000
Stock (1 January 19-2)	25,200	
General expenses	11,020	
Purchases and sales	164,764	233,384
Bad debts written off	2,400	
Debenture interest	900	
Discounts	325	640
Salaries	24,210	
Insurance	300	
Provision for depreciation:		
plant and machinery		16,000
motor vehicles		7,200
Directors' fees	17,000	
Interim preference dividend paid	320	
Profit and loss account (1 January 19-2)		3,300
Provision for bad debts (1 January 19-2)		530
	345,924	345,924

Additional information:

- stock at 31 December 19-2 is valued at £28,247

- depreciation on plant and machinery is to be provided for at the rate of 10 per cent per annum calculated on cost

- depreciation on motor vehicles is to be provided for at the rate of 20 per cent per annum using the reducing balance method

- insurance prepaid at 31 December 19-2 amounted to £60

- general expenses owing at 31 December 19-2 amounted to £110

- the provision for bad debts is to be increased to £750

- the directors propose to pay an ordinary dividend of 6 per cent to the ordinary shareholders and to pay the remaining dividend due to the preference shareholders

- £2,000 is to be transferred to General Reserve

You are to prepare appropriate final accounts for the year ended 31 December 19-2, together with a balance sheet at that date.

14 Interpretation of financial statements

introduction

The ability to interpret financial informationis an important aspect of finance. Questions which can be answered from a basic financial interpretation include:

Did the organisation perform better this year than last year?
Is organisation A better than organisation B?
How efficiently is the organisation managing the resources it uses?

Interpretation is carried out by calculating accounting ratios and percentages, and then using the results to draw relevant conclusions. A number of the more important ratios, and percentages are considered below; however, it is not always possible to apply all the calculations to every set of financial statements, although they can all be used on the accounts of trading organisations such as sole-traders, partnerships (see Chapter 12), and limited companies (see Chapter 13). It is important to note that interpretation consists of far more than simply calculating a series of ratios and percentages; appropriate conclusions need to be drawn and presented in the form of a written or verbal report.

To help in the task of interpretation, we will consider the calculations under five headings:

*   *profitability* – the amount of profit the organisation makes
*   *capital strength* – the amount of money invested by the owner(s) in comparison with outside borrowing (this is also known as *gearing)*
*   *liquidity* – the availability of cash, or near cash, in an organisation
*   *activity* – the control of stocks, debtors and creditors
*   *investment ratios* – indicators to investors as to how profitable a business is, and what rate of return it gives on money invested

In this chapter we will also consider

*   the people and organisations who will be interested in financial ratios and percentages

*   the presentation and analysis of sales figures

people interested in accounting ratios

A number of parties are interested in accounting ratios calculated from financial statements. The ratios they will examine will differ and the reasons for their interest can be very different:

the management The management of a business will want to know the current financial state of the business and the controls needed as the business develops. Management will therefore look at:

- *liquidity* – the ability of the company to meet its everyday running expenses and debt obligations
- *activity* – indicators of how well stock levels are being controlled, how efficiently customer debts are chased up, and how promptly suppliers are paid
- *profitability* – the management will be responsible to the owners of the business (they may *be* the owners of the business) and will need to ensure that profitability is maintained wherever possible

the bank The bank manager will want to be reassured that any money lent to the business will be repaid when due. The bank will be particularly interested in:

- *capital strength* – how dependent is the business on outside borrowing?
- *profitability* – what are the prospects of borrowing being repaid in the future?
- *liquidity* – what are the prospects of short-term borrowing being repaid in the present?

the investor A person investing in a business will be particularly interested in the return that will be received:

- *profitability* – what profits are being made ?
- *investment ratios* – what is the level of return given to the investor, and how does it compare with that of similar businesses?

the employee The employer will want to motivate the employee and instil loyalty by showing that the business is doing well, particularly in terms of:

- *profitability* – the employee may receive a part of the profit in a 'profit-sharing' scheme
- *capital strength* – the employee will be reassured to know the extent of the total Net Assets of a business, as shown on the balance sheet

We will first look at how these ratios and percentages are calculated, and will then apply a number of them to a Case Study of a sole trader business: 'Financial Statements of J Brown' .

profitability

gross profit percentage

$$\frac{Gross\ profit\ for\ year}{Sales\ for\ year} \times \frac{100}{1} = Gross\ profit/sales\ percentage$$

This expresses, as a percentage, the gross profit in relation to sales. For example, a gross profit percentage of 20 per cent means that for every £100 of sales made, the gross profit is £20.

The gross profit percentage should be similar from year-to-year for the same organisation. It will vary between organisations in different areas of business, eg the gross profit percentage on jewellery is considerably higher than that on basic items of food. A significant change from one year to the next, particularly a fall in the percentage, needs further investigation.

net profit percentage

$$\frac{Net\ profit\ for\ year}{Sales\ for\ year} \times \frac{100}{1} = Net\ profit/sales\ percentage$$

As with gross profit percentage, the net profit percentage should be similar from year-to-year for the same business, and should also be comparable with other firms in the same line of business. Ideally the net profit percentage should show a slight increase, which indicates that the profit and loss account costs are being kept under control. Any significant fall should be investigated to see if it has been caused by an increase in one particular expense, eg wages and salaries, advertising, etc.

A large expense item can always be expressed as a percentage of sales, eg

$$\frac{Specified\ expense}{Sales\ for\ year} \times \frac{100}{1} = Expense/sales\ percentage$$

For example, the relationship between advertising and sales might be found to be 10 per cent in one year, but 20 per cent the next year. This would probably indicate that an increase in advertising had failed to produce a proportionate increase in sales.

return on capital employed

$$\frac{Net\ profit\ for\ year}{Capital\ employed\ at\ start\ of\ year} \times \frac{100}{1} = Percentage\ return\ on\ capital\ employed$$

This expresses the net profit of the business in relation to the owner's capital. For this calculation, the capital at the start of the year should, ideally, be used but, if this is not known, the year-end figure can be used. The percentage return is best thought of in relation to other investments, eg a building society might offer a return of eight per cent, or a bank might offer five per cent on a deposit account. A person running a business is investing a sum of money in that business, and the net profit is the return that is achieved on that investment. However, it should be noted that the risks in running a business are considerably greater than depositing the money with a building society or bank, and an additional return to compensate for the extra risk is needed.

The calculation of return on capital employed can be varied to consider not only the owner's capital, but also to include any long-term loans, because they are a part of the semi-permanent capital of the organisation.

capital strength - gearing

It is useful to be able to see to what extent an organisation relies on outside borrowing and to what extent it is financed by the owner(s)' capital and accumulated profit. The relationship between these two figures demonstrates the *capital strength* of the organisation – the *gearing* as it is commonly known. The gearing percentage is usually calculated as follows:

$$\frac{Outside\ borrowing\ (eg\ bank\ loans)}{Capital}\ x\ 100\ =\ gearing\ percentage$$

If the percentage is over 100% it means that the organisation is borrowing *more* than the amount of the owner's capital, a vulnerable situation, if, say, the borrowing had to be repaid in a short space of time. High gearing also means that the business will be paying substantial amounts in interest. Note: gearing can also be expressed as a ratio (ie outside borrowing : capital).

liquidity

working capital ratio/current ratio

$$\frac{Current\ assets}{Current\ liabilities}\ =\ Working\ capital\ ratio\ (also\ known\ as\ the\ current\ ratio\ )$$

Using figures from the balance sheet, this ratio measures the relationship between current assets and current liabilities. Working capital (calculated as *current assets minus current liabilities*) is needed by all organisations in order to finance day-to-day trading activities. Sufficient working capital enables an organisation to hold adequate stocks, allow a measure of credit to its customers (debtors), and to pay its suppliers (creditors) as payments fall due.

Although there is no ideal working capital ratio, an often accepted ratio is about 2:1, ie £2 of current assets to every £1 of current liabilities. However, an organisation in the retail trade may be able to work with a lower ratio, eg 1.5:1 or even less, because it deals mainly in sales for cash and so does not have a large figure for debtors. A working capital ratio can be *too* high: if it is above 3:1 an investigation of the make-up of current assets is needed: eg the organisation may have too much stock, too many debtors, or too much cash at the bank, or even too few creditors.

liquid capital ratio

$$\frac{(Current\ assets\ -\ stock)}{Current\ liabilities}\ =\ Liquid\ capital\ ratio\ (also\ known\ as\ the\ acid\ test\ )$$

This ratio (also known as the *quick ratio* or *acid test ratio*) includes the current assets and current liabilities from the balance sheet, but stock is omitted. This is because stock is the most illiquid current asset: it has to be sold, turned into debtors, and then the cash has to be collected from the debtors. Also, some of the stock included in the balance sheet figure may be unsaleable or obsolete.

The balance between liquid assets, that is debtors and cash/bank, and current liabilities should, ideally, be about 1:1, ie £1 of liquid assets to each £1 of current liabilities. At this ratio an organisation is expected to be able to pay its current liabilities from its liquid assets, a figure below 1:1, eg 0.75:1, indicates that the organisation would have difficulty in meeting pressing demands from creditors. However, as with the working capital ratio, certain types of organisation are able to operate with a lower liquid capital ratio than others.

With both the working capital and the liquid capital ratios, trends from one year to the next need to be considered, or comparisons made with similar organisations.

activity

stock turnover

$$\frac{Average\ stock}{Cost\ of\ goods\ sold} \quad x\ 365\ days = \quad Stock\ turnover\ (in\ days)$$

This calculation uses information from the trading account: average stock is usually found by taking the average of the opening and closing stocks, ie (opening stock + closing stock) ÷ 2; cost of goods sold is the figure before gross profit is ascertained. Stock turnover is the average number of days in the financial year that the stock is held by the business. For example, a market trader selling fresh flowers who finishes each day when sold out will have a stock turnover of one day. By contrast a furniture shop may have a stock turnover of 90 days, the average length of time for which an item of furniture is held in the shop before being sold. The lower the stock turnover, the more efficient the organisation, for the same *type* of business.

debtors' collection period

$$\frac{Debtors}{Credit\ sales\ for\ year} \quad x\ 365\ days\ = \quad Debtors'\ collection\ time\ (in\ days)$$

This calculation shows how long, on average, debtors take to pay for goods sold to them by the organisation. The figure of *credit sales for the year* may not be disclosed in the trading account, in which case the sales figure should be used. Some organisations make the majority of their sales on credit but others, such as shops, will have a considerably lower proportion of credit sales.

The debtors collection period can be compared with that for the previous year, or with that of a similar organisation. In the UK, most debtors should make payment within 30 to 60 days; however, sales made abroad will take longer for the proceeds to be received. A comparison from year-to-year of the collection period is a measure of the organisation's efficiency at collecting the money that is due to it.

creditors' payment period

$$\frac{Creditors}{Credit\ Purchases} \quad x\ 365\ days\ = \quad Creditors'\ payment\ time\ (in\ days)$$

This calculation is the 'other side of the coin' to that of debtors: here we are measuring the speed it takes to pay creditors. While creditors can be a useful temporary source of finance, delaying payment too long may cause problems.

investment ratios

Investment ratios are useful indicators for investors who intend to buy holdings of shares in limited companies. These ratios are also of interest to people who already own shares and who receive the annual report of the company. It must be stressed that the list of ratios set out below is by no means exhaustive; it does however include the main indicators to be found in the annual reports of companies and in the financial pages of the daily press. You will note that the word 'ratios' is applied in a loose sense; many of the indicators are expressed in terms of pence or percentages.

dividend per share

$\dfrac{Dividends\ for\ year}{Number\ of\ shares\ issued}$ = *Dividend per share (pence)*

Investors receive a return on their investment in the form of dividend payments, often twice a year: the *interim* dividend and the *final* dividend. The money amount of the dividends is calculated as a number of *pence* per share (the price of shares is always expressed in pence). Investors will clearly be interested in this figure as it represents what they will be receiving before deduction of tax.

earnings per share

$\dfrac{Net\ profit,\ after\ corporation\ tax\ and\ preference\ dividends}{Number\ of\ issued\ ordinary\ shares}$ = *Earnings per share (pence)*

Earnings per share (or EPS) measures the amount of profit *earned* by each share, after corporation tax and preference dividends. Comparisons can be made with previous years to provide a basis for assessing the company's performance. It must be borne in mind that profit per share is not the same as dividend per share. The profit per share will not be paid out in full as dividends, some of the profit will be retained in the company for reinvestment and expansion.

dividend cover

$\dfrac{Net\ profit,\ after\ corporation\ tax\ and\ preference\ dividends}{Ordinary\ dividends}$ = *Dividend cover*

This figure shows the margin of safety between the amount of profit a company makes and the amount paid out in dividends. The figure must be greater than 1 if the company is not to use past retained profits to fund the current dividend. For example, a figure of 5 as dividend cover indicates that profit exceeds dividend by five times – a healthy sign. The share price pages in the financial press quote the dividend cover figure under the column headed 'cover' or its abbreviation 'cvr'.

price/earnings ratio

$\dfrac{Market\ price\ of\ ordinary\ share\ (in\ pence)}{Earnings\ per\ ordinary\ share\ (in\ pence)}$ = *Price/earnings ratio*

The price/earnings ratio (or P/E ratio, as it is often abbreviated) compares the current market price of a share and the earnings (after corporation tax) of that share. For example, if a particular share has a market price of £3, and the earnings per share in the current year are 30p, then the P/E ratio is 10. This simply means that a person buying the share for £3 is paying ten times the last reported earnings of that share. Investors make use of the P/E ratio to help them make decisions as to the 'expensiveness' of a share.

other indicators

Other figures of interest to investors and highlighted in the annual report of a company will include
- profit before taxation
- total assets
- shareholders' funds, ie the capital position of the company

Illustrated below are extracts from the 1991 Annual Report and Accounts of The Royal Bank of Scotland Group plc, a financial services group. Note how the figures are presented on a comparative year-to-year basis in graphical form.

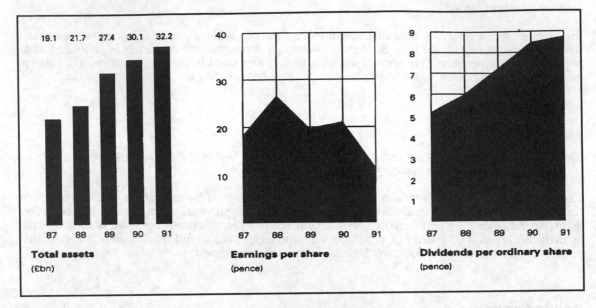

We will now apply the principles of accounting ratios to a Case Study of a sole trader business.

Case Study: financial statements of J. Brown

Situation

The accounts of J. Brown have been submitted to you for analysis.

**TRADING AND PROFIT AND LOSS ACCOUNTS
FOR THE YEAR ENDED 31 DECEMBER 19-1**

	£	£
Sales		150,000
Opening stock	10,000	
Purchases	66,000	
	76,000	
Less closing stock	16,000	
Cost of goods sold		60,000
Gross profit		90,000
Less:		
Wages and salaries	60,000	
Advertising	15,000	
Sundry expenses	5,000	
		80,000
Net profit		10,000

BALANCE SHEET AS AT 31 DECEMBER 19-1

	£	£	£
Fixed assets			
Premises			70,000
Machinery			30,000
			100,000
Current assets			
Stock		16,000	
Debtors		12,500	
		28,500	
Less Current liabilities			
Creditors	11,000		
Bank overdraft	24,500		
		35,500	
Working capital			(7,000)
NET ASSETS			93,000
FINANCED BY			
Capital			
Opening capital			90,000
Add net profit			10,000
			100,000
Less drawings			7,000
			93,000

Solution

Calculations

PROFITABILITY

Gross profit/sales percentage $= \dfrac{£90,000}{£150,000} \times \dfrac{100}{1} = 60\%$

Net profit/sales percentage $= \dfrac{£10,000}{£150,000} \times \dfrac{100}{1} = 6.7\%$

Wages and salaries/sales $= \dfrac{£60,000}{£150,000} \times \dfrac{100}{1} = 40\%$

Advertising/sales $= \dfrac{£15,000}{£150,000} \times \dfrac{100}{1} = 10\%$

Return on capital employed $= \dfrac{£10,000}{£90,000} \times \dfrac{100}{1} = 11.1\%$

CAPITAL STRENGTH/GEARING

Overdraft/Capital $= \dfrac{£24,500}{£93,000} \times \dfrac{100}{1} = 26\%$

LIQUIDITY

Working capital ratio $= \dfrac{£28,500}{£35,500}$ $= 0.8:1$

Liquid capital ratio $= \dfrac{£12,500}{£35,500}$ $= 0.35:1$

ACTIVITY

Stock turnover $= \dfrac{£13,000}{£60,000} \times 365$ $= 79$ days

Debtors' collection time $= \dfrac{£12,500}{£150,000} \times 365$ $= 30$ days

Creditors' payment time $= \dfrac{£11,000}{£66,000} \times 365$ $= 61$ days

Comments

PROFITABILITY

This business has a product with a high gross profit percentage of 60% (comparisons with the previous year/similar firms need to be made). Unfortunately the high gross profit percentage is not fully reflected in the fairly low net profit percentage. Wages form 40% of the selling cost and an investigation should be made by the owner of the business to see if savings can be made here; similarly the advertising percentage appears to be quite high. Nevertheless, the business has provided a satisfactory return on the owner's capital.

CAPITAL STRENGTH/GEARING

The size of the owner's capital (£93,000) is in excess of the overdraft (£24,500), which is the only external borrowing of the business, although as we will see, there may be a problem with this bank borrowing. The gearing percentage of 26% is nevertheless very satisfactory: the business should not be vulnerable to the withdrawal of loans.

LIQUIDITY

Both the working capital and the liquid capital are extremely low. The problems here seem to stem from the high bank overdraft, and the reasons for this need investigating.

ACTIVITY

The stock turnover is 79 days, and comparisons need to be made to see if this is satisfactory for the type of business. The debtors' collection time is satisfactory, indicating good control procedures. However, the creditors' payment time is twice as long. It may be that the bank refuses to pay any more cheques and this has resulted in the lengthy period of credit being taken: these are very real danger signals to the owner of the business and, of course, to the bank.

Conclusion

This appears to be a profitable business, although there may be scope for cutting down somewhat on the profit and loss account expenses of wages and salaries, and advertising. The business offers a reasonable return on capital, and the gearing is low. However, the business needs additional capital in order to reduce the bank overdraft and to pay any pressing creditors: this would help to restore the working capital and liquid ratios to more acceptable levels. It might be that the owner of the business should consider taking on a partner who may be able to inject more cash and thus help the liquidity problem.

problems of interpretation

It is important to appreciate that there are a number of problems which can make interpretation of financial statements more difficult:

- In order to be able to make true comparisons, financial statements of the same business need to be prepared on a *consistent* basis. This problem is highlighted even more when the financial statements of one organisation are compared with those of another: different accounting policies may have been followed, eg in respect of depreciation, and valuation of stock.

- Most financial statements are prepared on an historical cost basis, i.e. assets and liabilities are recorded at their original cost. Only recently have attempts been made to tackle the effects of inflation on financial statements.

- The financial statements record what has gone on in the past and are not a certain guide to what will happen in the future. Therefore decisions made on the basis of last year's financial statements may be invalid on the basis of changed circumstances – for example, consider the international price fluctuations of a barrel of oil and the effect this has on companies (and not just oil companies), or the effect of exchange rate fluctuations on companies which trade abroad.

- The balance sheet shows the assets and liabilities at one particular date, but may not be representative of the year as a whole – it may have been *window-dressed* for the financial year-end.

interpretation of sales figures

We have so far concentrated on the interpretation of financial statements by outside bodies. It must also be appreciated that the management of an organisation will examine the financial statements of that organisation on a regular basis looking at performance and efficiency, and taking action where appropriate. The management will also look critically at the *sales* performance of an organisation on a regular basis. The figures will be extracted from the accounting records and will be analysed under various headings appropriate to the organisation:

- sales by area
- sales by product
- sales by individual sales representatives or groups of representatives
- home sales/export sales
- sales achieved by different methods, eg retail outlets/mail order

The sales figures will need to be compared with the budgeted figures for the period set out in the *sales budget*. The subject of budgeting is covered fully in Chapter 21, but you should note at this point that projections of expected sales are regularly made by an organisation on the basis of factors such as

- the size of the market
- whether the market is growing or declining
- the market share of the organisation and whether it is increasing or decreasing
- what the competition is doing to increase its sales

Sales trends can be computed from these factors and a likely level of sales budgeted for. The actual sales figures when they are available can then be compared with the budgeted figures so that weak areas can be identified and appropriate action taken.

presentation of sales figures

Sales figures are more easily interpreted if they are presented in visual form. They are often presented in the form of tables, graphs, bar charts and pie charts. These visual formats can either be drawn up manually or as part of a graphics function of a computer database or spreadsheet. In the section which follows we look at the various ways in which sales figures may be presented.

interpretation and presentation of numbers

It has often been said that "a picture is worth a thousand words." Numerical information presented in visual form includes tables, graphs, bar charts, and pie charts. Numeracy skills involve you being able to *interpret* tables, graphs, bar charts, and pie charts, and also to be able to *choose the most appropriate format* when you are presenting numerical data.

from raw data to table

The starting point for any visual presentation of numbers is the 'raw' information, which will often be presented first in the form of a table.   We shall take as an example a Japanese car manufacturer, Niyota, which has manufactured two main models – the Corsair and the Tornado – over a period of four years. The sales figures are as follows:

Corsair Year 1 £1,000m; Year 2 £1,250m; Year 3 £1,500m; Year 4 £1,250m
Tornado Year 1 £1,500m; Year 2 £1,000m; Year 3 £500m; Year 4 £250m

The reader of these figures can understand them, but the sales trends are not immediately clear.   The first step in making the figures more presentable is to set them out in a table:

Niyota Cars - annual sales of Corsair and Tornado models

	Year 1 £m	Year 2 £m	Year 3 £m	Year 4 £m
Sales of Corsair	1,000	1,250	1,500	1,250
Sales of Tornado	1,500	1,000	500	250

These figures may then be presented by means of a line graph or a bar chart (see Fig.14.1)

line graph
Note that
- the graph is given a title
- the time scale is set out on the horizontal axis and a label added
- the sales figure in £m are set out on the vertical axis and a label added
- a key is produced to distinguish between the two lines

bar chart
Note that
- the chart is given a title
- the time scale is set out on the horizontal axis and labelled
- the sales figures in £m are set out on the vertical axis and labelled
- there is a distinctively shaded bar for each type of car
- the bars are of equal width
- a key is produced to distinguish between the two types of bar

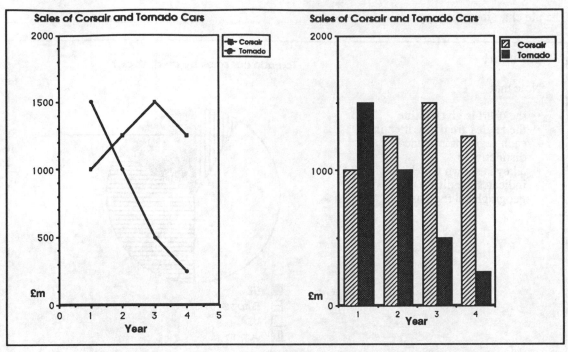

Fig 14.1 Line graph and bar chart showing sales of Niyota cars

pie chart

A pie chart (see Fig. 14.2 on the next page) is a circle divided into a number of parts, just as an edible 'pie' is divided into slices. Whereas the line graph and bar chart are useful in showing a *trend* over a period of time, a pie chart is used to illustrate how a single figure is made up from its constituent parts. For example total sales for an organisation for one year may be divided into sales by region, and illustrated by means of a pie chart.

A pie chart might be used, for example, to show the worldwide sales by region of Tornado Cars:

Sales of Tornado Cars by area in Year 1

Area	£m
UK	250
Europe	500
USA	625
Japan	125
Total sales	1,500

The total sales of £1,500m will become the whole circle of the pie divided into segments, each of which will proportionally represent a geographical sales figure. As the angle at the centre of a circle is 360° it is necessary to work out the angle for *each* segment individually before drawing in the 'slices' of the pie. The formula is as follows:

$$\frac{\textit{Figure for the part of the whole}}{\textit{Figure for the whole}} \times 360° = \textit{the angle at the centre for the segment (°)}$$

The angle for the UK sales 'slice', for example, is therefore $\frac{250}{1,500} \times 360 = 60°$

The pie chart therefore appears as follows:

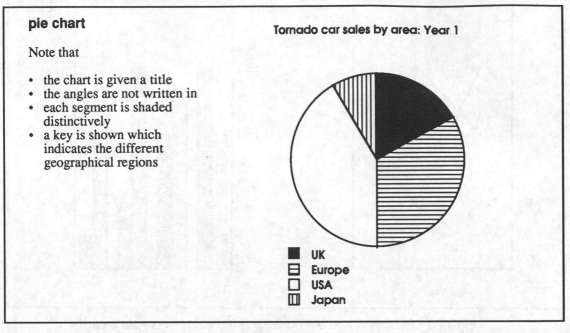

pie chart

Note that

- the chart is given a title
- the angles are not written in
- each segment is shaded distinctively
- a key is shown which indicates the different geographical regions

Tornado car sales by area: Year 1

■ UK
⊟ Europe
☐ USA
⊞ Japan

Fig. 14.2 Pie chart showing sales of Tornado cars by geographical area

Chapter Summary

❑ Accounting ratios and percentages are numerical values extracted from the financial statements of organisations.

❑ Accounting ratios and percentages are used by a wide variety of interested parties: the management of the organisation, the bank, the investor and employees.

❑ Accounting ratios and percentages can be used to measure
- profitability
- capital strength
- liquidity
- activity
- investment potential

❑ Comparisons need to be made between previous financial statements, or those of similar organisations.

❑ A number of limitations should be borne in mind when drawing conclusions from ratios. These include problems of consistency when preparing financial statements and the effects of inflation when reporting figures from year-to-year.

❑ The analysis and presentation of sales figures against budget projections is an important function within an organisation; such figures are often presented in graphical form.

✍ Student Activities

14.1 You are working as a trainee accountant and come across, in your firm's files, the following information relating to two businesses, A and B.

	BUSINESS A		BUSINESS B	
	£000s	£000s	£000s	£000s
PROFIT AND LOSS ACCOUNT EXTRACTS				
Sales		3,057		1,628
Cost of goods sold		2,647		911
Gross Profit		410		717
Expenses		366		648
Net Profit		44		69
SUMMARISED BALANCE SHEETS				
Fixed Assets		344		555
Current Assets				
Stock	242		237	
Debtors	6		269	
Bank/cash	3		1	
	251		507	
Less Current Liabilities	195		212	
Working Capital		56		295
NET ASSETS		400		850
FINANCED BY				
Capital		400		850

One business operates a chain of grocery supermarkets; the other is a heavy engineering company.

As a training exercise your boss asks you to:

• Calculate the following accounting ratios for both businesses:

  (a) gross profit percentage

  (b) net profit percentage

  (c) stock turnover (use balance sheet figure as *average* stock)

  (d) working capital (current) ratio

  (e) liquid capital ratio

  (f) debtors' collection period

  (g) return on capital employed

• Indicate which company you believe to be the grocery supermarket chain and which the heavy engineering business. Briefly explain the reasons for your choice based on the ratios calculated and the accounting information.

Present your findings in the form of a memorandum. Your boss is Gareth Davies, Senior Partner in Davies, Davies and Lloyd. Use your own name and today's date.

14.2 You work in the Accounts Department of Thomsons Sports Limited, a sports equipment wholesaler. Your department has recently been computerised and one of the programs provided is a spreadsheet. Your boss asks you to set up a spreadsheet for analysing the business' financial statements. He says that the management are particularly interested in

(a) return on capital employed

(b) gearing

(c) gross profit percentage

(d) net profit percentage

(e) current ratio

(f) liquid capital ratio

(g) debtor payment period (days)

(h) creditor payment period (days

(i) stock turnover (days)

Extracts from the figures for the last two years trading are as follows:

	19-8	19-9
	£	£
Sales	240,000	400,000
Cost of sales	160,000	300,000
Purchases	160,000	318,000
Gross profit	80,000	100,000
Net profit	60,000	70,000
Fixed assets	70,000	75,000
Stock	14,000	32,000
Debtors	24,000	40,000
Bank (not overdraft)	2,000	3,000
Creditors	20,000	40,000
Long-term bank loan	20,000	20,000
Share capital and reserves	70,000	90,000

You are to

(a) set up a spreadsheet model into which you can enter the figures set out above and extract by means of formulas the various accounting ratios and indicators

(b) write a report addressed to the Finance Director, Jim Thompson, setting out the accounting ratios in a table, including graphs and charts where appropriate, and commenting on the strengths and weaknesses of the figures.

Note: the use of computer spreadsheets is explained in Chapter 31.

14.3. You work for Laycocks Nurseries, a garden centre chain operating garden centres in four towns in the area: Mereford, Martley, Broadwood and Pencroft. You have recently received from your Sales Department an analysis of the sales of each garden centre over the last two years.

Garden Centre	Year 1 £000's	Year 2 £000's
Mereford	250	250
Martley	157	235
Broadwood	225	168
Pencroft	105	110
Total Sales	737	763

(a)   What trends are evident, and what questions might you ask your Sales Department?

(b)   Choose a suitable presentation method from: graph, bar chart, pie chart, and set out the figures contained in the table using your chosen method.

14.4 You work in the public relations department of H Schmidt Limited, the UK subsidiary of the German electronics company which has made substantial inroads into the UK market with its revolutionary Laserpunkt battery CD player.

Market Share: UK Market for CD Players

	19-1 £M	19-2 £M	19-3 £M
Japanese CD players	295	280	275
H Schmidt CD players	150	195	250
Others	140	130	115

(a) present this data in the form of a line graph

(b) comment on the trends exhibited

14.5 You are given the following figures for the sales of Dataservice Ltd over the last three years:

	Year 1 £	Year 2 £	Year 3 £
Sales	1,250,000	1,500,000	2,000,000
Total expenses	1,000,000	1,250,000	1,500,000

You are asked for the following information

(a)   What is the net profit for each of the three years?

(b)   What is the net profit as a percentage of the sales figure for each year? Note: round off your result, where appropriate, to the nearest percentage figure – do not take the percentages into decimal figures

(c)   Construct a line graph which shows both the sales and the profit for the three years

(d)   Construct a bar chart which shows the profit for the three years

(e)   What comments would you make about the performance of the company over the three years in respect of sales and profitability?

Assignment 5
Limited Company Accounts: Severn DIY Limited

LEARNING OUTCOMES COVERED:
Preparation of limited company final accounts, interpretation of accounts,
presentation of numerical information

SITUATION

Severn DIY Ltd. operates a chain of do-it-yourself shops throughout Gloucestershire and the County of Hereford and Worcester. The company employs some 20 full-time staff, together with a number working part-time. The three directors, who originally founded the company and continue to work in it full-time, believe they have an enlightened attitude to employee involvement in the business. They have encouraged the development of a 'works' committee which meets at regular intervals to review progress. In recent weeks some bad feeling has been shown at these meetings because the employees' representatives have been seeking a substantial pay rise (10%), something which the company management claims it cannot afford.

The company has an authorised share capital of 500,000 ordinary shares of £1 each. At 30 April 19-6 the following trial balance was extracted:

	Dr £	Cr £
Ordinary share capital		500,000
Property	350,000	
Fixtures and fittings at cost	90,000	
Motor vehicles at cost	60,000	
Debtors and creditors	349,800	178,700
Bank overdraft		18,350
10% Debentures		90,000
Stock (1 May 19-5)	252,000	
General expenses	110,200	
Purchases and sales	1,652,140	2,333,840
Bad debts written off	24,000	
Debenture interest	4,500	
Discounts	3,250	6,400
Salaries	242,100	
Insurance	3,000	
Provision for depreciation:		
fixtures and fittings		27,000
motor vehicles		21,600
Directors' fees	73,200	
Profit and loss account (1 May 19-5)		33,000
Provision for bad debts (1 May 19-5)		5,300
	3,214,190	3,214,190

The following additional information has been provided by the Accounts Department:

- stock at 30 April 19-6 is valued at £282,470

- depreciation of fixtures and fittings is to be provided for at the rate of 10 per cent per annum calculated on cost

- depreciation on motor vehicles is to be provided for at the rate of 20 per cent per annum using the reducing balance method

- insurance prepaid at 30 April 19-6 amounted to £600

- general expenses owing at 30 April 19-6 amounted to £1,100

- the provision for bad debts is to be increased to £7,500

- the company will pay the debenture interest of £4,500 due for the year ended 30 April 19-6 on 11 May 19-6

- the directors propose to pay an increased ordinary dividend of 6 per cent to the ordinary shareholders

STUDENT TASKS

1. As a clerk in the Accounts Department you are asked to prepare the trading and profit and loss accountfor the year ended 30 April 19-6, together with a balance sheet at the year-end. These financial statements are then circulated to the directors and the members of the works committee.

2. A confrontation between the management and the works committee is due to take place shortly. The group should subdivide into two:

   - *the management of Severn DIY Ltd*, who want to ensure that the company retains a strong financial position and does not have its profits eaten away by large salary increases

   - *the employee representatives* who claim that the shareholders and directors are doing very well already and can afford to pay increased salaries

   Each subgroup should prepare a case to support the contrasting viewpoint concerning the disputed pay increase. Reference should be made to the latest financial statements. Accounting ratios should be used and visual display of those ratios (bar charts, pie charts etc.) would be useful aids to the presentation of the opposing viewpoints.

   The following guide may be useful:

   Figures used to support management's case:
   - working capital ratio
   - liquid capital ratio
   - gearing
   - the ratio of salaries to net profit

   Figures used to support the works committee's case
   - return on capital employed
   - gross and net profit percentages
   - the level of existing and proposed directors' fees

3. Management and works committee should each present their case orally to the other and be prepared to answer questions publicly. Negotiations should then follow. If no agreement can be reached, the lecturer should be asked to arbitrate the dispute.

15 Cashflow statements

introduction

A balance sheet shows the financial state of a business at a particular date and is usually only prepared once a year. While it is possible to obtain a great deal of information on the progress of the business by comparing one year's balance sheet with that of the next year, it is more difficult to see what has gone on during the period between the two balance sheet dates.

A cashflow statement uses information from the accounting records (including profit and loss account) and balance sheet, and shows an overall view of money flowing in and out of a business during an accounting period.

Such a statement concentrates on the liquidity of a business and explains to the owner or shareholders why, after a year of good profits for example, there is a reduced balance at the bank or a larger bank overdraft, at the year-end than there was at the beginning of the year.

Cashflow statements are especially important because they deal with flows of money. It is invariably a shortage of money that causes most businesses to fail, rather than a poor quality product or service. The importance of the cashflow statement is such that all but the smallest companies are required to include this statement as a part of their accounts which they publish and send to shareholders. For sole traders and partnerships, the information that the statement contains is of considerable interest to the owner(s) and to a lender, such as a bank.

A cashflow statement can look either at what has gone on in a past accounting period (normally a year), or it can, based on a forecast trading and profit and loss account and balance sheet, demonstrate the effect on cashflow of future alternative courses of action.

cashflows

Cashflow statements are divided into five sections:
1. Operating activities
2. Returns on investments and servicing of finance
3. Taxation
4. Investing activities
5. Financing

The cashflows for the year affecting each of these main areas of business activity are shown in the statement.

1 operating activities

The main source of cashflow for a business is usually that which is generated from the operating (or trading) activities of the business.

The *net cash inflow from operating activities* is calculated by using figures from the profit and loss account for the year and the balance sheet at the beginning and the end of the year:

- net profit (before interest and tax)
- *add* depreciation for the year*
- *add* decrease in debtors, or *deduct* increase in debtors
- *add* increase in creditors, or *deduct* decrease in creditors
- *add* decrease in stock, or *deduct* increase in stock

*Depreciation is added to net profit because depreciation is a *non-cash expense,* that is, no money is paid out by the business in respect of depreciation charged to profit and loss account.

Note that changes in the main working capital items of stock, debtors and creditors have an effect on cash balances. For example, an increase in stock reduces cash, while a decrease in debtors increases cash.

2 returns on investments and servicing of finance

This section of the cashflow statement shows the cashflows relating to receipts and payments of interest and dividends, eg

- interest received
- interest paid
- dividends received
- dividends paid (drawings – for a sole trader or partnership business)

3 taxation

Here is shown the tax paid during the year.

4 investing activities

This section of the cashflow statement shows the cashflows relating to the purchase or sale of fixed assets, eg

- purchase or sale of plant and machinery
- purchase or sale of investments

5 financing

The financing section of the statement shows the cashflows in respect of shares and loans, eg

cash inflows
- increase in capital/share capital
- raising/increase of medium/long-term loans

cash outflows
- repayment of capital/share capital
- repayment of medium/long-term loans

Note that the change in cash/bank balances is not included in this section.

increase or decrease in cash

The subtotals from the five main areas of business activity are totalled to give the *increase/ (decrease) in cash* for the year. There then follows a reconciliation of the cash at the start of the year, plus the increase, or minus the decrease, for the year (as above), which then equals the balance of cash at the end of the year. Note that 'cash' includes cash itself and the balance at bank.

layout of a cashflow statement

A cashflow statement uses a common layout which can be amended to suit the particular needs of the business for which it is being prepared. The following layout is commonly used (specimen figures have been included):

CASHFLOW STATEMENT OF ABC LTD FOR THE YEAR-ENDED 31 DECEMBER 19-1

	£	£
Operating activities:		
Net profit (before tax and interest)	75,000	
Depreciation	10,000	
Decrease in stocks	2,000	
Increase in debtors	(5,000)	
Increase in creditors	7,000	
Net cash inflow from operating activities		89,000
Returns on investments and servicing of finance:		
Interest received	10,000	
Interest paid	(5,000)	
Dividends paid (note: amount *paid* during year)	(22,000)	
Net cash outflow from returns on investments and servicing of finance		(17,000)
Taxation:		
Corporation tax paid (note: amount *paid* during year)	(6,000)	
Tax paid		(6,000)
Investing activities:		
Payments to acquire fixed assets	(125,000)	
Receipts from sales of fixed assets	15,000	
Net cash outflow from investing activities		(110,000)
Net cash outflow before financing		(44,000)
Financing:		
Issue of share capital	225,000	
Repayment of capital/share capital	–	
Increase in loans	–	
Repayment of loans	(90,000)	
Net cash inflow from financing		135,000
Increase in cash		91,000*
Analysis of changes in cash during the year:		
Balance at start of year		(8,000)
Net cash inflow		91,000*
Balance at end of year		83,000

*These two figures are the same: they represent the change in cash (ie cash and bank balance) for the year.

Important note:
Money amounts shown in brackets indicate a deduction, or where the figure is a subtotal, a negative figure.

Case Study: Mrs Green – a sole trader

Situation

Mrs Green runs a children's clothes shop in rented premises in a small market town. Her balance sheets for the last two years are as follows:

BALANCE SHEET AS AT 31 DECEMBER

	19-1			19-2		
	£	£	£	£	£	£
	Cost	Dep'n	Net	Cost	Dep'n	Net
Fixed Assets						
Shop fittings	1,500	500	1,000	2,000	750	1,250
Current Assets						
Stocks		3,750			4,850	
Debtors		625			1,040	
Bank		220			-	
		4,595			5,890	
Less Current Liabilities						
Creditors	2,020			4,360		
Bank	-			725		
		2,020			5,085	
Working Capital			2,575			805
			3,575			2,055
Less Long-term Liabilities						
Loan from husband			-			1,000
NET ASSETS			3,575			1,055
FINANCED BY						
Capital			3,300			3,575
Add Net profit for year			5,450			4,080
			8,750			7,655
Less Drawings			5,175			6,600
			3,575			1,055

Note: Loan and overdraft interest paid in 19-2 was £450.

Mrs Green says to you: "I cannot understand why I am overdrawn at the bank on 31 December 19-2 when I made a profit of £4,080 during the year". She asks you to explain.

Solution

A cashflow statement will give Mrs Green the answer.

CASHFLOW STATEMENT OF MRS GREEN FOR THE YEAR-ENDED 31 DECEMBER 19-2

	£	£
Operating activities:		
Net profit (before interest)	4,530	
Depreciation for year	250	
Increase in stock	(1,100)	
Increase in debtors	(415)	
Increase in creditors	2,340	
Net cash inflow from operating activities		5,605
Returns on Investments and servicing of finance		
Interest paid	(450)	
Drawings paid	(6,600)	
Net cash outflow from returns on investments		
and servicing of finance		(7,050)
Taxation:		
Tax paid		–
Investing activities:		
Purchase of fixed assets	(500)	
Net cash outflow from investing activities		(500)
Net cash outflow before financing		(1,945)
Financing:		
Loan from husband	1,000	
Net cash inflow from financing		1,000
Decrease in cash		(945)
Analysis of changes in cash during the year:		
Bank balance at start of year		220
Net cash outflow		(945)
Balance at end of year		(725)

Points to note:

- Net profit for the year (before interest) is calculated as: net profit for 19-2 £4,080 *add* interest for 19-2 £450 *equals* £4,530

- Depreciation for the year of £250 is the amount of the increase in depreciation to date shown on the balance sheets, that is, £750 minus £500.

- In this example there is no tax paid (because Mrs Green is a sole trader who will be taxed as an individual, unlike a company which pays tax on its profits); however, the place where tax would appear is indicated on the cashflow statement.

- An increase in stock and debtors reduces the cash available to the business (because stock is being bought, debtors are being allowed more time to pay). In contrast, an increase in creditors gives an increase in cash (because creditors are allowing Mrs Green more time to pay).

- The change in the bank balance is summarised at the end of the cashflow statement: from £220 in the bank to an overdraft of £725 is a 'swing' in the bank of minus £945, which is the amount of the decrease in cash shown by the cashflow statement.

explanation to Mrs Green

In this example, the statement highlights the following points for the owner of the business:

* net cashflow inflow from operating activities is £5,605, whereas owner's drawings are £6,600; this state of affairs cannot continue for long
* fixed assets costing £500 have been purchased
* a long-term loan of £1,000 has been raised from her husband
* over the year there has been a decrease in cash of £945, this trend cannot be continued for long
* by the end of 19-2 the business has an overdraft of £725, caused mainly by the excessive drawings of the owner
* in conclusion, the position of this business has deteriorated over the two years, and corrective action will be necessary

Case Study: a limited company cashflow statement

Situation

The balance sheets of Newtown Trading Company Limited for 19-8 and 19-9 are as set out below. You are asked to prepare a cashflow statement for the year ended 31 December 19-9.

BALANCE SHEET AS AT 31 DECEMBER

	19-8			19-9		
	£ Cost	£ Dep'n	£ Net	£ Cost	£ Dep'n	£ Net
Fixed Assets	47,200	6,200	41,000	64,000	8,900	55,100
Current Assets						
Stocks		7,000			11,000	
Debtors		5,000			3,700	
Bank		1,000			500	
		13,000			15,200	
Less CurrentLiabilities						
Creditors	3,500			4,800		
Proposed dividends	2,000			2,500		
Corporation tax	1,000			1,500		
		6,500			8,800	
Working Capital			6,500			6,400
			47,500			61,500
Less Long-term Liabilities						
Debentures			5,000			3,000
NET ASSETS			42,500			58,500
FINANCED BY						
Ordinary share capital			30,000			40,000
Share premium account			1,500			2,500
Retained profits			11,000			16,000
SHAREHOLDERS' FUNDS			42,500			58,500

Note: Loan interest paid in 19-9 was £400.

Solution

NEWTOWN TRADING COMPANY LTD
CASHFLOW STATEMENT FOR THE YEAR-ENDED 31 DECEMBER 19-9

	£	£
Operating activities:		
Net profit (before interest) *	9,400	
Depreciation for year §	2,700	
Increase in stock	(4,000)	
Decrease in debtors	1,300	
Increase in creditors	1,300	
Net cash inflow from operating activities		10,700
Returns on investments and servicing of finance:		
Interest paid	(400)	
Drawings paid	(2,000)	
Net cash outflow from returns on investments		
and servicing of finance		(2,400)
Taxation:		
Corporation tax paid	(1,000)	
Tax paid		(1,000)
Investing activities:		
Payments to acquire fixed assets	(16,800)	
Net cash outflow from investing activities		(16,800)
Net cash outflow before financing		(9,500)
Financing:		
Issue of ordinary shares at a premium £10,000 + £1,000	11,000	
Repayment of debentures	(2,000)	
Net cash inflow from financing		9,000
Decrease in cash		(500)
Analysis of changes in cash during the year:		
Bank balance at start of year		1,000
Net cash outflow		(500)
Bank balance at end of year		500

Notes:
* Calculation of the net profit for 19-9 before interest, tax and dividends:

	£
increase in retained profits	5,000
interest paid in 19-9	400
proposed dividends, 19-9	2,500
corporation tax, 19-9	1,500
net profit before interest, tax and dividends	9,400

§ Depreciation charged: £8,900 – £6,200 = £2,700

Proposed dividends and corporation tax, which are current liabilities at 31 December 19-8, are paid in 19-9. Likewise, the current liabilities for dividends and tax at 31 December 19-9 will be paid in 19-0.

how useful is the statement?

The following points are highlighted by the statement:

- cashflow from operating activities is £10,700
- a purchase of fixed assets of £16,800 has been made, financed partly by operating activities, and partly by financing activities with an issue of shares at a premium
- the bank balance during the year has fallen by £500
- in conclusion, the picture shown by the cashflow statement is that of a business that is generating cash from its operating activities and using them to build for the future

Chapter Summary

❏ The objective of a cashflow statement is to show an overall view of money flowing in and out of a business during an accounting period.

❏ A cashflow statement is divided into five sections:
- operating activities
- returns on investments and servicing of finance
- taxation
- investing activities
- financing

❏ Most limited companies are required to include a cashflow statement as a part of their published accounts. They are also useful statements for sole traders and partnerships.

 Student Activities

15.1 John Smith has been in business for two years. He is puzzled by his balance sheets because, although they show a profit for each year, his bank balance has fallen and is now an overdraft. He asks for your assistance to explain what has happened. The balance sheets are as follows:

BALANCE SHEET AS AT 31 DECEMBER

| | 19-1 | | | 19-2 | | |
	£ Cost	£ Dep'n	£ Net	£ Cost	£ Dep'n	£ Net
Fixed Assets						
Fixtures and fittings	3,000	600	2,400	5,000	1,600	3,400
Current Assets						
Stocks		5,500			9,000	
Debtors		750			1,550	
Bank		850			-	
		7,100			10,550	
Current Liabilities						
Creditors	2,500			2,750		
Bank overdraft	-			2,200		
		2,500			4,950	
Working Capital			4,600			5,600
NET ASSETS			7,000			9,000

FINANCED BY	19-1		19-2
Capital	5,000		7,000
Add Net profit for year	8,750		11,000
	13,750		18,000
Less Drawings	6,750		9,000
	7,000		9,000

Note: Interest paid in 19-2 was £250.

You are to prepare a cashflow statement for the year-ended 31 December 19-2. Explain to John Smith the reason for the change in the bank balance.

15.2   Richard Williams runs a stationery supplies shop; his balance sheets for the last two years are:

BALANCE SHEET AS AT 30 SEPTEMBER

	19-5			19-6		
	£ Cost	£ Dep'n	£ Net	£ Cost	£ Dep'n	£ Net
Fixed Assets	60,000	12,000	48,000	70,000	23,600	46,400
Current Assets						
Stocks		9,800			13,600	
Debtors		10,800			15,000	
		20,600			28,600	
Less Current Liabilities						
Creditors	7,200			14,600		
Bank overdraft	1,000			4,700		
		8,200			19,300	
Working Capital			12,400			9,300
			60,400			55,700
Less Long-term Liabilities						
Bank loan			10,000			15,000
NET ASSETS			50,400			40,700
FINANCED BY						
Capital			50,000			50,400
Add Net profit/(loss)			10,800			(1,500)
			60,800			48,900
Less Drawings			10,400			8,200
			50,400			40,700

Note: Loan and overdraft interest paid in 19-6 was £2,200.

You are to prepare a cashflow statement for the year-ended 30 September 19-6. As his accountant, use the cashflow statement to write a reply to Richard Williams (address: The Stationery Shop, 32 Bank Street, Redgrove RD1 7GT) who says: "I don't know what has gone wrong – I have worked very hard to build up the business so that I can earn profits to repay the bank".

15.3 Martin Jackson is a shareholder in Retail News Ltd, a company that operates a chain of newsagents throughout the West Midlands. Martin comments that, whilst the company is making reasonable profits, the bank balance has fallen quite considerably. He provides you with the following information for Retail News Ltd:

BALANCE SHEET AS AT 31 DECEMBER

	19-4 £000	19-4 £000	19-5 £000	19-5 £000	19-6 £000	19-6 £000
Fixed Assets at cost		252		274		298
Add Additions during year		22		24		26
		274		298		324
Less Depreciation to date		74		98		118
		200		200		206
Current Assets						
Stock	50		64		70	
Debtors	80		120		160	
Bank	10		-		-	
	140		184		230	
Less Current Liabilities						
Creditors	56		72		78	
Bank	-		10		46	
Proposed dividends	16		20		16	
Corporation tax	4		5		8	
	76		107		148	
Working Capital		64		77		82
NET ASSETS		264		277		288
FINANCED BY						
Ordinary share capital		200		210		210
Retained profits		64		67		78
		264		277		288

Note: Interest paid was: £3,000 in 19-5, and £15,000 in 19-6.

You are to prepare a cashflow statement for the years ended for 19-5 and 19-6. Explain the reason for the change in the bank balance.

16 Financial statements – clubs and associations

introduction

We have seen in our studies of Finance that a business organisation aims to maximise *profit*. This aim is naturally and rightly self-centred. The aim of a social organisation, on the other hand, is to provide benefits for the *social* good.

A social organisation is the voluntary co-operation of individuals with a mutual interest to arrange social activities for the benefit of themselves and/or others.

For example, an angling club can arrange a good day's fishing, and on a more informal basis a group of individuals can arrange a holiday. In all cases the activity will be enjoyed and *financed* by the members.

In this chapter we will examine the affairs of the Crown Heath Cricket Club, a typical social organisation which, as we will see, is dependent solely on the drive and enthusiasm of its members and the support of the local village community to enable it to operate and to expand its activities.

Crown Heath Cricket Club

the present situation

The village of Crown Heath is very much a farming community; it boasts a fine old church, three pubs and a well-known cricket team. The team's activities are made possible by the Crown Heath Cricket Club, which is fortunate in being able to rent a clubhouse, equipped with a bar, from the Parish Council. The Club owns the furniture and fittings (£2,000 at cost) and sports equipment (£1,000 at cost).

The setting of the clubhouse by the village green is ideal for the team's many fixtures; yet the scene is far from idyllic: the building is cramped, a new changing room is needed, and a recent visit by a Fire Officer has pointed to major deficiencies in the building's fire doors. Before seeing how the situation is to be remedied, it is important to examine the Club's financial control and accounting records.

financial control of the club

The officers of the Club include the Chairman, Secretary and the Treasurer, who is a local bank manager. The Club has its own bank account, and any two of the officers can sign cheques on the account. The accounting records are very simple.

accounting records of the Club

Cash Book: Receipts and Payments Account

The cash book used, often called the *Receipts and Payments Account* is a simple version of the cash book used by businesses (see Chapter 28); it records amounts paid into and out of the bank account, and cash held by the Club. It is normally ruled off at the end of a financial year and does not therefore record refinements such as accruals and prepayments, or distinguish between capital and revenue expenditure.

The Receipts and Payments Account is very often the *only* accounting record kept by social organisations which meet infrequently or only handle small amounts of money. A more accurate method of accounting is preferable for the latter social organisation: the Treasurer of the Crown Heath Cricket Club produces final accounts as follows:

- income and expenditure account (profit and loss account)
- balance sheet

We will examine this process in detail for the accounting year ending on 31 December 19-8.

Receipts and Payments Account

First, a summary is made of the Cash Book at the end of the financial year:

Crown Heath Cricket Club
Receipts and Payments Account for the Year ended 31 December 19-8

RECEIPTS	£	PAYMENTS	£
Bank balance at 1 January	231	Rent	200
Subscriptions	875	Heating oil	900
Bar takings	2,700	Electricity	127
Donations	500	Bar expenses	1,250
Sale of Programmes	310	Printing of Programmes	175
		Sports equipment	510
		Groundsman's wages	1,050
		Sundry expenses	35
		Bank balance at 31 Dec.	369
	4,616		4,616

As we have seen, Treasurers of some social organisations go no further than this accounting summary. What are its shortcomings, and how can it be improved?

- The acquisition of assets, here sports equipment of £510, is recorded along with other expenses and does not appear on a balance sheet. The members *do not know what they own*.

- The summary ignores the fact that subscriptions of £875 include £70 paid by members in advance *for next year*.

- The summary ignores the fact that rent of £50 has been paid for the first quarter of *next year* (a prepayment).

Thus the Receipts and Payments Account is not an entirely true picture of the Club's affairs *for the year*. The Treasurer therefore converts this cash book summary into a more accurate view of the year's income and expenditure, an Income and Expenditure Account, comparable to a business' Trading and Profit and Loss Account.

income and expenditure account

In drafting this account, the Treasurer must make the following adjustments:

*   Adjust for prepayments (deduct £50 from the rent of £200 = £150).
    Note: an adjustment would be made for any accruals (expenses outstanding) by adding to the yearly total.
*   Adjust the subscriptions by deducting advance payments of £70 from the total of £875 = £805.
    Note: subscriptions outstanding are ignored for the year's accounts – they are often paid late, if at all.
*   Exclude any asset purchase not part of normal running expenses, here sports equipment of £510.
*   Net the contributions from fund raising activities, here:
    (a) bar takings £2,700 less bar expenses £1,250 = bar profit £1,450
    (b) sale of programmes £310 less printing costs £175 = profit £135
    Note: if the bar is run throughout the year, the Treasurer may keep a separate 'Bar Trading Account'. This is prepared on the same basis as the trading account of a business.

The revised account will appear as set out below, but note that it has been prepared in *vertical* format, like the Trading and Profit and Loss account of a business organisation. Income is listed at the top and expenditure deducted below. The surpus or 'profit' shown at the bottom is referred to as an 'excess of income over expenditure'. If a loss had been made, it would be referred to as an 'excess of expenditure over income.'

Crown Heath Cricket Club
Income and Expenditure Account for the year ended 31 December 19-8

	£	£
Income		
Members' subscriptions		805
Profit on bar		1,450
Profit on programmes		135
Donations		500
		2,890
Less expenditure		
Rent	150	
Heating oil	900	
Electricity	127	
Groundsman's wages	1,050	
Sundry expenses	35	
Depreciation	75	
		2,337
Surplus of income over expenditure		553

The £553 surplus for the year has largely been spent on sports equipment (£510) which then appears in the balance sheet. The balance sheet shown at the top of the next page is in the more common *vertical* format used for the balance sheets of business organisations. The balance sheet is also shown below this in the old-fashioned *horizontal* format which some clubs and organisations may still use. The horizontal format given here shows assets on the left and liabilities on the right.

vertical format balance sheet

Crown Heath Cricket Club
Balance Sheet as at 31 December 19-8

	£	£	£
Fixed Assets	Cost	Dep'n	Net
Furniture and equipment	2,000	1,100	900
Sports equipment	1,000	250	750
	3,000	1,350	1,650
Current Assets			
Bar stocks		835	
Prepayment of rent		50	
Bank		369	
Cash		120	
		1,374	
Less Current Liabilities			
Subscriptions paid in advance	70		
Creditors	356		
		426	
Working Capital			948
NET ASSETS			2,598
REPRESENTED BY			
Accumulated fund			2,045
Surplus of income over expenditure for year			553
			2,598

A social organisation does not have 'capital' as such. Instead, the term *Accumulated Fund* or *General Fund* is used to describe the difference between the total assets and total liabilities of the organization. In the case of the Crown Heath Cricket Club the Accumulated Fund of £2,045 represents the members' 'stake' in the Club at the beginning of the financial year.

horizontal format balance sheet

Crown Heath Cricket Club
Balance Sheet as at 31 December 19-8

	£	£	£		£
Fixed Assets	Cost	Dep'n	Net		
Furniture & fittings	2,000	1,100	900	**Accumulated Fund**	2,045
Sports Equipment	1,000	250	750	Surplus of income over	
	3,000	1,350	1,650	expenditure	553
					2,598
Current Assets				**Current Liabilities**	
Bar Stocks		835		Subscriptions paid in	
Prepayment of Rent		50		advance	70
Bank		369		Creditors	356
Cash		120	1,374		
			3,024		3,024

fund raising efforts: sources of finance

The Treasurer presents the accounts, audited by an accountant living in the village at the Annual General Meeting of the Club on 10 April 19-9. The members can see clearly from the Income and Expenditure Account what income has been received, and expenditure incurred. They know from the balance sheet exactly what the Club owes and what assets it owns.

On the face of it, the financial state of the Club is healthy. But, as was mentioned earlier, two large items of capital expenditure are required: an extension to the changing room costing £8,000, and new fire doors costing £500 to be installed within the next twelve months. The Treasurer mentions that the Local Authority will give a grant of 50% of the cost of the extension, as long as 25% of the total extension costs, ie £2,000, has been raised by the members themselves by the time the grant application is submitted. The Club therefore needs £2,500, ie £2,000 plus £500.

How is the money to be raised? The following points are decided at the meeting:

* the fire doors are more urgent and should have priority
* subscriptions can only cover revenue ('running') expenses
* borrowing from commercial sources is not feasible: there is no tangible security or steady source of repayment

Fund raising by the members is the obvious solution. There are various suggestions, each of which it is hoped will raise £500:

* a sponsored cricket match
* a midsummer party
* a car boot sale on the village green
* a 'buy a brick' campaign (specifically for the extension)
* a 'casino night' at the clubhouse

Members volunteer to run the various events and schemes. Because of the popularity of the Club in the neighbourhood, they are hopeful of raising the £2,500 required. A visit to the Club in twelve months' time may well reveal that the money has been raised, but also that more funds are required for a different purpose. So this short-term cycle of fund raising and renewal, typical of many social organisations, continues, and as long as it does, so the social organisation will survive.

Chapter Summary

❏ We have examined in this chapter the fortunes of one particular type of social organisation - the social sports club - which has large sums of money passing through its hands, and like a business organisation needs tight accounting control and a well organised financial planning process.

❏ Unlike a business, however, it does not base its activities on the profit motive, but operates for the social benefit of its members and the general public.

❏ The principal financial statements of a social organisation are
  * receipts and payments account
  * income and expenditure account
  * balance sheet

Student Activities

16.1 You have recently taken over as the Treasurer of the Hallow Male Voice Choir. The accounts of the previous year (to 31 December 19-8) have been prepared, but only as a Receipts and Payments Account as follows:

Hallow Male Voice Choir
Receipts and Payments Account for the year to 31 December 19-8

RECEIPTS	£	PAYMENTS	£
Bank balance as at 1 Jan. 19-8	112	Concert costs	1,250
Subscriptions	750	Conductor's fee	300
Music Festival prize	500	Music purchase	450
Concert ticket sales	825	Printing of programmes	60
Fund raising activities (raffles)	427	Bank balance as at 31 Dec19-8	554
	2,614		2,614

Additionally, you note that:

• £65 of subscriptions, included in the £750, are paid in advance for 19-9.

• The Club owes £40 for programme printing.

• Your committee wants you to set up a 'Concert Account' which will net the concert costs with the concert ticket sales.

• Stocks of music held, including that recently bought, are valued at cost of £1,125. All music used is owned by the Club and lent to members free of charge.

Your committee ask you to:

(a) Prepare an Income and Expenditure Account for the year and a Balance Sheet, showing an Accumulated Fund, at the year-end.

(b) Write accompanying notes, commenting on and explaining the sources of income, and how they have been spent, and concluding with recommendations for improving income by fund raising or by other means.

16.2 You have just taken over as Treasurer of Severn Social Club, an organisation strictly for the under-25s. The Severn Social Club arranges social events such as discos and short holidays abroad for its members. It is entirely self-supporting, and has earned itself a good reputation in the area as it also helps raise money for charity through its annual sponsored walk and other fund-raising activities

The Club has a major problem: the previous Treasurer, who resigned on 31 March 19-8, the end of the Club's financial year, has left the accounts in a poor state and the Club's bank account overdrawn by £5.10. The financial records are contained in a tatty box file and comprise:

- A bank statement (illustrated below) for the last financial year of the Club. The previous Treasurer has annotated the items on the statement (in the Particulars column) with details of the transactions.

- The following invoices relating to the financial year ending March 19-8: a printing bill of £23.50 and an advertising bill of £7.50, both overdue, and both for publicity.

- An invoice for second-hand disco equipment bought by the Club for £1,000 on 1 July 19-7. The equipment was a good buy, so you consider £1,000 also to be the present value of the equipment.

- An envelope marked 'Sponsored Walk Proceeds' containing £12.50 in cash. You suspect that the previous Treasurer has forgotten to pay the money into the bank. This cash and the disco equipment appear to be the only assets held by the Club.

- A list which shows that there were 120 members at 31 March 19-8. The subscription is £5 per year. The Treasurer has scribbled a note to the effect that, during the year, £50 of subscriptions were paid in advance.

As Treasurer, using the rather sparse financial information given, you are to draw up

- a Receipts and Payments Account for the year

- an Income and Expenditure account for the past financial year

- a Balance Sheet which shows the Accumulated Fund as at 31 March 19-8.

IN ACCOUNT WITH

National Bank plc

Branch.........Felpersham

TITLE OF ACCOUNT.....SEVERN SOCIAL CLUB

ACCOUNT NUMBER.....21097318

STATEMENT NUMBER   5

DATE	PARTICULARS	PAYMENTS	RECEIPTS	BALANCE
19-7		£	£	£
1 Apl	Balance b/f			219.15 Cr
8 Apl	Credit *subscriptions*		510.00	729.15 Cr
18 Apl	Credit *subscriptions*		50.00	779.15 Cr
21 Apl	Credit *subscriptions*		40.00	819.15 Cr
7 May	Chq 329710 *disco hire*	150.00		669.15 Cr
9 May	Chq 329711 *advert for dance*	17.50		651.65 Cr
9 May	Chq 329712 *hall hire and drink*	250.00		401.65 Cr
13 May	Credit *dance receipts*		612.00	1,013.65 Cr
21 Jun	Chq 329713 *walk expenses*	25.00		988.65 Cr
28 Jun	Credit *walk takings*		509.75	1,498.40 Cr
1 Jul	Chq 329714 *disco purchase*	1,000.00		498.40 Cr
5 Jul	Chq 329715 *donation to hospital*	500.00		1.60 Dr
19-8				
5 Jan	Credit *subscriptions*		50.00	48.40 Cr
17 Jan	Chq 329716 *treasurer's expenses*	25.00		23.40 Cr
12 Mar	Chq 329717 *publicity (advert)*	28.50		5.10 Dr
31 Mar	Balance c/f			5.10 Dr

17 Local Authority finance

introduction

So far in this book we have examined in detail the financial needs and operations of individuals and business organisations in the *Private Sector,* a term used to describe organisations which are not owned by, or which are not directly responsible to Central Government.

In this chapter we will consider the financing and financial statements of *Local Authorities* which are part of what is known as the *Public Sector,* a term used to describe bodies which are held in public ownership and overseen by Central Government. Other bodies in the Public Sector include Public Corporations such as the BBC and the Post Office, Government Departments, and the Health Authorities.

Local Authority is a term applied to local governing councils which operate both in the county areas and also in urban areas. In the county areas the Local Authority is normally structured in three tiers:
* the County Council
* the Borough or District Councils
* the Parish Councils

In the urban areas, on the other hand, only *one* level of council exists: in London there are separate Borough Councils (such as Brent or Westminster) and in other urban areas there are Metropolitan Borough Councils (such as Birmingham or Liverpool). Proposals for the reform of the structure of local government are currently being considered. It is likely that the County and Borough or District Councils will be replaced by single 'unitary' authorities. It is probable that this scheme will be introduced first in Wales.

Local Authorities taken as a whole have a wide range of services to administer. These include education, environmental health, planning, refuse collection, social services, transport, fire services, libraries and recreational facilities. Not all of these are actually carried out by the Local Authorities: in recent years Local Authorities have engaged in Compulsory Competitive Tendering (CTT), the system whereby services such as waste collection and catering have been offered for tender to private businesses. It has been proposed that this system be extended to other areas such as legal services and payroll.

In this chapter we will see how the Local Authorities finance these operations, and also how they prepare and present their accounts to the public.

financial objectives: budgeting for expenditure

Local Authorities, unlike businesses in the Private Sector, do not have the profit motive as a *major* objective, although of course they do strive for efficiency and cost saving. They do not rely for their survival on the level of demand in a competitive market. Therefore, they approach the subject of expenditure quite differently: they carefully budget for how much they need to spend on administration and services; then they tackle the problem of how they are going to raise those funds.

The budgeting process of a Local Authority is normally divided into four separate budgets:

The Revenue Budget is a compilation of projections of likely expenditure and income of the Local Authority services during the coming year. It is also responsible for setting the Council Tax.

The Capital Budget sets targets for spending on long-term assets such as roads and schools. Its time span is normally five years, although it can be longer. It is reviewed each year, ie a further year is added to the five year plan, making it a 'rolling' budget.

The Manpower Budget controls the level of staffing, the most expensive item for Local Authorities, which are essentially labour-intensive organisations.

The Cash Flow Budget, like the cash budget of an individual or business organization, projects and monitors the amount of money that is likely to be received or paid out over a given period. One important function is the management of repayment and interest for Local Authority Loan Debt.

Local Authority expenditure

Local Authority spending, like business expenditure, is of two types:
* *capital* expenditure for major projects such as roads and hospitals
* *revenue* expenditure for day-to-day running costs

capital expenditure
The sources of finance for *capital* expenditure are (in order of magnitude):
* loan debt
* specific Central Government grants
* contributions from Local Authority revenue
* sale of existing capital items
* leasing
* internally accumulated funds (Capital and Renewals Funds)

revenue expenditure
There are four main sources of finance for *revenue* expenditure; they are (in order of magnitude):
* Central Government grants: Revenue Support Grant (also known as the Standard Spending Grant)
* fees and charges for local services
* redistributed income from the Non-Domestic Rate (a levy on business property) collected by Local Authorities on behalf of Central Government
* local taxes: the Council Tax (previously the Community Charge) in England, Wales and Scotland

We will now look at the most important of these sources of finance: Central Government grants, charges for local services, local taxes, and Local Authority borrowing.

sources of Local Authority finance

Central Government grants
Central Government grants are of two types:
- Specific Grants
- Revenue Support Grant

Specific Grants
The Specific Grants, as the title suggests, are intended to assist specific requirements such as housing, police and transport.

Revenue Support Grant
Central Government calculates each year the amount of revenue expenditure which it considers each local authority *should* incur in providing what it calls the *standard level of service*. This is known as a *Standard Spending Assessment* (SSA). You may well ask how the Government performs this calculation. The answer lies in the application of complex formulas to all areas of revenue expenditure, based on population and other factors relevant to the area, to produce a total revenue spending figure:

Total of Standard Spending Assessments for England for 1992/93

	£m.
Education	18,352.7
Social Services	4,734.6
Police	2,686.9
Fire and Civil Defence	1,105.2
Highway Maintenance	1,806.0
Other Services (eg Flood Defence)	7,398.9
Financing of Local Authority borrowing	1,908.4
TOTAL STANDARD SPENDING	37,992.7

The Central Government then allocates a share of this total of Standard Spending Assessments to Local Authorities as the *Revenue Support Grant* in proportion to the adult population in each Authority. The grant is therefore *fixed* by Central Government. It is then up to each Local Authority to spend the grant as it thinks appropriate, and as efficiently – or inefficiently – as the financial management of the Authority allows. The Revenue Support Grant will not cover all the revenue expenditure undertaken by Local Authority. The difference is made up from

- fees and charges for local services
- payment by Central Government of money raised from the Uniform Business Rate
- local taxation: the Council Tax in England, Wales and Scotland

We will deal with these sources of income in turn.

charges for local services
A certain proportion, typically 25%, of a Local Authority's income comes from charges for services provided. Some services give a social benefit, others are more commercial in nature and may compete with private enterprise. Socially oriented income includes rent from council housing and elderly persons' homes, while income from more commercial sources includes revenue from car parks and caravan sites, lotteries and leisure centres.

Non-Domestic Rate (Business Rates)

Central Government taxes business premises and property by means of the *Non-Domestic Rate*. All business property has been valued for taxation purposes by the Inland Revenue and given a *rateable value* expressed in £s. Rateable value is a hypothetical annual rental value; it is *not* the market value of the property. A factory unit, for instance, may be given a rateable value of £50,000. The tax due to Central Government is calculated by applying a standard multiplier (the Non-Domestic Rating Multiplier) to the rateable value. This multiplier is 40.2p in the £ for the year 1992/1993, and will be raised annually in line with inflation. The rates due on the factory unit will therefore be:

£50,000 (rateable value) x 40.2p (1992/93 Non-Domestic Rating Multiplier) = £20,100 per year

The Non-Domestic Rate is collected by the Local Authorities and passed over to a central pool which Central Government then reallocates to Local Authorities to help fund their revenue expenditure. The allocation is made on the basis of the figure for the adult population in the Local Authority area.

local taxation: the Community Charge and the Council Tax

General Rates, Community Charge and the Council Tax: an historical note

Before April 1990 in England and Wales (and April 1989 in Scotland), local taxation was raised by Local Authorities by means of the *General Rates*. This levy was essentially a tax on the occupation of property, whether for domestic or business purposes. Each property was given a rateable value (in the same way as business property is now assessed for Non-Domestic Rate) and the rates calculated by applying so many pence in the £ to that rateable value. Thus a property was taxed according to its size rather than on the number of occupants. Whatever the advantages and disadvantages of the rating system, it was replaced for domestic properties in April 1990 in England and Wales (April 1989 in Scotland) by the *Community Charge*, or Poll Tax as it is commonly known, which was a local taxation on individuals of 18 years of age and over. In 1991 the Government announced that the Community Charge would be replaced in 1993 by a *Council Tax*, based in part on property values.

the Council Tax

what is the Council Tax?

The Council Tax, in force from 1 April 1993, is chargeable on all domestic property in England, Scotland and Wales. It is set by designated Local Authorities and the amount payable is determined by the value of the property concerned. Properties are valued according to a system of 'valuation bands' into which the properties are allocated by the Inland Revenue (see Fig. 17.1). Discounts are available, subject to the personal circumstances of the residents of the property.

ingredients of the Council Tax - calculation of discounts

The tax is composed of two parts:

- a property part
- a personal part

The *property part* comprises 50% of the Council Tax payable in a valuation band. With a few exceptions, all properties are liable for this part *in full*, whether occupied or not.

The *personal part* is based on the number of people aged 18 or over (adults) living at the property. Where two or more adults live in the property, this 50% of the Council Tax (the personal part) then becomes payable. There are, however, certain discounts applicable to the personal part of the tax if the number of adult residents is less than two:

- if there is only *one* adult resident in the property, only 50% of the personal part becomes payable – this is effectively *a discount of 25%* on the total Council Tax bill on the property
- if there are *no* adult residents in the property, no personal part is payable – this is effectively *a discount of 50%* on the total Council Tax bill on the property

As you will see, the 50% property part of the Council Tax is payable in full, whether or not the property is occupied.

valuation bands

The Inland Revenue, assisted by private valuers, has placed all domestic properties into a range of eight valuation bands (designated by the letters A – H). These represent the amounts which the properties would have been expected to realise if they had been sold on 1 April 1991. Each property is shown in a Valuation List which shows the appropriate band for that property.

setting of the tax

It should be noted that property values vary widely in different parts of the country: £200,000 can buy a terraced house in Central London and also a five-bedroomed country residence in the Cotswolds. Therefore, while the amounts set out in valuation bands A – H, remain fixed (see Fig. 17.1), it is up to the Local Authority to set the Council Tax to reflect the number of properties in each band, and also the amount required to cover their Budget requirements not met from other sources of income. As a result, levels of Council Tax will vary from Authority to Authority.

Local Authorities set the Council Tax as a single amount for a property occupied by two or more adults in band D. The levels of tax in the other bands are calculated according to proportions set down by Act of Parliament. These appear as proportional factors in the third column of the table below, which shows Council Tax calculated on the basis of £400 for two adults or more at band D.

Council Tax calculation – Band D set at £400					
Band	Value Range (£) (as at 1 April 1991)	Proportional Charges	Approximate Level of Charge (£)		
			Empty house	One Adult	Two or More Adults
A	up to 40,000	6	134	200	267
B	40,001 – 52,000	7	156	233	311
C	52,001 – 68,000	8	178	267	356
D	68,001 – 88,000	9	200	300	400
E	88,001 – 120,000	11	245	367	489
F	120,001 – 160,000	13	289	434	578
G	160,001 – 320,000	15	334	500	667
H	320,001 and above	18	400	600	800

Fig. 17.1 Council Tax valuation bands and example tax calculation

status discounts

Certain groups of people are disregarded for the purposes of calculating the total number of people in the property, and therefore the person liable to pay the tax may be entitled to a discount, even though more than one adult is living there. These groups are:

* students
* student nurses
* apprentices
* Youth Training trainees
* people previously exempt from the Community Charge:
  - the severely mentally impaired
  - prisoners
  - members of religious communities
  - persons resident in hospitals and homes
  - children
  - carers
  - residents of hostels
  - school leavers
  - members of international headquarters and defense organisations

students

In addition to the status discounts shown above, a property which is *wholly* occupied by students is exempt from the Council Tax.

who is liable to pay the Council tax?

There are some circumstances where it is not clear – on the face of it – *who* in the household is liable to pay the tax. For example, who pays in the cases of landlord and tenant, relatives living with a family, live-in nannies, and so on? A summary of the order of liability to pay is as set out below, but note that the person must normally be *in occupation* to be liable:

1. *freeholder*   Most residential land is *freehold*, ie the person who buys it – the *freeholder* – has an absolute right to it and can pass it on to his or her heirs. Most house owners are freeholders and will therefore be 'first in line' to pay the tax, and may be taken to court if they do not!

2. *leaseholder*   If the freeholder lets out his property, he does so by means of a *lease*, and the person to whom the lease is made out is known as the *leaseholder*, and the property is known as *leasehold*. Many flats are leasehold, and if you buy or rent a leasehold flat, you will be liable to pay the Council Tax, assuming the freeholder is not resident.

3. *resident*   Residents of a property, eg relatives, are only liable to pay the Council Tax if the owner (freeholder/leaseholder) is not living there – an unlikely event. However, the non-resident owner *is* liable to pay if the property is
   * a residential care home
   * a religious community
   * a house in multiple occupation
   * occupied by resident staff
   * occupied by a minister of religion

council tax benefit

This is a means tested deduction from the bill for the property and is up to a maximum of 100% for people on low income or on Income Support. The number of non-dependents living in the household affects the benefit.

second adult rebates

If there is a second adult living in the property who

• is not a husband or wife or tenant
• is on low income

the first adult may be granted a rebate to make up for the 25% discount lost (see page 181). The rebate is up to 25% if the second adult is on Income Support or earns less than £130 a week.

controls over Local Authority Spending

The sources of funding for Local Authority revenue spending are set out in the diagram below. Note that the levels of the Government sources of funding – the Revenue Support Grant and the Non-Domestic Rate – are outside the control of the Local Authority.

Money contributed by the Government (fixed amounts)	Money raised from within the Local Authority (amounts decided upon by Local Authority)
Revenue Support Grant	Council Tax
Redistributed Non-Domestic Rate	Fees and Charges for Local Services

Council Tax 'Capping'

It therefore follows that if a Local Authority wishes to spend more than the Government considers that it should (ie more than the *standard level of service* which forms the basis for the calculation of the Revenue Support Grant) the extra money will have to be found from

• fees and charges for local services
• the Council Tax set by the Local Authority

In the main, the extra money will be obtained from the Council Tax. In order to prevent Local Authorities from spending too much and consequently levying a very high Council Tax, the Government has the power to 'cap.' This process involves the Secretary of State for the Environment setting formulas for limits on expenditure in relation to the Standard Spending Assessment. The Authority concerned must submit revised expenditure figures in order to comply with the imposed spending limits. As a *consequence* of this the Council Tax will be set at a lower level. The process of 'capping' might therefore be more accurately termed 'expenditure capping.'

forms of Local Authority borrowing

As we saw earlier, Local Authorities also finance their operations from loans that they raise.

Local Authority Mortgages
A Local Authority Mortgage is a loan evidenced in the form of a signed and sealed legal document. Mortgages are available from:

- local investors
- large institutions (eg pension funds, insurance companies)
- Public Works Loan Board (PWLB)

The period of mortgage loans can vary from 10 to 80 years; repayment can be in instalments, or at maturity, ie the end of the loan.

Local Authority Stock Issues
Local Authority Stock is issued and traded on the Stock Exchange, and thus can be bought by the public in the same way as public limited company shares and Government Stock. Stock is only issued by the larger Local Authorities.

Local Authority Bonds
Local Authority Bonds are sold directly 'over the counter' to private investors, and can take the form of 'local', 'yearling' and 'negotiable' bonds. They are issued for periods of up to a year (hence 'yearling') and may be renewed as they mature.

Temporary Loans
Financial institutions, large companies and other Local Authorities sometimes have short-term surpluses of cash which they place with money brokers. These funds are then lent by the brokers to similar institutions with a cash requirement. Local Authorities can borrow such funds for periods from one day to one year; they will issue 'deposit receipts' in return for the loans.

Local Authority loan administration: the Loans Fund

A Local Authority has many services to finance, and it is therefore clear that it would be administratively difficult to apply any particular loan to any particular service. The Local Government Act 1972 has therefore provided that a Local Authority may set up a Loans Fund, often known as a 'Consolidated Loans Fund'.

A Loans Fund is a 'pool' of money into which all money raised from borrowing is paid, and out of which the Local Authority draws money to finance capital expenditure and repay borrowing. The departments (individual services) which borrow money from the Loans Fund are known as the 'borrowing accounts'; these are required to repay the loans to the Loans Fund over a period related to the life of the asset purchased.

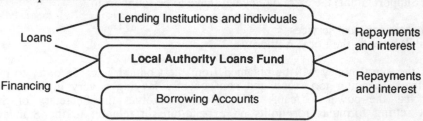

The Loans Fund is, therefore, a very useful arrangement as it enables the Local Authority to average out the cost of its many forms of borrowing in terms of interest rates and administrative expenses.

financial control of a Local Authority

When examining finance for individuals and business organizations we have seen that financial control is important for efficiency and profitability. Local Authorities also aim to be efficient, and not wasteful with the resources they have at their disposal, largely because they are accountable to Central Government and the local taxpayers for those resources. Local Authorities are therefore subject to both internal and external controls, some of them set down in law.

internal financial control of a Local Authority

There is no legally defined structure for the financial organization of a Local Authority, but the following hierarchy is fairly typical:

The Finance Committee directs financial policy and makes recommendations to the Council. Its functions include the supervision of borrowing, investment, banking operations, and expenditure.

The Director of Finance, also known as the Treasurer is an important figure in Local Authority finance. His position may be compared with that of a Finance Director of a large public limited company. He has overall control of the day-to-day running of the Finance Division, and is directly responsible to the Finance Committee.

The Finance Department is subdivided into operational divisions such as collection of revenue, expenditure, wages and salaries. Its accounting functions include budgetary control (the recording of transactions) and financial planning (the planning of future needs).

Internal Audit is carried out by a separate section of the Finance Department, and is required by law. Its function is to monitor and ensure the efficiency and accuracy of the Local Authority's accounting system, compliance with law and council policies, prevention and detection of fraud.

external financial control: the Audit Commission

External audit of Local Authorities, like internal audit, is required by law, principally the Local Government Finance Act 1982, which established the Audit Commission. This independent body, which has the motto of the three Es – economy, efficiency, effectiveness – aims to achieve 'value for money' from the Local Authorities. It does this by appointing either a District Auditor or an Approved Auditor.

District Auditors are members of the Audit Inspectorate, which is part of the Civil Service. They each have responsibility for a certain geographical area.

Approved Auditors are members of a recognised Accounting Body, approved by the Secretary of State. These bodies include The Institute of Chartered Accountants in England and Wales, The Chartered Association of Certified Accountants, and The Chartered Institute of Public Finance and Accounting (CIPFA).

The Audit Commission publishes data which which enables useful comparison to be made of performance and the efficiency of the provision of services by Local Authorities with similar geographic locations and demographic patterns.

duties of an external auditor

An approved or district auditor must examine the accounts for a number of reasons:
- to ensure that fraud, waste and inefficiency are kept to a minimum
- to ensure that the accounts are drawn up in accordance with accepted accounting practices
- to ensure consistency in the running of the accounts and that internal audit is adequate
- to ensure the accuracy of the Authority's claims for Government grants and subsidies
- to undertake 'value for money' exercises

the internal accounts of a Local Authority

The published accounts of a Local Authority, which we shall describe in the next section, are prepared from the day-to-day accounting records. These may be summarised as follows:

Cash Accounts are comparable with the 'bank' account maintained by a business in its Cash Book. These accounts record all receipts and payments passed through the bank; separate accounts are kept for capital and revenue transactions.

Income Accounts and Expenditure Accounts record separately, in addition to the Cash Account, income received, on a cash payment or credit basis, and all payments made by the Local authority in respect of capital items, goods and services, and wages and salaries.

Revenue Accounts are compiled from Income and Expenditure accounts, and are basically the Profit and Loss accounts of individual services or departments. They show:
• income: government grants, charges and fees
• expenditure: salaries, running expenses (not capital items), interest and repayment of loans
• any surplus or deficit

Capital Accounts are also compiled from the Income and Expenditure accounts, but record capital items in specified services or departments. They are comparable to the fixed asset accounts of businesses.

the published accounts of a Local Authority

The Local Government Planning and Land Act 1980 states that all Local Authorities must produce an Annual Report, and that the Report must contain the relevant accounts. The District or Borough Council and the County Council therefore both publish Accounts as at 31 March each year, the accounts being set out according to a CIPFA Code of Practice issued in June 1987.

As we have seen when examining the aims of the Audit Commission, the present emphasis in viewing the accounts of Local Authorities is on efficiency. The Accounts will therefore contain a number of 'performance indicators' which tell the reader how well the Local Authority is performing in comparison with the year's budget and the previous year's figures. The most important items in the Accounts will be:

• the Finance Director's Report on the Accounts
• the Auditor's Report on the Accounts
• details of revenue income and expenditure by service, including performance indicators
• a Revenue Account Summary
• a Capital Account Summary by service, showing sources of finance
• general statistics and performance indicators for services
• a manpower summary
• a Consolidated Balance Sheet (see Fig. 17.2 on the next page)
• a Consolidated Statement of Revenue and Capital Movements

The published accounts will normally be distributed to:

• town halls, county halls, public libraries
• the local press (with a press release)
• interested groups who have requested a copy
• employees of the Local Authority

CONSOLIDATED BALANCE SHEET

The Balance Sheet summarises the state of the County Council's affairs at 31 March 1991 and incorporates the balances of the County Fund but excludes the Superannuation and Trust Funds.

31.3.90		31.3.91
£000		£000
92,819	Fixed Assets	99,992
150	Deferred Charges	129
1,221	Long term debtors	1,475
94,190	Total Long Term Assets	101,596
	Current Assets	
2,464	Stocks	2,251
17,013	Debtors	19,043
11,915	Temporary Investments	13,685
259	Cash in hands of accounting officers	273
31,651		35,252
	Less Current Liabilities	
29,062	Creditors	31,440
5,955	Temporary Loans	7,462
6,387	Cash overdrawn	8,198
41,404		47,100
(9,753)	Net Current Liabilities	11,848
84,437		89,748
	Financed by:	
56,388	Long-term borrowing	67,482
53	Deferred capital receipts	52
8,833	Capital receipts unapplied	-
-	Provision for credit liabilities	7,449
11,084	Reserves	13,502
502	Provisions	202
7,577	Revenue Balances	1,061
84,437		89,748

Fig.17.2
County Council of Hereford and Worcester
Consolidated Balance Sheet as at 31 March 1991

Chapter Summary

❑ The Public Sector comprises bodies in 'public' ownership such as Central Government Departments, Public Utilities, Public Corporations and the Local Authorities.

❑ Local Authorities, which include the County Council, District and Borough Councils, and Parish Councils in the counties, Metropolitan councils in urban areas, and the London Boroughs, do not aim to make a profit.

❑ Budgets have to be prepared for both revenue and capital spending.

❑ Sources of finance include government grants, charges for services, the Council Tax, and borrowing from institutions and individuals.

❑ Local Authorities are under tight financial control and publish Annual Accounts, the form of which is different from those of business organisations.

❑ The present aim for a Local Authority is to give 'value for money'.

 Student Activities

17.1   Obtain a financial information leaflet from the Treasurer's Department of your local charging authority. (This leaflet may be called something along the lines of 'Your Local Authority Budget Explained' or 'Budget Information')

As an exercise in the presentation of financial information

(a)   draw up pie charts showing the breakdown of local authority spending and sources of income

(b)   draw up bar charts showing the increase or decrease in spending from the previous to the present year

If possible use a computer spreadsheet or database with graphics facilities to prepare this visual information

17.2   Obtain the Annual Report and Accounts of your local County Council (or equivalent), and compare them with the Annual Report and Accounts of a public limited company. Pay particular attention to:

(a)   The overall appearance and presentation – are shareholders and local taxpayers given the same style of document?

(b)   The items reported in the financial statements – how do they differ?

(c)   The apparent financial objectives of the two bodies – how do they differ, and in what ways are they the same? (Look at the Chairman's/Treasurer's Report.)

(d)   The auditors – who are they in each case; are they public sector or private sector accountants?

section four
business planning and
budgeting

In this section we look at the financial aspects which assist the owners or managers of a business – or other organisation – in the planning and budgeting process. The topics include:

- management accounting – including fixed and variable costs
- overhead costs – allocation, apportionment and absorption
- standard costing – including variance analysis
- budgets – planning and control
- financial planning – the Business Plan
- investment appraisal techniques

In each case we will demonstrate the importance of these topics in the provision of financial information to owners/managers so that correct decisions can be made.

18 Management accounting

introduction

Management accounting can be defined as:

the presentation of accounting information in such a way as to assist management in the formation of policies and in the day-to-day planning and control of an undertaking.

It is concerned, therefore, with providing the management of an organisation with recommendations, based on accounting information, in order to help in making day-to-day decisions and in longer-term planning. This is different from much of what has been studied so far in Finance, which has been concerned with financial transactions and statements that have *already taken place*. Management accounting uses information from past transactions as an aid to making decisions for the future.

Management accounting needs certain basic information from which to work. It needs to know accurate costs of individual products or services, together with the total costs of running the organisation: such information is found from the costing records. Nowadays the use of costing information to make decisions is assuming increasing importance as businesses seek to maximise profits and public sector organisations are required to provide the best services at lowest cost. To this end, many businesses have specialist costing sections and employ cost clerks. Here the information required is gathered together so that it is available to help in the decision-making process of management accounting.

In this chapter we will look at a number of specific areas related to *how much* it will cost to produce an item, and calculating whether it is *worth* doing so. In particular we will consider:

- the elements of cost
- the manufacturing account
- fixed and variable costs
- break-even calculations
- marginal costing and absorption costing

Case Study: S & T Manufacturing Co

Situation

The following information is given for S & T Manufacturing Co, a two-product (S and T) company, for the year 19-1:

			£	£
Sales:	S			100,000
	T			200,000
				300,000
Less:	Cost of materials:	S	50,000	
		T	95,000	
	Labour costs:	S	40,000	
		T	50,000	
	*Cost of overheads:	S	20,000	
		T	30,000	
				285,000
Profit				15,000

* Overheads include factory rent, depreciation of machinery, and other factory costs.

Try presenting this information in a way which will be of more use to the management of this business. What conclusions do you draw for this business?

Solution

The information is best presented in a way which analyses the profit of each product:

	S £	T £	Total £
Cost of materials	50,000	95,000	145,000
Labour costs	40,000	50,000	90,000
Cost of overheads	20,000	30,000	50,000
Cost of Goods Sold	110,000	175,000	285,000
Sales	100,000	200,000	300,000
Less Cost of Goods Sold	110,000	175,000	285,000
Profit/(Loss)	(10,000)	25,000	15,000

On the basis of this information, product S should be discontinued because it is making a loss. However, this may be a simplistic solution, and other factors will have to be considered, eg sales of product T may be linked to sales of product S; the overheads of T are likely to increase if S is discontinued.

elements of cost

For a manufacturing business, there are three main elements of cost:

- **direct (or raw) materials,** ie those materials that go to make up the finished product

- **direct labour,** ie the cost of the workforce engaged in production (note that the wages of those who supervise the production workers are an overhead, not a direct cost, and are often described as 'indirect labour')

- **factory overheads,** ie all other costs of manufacture, eg wages of supervisors, rent of factory, depreciation of factory machinery, heating and lighting of factory

The total of these three costs gives a manufacturing cost and it would be usual to present the costs, at the end of a financial year, in the form of a manufacturing account.

manufacturing account

The layout of a manufacturing and trading account (with sample figures) is as follows:

MANUFACTURING AND TRADING ACCOUNTS OF ACE MANUFACTURING CO
FOR THE YEAR ENDED 31 DECEMBER 19-1

	£	£
Opening stock of raw materials		5,000
Add Purchase of raw materials		50,000
		55,000
Less Closing stock of raw materials		6,000
COST OF RAW MATERIALS USED		49,000
Direct labour		27,000
PRIME COST		76,000
FACTORY OVERHEADS		
Rent of factory	5,000	
Indirect labour	18,000	
Depreciation of factory machinery	10,000	
Factory light and heat	4,000	
		37,000
		113,000
Add Opening stock of work-in-progress		4,000
		117,000
Less Closing stock of work-in-progress		3,000
MANUFACTURING COST OF GOODS COMPLETED		114,000
Sales		195,000
Opening stock of finished goods	8,000	
Manufacturing cost of goods completed	114,000	
	122,000	
Less Closing stock of finished goods	7,000	
COST OF GOODS SOLD		115,000
Gross Profit		80,000

Points to note:

- The total of raw materials and direct labour is known as *prime cost,* ie the basic cost of the product before factory overheads are added.

- *Manufacturing cost* is simply the total of the costs for the accounting period.

- A manufacturing account forms one part of the year-end financial statements for a manufacturing business, and precedes the trading account. The latter is prepared in the usual way except that manufacturing cost takes the place of purchases; also, for the trading account, the opening and closing stocks are the *finished goods* held by a business.

- Manufacturing businesses usually hold stocks of goods in three different forms:

  - *raw materials:* commodities and components purchased from suppliers required in manufacturing the finished product

  - *work-in-progress:* products in course of manufacture at a particular moment in time

  - *finished goods:* products on which the manufacturing process has been completed and which are ready for sale

  Note that, with raw materials, there may be the cost of *carriage in* to be added, and an amount for *purchases returns* to be deducted.

  Raw materials and work-in-progress appear in the manufacturing account, while finished goods stock is in the trading account. The closing stock valuation of *all three* form the year-end stocks to be shown in the balance sheet.

- Certain expenses might be allocated between the manufacturing account and profit and loss account – for example, business rates might be allocated two-thirds to the factory and one-third to the office.

unit cost of goods manufactured

When the manufacturing cost has been ascertained, the unit cost can be calculated as follows:

Unit cost = Manufacturing cost of goods completed
          Number of units completed

For example, if the manufacturing account on page 192 represented production of 200,000 units, the unit cost for the year was:

Unit cost = £114,000 = £0.57 per unit
          200,000

Businesses have many different costs: for example, the costs shown in a manufacturing account usually include raw materials, labour (direct and indirect), factory rent, depreciation of factory machinery, etc. What would be the effect on such costs if production was, for example, doubled? Would total manufacturing costs also double? The answer is that they would not: total costs would increase, with certain costs increasing proportionately to the increase in production, while others will remain unchanged. This is because certain costs are *variable* with changes in the level of production, while others are *fixed* and are not affected, in the short-term at least, with production changes.

fixed and variable costs

The two main variable costs for a manufacturing business are raw materials and direct labour. With both of these, as production increases so more of each will be needed in direct proportion to the increase. In practice such increases may not be quite so direct, eg the purchase of raw materials in larger quantities may enable the manufacturer to obtain discounts in bulk. Also, we usually regard direct labour as varying with production: where payment is made on a piecework basis, ie each production worker is paid a certain amount for each unit made, this will be true; however, piecework is not common nowadays – most production workers are paid a basic wage, plus a production bonus which varies with overall output. Despite this, there is a close relationship between goods produced and the costs of direct labour.

All costs for any organisation can, therefore, be categorised as *fixed* or *variable*. Fixed costs remain constant despite other changes; variable costs alter with changed circumstances, such as increases in production or sales. However, these 'rules' are only true within certain, restricted limits; for example, a rapidly expanding business must eventually reach the point at which more premises are needed, and then rent, and other costs, will increase. In the short term, though, it is correct to classify costs between those that are fixed and those that are variable.

break-even point

A knowledge of fixed and variable costs is important when calculating the *break-even point* of a business.

Break-even is the point at which neither a profit nor a loss is made.

Case Study: break-even

Situation

A business manufactures soft toys, and is able to sell all that can be produced. The variable costs (materials and direct labour) for producing each toy are £10 and the selling price is £20 each. The fixed costs of running the business are £5,000 *per month*. How many toys need to be produced and sold each month for the business to break-even?

Solution

This problem can be solved by calculation, by constructing a table, or by means of a graph.

❑ calculation

Selling price per unit	£20
Less variable costs per unit	£10
Contribution per unit	£10

Each toy sold gives a *contribution* (selling price, less variable costs) of £10. This contributes towards the fixed costs and, in order to break-even, the business must have sufficient £10 'lots' to meet the fixed costs. Thus, with fixed costs of £5,000 per month, this business must sell £5,000 ÷ £10 = 500 toys each month. The break-even formula is:

$$\frac{\text{Total fixed costs (£)}}{\text{Contribution per unit (£)}} = \text{Break-even point (number of units)}$$

❑ Table

Units of production	Variable costs	Fixed cost	Total cost	Revenue	Profit/(loss)
	£	£	£	£	£
100	1,000	5,000	6,000	2,000	(4,000)
200	2,000	5,000	7,000	4,000	(3,000)
300	3,000	5,000	8,000	6,000	(2 000)
400	4,000	5,000	9,000	8,000	(1,000)
500	5,000	5,000	10,000	10,000	nil
600	6,000	5,000	11,000	12,000	1,000
700	7,000	5,000	12,000	14,000	2,000

❑ Graph

A graphical presentation uses money amounts as the common denominator between fixed costs, variable costs, and sales revenue. The graph appears as follows:

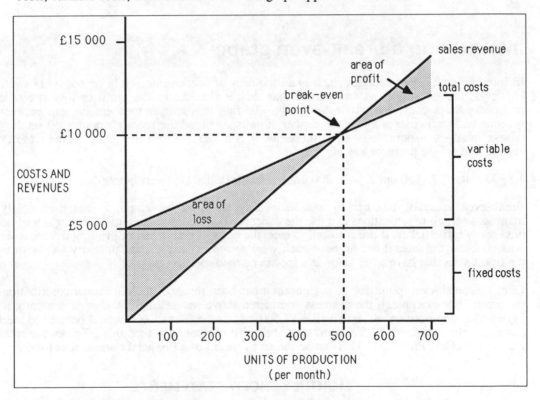

Notes:

- With a break-even graph, it is usual for the vertical axis (the 'y' axis) to show money amounts; the horizontal axis ('x') shows units of production/sales.

- The fixed costs are unchanged at all levels of production, in this case they are £5,000.

- The variable costs commence, on the 'y' axis, *from the fixed costs amount,* not from 'zero'. This is because the cost of producing zero units is the fixed cost.

- The fixed costs *and* the variable costs form a *total costs line.*

- The point at which the total costs and sales revenue lines cross is the break-even point.

hints for drawing a break-even graph

- In an accountant's break-even chart *all lines are straight*. This means that only two points need be plotted for each line; for example, with sales, choose a number that is fairly near to the maximum expected, multiply by selling price per unit, and this is the point to be marked on the graph. As the sales line always passes through zero, you now have two points along which to draw a straight line.

- When drawing a break-even graph it is often difficult to know what total value to show on each axis, ie how many units, and/or how much in costs and revenues? As a guide, look for a maximum production or sales level that will not be exceeded: this will give the 'x' axis. Multiply the maximum sales, if known, by the unit selling price to give the maximum sales revenue for the 'y' axis. If the figure for maximum sales is not known, it is recommended that the break-even point is calculated before drawing the graph so that the extent of the graph will be known.

- A common error is to start the variable costs from the zero point instead of the fixed costs line.

interpreting a break-even graph

In interpreting a break-even graph, it is all too easy to concentrate solely on the break-even point. However, the graph tells us much more than this: it also shows the profit or loss at any level of production/sales contained within the graph. To find this, simple measure the gap between sales revenue and total costs at a chosen number of units, and read the money amounts off on the 'y' axis (above break-even point it is a profit; below, it is a loss). From the graph in the Case Problem above, read off the profit or loss at:

1. 700 units,   2. 650 units,   3. 200 units,   4. 400 units (answers below).

Break-even analysis, whether by calculation, by table, or by graph, is not used solely by a manufacturer: all organisations can use the concept. For example, a youth club might wish to know how many raffle tickets it needs to sell to meet the costs of prizes and of printing tickets; a shop will wish to know the sales it has to make each week to meet costs; a local authority will wish to know the ticket sales that have to be made at a sports centre to meet costs.

Once the break-even point for an organisation has been reached, the *additional* contributions form the profit. For example, if the business considered above was selling 750 toys each month, it would have a total contribution of 750 x £10 = £7,500; of this the first £5,000 would be used to meet fixed costs, and the remaining £2,500 represents the profit (we can also read this off from the break-even graph in the Case Problem). This can be shown by means of a financial statement as follows:

MONTHLY PROFIT STATEMENT

	£
Sales (750 toys at £20 each)	15,000
Less variable costs (750 toys at £10 each)	7,500
Contribution (to fixed costs and profit)	7,500
Less monthly fixed costs	5,000
Profit for month	2,500

Answers: 1. £2,000 profit,   2. £1,500 profit,   3. £3,000 loss,   4. £1,000 loss

limitations of a break-even graph

The problem of break-even analysis is that it assumes that the relationship between sales revenue, variable costs and fixed costs, remains the same at all levels of production. This is a rather simplistic view because, for example, in order to increase sales, a business will often need to offer bulk discounts, so reducing the sales revenue per unit at higher levels. The limitations of a break-even graph (and also break-even calculations) can be summarised as follows:

(a) All costs and revenues are expressed in terms of straight lines. However, this is relationship is not always so. As indicated above selling prices may vary at different quantities sold; in a similar way, variable costs alter at different levels as a business takes advantage of lower prices to be gained from bulk buying, and/or more efficient production methods.

(b) Fixed costs do not remain fixed at all levels of production: for example, a decision to double production is likely to increase the fixed costs.

(c) It is not possible to *extrapolate* the graph; by extrapolation is meant extending the lines on the graph beyond the limits of the activity on which the graph is based. For example, in the Case Study just considered, the graph cannot be extended to, say, 1,000 units of production and the profit read off at this point. The relationship between sales revenues and costs will be different at much higher levels of production.

(d) The profit or loss shown by the graph or calculations is probably only true for figures close to current production levels – the further away from current figures, the less accurate will be the profit or loss shown.

(e) A further disadvantage of break-even analysis is that it concentrates too much attention on the break-even point. While this aspect is important to a business, other considerations such as ensuring that production is as efficient as possible, and that costs are kept under review, are just as important.

break-even: margin of safety

The margin of safety is the amount by which sales exceed the break-even point. For example, in the Case Study, current production was 750 units, while the break-even point was found to be 500 units. Thus the margin of safety is 250 units, or expressed as a percentage:

$$\frac{\text{Production beyond break-even point}}{\text{Units to break-even}} = \frac{250}{500} = 50\% \text{ margin of safety}$$

marginal costing and absorption costing

Marginal costing and absorption costing are used in cost accounting as an aid to management decision-making:

* **marginal cost** *is the cost of producing one extra unit and will, generally, comprise the variable costs of production*

  Marginal costing recognises that fixed costs vary with time rather than activity, and attempts to identify the cost of producing one extra unit. For example, the rent of a factory relates to a certain time period, eg one month, and remains unchanged whether 100 units are made or whether 500 units are made (always assuming that the capacity of the factory is at least 500 units); by contrast, the production of one extra unit will incur an increase in variable costs, ie direct materials and direct labour – this increase is the *marginal cost*.

- **absorption cost** is the total cost divided by the number of units produced

Absorption costing absorbs all costs – both direct and indirect – into each unit of production. Thus each unit produced in the factory making 100 units will bear a greater proportion of the factory rent than will each unit when 500 units are made in the same time period.

Case Study: Wyvern Bicycle Co

Situation

The following monthly figures have been extracted by the cost accountant of the Wyvern Bicycle Co:

Monthly manufacturing costs for producing 100 bicycles

	£
Direct materials (£20 per bicycle)	2,000
Direct labour (£25 per bicycle)	2,500
	4,500
Factory overheads	3,500
Total factory cost of producing 100 bicycles	8,000

The selling price to retailers is £100 per bicycle.

(a)   What is the factory cost of producing one bicycle?

(b)   A major retail store offers to buy

either   (1)   50 bicycles each month at a price of £60,

or   (2)   100 bicycles each month at a price of £40.

How would you advise the management? (It is to be assumed that these sales will be produced in addition to existing production, with no increase in fixed costs.)

Solution

(a)   The factory cost is:

Absorption cost basis: £8,000 ÷ 100 units = £80 per bicycle

Marginal cost basis: £20 (direct materials) + £25 (direct labour) = £45 per bicycle

(b) 1 Although below absorption cost, the offer is above marginal cost and increases profits by the extra contribution brought in, ie (£60 - £45) x 50 bicycles = £750 extra profit.

   2 This is below absorption cost and below marginal cost; therefore, there will be a fall in profit if this order is undertaken of (£45 - £40) x 100 bicycles = £500 fall in profit.

Summary profit statements are as follows:

	Existing production	Existing production + 50 units @ £60 each	Existing production + 100 units @ £40 each
	£	£	£
Sales revenue (per month):			
100 bicycles at £100 each	10,000	10,000	10,000
50 bicycles at £60 each	–	3,000	–
100 bicycles at £40 each	–	–	4,000
	10,000	13,000	14,000
Less production costs:			
Direct materials (£20 per unit)	2,000	3,000	4,000
Direct labour (£25 per unit)	2,500	3,750	5,000
Fixed factory overheads	3,500	3,500	3,500
GROSS PROFIT	2,000	2,750	1,500

The conclusion is that the first special order should be undertaken, and the second declined.

The general rule is that, once the fixed costs have been recovered, provided additional units can be sold at a price above marginal cost, then profits will increase.

Chapter Summary

❑ Management accounting helps with decision-making in a business by looking at what has gone on in the past and using the information to estimate future costs.

❑ For a manufacturing business, the three main elements of cost are raw materials, direct labour, and factory overheads. The three costs are shown in a manufacturing account which precedes a trading account in the year-end financial statements.

❑ Most manufacturing costs are either fixed or variable, and the relationship between the two can be used to calculate, tabulate, or show by means of a graph, the break-even point.

❑ Marginal and absorption costing help a business with decision-making when faced with orders at 'special prices'.

Another aspect of management accounting is to ensure that factory overheads are charged to production; this is considered in the next chapter – Chapter 19 'Overhead Costs'.

Student Activities

18.1   Which of the following costs are variable, and which are fixed?

- Raw materials
- Factory rent
- Depreciation on factory machinery
- Direct labour, eg production workers paid on a piecework basis
- Indirect labour, eg supervisors' salaries
- Commission paid to sales staff

Taking the costs in turn, explain to Louise Smith, who is about to set up a furniture manufacturing business, why you have classified each as either fixed or variable. Answer her comment, "What difference does it make anyway, they are all costs that have to be paid".

18.2   D. Bradman, a manufacturer of cricket bats, has the following *monthly* costs:

	£
Material cost	8 per bat
Labour cost	12 per bat
Selling price	35 per bat
Fixed expenses	£12,000

You are to:
- Draw up a schedule showing costs, revenue and profit or loss for production of bats in multiples of 100 up to 1,200.
- Draw a graph showing the break-even point.
- Prove your answer by calculation.
- Read off the graph the profit or loss if (a) 200 bats, and (b) 1,200 bats are sold each month: prove the answer by calculation.

Sales are currently 1,000 bats each month. Supermail, a mail-order company has approached the manufacturer with a view to buying:

either   200 bats each month at a price of £25 each,

or   500 bats each month at a price of £18 each.

You are to evaluate this order by means of a manufacturing cost statement and advise which order, if either, should be accepted. For both orders the extra production can be carried out within the existing factory.

18.3   Bert Peters is the owner of a petrol filling station which has the following *weekly* costs:

Cost of petrol (including tax) from oil company	50p per litre
Selling price	55p per litre
Fixed expenses	£750

You are the accountant of the business and are asked to:
- Draw a schedule showing costs, revenue and profit or loss for sale of petrol in multiples of 1,000 litres up to 20,000 litres.
- Draw a graph showing the break-even point.
- Prove your answer by calculation.
- Read off the graph the profit or loss if (a) 12,000 litres, and (b) 18,000 litres are sold each week: prove the answer by calculation.

Sales are currently 20,000 litres each week and the filling station is open from 7 am until 11 pm. The owner is considering changing the hours to 8 am until 10 pm. He has estimated that, by doing this, fixed expenses can be reduced to £650 per week, but sales will fall to 18,500 litres.

You are asked to evaluate this proposal by means of financial statements and advise the owner of the decision he should take.

18.4 From the following figures relating to Crown Heath Woodcrafts you, as the accountant, are to prepare manufacturing and trading accounts for the year-ended 31 December 19-8 to show clearly:

- cost of raw materials used
- prime cost
- manufacturing cost
- cost of goods sold
- gross profit

	£
Stocks at 1 January 19-8	
Raw materials	10,500
Finished goods	4,300
Stocks at 31 December 19-8	
Raw materials	10,200
Finished goods	3,200
Expenditure during year:	
Purchases of raw materials	27,200
Factory wages - direct	12,600
Factory wages - indirect	3,900
Factory rent and rates	1,200
Factory power	2,000
Depreciation of factory machinery	900
Repairs to factory buildings	300
Sundry factory expenses	900
Sales during year	60,400

18.5 The following figures relate to the accounts of Barbara Francis, who operates a furniture manufacturing business, for the year ended 31 December 19-3:

	£
Stocks of raw materials, 1 January 19-3	31,860
Stocks of raw materials, 31 December 19-3	44,790
Stocks of finished goods, 1 January 19-3	42,640
Stocks of finished goods, 31 December 19-3	96,510
Purchases of raw materials	237,660
Sale of finished goods	796,950
Rent and rates	32,920
Manufacturing wages	234,630
Manufacturing power	7,650
Manufacturing heat and light	2,370
Manufacturing expenses and maintenance	8,190
Salaries	138,700
Advertising	22,170
Office expenses	7,860
Depreciation of plant and machinery	7,450

Three-quarters of the rent and rates are to be treated as a manufacturing charge.

As Miss Francis' accountant, you are to prepare manufacturing, trading and profit and loss accounts for the year-ended 31 December 19-3, to show clearly:

- the cost of raw materials used,
- prime cost,
- cost of factory overheads,
- manufacturing cost of goods completed,
- cost of goods sold,
- gross profit for the year,
- net profit for the year.

Explain, by memorandum, to Miss Francis why you have presented the accounts in such a form, and what they show.

19 Overhead costs

introduction

In the previous chapter, we saw that the three elements of cost are direct materials, direct labour, and overheads. The first two of these – direct materials and direct labour – can be charged directly to the product in which they are involved, eg the materials used for making product 'A' are charged directly in the costing to that product. However, overheads cannot be charged directly to particular units of production but must, instead, be shared between all units to which they relate.

In this chapter we shall look at ways in which overheads are charged to production, and some of the problems that may occur. Firstly though, there are two costing terms to define: *cost units* and *cost centres*.

cost units

Cost units are units of production to which costs can be charged .

Thus a cost unit can be a *unit of production,* such as a car, an item of furniture, a television, etc, or it can be a *unit of service,* such as a passenger-mile on a bus, a transaction on a bank statement, an attendance at a swimming pool, an operation in a hospital, etc.

cost centres

Cost centres are sections of a business to which costs can be charged.

In manufacturing business a cost centre is a particular department of a factory, even a whole factory, or a particular stage in the production process. In hospitals, a ward or a unit is a cost centre, while in a college, a department is a cost centre.

a classification of overheads

With overheads the important point to remember is that all the overheads of a business, together with the direct costs of materials and labour, must be covered by money flowing in from sales made. For example, a business makes a product which sells for £20 per unit, and the cost of direct materials is £5 and direct labour is £6.50. Taking the cost of direct materials and direct labour from the selling price gives:

£20 – (£5 + £6.50) = £8.50

The £8.50 from each unit sold is a *contribution* to cover the overheads and provide a profit for the owner(s) of the business. In other words, sufficient units have to be sold to produce a total contribution to meet the total overheads of the business and to contribute to the profits of the business. We have already looked at this concept of contribution in the previous chapter, where it was used to help in calculating the break-even point of a business.

Overheads are usually classified *by function* under headings such as:

* *factory or production,* eg factory rent and rates, indirect labour, indirect materials, heating and lighting of factory
* *selling and distribution,* eg sales reps' salaries, packing costs, vehicle costs
* *administration,* eg office rent and rates, office salaries, heating and lighting of office
* *finance,* eg bank interest, discount allowed

In order to determine how much has been spent on overheads, it will be necessary to use the financial accounting records: for example, the expenses accounts will show the amount for rent, rates, salaries, wages, heating, lighting, vehicle costs, etc. Some figures, such as those for wages, and for purchases, will need to be analysed to see which part of the total cost is a direct expense (to be charged directly to the appropriate cost units), and which is the indirect expense (to be charged to overheads).

Once the various overheads have been classified, they are then either *allocated* or *apportioned* to cost centres.

allocation of overheads

Allocation of overheads is the charging to a cost centre of those overheads that have been directly incurred by that cost centre.

For example, in a large organisation a whole factory might be a cost centre and so the rent and rates of that factory will be allocated to it as a separate cost centre. Another example would be where a department is the cost centre; here the costs of a supervisor working solely within one department would be allocated to that department.

apportionment of overheads

Apportionment is where cost centres are charged with a proportion of overheads.

For example, a department which is a cost centre within a factory will be charged a proportion of the factory rent and rates. Another example is where a supervisor works within two departments, both of which are separate cost centres: the indirect labour cost of employing the supervisor will be charged between the two cost centres. With apportionment, a suitable basis must be found to apportion overheads between cost centres. Different methods might be used for each overhead.

Case Study: Laser Engineering

Situation

A friend of yours, Natalie Wood, has recently established a 'hi-tech' engineering business which uses some of the latest laser equipment in one department, while another section of the business continues to use traditional machinery.   You have been helping her with various aspects of the business and she now asks you which overheads of the business should be allocated or apportioned. Details of the factory are as follows:

Department A is a 'hi-tech' machine shop equipped with machinery which has cost £40,000.   This department has 200 square metres of floor area.   There are three machine operators supervised by the foreman who spends one-third of his time in this department.

Department B is a 'low-tech' part of the factory equipped with machinery which has cost £10,000. The floor area is 300 square metres. There are two workers who spend all their time in this department, supervised by the foreman for two-thirds of his time.

The overheads to be allocated or apportioned are as follows:

1.   Factory rates, £12,000
2.   Wages of the foreman, £15,000
3.   Factory heating and lighting, £2,500
4.   Depreciation of machinery, £10,000
5.   Buildings insurance, £2,000
6.   Insurance of machinery, £1,500
7.   Specialist materials for cleaning the laser equipment, £2,500

How would you suggest each of these should be allocated or apportioned to each department?

Solution

The recommendations are:

1.   Factory rates – apportioned on the basis of floor area, ie 40% to Department A, and 60% to Department B.
2.   Foreman's wages – apportioned on the basis of time spent, ie one-third to Department A, and two-thirds to Department B. If the time spent was not known, a suitable basis would be the number of employees.
3.   Factory heating and lighting – apportioned on the basis of floor area.
4.   Depreciation of machinery – apportioned on the basis of machine value,
      ie four-fifths to Department A, and one-fifth to Department B.
5.   Buildings insurance – apportioned on the basis of floor area.
6.   Insurance of machinery – apportioned on the basis of machine value.
7.   Specialist materials for cleaning the laser equipment – allocated to Department A, the cost centre which directly incurred the cost.

It is important to note that there are no fixed rules for the apportionment of overheads – the only proviso is that the basis used should be equitable, ie that a fair proportion of the overhead is charged to the department.

The apportionment for Laser Engineering would take place as follows:

Cost	Basis of apportionment	Total £	Dept A £	Dept B £
Factory rates	Floor area	12,000	4,800	7,200
Wages of foreman	Time spent	15,000	5,000	10,000
Heating and lighting	Floor area	2,500	1,000	1,500
Machinery depreciation	Machine value	10,000	8,000	2,000
Buildings insurance	Floor area	2,000	800	1,200
Machinery insurance	Machine value	1,500	1,200	300
Specialist materials	Allocation	2,500	2,500	-
		45,500	23,300	22,200

service departments

Many factories have service departments, such as stores, maintenance, transport, etc. Each service department is likely to be a cost centre, to which a proportion of overheads is charged. As service departments do not themselves have any cost units to which their overheads may be charged, the costs of each service department must be *re-allocated* to the production departments (which do have cost units to which overheads can be charged). A suitable basis of re-allocation must be used; for example, the overheads of a maintenance department might be reallocated to production departments on the basis of value of machinery, or on the basis of time spent in each production department; the overheads of a stores department might be reallocated on the basis of value of stores issued to production departments. Fig. 19.1 summarises the ways in which production overheads are allocated or apportioned to production cost centres.

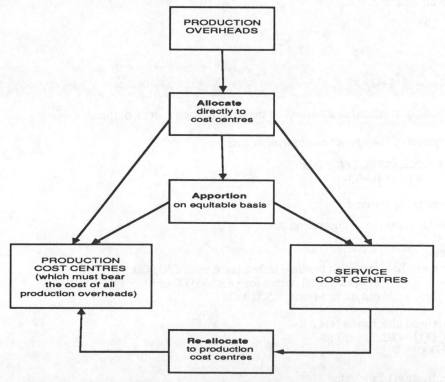

Fig. 19.1 Allocation and apportionment of production overheads

overhead absorption

Once overheads have been allocated or apportioned to production cost centres, the final step is to ensure that the overheads are changed to cost units. In the language of cost accounting this is known as *absorption* ie the cost of overheads is charged to cost units which pass through that particular production department.

There are plenty of examples of overhead recovery in everyday life – it is not something used solely by large factories. For example, if you take a car to be repaired at a garage, the bill will be presented as follows:

Parts	£35.50
Labour: 3 hours at £15 per hour	£45.00
Total	£80.50

Within this example bill are the three main elements of cost: materials (parts), labour and overheads. The last two are combined as labour – the garage mechanic is not paid £15 per hour; instead the labour rate might be £6 per hour, with the rest, ie £9 per hour, being a contribution towards the overheads of the garage. Other examples are accountants, solicitors, etc who charge a 'rate per hour', part of which is used to contribute to the cost of overheads.

In order to absorb the overheads of a department, there are two steps to be followed:
1. Calculation of the overhead absorption rate.
2. Application of this rate to cost units.

Although there are a variety of methods available to a business, three commonly used overhead absorption methods are:
- units of output
- direct labour hour
- machine hour

units of output

Using this method overhead is absorbed on the basis of each unit of output.

1. *Calculation of the overhead absorption rate:*

$$\frac{\text{total cost centre overheads}}{\text{total cost units}}$$

2. *Application of the rate:*

   cost units x overhead absorption rate

   example
   Department X: total cost centre overheads for year, £50,000
   expected total output for year, 20,000 units
   output in March, 1,500 units

   1. Overhead absorption rate:
      $$\frac{£50,000}{20,000} = £2.50 \text{ per unit}$$

   2. Application of the rate:
      1,500 x £2.50 = £3,750 of overhead absorbed in March

direct labour hour

With this method, overhead is absorbed on the basis of the number of direct labour hours worked.

1. *Calculation of the overhead absorption rate:*

$$\frac{\text{total cost centre overheads}}{\text{total direct labour hours (in cost centre)}}$$

2. *Application of the rate:*

direct labour hours worked   x   overhead absorption rate

example

Department Y: total cost centre overheads for year, £20,000
                        expected direct labour for year, 5,000
                        actual direct labour hours in March, 450

1. Overhead absorption rate:
$\frac{£20,000}{5,000}$ = £4 per direct labour hour

2. Application of the rate:
450 hours x £4 = £1,800 of overhead absorbed in March

machine hour

Here the overhead is absorbed on the basis of machine hours.

1. *Calculation of the overhead absorption rate:*

$$\frac{\text{total cost centre overheads}}{\text{total machine hours (in cost centre)}}$$

2. *Application of the Rate:*

machine hours x overhead absorption rate

example

Department Z: total cost centre overheads for year, £108,000
                        expected machine hours for year, 36,000
                        actual machine hours in March, 3,500

1. Overhead absorption rate:
$\frac{£108,000}{36,000}$ = £3 per machine hour

2. Application of the rate:
3,500 hours x £3 = £10,500 of overhead absorbed in March

which method to use?

Only one overhead absorption rate will be used in a particular cost centre and management must choose the method that suits their particular business.

Where units of production are identical, eg in mass production factories, the units of output method is appropriate. However, it would be entirely unsuitable where different types and sizes of products pass through the same department, because each unit would be charged the same rate.

The direct labour hour method is a very popular method (eg the garage mentioned earlier) because overheads are absorbed on a time basis. Thus the cost unit that requires twice the direct labour of another cost unit will be charged twice the overhead. However this method will be inappropriate where some units are worked on by hand while others quickly pass through a machinery process and require little direct labour time.

A machine hour rate is particularly appropriate where expensive machinery is used in the department. However, it would not be a suitable method where not all products pass through the machine but some are worked on by hand: in the latter case, no overheads would be charged to the cost units.

pre-determined overhead rates

Overhead absorption rates are *set in advance* by making forecasts of production and costs. The making of forecasts is known as *budgeting,* and this topic is discussed fully in Chapter 21.

It is quite likely that actual overhead absorbed will be different from the estimates made at the beginning of the year. Thus overhead will either be *under-absorbed,* or *over-absorbed;* under-absorption means that less overhead has been recovered than has been incurred; over-absorption means that more overhead has been recovered than incurred.

example

Department W: overhead absorption rate (based on units of output): £2.50 per unit
        expected total output for year: 20,000 units
        actual output in year: 21,000 units

- Total overheads for the department are 20,000 units x £2.50 per unit = £50,000

- Actual overhead absorbed: 21,000 units x £2.50 per unit = £52,500

- Over-absorption of overhead: £52,500 - £50,000 = £2,500

The management of a business will constantly monitor actual production and will seek reasons for variances between this and budgeted production. While over-absorption of overheads, on first impressions, seems to be a 'bonus' for a business – profits will be higher – it should also be remembered that the overhead rate has been set too high. As a consequence, sales might have been lost because the selling price has been too high.

Chapter Summary

❏ Cost units are units of production to which costs can be charged.

❏ Cost centres are sections of a business to which costs can be charged.

❏ Direct costs, such as materials and labour, are charged directly to cost units.

❏ Overheads are allocated to cost centres that have directly incurred the overhead.

❏ Overheads are apportioned between cost centres, using an equitable basis.

❏ Cost centre overheads are charged to cost units by methods which include units of output, direct labour hour and machine hour.

❏ The objective of overhead absorption is to ensure that overheads are recovered by the cost units which pass through the cost centre.

❏ With pre-determined overhead rates, there may be either under-absorption or over-absorption of overheads.

The next chapter looks at ways in which costs can be established at the beginning of a manufacturing process by means of standard costs. It also analyses the variances that might occur between the standard cost and the actual cost.

 Student Activities

19.1 ABC Ltd. is a manufacturing business with three cost centres: Departments A, B and C. The following are the expected factory expenses for next year:

Rent and rates	£7,210
Depreciation of machinery	£10,800
Foreman's salary	£12,750
Insurance of machinery	£750

Departmental information is:

	Dept A	Dept B	Dept C
Floor area (sq. m)	300	150	250
Value of machinery	£25,000	£15,000	£10,000
Number of production-line employees	8	4	3

You are to:

(a) Apportion the expenses to the cost centres, stating the basis of apportionment.

(b) The factory works a 37 hour week for 48 weeks in a year. What is the overhead absorption rate (to two decimal places) of each department, based on direct labour hours?

19.2 Messrs. Rossiter and Rossiter is a firm of chartered accountants, with two partners. Overhead costs for next year are estimated to be:

Office rent	£5,000
Secretarial salaries	£15,000
Rates	£2,400
Heating and lighting	£1,200
Stationery	£1,000
Postages and telephone	£2,550
Car expenses	£2,800

The two partners plan to work for 47 weeks next year. They will each be in the office for 40 hours per week, but will be working on behalf of their clients for 35 hours per week.

(a) What is the overhead absorption rate per partner hour?

(b) If each partner wishes to earn a salary of £20,000 per year, what is the combined rate, which includes overheads and their salaries?

19.3 Osborne Engineering Ltd offers specialist engineering services to the car industry. It has two production departments – machinery and finishing – and a service department which maintains the machinery of both departments. Expected costs for next year are:

	£
Rent and rates	2,760
Buildings insurance	660
Insurance of machinery	825
Lighting and heating	1,860
Depreciation of machinery	5,500
Supervisory salaries	15,000
Maintenance department salary	8,000
Factory cleaning	2,400

The following information is available:

	Machinery	Finishing	Maintenance
Floor area (square metres)	300	200	100
Number of employees	6	3	1
Value of machinery	£20,000	£7,500	-

The factory works a 40-hour week for 47 weeks each year.

You are to:

(a) Prepare an analysis of overheads showing the basis of apportionment and allocation to the three departments of the business.

(b) Re-allocate the service department overheads to production departments on the basis of value of machinery.

(c) Calculate an overhead absorption rate based on direct labour hours for each of the two production departments.

19.4 Steel Forgings (Rowcester) Ltd. is a heavy engineering business making parts for the car industry. The factory works a 40 hour week and is divided into three manufacturing divisions, with each making a different type of forging. Details are as follows:

	Division 1	Division 2	Division 3
Cost of 1 tonne of raw materials	£65	£70	£75
Number of direct workers	5	4	6
Wagew rate (per hour)	£5.50	£6.00	£6.50
Labour hours required to output			
1 tonne of finished goods	8 hours	10 hours	12 hours
Power costs per tonne of finished goods	£15	£18	£14

Factory overhead	£1,500 per week (to be apportioned between divisions on the basis of number of direct workers).
Administration overhead	£1,000 per week.
Selling costs	£750 per week.

Selling prices are established by marking up the factory cost by 50%.

You are to:

(a) Calculate the gross profit per week for each division.

(b) Calculate the net profit per week for the company as a whole.

19.5 A friend of yours is about to start in business making garden seats. She plans to make two different qualities – 'standard' and 'de luxe'. Costs per unit for raw materials and direct labour are expected to be:

	'Standard'	*'De Luxe'*
Direct materials	£12.50	£20.00
Direct labour:		
6 hours at £4.00 per hour	£24.00	–
7 hours at £5.00 per hour	–	£35.00
	£36.50	£55.00
Machine hours	2	5

Factory overheads are expected to be £1,000 per month.
Production (per month) is expected to be 80 'standard' seats and 40 'de luxe' seats.

You are to:

(a) Suggest three different methods in which overheads can be absorbed.

(b) Calculate the factory cost of each of the two qualities of garden seats using the three different methods of overhead absorption.

(c) Compare the results of your calculations and suggest to your friend the most appropriate method of overhead absorption for this business.

20 Standard costing and variance analysis

introduction

All businesses need methods of controlling the costs of materials, labour and overheads that go to make up the finished product. Imagine a car factory where the cost and amount of the materials to make the car is not known; where the hours of work and the rates of pay are not known; where the cost of the overheads is not known. Under such circumstances, the costs could not be controlled, and it would also be impossible to quote a price for the product to a customer. Manufacturing firms usually establish a *standard cost* for their 'production line' products.

In this chapter we look at the calculation of *standard cost*. We also analyse how actual cost varies from standard cost, a process known as *variance analysis*.

standard cost

A standard cost is a pre-determined cost, based on expected effective working conditions, in the period ahead, of materials, labour and overhead costs. It can be used as a method of cost control through variance analysis, and also for establishing selling prices.

- **materials** The quantity of each material to be used in production, and the price of such materials is pre-determined. *Standard materials cost* is the expected quantity multiplied by expected material price.

- **labour** The labour hours required to manufacture a quantity of goods, and the cost of the labour is pre-determined. *Standard labour cost* is the expected labour hours multiplied by expected wage rates.

- **overheads** The expected quantity of goods produced divided into the expected overheads will determine the *standard overhead cost*.

setting standards

In standard costing, it is important that care should be taken over the setting of standards. Poorly set standards will be worse than useless to the management of a business when they come to use the figures in an analysis.

The main people within a business who can provide information to enable standards to be set are:

*   **buyers** The buying department of a business will be able to determine prices, and their future trends, of materials used.

*   **personnel** This department will have current wage rates, together with bonus and overtime details, of the various grades of worker; forecasts of changes can also be ascertained.

*   **management services** Often called *work study,* this department will determine the standard amount of time that each work-task in the manufacturing process should take.

*   **production** This department has overall responsibility for production and will know the quantities of raw materials required for each unit of production and is likely to have knowledge of overhead costs.

Case Study: DMS Engineering Limited

Situation

This company manufactures car bumpers. It has been asked by its major customer, Okasa (Japan) Ltd. to prepare a quotation for bumpers for a new car, which is code-named 'OK10'. The elements of cost for 100 bumpers have been calculated by DMS Engineering as:

Materials:	Polycarbonate (of specified quality), 200 kilos at £1.10 per kilo
	Matt black finishing material, 10 litres at £5.40 per litre
Labour:	10 hours at £5.75 per hour
	3 hours at £8.50 per hour
Overheads:	13 hours at £20 per hour

Calculate:
*   The standard cost of producing 100 bumpers.
*   If DMS Engineering Ltd. add 20% profit on to their total cost, what will be the cost of one bumper to Okasa (Japan) Ltd?

Solution

	£	£
Materials		
Polycarbonate: 200 kilos at £1.10 per kilo		220.00
Finishing material: 10 litres at £5.40 per litre		54.00
		274.00
Labour		
10 hours at £5.75	57.50	
3 hours at £8.50	25.50	
		83.00
		357.00
Overheads		
13 hours at £20 per hour		260.00
Total cost		617.00
Profit (20% of total cost)		123.40
Total selling price		740.40

Therefore one bumper costs £740.40 ÷ 100 = £7.40

variance analysis

Having established standard costs, the management of a business needs to put these to use by comparing the standards set with the costs that actually occurred. The outline of the procedure is as follows:

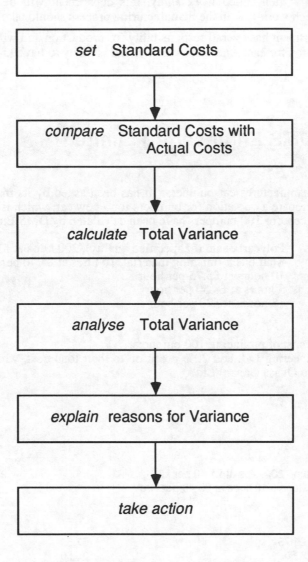

A variance can be either *favourable* or *adverse:*

- a *favourable* variance occurs when actual costs are lower than standard costs.
- an *adverse* variance is when actual costs are higher than standard costs.

The total variance can be analysed into a number of sub-variances, principally concerned with the three main elements of cost: materials, labour and overheads. These are illustrated in the diagram on the next page.

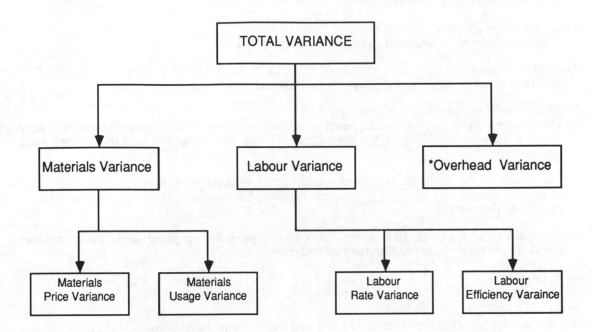

* The overhead variance can be analysed in a variety of ways – principally the distinction can be made between those overheads that are fixed and those that are variable. However, the analysis of such variances is outside the scope of a general finance textbook such as this, and it may be that your further studies of cost and management accounting will lead you to this topic.

materials variances

The variances for materials costs are:

variance
• materials variance

sub-variances
• materials price variance
• materials usage variance

The money amounts of each variance are calculated from the areas indicated in the following diagram:

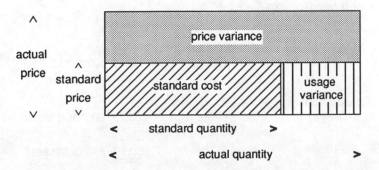

Materials price variance
    (actual price   –   standard price)   x   actual quantity

Materials usage variance
    (actual quantity   –   standard quantity) x   standard price

Materials variance
    (actual quantity x   actual price)   –   (standard quantity x standard price)

Notes from the diagram on the previous page:
- The change in the price of materials, based on the quantity actually used, forms the materials price variance – shaded � in the diagram. This variance is the responsibility of the buying department.

- The change in the actual quantity used, based on the standard price, forms the materials usage variance – shaded ⊞ in the diagram. This variance is the responsibility of the production department.

- For clarity of presentation, the diagram shows adverse price and usage variances; these variances can also be favourable, ie less than the standard cost.

example

A manufacturer of clay garden gnomes has prepared the following information:
- the standard price of clay used to make the gnomes is 50p per kilo
- the standard usage is 2 kilos per gnome

The results achieved for last month's production are:
- the actual price of clay used was 60p per kilo
- the actual usage was 1½ kilos per gnome

Here both the price and usage have differed from the standard to give the following *materials variance*:

$$(1½ \text{ kgs} \times 60p \text{ per kg}) \quad – \quad (2 \text{ kgs} \times 50p \text{ per kg}) \quad =$$
$$90p \quad\quad\quad – \quad\quad\quad £1.00 \quad\quad = £0.10 \text{ FAVOURABLE}$$

Note: A favourable variance is a negative figure, eg 90p – £1.00 = –£0.10; this means that the actual cost is *less* than the standard cost. By contrast, an adverse variance is a positive figure, ie the actual cost is *more* than the standard cost.

While the overall materials variance is favourable by £0.10, as both price *and* usage differ from standard, the sub-variances must be calculated:

Materials price variance
    (actual price   –   standard price)   x   actual quantity
    (60p   –   50p)   x   1½ kgs   = £0.15 ADVERSE

Materials usage variance
    (actual quantity – standard quantity) x standard price
    (1½ kgs   –   2 kgs)   x   50p   = £0.25 FAVOURABLE

MATERIALS VARIANCE   <u>£0.10</u> FAVOURABLE

labour variances

The variances for labour costs are:

variance
- labour variance

sub-variances
- labour rate variance
- labour efficiency variance

The money amounts of each variance are calculated from the areas indicated in the following diagram:

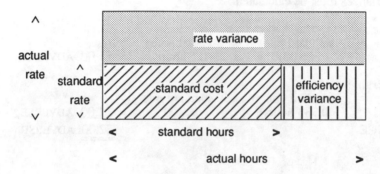

Labour rate variance
      (actual rate   –   standard rate)   x   actual hours

Labour efficiency variance
      (actual hours   –   standard hours)   x   standard rate

Labour variance
      (actual hours   x   actual rate)   –   (standard hours x standard rate)

Notes from the above diagram:
- The change in the labour rate, based on the actual hours, forms the labour rate variance – shaded   in the diagram. This variance is the responsibility of the personnel department.

- The change in the actual hours, based on the standard hours, forms the labour efficiency variance – shaded   in the diagram. This variance is the responsibility of the production department.

- For clarity of presentation, the diagram shows adverse rate and efficiency variances; these variances can also be favourable, ie less than the standard cost.

example
A manufacturer of clay garden gnomes has prepared the following information:
- the standard cost of direct labour is £6.00 per hour
- the standard efficiency is production of one gnome every 20 minutes (0.333 of an hour)

The results achieved for last month's production are:
- the actual cost of direct labour was £8.00 per hour
- the actual production was one gnome every 30 minutes (0.5 of an hour)

Here both the rate and efficiency have differed from the standard to give the following *labour variance*:

(0.5 hours x £8.00 per hour) –   (0.333 hours x £6.00 per hour) =
         £4.00   –   £2.00   = £2.00 ADVERSE

Note: The calculation gives a positive figure of £2.00; this means that the actual cost is *more* than the standard cost, ie it is adverse. By contrast, a favourable variance is a negative figure, ie the actual cost is *less* than the standard cost.

While the overall labour variance is adverse by £2.00, as both rate *and* efficiency differ from standard, the sub-variances must be calculated:

Labour rate variance
         (actual rate   –   standard rate)   x   actual hours
             (£8.00   –   £6.00)   x   0.5 hours   = £1.00 ADVERSE

Labour efficiency variance
         (actual hours   –   standard hours)   x   standard rate
             (0.5 hours   –   0.333 hours)   x   £6.00   = £1.00 ADVERSE
LABOUR VARIANCE   £2.00 ADVERSE

conclusion

Standard costs are set in order to give the individual departmental managers, responsible for aspects of the organisation's output, suitable targets to aim for. When actual costs are compared with standard costs, an analysis can be carried out to see why the variances have occurred, and to see what can be done about them for the future.

Chapter Summary

❏   Standard costs are established for the main elements of cost: materials, labour and overheads.

❏   Actual costs incurred are recorded.

❏   A comparison is made between standard costs and actual costs, and variances are calculated.

❏   Material variances are analysed into:
   • price variance: (actual price - standard price) x actual quantity
   • usage variance: (actual quantity - standard quantity) x standard price

❏   Labour variances are analysed into:
   • rate variance: (actual rate - standard rate) x actual hours
   • efficiency variance: (actual hours - standard hours) x standard rate

❏   Investigation should be made in order to find out why the variances have occurred and corrective action taken.

The next chapter looks at how standard costs can be incorporated into the budget of an organisation, the preparation of budgets, and their uses in the control of a business.

Student Activities

20.1 (a)   What is meant by the term 'standard costing'?

(b)   What are the advantages to a business in using such a costing scheme?

20.2 Calculate the materials variance for each of the following, and analyse the variance between a price variance and a usage variance. (Indicate whether each variance is *adverse* or *favourable*.)

> *Material: sheet steel*
> | | |
> |---|---|
> | Standard usage | 0.5 sq. metres |
> | Standard price | £5 per sq. metre |
> | Actual usage | 0.5 sq. metres |
> | Actual price | £6 per sq. metre |
>
> *Material: alloy*
> | | |
> |---|---|
> | Standard usage | 2 kgs |
> | Standard price | £1.50 per kg |
> | Actual usage | 2.5 kgs |
> | Actual price | £1.50 per kg |
>
> *Material: flour*
> | | |
> |---|---|
> | Standard usage | 0.5 kgs |
> | Standard price | 50p per kg |
> | Actual usage | 0.6 kgs |
> | Actual price | 40p per kg |
>
> *Material: gelling fluid*
> | | |
> |---|---|
> | Standard usage | 3 litres |
> | Standard price | £1.50 per litre |
> | Actual usage | 2.5 litres |
> | Actual price | £2 per litre |

20.3 Calculate the labour variance for each of the following, and analyse the variance between a rate variance and an efficiency variance. (Indicate whether each variance is *adverse* or *favourable*.)

> *Casting*
> | | |
> |---|---|
> | Standard hours | 5 hours |
> | Standard wage rate | £6 per hour |
> | Actual hours | 6 hours |
> | Actual wage rate | £6 per hour |
>
> *Machining*
> | | |
> |---|---|
> | Standard hours | 2 hours |
> | Standard wage rate | £6.50 per hour |
> | Actual hours | 2 hours |
> | Actual wage rate | £7.50 per hour |
>
> *Finishing*
> | | |
> |---|---|
> | Standard hours | 1 hour |
> | Standard wage rate | £6 per hour |
> | Actual hours | 1.25 hours |
> | Actual wage rate | £6.40 per hour |

Packing

Standard hours	1 hour
Standard wage rate	£4 per hour
Actual hours	0.75 hours
Actual wage rate	£3.60 per hour

20.4 From the following data you are to calculate:

    (a) materials price variance
    (b) materials usage variance
    (c) total materials variance

(Indicate whether each variance is *adverse* or *favourable*.)

	Standard Price	Standard Usage	Actual Price	Actual Usage
Material A	£5 per kg	10 kgs	£4 per kg	12 kgs
Material B	£20 per unit	12 units	£22 per unit	10 units
Material C	£10 per litre	6 litres	£9 per litre	5 litres
Material D	£2 per metre	3 metres	£3 per metre	2.5 metres

20.5 From the following data you are to calculate:

    (a) labour rate variance
    (b) labour efficiency variance
    (c) total labour variance

(Indicate whether each variance is *adverse* or *favourable*.)

	Standard Hours	Standard Wage Rate	Actual Hours	Actual Wage Rate
Job No. 1	8	£5.00	7	£5.50
Job No. 2	3	£4.50	4	£5.00
Job No. 3	24	£6.00	30	£5.75
Job No. 4	12	£8.00	15	£8.50

20.6 The cost accountant of Rowcester (Engineering) Ltd. estimates that a particular job – to produce 10 identical castings for a customer – will require the following:

> *Job No. 12345: 10 castings*
> Materials:
>   55 kgs of ordinary steel at £3.50 per kg.
>   20 kgs of high-tensile steel at £10.00 per kg.
>
> Labour:
>   10 hours foundry-workers' wages at £6.00 per hour
>   25 hours in the machine shop at £7.50 per hour
>
> Overheads:
>   £225.00

When the job is finished, it is found that actual results were:

Materials:
  60 kgs of ordinary steel at £3.00 per kg.
  22 kgs of high-tensile steel at £12.00 per kg.

Labour:
  12 hours foundry-workers' wages at £6.50 per hour.
  22 hours in the machine shop at £7.25 per hour.

Overheads:
  £225.00

Tasks

(a) You are to prepare a statement which shows:
  1. the standard cost of the job
  2. the actual cost of the job
  3. the variances from standard, analysed between the sub-variances

(b) 1. Based on the standard cost, a price was quoted to the customer which gave Rowcester (Engineering) Ltd a profit of £255. What will be the actual profit earned?

  2. To what use will the cost accountant put the actual cost of the job calculated in (a) above?

20.7 Eveshore Packaging Ltd. make cartons for the food industry. A job that has just come in is to make 10,000 cartons for fruit juices. The cost accountant estimates that the materials and labour required will be:

Materials:
  2,000 sq. metres of card at £15 per 100 sq. metres
  50 litres of wax coating at £4.50 per litre

Labour:

Cutting	30 hours at £3.50 per hour
Waxing	20 hours at £4.50 per hour
Finishing	16 hours at £5.00 per hour

The actual costs of the job are:

Materials:
  1,950 sq. metres of card at £15.60 per 100 sq. metres
  45 litres of wax coating at £4.75 per litre

Labour:

Cutting	35 hours at £3.25 per hour
Waxing	19 hours at £5.00 per hour
Finishing	15 hours at £5.50 per hour

You are to prepare a statement which shows:

(a) the standard cost of the job
(b) the actual cost of the job
(c) the variances from standard, analysed between the sub-variances

21 Budgets and budgetary control

introduction

Businesses and other organisations need to plan for the future. In large businesses such planning, usually known as *corporate planning,* is very formal while, for smaller businesses, it will be less formal. Planning for the future falls into three time scales:

- *long-term:* from about three years up to, sometimes, as far as twenty years ahead
- *medium-term:* one to three years ahead
- *short-term:* for next year

Clearly, planning for these different time scales needs different approaches: the further on in time, the less detailed can be the plans. In the medium and longer term, a business will establish broad *corporate objectives.* Such corporate objectives do not have to be formally written down, although in a large organisation they are likely to be; for smaller businesses, corporate objectives will certainly be thought about by the owners or managers. This is very similar to each one of us having personal objectives, which we are likely to think about, rather than write down.

In this chapter we are concerned with planning for the more immediate future, ie the next financial year. Such planning takes note of the broader corporate objectives and sets out how these are to be achieved in the form of detailed plans known as *budgets.*

what is a budget?

A budget is a planning and control tool relevant to the management of an organisation

The main purposes of budgeting are:

- to assist in the assessment and evaluation of different courses of possible action
- to create motivation by expressing a proposed plan of action in terms of targets
- to monitor the effectiveness of performance being accomplished against the budget, and to report variances

Most budgets are prepared for the forthcoming financial year, and are usually broken down into shorter time periods, commonly monthly. This enables control to be exercised over the budget: as time passes by, so the business' actual results can be compared to the budget; discrepancies between the two can be investigated.

what budgets are prepared?

The end result of the budgeting process is the production of a *master budget* which takes the form of budgeted operating statements (trading and profit and loss account) together with a budgeted balance sheet at the end of the budgetary period. However, before the master budget can be produced, a number of subsidiary budgets covering all aspects of the business need to be prepared, eg sales, purchases, production, overheads, cash. Fig 21.1 on the next page shows a number of subsidiary budgets and their relationship to the master budget.

limiting factors

From Fig. 21.1, it can be seen that sales is, for most businesses, the starting point for the budget; this is because sales is often the limiting factor. A limiting factor is some aspect of the business which prevents further expansion. Other limiting factors include shortages of:

* raw materials
* skilled labour
* factory space
* capital
* expenditure on research and development

Whatever the limiting factor, the budget needs to be designed to incorporate any restrictions imposed by that factor.

Case Study: Fitta Fabricators Ltd. – production budget

Situation

Jim Lewis is the production manager of Fitta Fabricators Ltd, manufacturers of the Fitta De Luxe Exercise Cycle. The sales manager has just presented Jim with the budgeted sales for the forthcoming twelve months to 31 December 19-1, as follows:

January	150 units
February	150 "
March	200 "
April	400 "
May	400 "
June	400 "
July	500 "
August	300 "
September	200 "
October	200 "
November	700 "
December	425 "

Stock in the warehouse on 1 January at the start of the year is budgeted to be 100 units. Jim's problem is that the factory, working at normal capacity, can produce 350 units each month. More units can be made if overtime is paid, but the directors are not keen to see this happen, just as they do not like to see too much under-utilisation of the factory. Jim has to work out an even production budget which will keep the factory working at near or full capacity, but without incurring too much overtime. He has three other constraints:

* month-end stock must never fall below 100 units
* the warehouse is fairly small and cannot hold more than 600 units
* the factory is closed for half of August

Jim asks you to help him plan the production budget (see page 225 for the solution)

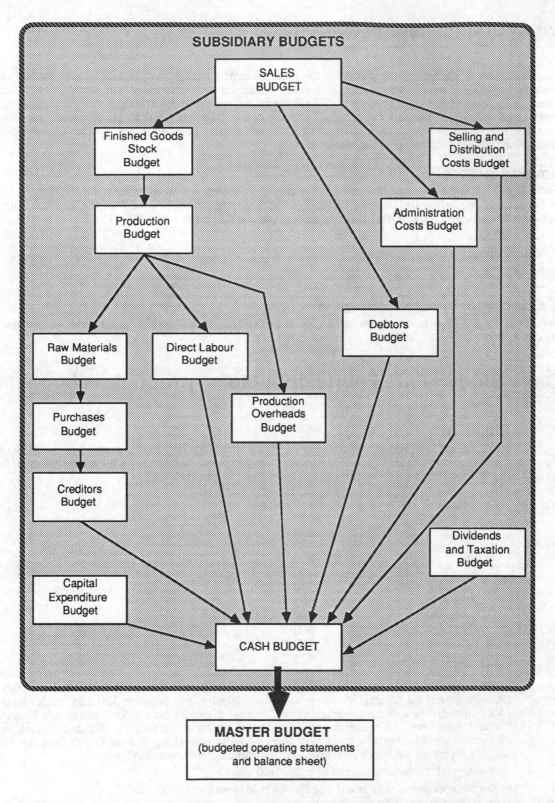

Fig. 21.1 Subsidiary budgets and the master budget

Solution

FITTA FABRICATORS LTD
Production Budget (units) for the year-ended 31 December 19-1

UNITS	JAN	FEB	MAR	APR	MAY	JUN	JUL	AUG	SEP	OCT	NOV	DEC
Opening stock	100	275	450	600	550	500	450	300	175	325	475	125
Add Units produced	325	325	350	350	350	350	350	175	350	350	350	400
Less Sales	150	150	200	400	400	400	500	300	200	200	700	425
Closing stock	275	450	600	550	500	450	300	175	325	475	125	100

Notes:
- January and February: under-production by 25 units each month.
- December: overtime payments in respect of 50 units.

budgetary planning

The planning of a budget is co-ordinated by a member of the accounts or finance department of a business organisation. However, managers of individual departments are made responsible for preparing budgets for their own departments. Many larger organisations take a highly formal view of planning the budget and form a *budget committee*. Fig. 21.2 shows a diagrammatic approach to budgetary planning.

An important aspect of budgetary planning is to test for feasibility before submitting the master budget for the approval of the owner, senior management, or board of directors. The test of feasibility would check, for example, that the sales budget and the production budget linked together (so that stock-piling or stock shortages do not occur), that the production budget is within the capacity of the facilities available, that the cash budget does not show excessive short-term borrowing which could be avoided by rescheduling major purchases.

budgetary control

Once a budget has been approved by the owner, senior management, or board of directors it becomes the official plan of the business for the period of the budget. There is no point in a business spending a lot of time and effort in preparing a budget if it is not used as a control mechanism throughout the period: this aspect is known as *budgetary control*.

The main aspect with which budgetary control is concerned is in comparing actual results with what was planned to happen in the budget. Fig. 21.2 also shows how budgetary control should be used to provide information both to those who are responsible for managing budgets and to the owner or board of directors.

advantages of budgets

performance targets are established
The process of budgeting establishes targets:
- for the business or organisation as a whole – in the form of a master budget
- for section managers – in the form of subsidiary budgets

comparisons can be made between budget and actual performance
By comparing the budget with what happens in reality allows:
- management to know that a variance has occurred
- an investigation to take place into the causes of the variance
- action to take place to correct the reason for the variance

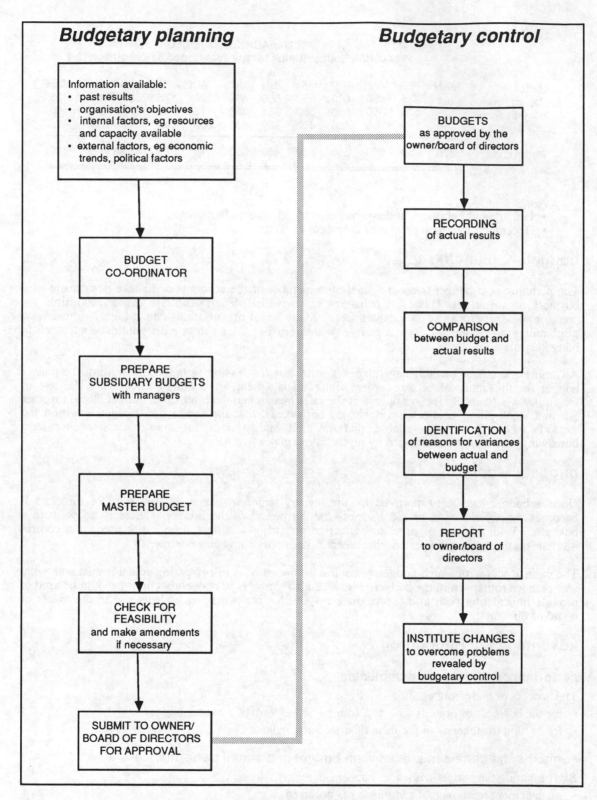

Fig. 21.2 Budgetary planning and control

planning is beneficial

It is too easy for a business or other organisation to meander along from day-to-day and week-to-week without any real idea of where it is going. A budget forces the management to think ahead and this, in turn, leads to better use of the resources of the organisation.

For a budget to be useful, it must be a realistic forecast of what can be achieved. If it is not, then the people who have to work to the budget will simply 'give up' and will not try to achieve the targets set. At the same time, the senior management, starting at the top with the owner or board of directors, must be convinced of the usefulness of the budget. If budgeting is seen as a necessary chore to be undertaken without much enthusiasm, then this attitude will soon permeate down through the organisation.

fixed and flexible budgets

fixed budgets

A fixed budget is one that is set at the start of the budgetary period and remains unchanged whatever the level of activity. For example, a budget is set for production of 10,000 units each month; actual production is 9,000 units per month. A fixed budget will compare the budgeted costs of producing 10,000 units with the actual costs of 9,000. Therefore the total variable costs, ie the *actual* figures, will be different from those budgeted for.

flexible budgets

A way of overcoming the difficulty caused by a fixed budget is to use a *flexible budget*. This recognises the different behaviour patterns of fixed costs and variable costs, depending on the level of output. Thus, an amended budget is produced on the basis of costs expected to be incurred at different production levels. For instance, in the example given above, a flexible budget would be produced for a production level of 9,000 units per month – the variable costs, eg materials, labour, and parts of the overhead, would be altered or 'flexed' to a level of 9,000 units. Then the actual costs can be compared directly with those of the flexible budget.

Case Study: fixed and flexible budgets

Situation

John Brown (Manufacturing) Ltd makes barbecue sets for garden use. The monthly budget has been prepared as follows:

Sales per month 1,000 barbecues at £20 each.

Production costs:

materials	£5 each
labour	£4 each
variable overheads	£1 each
fixed overheads	£7,500 per month

Because of poor weather, sales are down to 700 units each month and you have been asked to help in the preparation of revised budgets. Accordingly you should prepare a statement to show:

• the original monthly budget, showing the budgeted profit
• the flexible budget for production levels of 700 units each month

Solution:

JOHN BROWN (MANUFACTURING) LTD MONTHLY BUDGET

	FIXED BUDGET	FLEXIBLE BUDGET
Sales volume	1,000 units	700 units
Production volume	1,000 units	700 units
	£	£
Sales revenue (£20 each)	20,000	14,000
less : materials (£5 per unit)	(5,000)	(3,500)
labour (£4 per unit)	(4,000)	(2,800)
variable overheads (£1 per unit)	(1,000)	(700)
Contribution to fixed costs	10,000	7,000
less: fixed costs	(7,500)	(7,500)
Budgeted profit/(loss)	2,500	(500)

zero-based budgeting

The starting point for most budgets is to commence with last year's budget and then to 'add a few per cent to allow for inflation'. Such a policy, which is particularly prevalent in local and public authorities, has the major disadvantage that inefficiencies, provided they take place within the terms of the budget, remain 'in the system'.

One way to avoid this is to use *zero-based budgeting*. With this system, the budget starts from zero, and each item going into the budget has to be justified on the basis of business activity. For example, a stationery budget for an office, instead of starting with last year's figure and 'adding a bit', will start at zero and the manager of the office must justify each item which goes into the budget. The advantage of such a system is that managers have to justify their own budget.

cash budgets (cash flow forecasts): purpose and format

We have seen that the cash budget is the subsidiary budget that brings together all the other individual budgets. From a cash budget (which is often known as a *cash flow forecast)* can be produced the *master budget*. This takes the form of forecast financial statements:

* projected trading and profit and loss account
* projected balance sheet

In the next chapter we will examine in a practical way how these projections are brought together in a *Business Plan* prepared by a business applying to the bank for finance. First, however, it is necesssary to explain the theory of a cash budget.

The purpose of a cash budget is to detail the expected cash/bank receipts and payments, usually on a month-by-month basis, for the next three, six or twelve months (or even longer), in order to show the estimated bank balance at the end of each month throughout the period.

From the cash budget, the managers of a business can decide what action to take when a surplus of cash is shown to be available or, as is more likely, when a bank overdraft needs to be arranged.

The format of a cash budget, with sample figures, is set out on the next page.

		Jan £000	Feb £000	Mar £000	etc. £000
Receipts					
eg	sales receipts	150	150	161	170
	other receipts (loans, capital, interest)	70	80	75	80
Total receipts for month (A)		220	230	236	250
Payments					
eg	to creditors	160	165	170	170
	expenses	50	50	50	60
	fixed assets		50		
Total payments for month (B)		210	265	220	230
Net cashflow (Receipts less Payments, ie A-B)		10	(35)	16	20
Add bank balance at beginning of month		10	20	(15)	1
Bank balance (overdraft) at end of month		20	(15)	1	21

As you can see, a cash budget consists of three main sections:

• receipts for the month
• payments for the month
• summary of bank account

The *receipts* are analysed to show the amount that is expected to be received from sources such as cash sales, debtors, sale of fixed assets, loans and capital introduced. *Payments* will show how much is expected to be paid for cash purchases, to creditors, expenses, purchases of fixed assets, repayment of capital and loans. The summary at the bottom of the budget shows *net cashflow* (total receipts less total payments) added to the bank balance at the beginning of the month, resulting in the estimated closing bank balance at the end of the month. An overdrawn bank balance is shown in brackets.

Important Note: The main difficulty in the preparation of cash budgets lies in the *timing* of receipts and payments – for example, debtors may pay two months after date of sale, or creditors may be paid one month after date of purchase: the information given in each case should be studied carefully to ensure that such receipts and payments are correctly recorded. Note too that the cash budget, as its name suggests, deals only in cash; thus non-cash items, such as depreciation should never be shown. Similarly, where cash discounts are allowed or received, only the actual amount of cash expected to be received or paid should be entered.

cash budgets: limitations

While a cash budget is a very useful guide, it is only as good as the estimates on which it is based. A cash budget which is based on optimistic sales for the next six or twelve months will show an equally optimistic picture of the bank balance; a budget that looks too far into the future will probably prove to be inaccurate in later months. As with all budgets it is necessary to make comparisons between actual and budget figures: variances need to be investigated. Indeed, many cash budget and cash flow forms have columns for both *projected* and *actual* figures.

A cash budget does *not* indicate the profits, or losses, being made by a business. It does not follow that a cash budget which reveals an increasing bank balance necessarily indicates a profitable business. To supplement the cash budget, as noted earlier, it is usual to prepare a *master budget,* in the form of forecast final accounts, and this aspect is considered by looking at a practical example in the next chapter.

cash budgets and 'what if?' questions

A cash budget is prepared on the basis of certain assumptions, for example:
* debtors pay, in full, in the month following sale
* purchases from suppliers are paid for two months after the month of purchase

Often the managers of a business will wish to change the assumptions on which the cash budget is based by saying 'what if?' For example:
* *What if* half our debtors take two months to pay?
* *What if* we buy a new machine three months earlier than planned?
* *What if* we take advantage of cash discounts offered by our creditors and pay within, say, 14 days of purchase?

Each of these examples will change the cash budget substantially, and any two of the three, or all three together, is likely to have a considerable effect on a previously calculated budget, and may lead to an increased bank overdraft requirement.

To answer *'what if?'* questions, the whole cash budget has to be re-worked on the basis of the new assumptions. The reason for this is that, as the estimates of receipts and payments change each month, so the estimated closing month-end bank balance changes. This is where a computer spreadsheet is ideal for the preparation of cash budgets: each change can be put in, and the computer can be used to re-work all the calculations. A printout can be taken of each assumption and then passed to the interested parties for their consideration. In the next chapter we look at how a cash budget can be input into a computer spreadsheet.

Chapter Summary

❑ A budget is a planning and control tool relevant to the management of an organisation.

❑ Subsidiary budgets are prepared for each main activity of the business; these come together in the master budget which takes the form of budgeted operating statements and balance sheet.

❑ Budgetary planning establishes the targets and, when approved by the owners/board of directors, the budget becomes the official plan of the organisation for the budget period.

❑ Budgetary control uses the budget to make comparisons between actual results and budgeted results. Investigation of variances can be carried out and corrective action can be taken.

❑ A cash budget (or cash flow forecast) records the expected cash receipts and payments, usually on a monthly basis, for a period ahead of up to one year.

❑ The bank summary section of a cash budget shows the expected month-end bank balance. From this it is possible to see if short-term overdraft facilities need to be arranged.

In the next chapter we examine on a practical basis how a business approaching a bank for finance prepares a Business Plan which will contain, among other information, a cash budget, a projected trading and profit and loss account, and a forecast balance sheet.

Student Activities

21.1 Radionics Ltd is a manufacturer of radios. Most parts for the radios are bought in and assembled at the company's factory, which is situated on a modern industrial estate near Slough. The directors are currently planning the company's progress over the next twelve months.

You are a trainee in the accounts department of Radionics Ltd. You have been asked by your boss, the Finance Director, Mr. R. Perrin, to prepare a short paper for him to present at the next board meeting of the company which is to be held next week. The paper is to cover the following points:

- the different budgets that the company should prepare for the forthcoming year
- any limiting factors that the directors must bear in mind when considering budget proposals, and how such factors are likely to affect the company

21.2 Shades Ltd manufactures good quality sunglasses at its 'hi-tech' factory unit near Cambridge. Although there is some all-year round demand for sunglasses, highest demand is in late spring, and in summer. Because of the quality of the product, and the high skills needed from the workforce, there is little possibility of increasing production to meet peak demand; instead the company adopts a policy of keeping the factory working at full or near-full capacity throughout the year. The disadvantage of this policy is that completed stock needs to be warehoused until demand increases. Overtime can be worked to increase production by a maximum of 10%.

The sales director has been preparing a sales budget (in numbers of units of sunglasses) expected to be sold in the forthcoming year. Here is her budget:

January 5,500; February 4,500; March 3,500; April 4,000; May 7,000; June 12,500; July 15,000; August 10,000; September 2,000; October 3,000; November 5,000; December 5,000.

The production director now has to work out a production budget, taking into account the following:

- Stock at 1 January is 8,500 units
- Maximum monthly output without working overtime: 7,500 units. However, the factory is closed for one week in April (Easter), for two weeks in August (annual holiday), and for one week at Christmas. Each week of holiday loses one-quarter of that month's production.
- At the end of each month there must always be in stock two-thirds of the next month's budgeted sales.
- Overtime can be worked to produce a maximum increase in output of 10%.

You are to:

(a) Prepare a month-by-month production budget for Shades Ltd which:
 - shows when and how much overtime working will be necessary
 - shows closing stock (in units) at each month-end

(b) What are the limiting factors suffered by Shades Ltd, from the point of view of both production and sales?

21.3   (a) Explain what is meant by:
  - fixed budgets
  - flexible budgets

What is the main objective of preparing flexible budgets?

(b) Seats Ltd manufactures chairs which sell to schools and colleges throughout Britain.   The company is currently producing budgets for the next year.   The sales director is budgeting for sales of 90,000 chairs; the selling price is £10 each.   Production costs are budgeted as being:

  - materials £2.50 per chair
  - labour £2.75 per chair
  - variable overheads £0.50 per chair
  - fixed overheads £242,000 per year

However, a general election was announced a few days ago, and conversation at today's board meeting of the company's directors goes as follows:

"The outcome of the election looks unpredictable".

"If the government is re-elected, they are committed to a 10% cut in education spending."

"On the other hand, if the opposition party win, they have pledged to increase education spending by 25%."

"Until we get further information we had better assume that our sales will be affected by the same percentages."

As an accounts assistant, you are to:

(i) Prepare the fixed budget for the year based on sales of 90,000 chairs, to show budgeted profit
(ii) Prepare two flexible budgets based on the changes in educational spending proposed by each of the main political parties
(iii) Write a memorandum to the directors explaining the reason for the different budgeted profit figures.

21.4   Greenlawn Ltd manufactures a combined lawn weedkiller and fertiliser at its recently completed chemical works in Birmingham.   Output last year was 1,000,000 litres which sold for £5 per litre. However, this is well below the production capacity of the works and it is planned to increase production, and reduce the selling price.

The company wishes to prepare flexible budgets for output of 1,500,000 litres, 2,000,000 litres, and 2,500,000 litres (which is the maximum capacity of the works).

The selling price is to be reduced by 50p per litre for each increase in output.   Variable costs are £2,000,000 at an output level of 1,000,000 litres; fixed costs are £1,500,000; semi-variable costs are £750,000 at the present capacity, and are expected to increase by equal increments to £1,500,000 at the maximum production level.

You are to:

(a) Prepare a budget based on last year's level of output
(b) Prepare flexible budgets at the different production levels, showing budgeted profit
(c) Advise the management of Greenlawn Ltd of the production level which they should set for next year

22 Financial planning – the Business Plan

introduction

In Chapters 4 to 6 we looked at the sources of business finance and the fact that a business normally approaches a lender for funds by writing a formal *Business Plan*. In subsequent chapters we have looked at the financial statements of businesses and gained an understanding of how those statements are prepared. We have also examined the theory and practice of budgeting in Chapter 21.

These concepts are brought together in the financial section of the *Business Plan* which will contain the following projected statements:

- a *profit and loss forecast* – a budget projection of expected sales, expected costs and expected profits (part of the *master budget* – see the last chapter)
- a *cash flow forecast* – also known as the *cash budget* — a projection of cash received and cash spent month-by-month and a calculation of what the monthly bank balance is likely to be
- a *balance sheet* from the figures projected in these two forecasts

Clearly the cash flow forecast and the profit and loss forecast are quite different. The profit and loss forecast sets out the likely level of *profit* of a business whereas the cash flow forecast projects the likely *need for finance* or an estimated *surplus* by showing a shortfall or a surplus at the bank. A potential lender will want to see both forecasts: the profit and loss forecast shows the profits that will be earned; the cash flow forecast shows the amount of any borrowing that will be needed or cash that can be re-invested.

A business can also project a *balance sheet* from the figures in these two forecasts. This will be useful for a potential lender, who will be able to analyse the accounting ratios derived from the projected balance sheet.

In this chapter we therefore look in detail at

- the format of a business plan
- the completion of the cash flow forecast and profit and loss forecast
- the use of a computer spreadsheet for the cash flow forecast
- the projection of a balance sheet from the forecast figures

We will look in a Case Study at how a new business – a computer software shop – completes a Business Plan and makes a successful application to the bank for finance.

what is a Business Plan?

A Business Plan is a formal document, often submitted in the form of a ring binder file, which presents the business to a prospective lender or investor.

Not all business plans confirm to an identical format, but the following sections will normally be found in any well thought-out plan:

- a summary and list of contents of the Plan
- personal details of the borrower(s)
- history and background of the business
- a description of the product or service
- the market for the product or service
- financial considerations and background
- financial requirements
- profit and loss forecast, cash flow forecast, and any other relevant financial data

when and why is a Business Plan needed?
A Business Plan is needed either when you are starting up in business, or alternatively when you need to expand an existing business. It could be argued that every business should produce a Business Plan: it is an invaluable exercise in thinking through what you are planning to do; it enables *you,* as well as a prospective lender, to evaluate the proposal.

professional advice in compiling a Business Plan
A Business Plan is clearly a long and complex document. Professional advice in its compilation is highly recommended and available from a number of sources:

The accountant will be the most valuable source of information. He or she will be able to advise on the structure, assist in the drawing up of the financial projections, and may accompany you on your interviews with prospective lenders. An accountant will charge a fee for these services.

The bank manager will be pleased to give advice and also to provide free literature. Bank advice is *normally* free of charge, although the customer is well advised to enquire if a consultation fee is to be charged.

the Business Plan: structure and contents

summary
An introductory page which the prospective lender can read in a short space of time. It will outline the nature of the business, why it is better than the competition, how much finance will be needed, and for what purpose and period. A list of contents of the plan could usefully be included here.

the borrower
Brief personal details of the owner(s) of the business: name, age, qualifications, expertise, contact addresses and telephone numbers.

the business

This section will give details of the history and background of the business, its legal entity (sole trader, partnership or limited company), the length of time it has been trading (if this is the case), the premises it occupies (or will occupy), insurance arrangements and personal details (eg qualifications) of the management team. If the business is already trading, three years' final accounts should be enclosed.

the product or service

This section will include a description, in layman's language, of the product or service. It will include any promotional literature or illustrations that may be available. A positive approach is recommended: the section should state why the product or service is good.

the market

This section should show that detailed research has been carried out into the relevant market. The following questions should be answered:

- Who are the competitors? Why is the proposed product or service better than the competition?
- What market share is the business aiming at? Is the market expanding?
- How is the product or service to be marketed?
- What is the pricing policy? Is it competitive?
- Are there any orders already promised or received?
- What are the projected sales figures for the next six and twelve months?

financial considerations

The prospective lender will want to know:

- What credit will be given to the business by suppliers?
- What credit will the business give to customers?
- What assets does the business own? What is their value? Are they mortgaged?

assets required and financial needs

This should be a summary, based on the cash flow forecast (see below), detailing where applicable:

- the amount the proprietor is contributing
- the short-term requirement and the purpose, eg stock, initial expenses
- the medium/long-term requirements, and the purpose, eg premises, machinery, vehicles
- proposals for repayment
- assets available for security purposes (see 'financial considerations' above)

financial projections – format

The projections will normally include a six or twelve month projected trading and profit and loss account and a cash flow forecast. What is the format for these forecasts? The answer is that there is no defined format, but most forecasts will be set out along the lines of the illustrations on the pages which follow. These show the figures for a six month period as follows:

- *Inkpen Designs Limited* – a cash-flow forecast of an existing business applying for a short-term loan of £5,000 for new machinery purchased in March
- *R & S Engineering Limited* – a profit and loss forecast for an existing business

Guidance is also given on how to use a computer spreadsheet to present the cash flow forecast.

The major banks publish useful guides to setting up in business, and their information packs usually include blank forms for profit and loss forecasts and cash flow forecasts, together with accompanying notes on how to complete the forms. The bank information has the advantage of being free of charge. As we have already noted, accountants will also advise on how to present the forecasts, but will usually charge for the service.

Profit and loss forecast

name.......... R & S Engineering Limited ....period beginning......... 1 Jan 19-9

	January £	February £	March £	April £	May £	June £	TOTAL £
Sales	5,000	5,000	6,000	5,000	5,000	5,000	31,000
Less: Cost of Sales	2,500	2,500	3,500	2,500	2,500	2,500	16,000
Gross Profit	2,500	2,500	2,500	2,500	2,500	2,500	15,000
Gross Profit %	50	50	42	50	50	50	48
Expenses							
Wages	500	500	500	500	500	500	3,000
Rent/Rates	150	150	150	150	150	150	900
Insurance	40	40	40	40	40	40	240
Electricity	25	25	25	25	25	25	150
Telephone	35	35	35	35	35	35	210
Other services	55	55	55	55	55	55	330
Vehicle expenses	50	50	50	50	50	50	300
Stationery	10	10	10	10	10	10	60
Postages	55	55	55	55	55	55	330
Bank charges							
Interest charges							
Professional fees						100	100
Advertising	50	50	50	50	50	50	300
Sundries	35	35	35	35	35	35	210
Depreciation	100	100	100	100	100	100	600
Total Expenses	1,105	1,105	1,105	1,105	1,105	1,205	6,730
Net Profit/ (Loss)	1,395	1,395	1,395	1,395	1,395	1,295	8,270

completing the profit and loss forecast

definition

A profit and loss forecast is a budgeted projection of expected sales, expected costs and expected profit on a monthly basis over a specific period of time – here six months. Because sales and purchases are made on credit (they are paid for later) the forecast shows the profit position rather than the cash position of the business. You will note that the forecast combines the *trading* and the *profit and loss* accounts.

time period

The time period shown can be either six or twelve months. The vertical columns show the months, and on the extreme right-hand side, a total figure for the time period. Some profit and loss forecast forms have two columns for each month: one for the projected figures and one for the actual figures, so that the projections and actual figures can be compared during the time period. For the sake of simplicity the budgeted figures only are shown in the illustration here.

sales

Sales is the *invoiced* value of the sales during the month. It is *not* the amount of money received for sales during the month. It does *not* include VAT (for VAT–registered businesses)

cost of sales

Cost of sales (also known as *cost of goods sold*) is the direct cost of what has been sold during the month. The figure is normally based on the purchases adjusted for opening and closing stock (add opening stock, deduct closing stock). This figure obviously does not include capital items – such as machinery purchased – but only the cost of the normal stock-in-trade. It does *not* include VAT (where the business is registered for VAT).

gross profit

Gross profit is calculated by deducting cost of sales (cost of goods sold) from sales. It is useful (as here) to calculate the gross profit percentage to show the margin achieved by the business. The formula is

$$\frac{gross\ profit}{sales} \times 100 = gross\ profit\ \%$$

expenses

The figures entered in the expenses section represent the monthly cost of the expenses incurred, whether or not the bills have actually been paid. You will see from the example that some items, electricity for example, are averaged out over the six month period, even if they are paid for quarterly. VAT is not included in the expenses figures.

depreciation

As you will have seen when studying financial statements, depreciation is a non-cash expense. It must, however, be included on the profit and loss forecast as it represents the cost to the business of the wear and tear of the fixed assets over their useful lives.

total expenses

The total expenses figure is the total of all the items below the gross profit calculation. It must be stressed again that this figure does *not* represent cash paid out – it is the total of the expenses *incurred* during the month, and in all probability paid for later.

net profit/(loss)

The net profit is calculated as follows:

gross profit minus total expenses = net profit

A negative figure represents a net *loss* and will be shown in brackets.

Cash flow forecast

name...... Inkpen Designs Limited ....period beginning...... 1 Jan 19–9

	January £	February £	March £	April £	May £	June £	TOTAL £
RECEIPTS							
Cash sales	500	500	500	500	500	500	3,000
From debtors	4,000	5,000	3,000	4,000	4,500	4,000	24,500
Capital							
Loans			5,000				5,000
TOTAL RECEIPTS (A)	4,500	5,500	8,500	4,500	5,000	4,500	32,500
PAYMENTS							
Cash purchases	400	200	400	300	400	400	2,100
Credit purchases	2,000	2,500	3,000	2,000	2,000	1,000	12,500
Capital items			5,000				5,000
Wages	500	500	500	500	500	500	3,000
Rent/Rates			3,000				3,000
Insurance		550					550
Electricity			240				240
Telephone				300			300
VAT			500			500	1,000
Vehicle expenses	50	65	140	75	450	55	835
Stationery	10	20	55	17	230	20	352
Postages	50	70	150	50		50	370
Bank charges			145				145
Interest charges					120		120
Professional fees		750					750
Advertising	45	125	134	44	68	185	601
Sundries	34	54	63	67	21	25	264
TOTAL PAYMENTS (B)	3,089	4,834	13,327	3,353	3,789	2,735	31,127
NET CASH FLOW (A-B)	1,411	666	(4,827)	1,147	1,211	1,765	1,373
OPENING BANK BALANCE	(1,250)	161	827	(4,000)	(2,853)	(1,642)	(1,250)
CLOSING BANK BALANCE	161	827	(4,000)	(2,853)	(1,642)	123	123

completing the cash flow forecast

definition

A cash flow forecast (also known as a cash budget) is a projection of cash received and cash spent month-by-month and a calculation of what the monthly bank balance of the business is likely to be. A cash flow forecast is a useful guide in projecting

- how much and for how long a business may need to borrow from the bank (if there is a cash shortfall)
- when that borrowing is likely to be repaid

The cash flow forecast is normally projected for six or for twelve months, and sometimes a monthly column is left blank for the insertion of the actual figures adjacent to the forecast figures, so that the situation can be monitored and corrective action taken if it becomes necessary.

VAT

Unlike the profit and loss forecast, the cash flow forecast includes VAT amounts on sales, purchases and expenses. For VAT-registered businesses any payment of VAT will be entered as a cash outflow (see the entries of £500 under March and June in the illustration)

sales receipts

Receipts from *cash sales* are entered in the column for the month in which the sales are made. *From debtors* represents receipts from sales made in previous months. When completing the forecast the average time debtors take to pay should be calculated and entered accordingly: in the example it is assumed that credit sales are paid for two months after the invoice is issued. The March receipts of £3,000 therefore represent sales *invoiced* in January but *paid for* in March.

other receipts

Any capital introduced by the owner(s) of the business and any loans made to the business will be included in the total receipts calculation in the month in which they are paid into the bank account. In the illustration a loan of £5,000 has been been granted in March.

payments

Items in the payments section include purchases and expenses (items *included* in the profit and loss forecast) and also expenditure on capital items (*not* included in the profit and loss forecast), for example:

February: insurance £550; professional fees (the audit) £750

March:　computer purchased (capital item) £5,000; business rates £3,000; electricity £240; bank charges £145

Remember that payments for items purchased are entered in the month in which payment is made, not in the month of supply or invoice.

the bank balance

The bottom line of the cash flow forecast shows the all-important figure of the closing bank balance (the balance at the end of the month). A figure in brackets indicates a borrowing requirement. The *closing* bank balance is arrived at by adding the *opening* bank balance (ie the balance at the end of the previous month) to the *net cashflow*. The net cashflow is simply the total payments figure (B) deducted from total receipts (A).

In the illustration the closing bank balance line shows that an overdraft of up to £4,000 will be required in March and April in addition to the loan of £5,000 shown in the Receipts section. This overdraft will be repaid by the end of June.

the cash flow forecast on a computer spreadsheet

If you are unfamiliar with computer spreadsheets you are advised to study Chapter 31 at the back of this book before reading the next two pages.

The calculations on a cash flow forecast are not particularly difficult, but they do take a long time if you are tackling the task with only pen, paper and calculator. Imagine the situation if you finish the forecast and then find that you have to revise the sales figures: you will have to re-calculate the Total Receipts line, the Net Cash Flow line and all the bank balances. The task is, of course, made simple when you have input the worksheet onto a computer spreadsheet program. You will be able to change any figure, and the computer will do all the recalculations automatically, for example:

• projections of different levels of sales – optimistic, realistic and pessimistic
• projections of different levels of expenditure
• the effect of buying an asset at different times

In each case you will be able to see the effect on the critical figure of the closing bank balance which indicates the amount of money the business may have to borrow.

On the next page (Fig. 22.1) we set out a simple six-month cash flow forecast model based on the forecast illustrated on the previous page. The figures shown are simple so that you can see the way the forecast works arithmetically.

notes on completion of the spreadsheet

• Row 1 includes the name of the business and the heading 'Cash Flow Forecast'
• Row 2 shows the period involved, eg January – June 19-3
• Rows 3, 11, 13, 14, 33, 34 and 36 are left blank to make the presentation clearer
• Column A is used for labels
• Columns B to G show the six months of the forecast
• Column H shows the totals

use of formulas in the spreadsheet – column C

Extensive use is made here of the addition of a range of cells. You will need to check your computer manual to find the formula to use. The formula used here is *=Sum(C7:C10)* where all the cells between C7 and C10 are added together. Column C is used below for illustrative purposes. The formulas are as follows:

• Row 12 – Total Receipts	*=Sum(C7:C10)*
• Row 35 – Total Payments	*=Sum(C16:C32)*
• Row 37 – Net Cash Flow	*=C12 - C35*
• Row 38 – Opening Bank	*=B39* – ie the closing bank balance of the *previous* month. Note that B38 is a value cell into which is entered the opening bank balance for the period.
• Row 39 – Closing Bank	*=C37+C38*
• Column H – Total column	Each row is totalled, eg cell H7 is *=Sum(B7:G7)*. Column H is also totalled vertically, in the same way as the other columns, except that cell H38 is *=B38* and cell H39 is *=G39*
• Row 29 – Interest	This figure may be estimated and entered as a value, or can be approximated by formula. If interest for January is charged at the end of the month, the formula in cell B29 will be *=(B39*K2/100)/12*. K2 (column K row 2) is the reference of a value cell into which can be entered the current interest rate.

	A	B	C	D	E	F	G	H	
1	Name of Business: Cash Flow Forecast								
2	Period: month - month 19--								
3									
4		Jan	Feb	Mar	Apl	May	Jun	Total	
5		£	£	£	£	£	£	£	
6	RECEIPTS								
7	Cash sales	10	10	10	10	10	10	60	
8	Cash from debtors	10	10	10	10	10	10	60	
9	Capital							0	
10	Loans							0	
11									
12	TOTAL RECEIPTS	20	20	20	20	20	20	120	
13									
14									
15	PAYMENTS								
16	Cash purchases	1	1	1	1	1	1	6	
17	Credit purchases	1	1	1	1	1	1	6	
18	Capital items	1	1	1	1	1	1	6	
19	Wages	1	1	1	1	1	1	6	
20	Rent/rates	1	1	1	1	1	1	6	
21	Insurance	1	1	1	1	1	1	6	
22	Electricity	1	1	1	1	1	1	6	
23	Telephone	1	1	1	1	1	1	6	
24	VAT	1	1	1	1	1	1	6	
25	Vehicle expenses	1	1	1	1	1	1	6	
26	Stationery	1	1	1	1	1	1	6	
27	Postages	1	1	1	1	1	1	6	
28	Bank charges	1	1	1	1	1	1	6	
29	Interest	1	1	1	1	1	1	6	
30	Professional fees	1	1	1	1	1	1	6	
31	Advertising	1	1	1	1	1	1	6	
32	Sundries	1	1	1	1	1	1	6	
33									
34									
35	TOTAL PAYMENTS	17	17	17	17	17	17	102	
36									
37	NET CASHFLOW	3	3	3	3	3	3	18	
38	OPENING BANK	100	103	106	109	112	115	100	
39	CLOSING BANK	103	106	109	112	115	118	118	
40									
41									
42									
43									
44									

Fig. 22.1 Example of a computer spreadsheet model for a cash flow forecast

Case Study: Ian Phillips trading as 'Software Stores'

Situation

Ian Phillips is an expert in computer software. He has worked until recently for a leading British software house which made him redundant four months ago. He has £10,000 available from his redundancy money and savings to invest as capital, and wishes to set up a computer software retail outlet in a new shopping arcade, which is offering units at preferential rates. He has named his venture 'Software Stores'. It will open on 1 January 19-9. His customers will include the general public and also local businesses who need expert guidance on the setting up of business packages. He wishes to raise finance from the bank but is not sure how much he needs. He therefore approaches, on a friend's recommendation, Jim Stoner, a local accountant, who is known to specialise in small business finance.

Jim Stoner extracts the following information from his client.

income

- Ian Phillips has capital of £10,000 in the building society to introduce into the business
- expected cash sales from callers at the shop £3,000 per month
- expected credit sales from business software £1,000 per month on 60 days' credit (ie sales in January will be paid for in March)

expenditure

- initial purchase of stock of £5,000 to be paid for immediately by cheque (stock will be reduced to a level of £3,250 at the end of each month, following estimated sales of £1,750 [at cost] of stock each month)
- thereafter stock purchases to be £1,750 each month:
  (a) in February and March paid for immediately by cheque
  (b) April onwards, all purchases on 30 days' credit (eg April's purchases paid for in the month following purchase, ie in May)

  The reason for (a) and (b) is that credit will often only be granted by suppliers *after* the business has shown that it is creditworthy, usually after a few months' trading
- shop fixtures and fittings (fixed assets) £5,250, to be paid for in February
- equipment purchases (fixed assets) £4,500, to be paid for in January
- monthly payments:
  rent and rates £575, insurance £50, electricity £25, stationery £10, postages £15, drawings £750
- the telephone will cost £135 (a fixed asset); the monthly running cost will be £15
- advertising will cost £150 in January and £30 in subsequent months
- drawings will be £750 per month
- bank charges: arrangement fee of £100 and quarterly charges of £75 in March and June
- bank overdraft interest will also be charged quarterly, at 15% p.a.
- depreciation of fixed assets is to be charged (in the profit and loss account) at £750 (£125 per month); *as it is a non-cash item it does not appear in the cash flow forecast*

processing of the figures

Jim Stoner helps Ian to draw up a cash flow forecast and a forecast profit and loss account (illustrated on the following pages). Ian uses his spreadsheet program to calculate the cash flow forecast. Jim recommends that Ian does not register for VAT until the level of sales justifies it. It is therefore ignored for the present in the calculations.

Cash flow forecast

name...Ian Phillips t/a Software Stores....**period beginning**..1 Jan 19-9...

	January £	February £	March £	April £	May £	June £	TOTAL £
RECEIPTS							
Cash sales	3,000	3,000	3,000	3,000	3,000	3,000	18,000
Cash from debtors			1,000	1,000	1,000	1,000	4,000
Capital	10,000						10,000
Loans							
TOTAL RECEIPTS (A)	13,000	3,000	4,000	4,000	4,000	4,000	32,000
PAYMENTS							
Cash purchases	5,000	1,750	1,750				8,500
Credit purchases					1,750	1,750	3,500
Capital items	4,635	5,250					9,885
Wages							
Rent/Rates	575	575	575	575	575	575	3,450
Insurance	50	50	50	50	50	50	300
Electricity	25	25	25	25	25	25	150
Telephone	15	15	15	15	15	15	90
VAT							
Vehicle expenses							
Stationery	10	10	10	10	10	10	60
Postages	15	15	15	15	15	15	90
Bank charges	100		75			75	250
Interest charges			65				65
Professional fees							
Advertising	150	30	30	30	30	30	300
Drawings	750	750	750	750	750	750	4,500
TOTAL PAYMENTS (B)	11,325	8,470	3,360	1,470	3,220	3,295	31,140
NET CASHFLOW (A-B)	1,675	(5,470)	640	2,530	780	705	860
OPENING BANK BALANCE	0	1,675	(3,795)	(3,155)	(625)	155	0
CLOSING BANK BALANCE	1,675	(3,795)	(3,155)	(625)	155	860	860

Profit and loss forecast

name..... Ian Phillips t/a Software Stores .....period beginning..... 1 Jan 19-9 .....

	January £	February £	March £	April £	May £	June £	TOTAL £
Sales	4,000	4,000	4,000	4,000	4,000	4,000	24,000
Less: Cost of Sales	1,750	1,750	1,750	1,750	1,750	1,750	10,500
Gross Profit	2,250	2,250	2,250	2,250	2,250	2,250	13,500
Gross Profit %	56	56	56	56	56	56	56
Expenses							
Wages							
Rent/Rates	575	575	575	575	575	575	3,450
Insurance	50	50	50	50	50	50	300
Electricity	25	25	25	25	25	25	150
Telephone	15	15	15	15	15	15	90
Other services							
Vehicle expenses							
Stationery	10	10	10	10	10	10	60
Postages	15	15	15	15	15	15	90
Bank charges	50	40	40	40	40	40	250
Interest charges			65				65
Professional fees							
Advertising	50	50	50	50	50	50	300
Sundries							
Depreciation	125	125	125	125	125	125	750
Total Expenses	915	905	970	905	905	905	5,505
Net Profit (Loss)	1,335	1,345	1,280	1,345	1,345	1,345	7,995

notes on completion of the profit and loss forecast

sales
Total monthly sales of £4,000 comprise cash sales of £3,000 and invoiced credit sales of £1,000.

cost of sales
The monthly cost of sales is the cost of the stock actually sold, here £1,750. The formula is
cost of sales = opening stock + purchases - closing stock

wages
There is no entry here because Ian's drawings do not feature in the profit and loss account, but are deducted in the capital section of the balance sheet (see below).

expenses
The expenses are spread out over the six month period and allocated to each month, and not necessarily when they are incurred

telephone
The cost of £135 becomes a fixed asset and only the running costs (£15 per month) are shown in the profit and loss account

interest
The estimated bank account interest is shown in the March column as it is a charge for the January – March quarter

depreciation
The depreciation is shown as a monthly charge of £125

Jim Stoner suggests that Ian draws up a projected balance sheet as at the end of the six month period so that the bank manager can look at the figures and carry out some ratio analysis:

PROJECTED BALANCE SHEET OF IAN PHILLIPS TRADING AS SOFTWARE STORES AS AT 30 JUNE 19-9

	Cost £	Dep'n £	Net £
Fixed Assets			
Office equipment	4,635	350	4,285
Fixtures and fittings	5,250	400	4,850
	9,885	750	9,135
Current Assets			
Stock		3,250	
Debtors		2,000	
Bank		860	
		6,110	
Less Current Liabilities			
Creditors		1,750	
Working Capital			4,360
NET ASSETS			13,495
FINANCED BY			
Capital			10,000
Add net profit			7,995
			17,995
Less drawings			4,500
			13,495

note
all the figures for the balance sheet can be found in the workings for the forecast profit and loss account and cash flow forecast:

- *stock* is the closing stock figure from the cost of sales calculation

- *bank* is the closing bank balance from the cash flow forecast

- *debtors* is two months' credit sales not yet paid for

- *creditors* is the one month's purchases not yet paid for

completion of the Business Plan

Ian, now that he has completed his financial projections, will compile the Business Plan. The sections will include:

- personal details of himself, his experience and qualifications
- a description of the business and the type of software he is proposing to sell
- an analysis of the market, and his pricing strategy
- his financial requirements – the bottom line of the cash flow forecast shows that he needs an overdraft of approximately £4,000 in February which will be repaid out of sales receipts by the end of May
- his financial projections – the profit and loss forecast, cash flow forecast and his projected balance sheet
- assets he has available for bank security – a £10,000 life policy and his house (already mortgaged to the Abbeyfax Building Society)

He arranges an interview with his bank manager to whom he sends a copy of the Business Plan, so that the bank manager can study it before the interview. The manager will look carefully at the financial forecasts and see from the bottom line of the cash flow forecast that the borrowing can be repaid. The manager will also see from the forecast profit and loss account and balance sheet that the ratios are favourable: net profit percentage is 33%, the current ratio 3.5 : 1, and the liquid capital ratio 1.6 : 1.

the interview with the bank

Ian visits the bank with his accountant and they are interviewed together by one of the bank's business managers who has a number of questions to ask:

Do you know the software market well enough to be able to know what to stock in your shop? How will you keep up-to-date? Is the market steady, or might you be left with a lot of out-of-date stock?

Is your projected level of sales realistic? What would happen to your proposed overdraft if your sales were 10% lower than anticipated? Have you got any orders or customers lined up?

Have you estimated the costs of running the shop realistically? Is your figure for business rates up-to-date?

Can you live on your proposed drawings of £750 a month? Could you make do with less if the business did not do as well as expected? Has your wife got a job?

Ian, helped by his accountant, is able to give satisfactory answers to these questions and the bank manager, who has already looked at the business plan, makes an offer:

- an overdraft limit of £4,000 for the six months January to June
- an interest charge of base rate plus 5% (a total interest charge of 10% + 5% = 15% p.a.)
- an arrangement fee of £100
- a charge over Ian's life policy as security for the borrowing (the house is not required as security because the proposed business borrowing is only short-term)

conclusion

The offer is accepted and the bank manager then outlines other ways in which the bank can help: arranging insurance, pensions, and a variety of banking facilities. The interview is typical of a business lending situation. One point remains very clear: without the presentation of the business and the financial planning that went into the Business Plan, the bank manager would have had a more difficult decision to make. The Business Plan gives both the owner and the bank greater confidence in the venture.

Chapter Summary

❑ The writing of a Business Plan is an invaluable exercise for anyone wishing to start or expand a business.

❑ The bank and, most particularly, an accountant, should be consulted when compiling a Business Plan.

❑ The Business Plan contains sections setting out
  • details of the borrower and his or her business objectives
  • a description of the business and the product
  • the market and the pricing policy
  • financial documents: profit and loss forecast, cash flow forecast and other projections such as a balance sheet

❑ A computer spreadsheet program speeds up the production of the financial forecasts and should be used wherever possible

❑ A Business Plan, when properly presented to a prospective lender of funds, can considerably improve the chances of obtaining finance, and the speed with which the finance may be offered.

❑ It is advisable to send a copy of the business plan to a prospective lender in advance of any interview so that he or she will have time to assess the proposition fully.

 Student Activities

22.1 You are an accountant, Gareth Davies, of Davies, Davies and Lloyd, 4 Bank Chambers, High Street, Weatherbury, DT6 7TY. A financially unsophisticated client, Basil Noakes of 10 Springfield Avenue, Mellstock, Dorset, DT3 8HY, is trying to raise money to start a craft studio in his village. He needs approximately £10,000 to finance the venture; he has £5,000. Draft a letter telling him, *in brief,* the main sources of finance and the advantages of his presenting a business plan. Your letter should contain a description of the contents of a business plan.
Note: details of the main sources of finance are set out in Chapter 6.

22.2 Using a computer spreadsheet program, input the cash flow figures contained in the Case Study, Ian Phillips T/A Software Stores. What will be the effect on the cash flow if you

(a)　increase sales by 20%?
(b)　decrease sales by 20%?

Examine the expenses items critically. If there is a problem when sales decrease, what items would you change, or could you change? Use the computer spreadsheet to calculate a realistic alternative.

22.3 You are planning to set up in business at the beginning of the year 19-8. Your enterprise is a small bookshop which you will call 'Anne's Bookshop'.

You plan to introduce capital of £6,000 in January. You also intend to purchase for cash an initial stock of books costing £5,000, together with fixtures and fittings costing £3,750, also to be paid for in January.

You hope to start trading in January 19-8 and you have estimated sales for the first six months as follows:

January £3,000; February £2,400; March £3,600; April £4,500; May £4,200; June £3,900. All sales will be for cash. You plan to work to a gross profit margin of one-third of the selling price. Towards the end of each month you will replenish the stock to ensure that, at the month-end, it will be restored to £5,000. Your suppliers for book purchases, excluding the initial cash stock purchase, will allow one month's credit (eg purchases made in January will be paid for in February).

You estimate the monthly overheads of the shop will be rent and rates £250, wages £280, heat/light/telephone £95. You plan to withdraw for your own use drawings of £500 per month. Your accountant has advised you to depreciate fixtures and fittings at the rate of 20% per annum (straight line method).

Your accountant also advises you to prepare, for the six months ending 30 June 19-8:

- a cash flow forecast (using a spreadsheet if it is available)
- a profit and loss forecast
- a projected balance sheet as at 30 June 19-8

These documents will form part of the Business Plan which you will submit to the bank as part of your application for the finance, which your accountant suspects you will need. Prepare the documents and pass them to your accountant for checking.

Assignment 6
Business Planning: the Medfact brochure

LEARNING OUTCOMES COVERED:
Business planning: projected cash flow, profit and loss statement, balance sheet, the Business Plan, presenting a case to the bank

SITUATION

You are an accountant in the firm of Price Charterhouse, 67 Brewers Walk, Stourford, ST6 9UT, and have been asked to advise a client, John Carr.

John Carr has been unemployed for 12 months and intends to set up a mail order holiday guide business. He used to work in a travel agency, and knows the travel business well. He plans to sell an A4 format holiday resort guide giving invaluable information about all the popular resorts in the Mediterranean area. The guide and the business will be given the name 'Medfact'.

John Carr will operate under the local TEC Enterprise Allowance Scheme which will pay him £40 a week for the first year of operation. He has £2,500 of his own in a building society account, saved when he was in employment.

You have talked through the figures with him and he has produced the following estimates for his first six months' trading (1 January to 30 June 19-8):

- he will introduce capital on 1 January of £2,500
- opening stocks of Medfact guides will cost £2,000 and be paid for by cheque
- estimated sales for the first six months (based on a peak month of May) are:

January	£1,000
February	£1,600
March	£1,800
April	£2,000
May	£4,000
June	£2,400

- most sales are for cash, but he does expect to sell 25% of his guides through travel agents, and will have to wait a month for payment from them

- his Medfact guides cost 50% of his selling price; stocks of guides will be replaced each month so that the closing stock value will always be £2,000; January's stock purchases of guides will therefore be £1,000 (sales figure) x 50% = £500

- purchases will be made from his suppliers who allow 1 month's credit (apart from the initial cash purchase of stock)

His expenses (which are paid for as they are incurred) are:

- advertising £500 per month, except for April when he will spend £800

- post and packing £200 for January, February and March, £300 for April, May and June

- sundry expenses will be £10 per month, except for April when they will be £40

- you should ignore interest costs

Also,

- he wishes to buy office equipment for £1,000 by cheque in January; the equipment is expected to last for five years

- drawings from the bank account will be £180 per month (the Enterprise Allowance £40 per week will *not* be passed through the business) – his wife is a qualified teacher and her salary will subsidise him while the business is starting up

- John Carr suspects that he will have to approach the bank for finance in the early months of operation of the business. You realise that a Business Plan will have to drawn up, and you therefore advise him accordingly.

STUDENT TASKS

1. Write a letter to Mr John Carr (10 Gatwick Avenue, Stourford, ST4 3RF) explaining what a Business Plan is, and what Mr Carr will have to do to prepare one.

2. Construct a cash flow forecast for the first six months of operation of the business. Use a spreadsheet program if it is available.

3. Draw up a forecast profit and loss account for the six months to 30 June 19-8, and a projected balance sheet as at 30 June 19-8.

4. State in your letter how much Mr Carr may need to borrow from the bank, and what form the borrowing should take. The letter will enclose the cash flow forecast and the projected profit and loss statement and balance sheet as supporting evidence.

23 Investment appraisal

introduction

You will already know from your other studies in this and other areas that all resources are limited in supply. As a result there is a need to use resources in such a way as to obtain the maximum benefits from them. To do this it is necessary to choose between various alternatives available; for example, on a personal level, we have to make decisions such as:

Should I save my spare cash in a bank or in a building society?
Should I save up for a car, or should I buy on hire purchase?
Which make of car, within my price range, should I buy?
Should I rent a house or should I buy, taking out a mortgage?

While these decisions are personal choices, the management of businesses of all sizes is constantly faced with making choices, as are local authorities and central government.

The management of any business is constantly having to make decisions on *what* to produce, *where* to produce, *how* to produce, and *how much* to produce. Similar considerations must be the concern of organisations providing services. For each major choice to be made, some method of appraisal has to be applied to ensure that, whatever decisions are taken, they are the right ones. This means that it is necessary to look at all the alternatives available and to choose the one that is going to give the most benefit to the organisation. For example, a business may have to decide whether to replace its existing machinery with new, more up-to-date machinery. If it decides on new machinery, it then has to choose between different makes of machine and different models, each having a different cost and each capable of affecting output in a different way. At the same time a decision has to be made whether to pay cash outright, to buy on hire purchase, or to lease.

The objective of investment appraisal is to enable an organisation to decide whether or not to invest in a particular project and, where there are a number of viable alternatives, in which of them to invest.

what is an investment?

An investment is the spending of money now in order to receive benefits (or reduce costs) in future years. It is illustrated as follows:

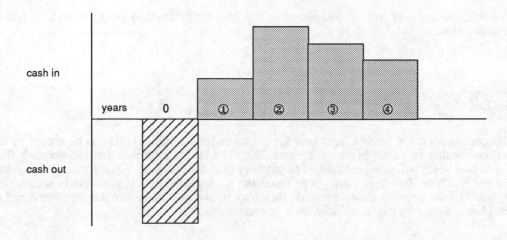

Here the capital expenditure now (shown as 'year 0') brings benefits (or reduced costs) in future years. The business or organisation needs to apply investment appraisal techniques to ensure that the investment decision is the correct choice.

Case Study: a new machine

Situation

An organisation needs a new machine and has to make the choice between Machine Y and Machine Z. The initial cost and the net cash flow (income, less running expenses but *not* depreciation) to the business have been ascertained for each machine as follows:

	MACHINE Y	MACHINE Z
Initial cost	£20,000	£28,000
Net cash flow:		
Year 1	£8,000	£10,000
Year 2	£12,000	£10,000
Year 3	£5,000	£8,000
Year 4	£4,000	£9,000
Year 5	£2,000	£9,000

Only one machine is needed and, at the end of five years, the machine will have no value and will be scrapped. To finance the project, the organisation can borrow money at 10 per cent per annum. Which machine should be chosen?

Solution

Three techniques are in common usage to appraise a project such as this:

- payback
- accounting rate of return
- discounted cash flow

Each of these techniques will be considered in this chapter in order to help the organisation to make its decision.

payback

This technique, as its name implies, sees how long it takes for the initial outlay to be repaid by the net cash flow coming in. Thus Machine Y costs £20,000 and it is expected that the net cash flow over the first two years will equal the cost. The payback time for Machine Y is, therefore, two years, while that for Machine Z is three years. The faster the payback the better, particularly where high technology or fashion projects are concerned – they may be out-of-date before they reach the end of their useful lives. So, using payback, Machine Y is preferable.

advantages of payback

- it is easy to calculate
- it is easy to understand
- it places emphasis on the earlier cash flows, which are more likely to be accurate than later cash flows
- an ideal capital investment appraisal technique for high technology projects

disadvantages of payback

- all cash flows after the payback period are ignored
- within the payback period it fails to take into account the timing of net cash flows, eg Machine Y would still have had a payback of two years even if the cash flows for years one and two had been reversed

accounting rate of return

This method is calculated by:

$$\frac{(Total\ estimated\ cash\ flow^* - Initial\ cost)}{Estimated\ life\ of\ project} \quad x \quad \frac{100}{Initial\ cost}$$

* Scrap value or residual value, if any, at the end of the project would be taken into account.

This method gives a percentage accounting rate of return on the initial cost of the project. For Machine Y it is calculated as follows:

$$\frac{(£31,000 - £20,000)}{5\ years} \quad x \quad \frac{100}{£20,000} \quad = \quad 11\ per\ cent$$

For Machine Z the accounting rate of return is 12.9 per cent; so, using this method, Machine Z is slightly preferable.

advantages of accounting rate of return
* it is relatively easy to calculate
* all cash flows are used
* it is easy to understand the results

disadvantage of accounting rate of return
* the timing of cash flows is completely ignored, ie the same result would have been reached if the cash flows for Machine Y had been £1,000, £1,000, £1,000, £1,000 for each of the first four years, and £27,000 in year five

discounted cash flow

Discounted cash flow (DCF) is an investment appraisal technique which recognises that money has a time value. For example, supposing that today a friend asks you to lend her £1 and offers to repay you either tomorrow, or in one year's time, which will you choose? The answer is clear: you would want the money back sooner rather than later because, if you don't intend to spend it, you can always save it in a bank or building society, where it will earn interest. Thus, as you will probably know from your studies, the rate of interest represents the time value of money.

Using £1 as an example, if it is invested with a bank or building society at an interest rate of 10 per cent per year, it will increase as follows:

Original investment	£1.00
Interest at 10% on £1	£0.10
Value at end of first year	£1.10
Interest at 10% on £1.10	£0.11
Value at end of second year	£1.21

As you will appreciate this is the technique of compound interest, with which you will, no doubt, already be familiar. So, with interest rates of 10 per cent per year, we can say that the future value of £1 will be £1.10 at the end of year one, £1.21 at the end of year two, and so on; thus £1 set aside now will gain in value so that, at some time in the future, we will have access to a larger sum of money. However, supposing that we were to *receive* £1 at the end of year one, what is it worth to us now? To find the answer to this, we need to carry out the following calculation:

$$£1 \times \frac{100}{110*} = £0.91$$

* 100 per cent, plus the rate of interest (in this example, 10 per cent).

Therefore, if we had £0.91 now and invested it at 10 per cent per year, we would have £1 at the end of year one. We can say that the *present value* of £1 receivable in one year's time is £0.91. In the same way, £1 receivable in two years' time is £0.83, calculated as follows:

$$£1 \times \frac{100}{110} \times \frac{100}{110} = £0.83$$

We can build up a *table of factors* (for 10 per cent interest rates) as follows:

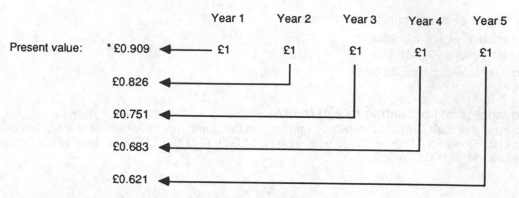

	Year 1	Year 2	Year 3	Year 4	Year 5
Present value: * £0.909 ←	£1	£1	£1	£1	£1
£0.826 ←					
£0.751 ←					
£0.683 ←					
£0.621 ←					

* taken to three decimal places, for greater accuracy.

Using your calculator, check that the table of factors above is correct. Put '1' into your calculator and multiply by 100 ÷ 110 for the first year; multiply the result by 100 ÷ 110 for the second year; and so on. As you are doing this, do not forget the basic principle that *money has a time value* and, from this, the further into the future that we expect to receive money, then the lower is its *present value*.

Let us now return to the problem of the organisation which has to choose between Machine Y and Machine Z. We will look at this assuming, firstly, a rate of interest or *cost of capital* of 10 per cent. (Cost of capital is the rate of return that an organisation expects on its money, or the rate of interest it has to pay when borrowing money.) For each machine, the expected net cash flows are multiplied by the relevant factor to give the *discounted cash flow;* the difference between total discounted cash flow and the initial cost is the *net present value* of the project.

For Machine Y the calculations are:

	Cash Flow		Discount Factor		Discounted Cash Flow
	£				£
Year 0*					(20,000)
Year 1	8,000	x	0.909	=	7,272
Year 2	12,000	x	0.826	=	9,912
Year 3	5,000	x	0.751	=	3,755
Year 4	4,000	x	0.683	=	2,732
Year 5	2,000	x	0.621	=	1,242
		Net Present Value (NPV)		=	4,913

* Year 0 is the commencement of the project when the initial costs are paid.

Note that the initial cost is shown in brackets because it is a *cost,* whereas the net cash flows are *positive amounts;* net present value is the sum of all cash flows.

For Machine Z the figures are:

	Cash Flow £		Discount Factor		Discounted Cash Flow £
Year 0					(28,000)
Year 1	10,000	x	0.909	=	9,090
Year 2	10,000	x	0.826	=	8,260
Year 3	8,000	x	0.751	=	6,008
Year 4	9,000	x	0.683	=	6,147
Year 5	9,000	x	0.621	=	5,589
			Net Present Value (NPV)	=	7,094

Here, with a cost of capital of 10 per cent, Machine Z is better, producing a considerably higher net present value than Y. Note that both machines give a positive net present value at 10 per cent: this means that either machine will be of benefit to the organisation but Machine Z is preferable; a negative NPV would indicate that a project should not go ahead.

Thus, using a discounted cash flow technique, future cash flows are brought to their value now; this means that, the further on in time that cash flows are receivable, the lower is the net present value. As this is often a difficult concept to grasp, to put it another way, future cash flows are all brought back to a common denominator which is *now*.

advantages of discounted cash flow

* all cash flows are used
* the timing of cash flows is taken into account
* using a table of factors the calculations are easy to make

disadvantages of discounted cash flow:

* the cost of capital rate is, in practice, difficult to ascertain
* the meaning of net present value is not always clear to users of the information
* the project with the higher net present value does not, in pure financial terms, always represent the better project

investment appraisal: conclusion

It is unlikely that an organisation will rely on one technique only; instead two or more criteria might be required before a project is given the go-ahead. Supposing, for example, that the organisation having to choose between Machines Y and Z applied the following criteria: 'projects must have a payback period not exceeding 2½ years, *and* must have a positive net present value at a 10 per cent cost of capital'. How do the two machines compare?

	MACHINE Y	MACHINE Z
Payback	2 years	3 years
NPV at 10 per cent	£4,913	£7,094

Under the criteria that the organisation has laid down, Machine Y would be chosen. However, Machine Z seems a better project on the net present value basis and is only rejected because it does not meet the payback requirement; also Machine Z has the better accounting rate of return (at 12.9 per cent, instead of 11 per cent for Machine Y). However, the capital expenditure required for Machine Z is £8,000 greater than Machine Y – something which NPV does not take fully into account. To obtain a better analysis, we need to use the technique of *internal rate of return*.

internal rate of return

The principles of discounted cash flow can be developed further in order to calculate the investment appraisal technique of *internal rate of return* (IRR) – this technique is also known as *DCF yield*. Note that internal rate of return is different from *accounting* rate of return.

The internal rate of return is the interest rate at which net present value exactly balances the initial investment. In other words, it shows the interest rate (or cost of capital) at which the investment 'breaks-even', ie income equals expenditure, but still applying DCF principles.

To calculate IRR we start with a cost of capital which gives a positive net present value – for example, 10 per cent cost of capital for Machine Y gives a NPV of £4,913. We increase the cost of capital by one or two percentage points each time until, eventually, it becomes negative. For example:

MACHINE Y

Cost of Capital	Present Value of Cash Flow	Initial Investment	Net Present Value
	£	£	£
10%	24,913	(20,000)	4,913
12%	23,946	(20,000)	3,946
14%	23,025	(20,000)	3,025
16%	22,177	(20,000)	2,177
18%	21,987	(20,000)	1,987
20%	20,619	(20,000)	619
22%	19,915	(20,000)	(85)

The net present value that balances the present value of cash flow with the initial investment lies between 20% and 22% – closer to 22% than 20%, so we can call it approximately 21.8%. For greater accuracy, we could make calculations using a cost of capital of 21.6% and 21.8%, but an answer to the nearest one or two percentage points is acceptable for most decisions.

Using the same techniques, the IRR for Machine Z is approximately 19.8%. Thus, Machine Y gives a higher IRR and is, thus, the preferred investment. The reason for this is that Machine Y requires a lower capital expenditure, and the timing of the cash flows is weighted towards the earlier years.

The decision criteria when using IRR is to:

• accept the higher IRR, where there is a choice between different investments
• accept projects with an IRR greater than the cost of borrowing (the cost of capital).

Thus, while IRR can be compared between two (or more) different investments, it can also be applied to cost of capital. In the example we have followed in this chapter, the cost of capital is 10%. The organisation could have gone ahead with either investment. However, if the cost of capital had been 20%, Machine Z would have been rejected and Machine Y accepted (with a 1.8% margin above cost of capital).

Chapter Summary

❑ Investment appraisal use a number of techniques to help in management decision making.

❑ The techniques include payback, accounting rate of return and discounted cash flow.

❑ Organisations often use a combination of two or more appraisal techniques before making decisions about major projects.

❑ Internal rate of return (also known as DCF yield) is used to rank projects, still applying the principles of discounted cash flow.

 Student Activities

TABLE OF DISCOUNTED CASH FLOW FACTORS

Cost of capital	10%	12%	14%	16%	18%	20%	22%	24%
Year 1	0.909	0.893	0.877	0.862	0.847	0.833	0.820	0.806
Year 2	0.826	0.797	0.769	0.743	0.718	0.694	0.672	0.650
Year 3	0.751	0.712	0.675	0.641	0.609	0.579	0.551	0.524
Year 4	0.683	0.636	0.592	0.552	0.516	0.482	0.451	0.423
Year 5	0.621	0.567	0.519	0.476	0.437	0.402	0.370	0.341
Year 6	0.564	0.507	0.456	0.410	0.370	0.335	0.303	0.275

23.1 Using the discounted cash flow technique, rework the calculations for Machines Y and Z, in the chapter, using the factors for (a) 14 per cent, and (b) 20 per cent per annum from the table above.

23.2 John Smith is considering two major investment projects for his engineering business. Only one project can be chosen and the following information is available:

	Project A	Project B
	£	£
Initial capital outlay	80,000	100,000
Net cash inflows, year: 1	40,000	20,000
2	40,000	30,000
3	20,000	50,000
4	10,000	50,000
5	10,000	49,500

The initial capital outlay will occur immediately and you may assume that the net cash inflows will arise at the end of each year. Smith's estimated cost of capital over the five year period is 12 per cent per annum.

To assist John Smith make his decision you, as his accountant are asked to:

• Produce numerical assessments of the two projects based on the following project appraisal techniques:
  (a) Payback
  (b) Net present value (NPV)
  (c) Accounting rate of return

• Comment on the relative merits of the project appraisal techniques, and advise John Smith on which investment project, if either, should be undertaken.   Present your advice in the form of a letter to your client, enclosing the calculations you have made for above.   His address is Unit 27, Factory Estate, Newtown, Wyvern County, WV2 1ER.

23.3   Ken Shah needs some printing equipment for his publishing firm. He has to choose between the following methods of acquisition:
• Purchase of the equipment for cash.
• Purchase under a hire purchase contract, involving an initial deposit and two annual payments.
• Hire of the equipment.

The following information is available:

Cash price of equipment	£10,000
Period of use in Shah's firm	5 years
Scrap value at end of use	£1,000
Initial deposit under hire purchase contract	£4,000
Two annual hire purchase payments due at end of first year and end of second year	£4,000 each
Hire of equipment, five annual hire charge payments due at end of each year	£2,500 each

Shah's estimated cost of capital over the five year period is 10 per cent per annum.

You are his Finance Director and to assist Ken Shah make his decision, you are asked to:
• Produce numerical assessments of the three methods of acquisition using discounted cash flow techniques.
• Advise Ken Shah, in the form of a memorandum, of the best method of acquisition.

23.4   Calculate the internal rate of return (DCF yield) to the nearest two per cent for projects A and B in question 23.2.

Comment on the IRR for both projects.

Assignment 7
Management Accounts : Fitta Fabricators Limited

LEARNING OUTCOMES COVERED:
Management accounting: break-even calculations, marginal and absorption costing, investment appraisal

SITUATION

You are working in the accounts department of Fitta Fabricators Ltd. The company manufactures a single product, the 'Fitta De Luxe' exercise cycle. Demand for this product increases each year as a result of the growing awareness of the importance of healthy living. The company has, as a result, increased its production capacity and, up until now, little thought has been given to the costing involved in manufacturing the product. However, some figures have recently been collected which show, at current production levels of 5,500 units per year, the following:

Raw material costs	£12 per unit
Direct Labour costs	£10 per unit
Selling price (to retail outlets)	£65 per unit (all units produced can be sold)
Fixed factory costs, and other overheads	£156,950 per year

An enquiry has been received from a company which operates a major mail-order catalogue. The company is considering the inclusion of the 'Fitta De Luxe' in their next catalogue. It is expected that they can sell 1,500 units to new customers who would not have bought the product elsewhere. However, they are seeking a discount, in view of the quantity of the order, and offer a price of £45 per unit. If this order is undertaken, the accountant of Fitta Fabricators Ltd considers that the unit variable costs would remain unchanged but that fixed costs would increase by 10 per cent, being the cost of additional factory and warehouse buildings that would have to be rented.

The company is considering the purchase of a new machine to replace an old piece of equipment which bends and shapes the tubular steel of the exercise cycle. The slowness of the old machine often causes production hold-ups and it is expected that the new machine will overcome such problems. There is no doubt that the company should install the new machine, but it can't decide whether to buy outright, buy on hire purchase, or to lease it. The relevant information is:

Outright purchase at a cost of £10,000.

Hire purchase, with a deposit of £3,000 payable immediately and three annual instalments of £3,500 payable at the end of each of the first three years.

Lease, with six annual leasing payments of £2,500 payable at the end of each year.

The machine is expected to last for six years, after which it will be worn out and have a nil scrap value.

The company has an agreed overdraft facility with the bank on which the bank charges interest at 10 per cent. Whichever method of acquisition is chosen, the payment(s) will be made through the bank account.

STUDENT TASKS ————————————————————————————

Write a memorandum to the accountant of Fitta Fabricators Ltd, your section boss; it should incorporate:

1.   A break-even graph on the basis of current production costs; prove your answer by calculation.

2.   An explanation of whether or not the proposed contract for the mail-order company should be undertaken. As part of your submission, prepare schedules showing:

   •   the expected net profit for a full year at existing production levels

   •   the expected net profit for a year if the new contract is taken on

3.   An investigation of hire-purchase and leasing as methods of acquiring a fixed asset such as a machine. Obtain leaflets, newspaper articles, etc. and set out the advantages and disadvantages, to a company, of each method.

4.   Discounted Cash Flow projections preparing figures to show the net present value under each option (tax is to be ignored) and ranking the choices in preferred order (starting with the best) as indicated by this one project appraisal technique.

   Note: use the table of factors on page 257.

section five
financial record keeping

In this section we look at how routine day-to-day transactions are processed and recorded by the book-keeping and accounts section of an organisation. The sequence of events is normally as follows:

- processing of business documents – either issued or received
- recording of documents in day books
- transfer of information from the day books into double-entry accounts
- balancing of accounts and extraction of the trial balance

We have already used the trial balance in the preparation of financial statements (see Section 3 of this book). It is important therefore, that financial record keeping should be accurate so that the financial statements themselves present a true picture of the organisation's financial affairs.

24 Business documents

introduction

When an organisation buys goods or services, it will eventually have to pay for them. Most goods and services are supplied *on credit:* the goods arrive or the service is supplied first, and payment is made later, often after thirty days. The *principle* is the same as when a person pays the milkman at a later date for milk delivered, or the newsagent for papers delivered.

The process involves a number of distinct stages – order, supply, request for payment, and payment. At each stage a *business document* is normally issued, the most well-known of which is the invoice, which tells the organisation buying the goods or services how much they cost, and what charges or discounts (if any) are applicable.

The business documents can either be produced manually or by computer on *paper* – the traditional and most common method, or as *electronic messages* between the supplier's and the buyer's computers, a system known as Electronic Data Interchange (EDI).

In this chapter we will look at the paper-based system of business documents, partly because it is the more common system, and partly because it forms the basis for EDI. We will also explain the basics of computer accounting and the EDI system. The financial documents to be examined are

- purchase order
- delivery note
- invoice
- credit note
- statement and remittance advice

the buying and paying process in the organisation

The size of an organisation largely determines who deals with the business documents. In a larger organisation there may be a *purchasing department* which deals with ordering goods, a *sales department* which sells the goods, and an *accounts department* which makes the payments. In a smaller organisation these functions may be left to individuals, eg the buyer and the accounts clerk. In a sole-trader business, the sole trader usually prepares the documents, or possibly employs a clerk to undertake the work.

business documents

There are a number of business documents – including the invoice – with which you will need to be familiar when dealing with ordering and paying for goods. In this chapter we will look at the business documents set out below by means of a Case Study which follows the ordering of copier paper by Martley Machine Rental Limited, the delivery of the paper, the return of some of the paper, and the final settlement by cheque.

purchase order   the official order form which the buyer uses to order the goods required

delivery note   the document which accompanies the goods and gives details of the goods supplied – it is normally signed by the recipient when the goods are delivered

invoice   the document which is sent by the seller to the buyer stating how much is owed and when it has to be paid

credit note   a document sent by the seller to the buyer if the amount owing (as shown on the invoice) has to be reduced for any reason, for example
• the goods were damaged in transit
• some of the goods have been returned by the buyer
• not all of the goods were sent
• a higher price has been charged in error

statement   a document sent by the seller to the buyer, normally at the end of every month, giving details of invoices issued, credit notes issued and payments made (just as a bank sends a regular statement to its customers showing money paid in and money paid out)

remittance advice   a form which will be sent with the buyer's payment when the invoice(s) or statement is settled; a remittance advice may be a separate piece of paper prepared by the buyer, or it can be a tear-off slip sent with the supplier's statement

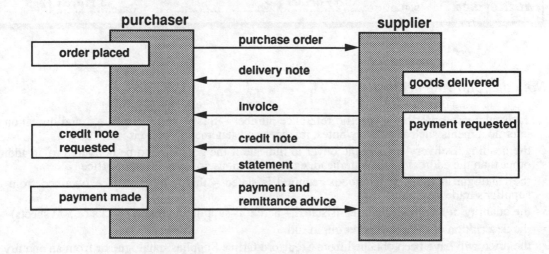

Fig.24.1 Summary of the flow of business documents

Case Study: business documents

purchase order

In the this Case Study, Martley Machine Rental Limited are ordering from Stourford Office Supplies some paper for their laser printer. The purchasing department or buyer at Martley Machine Rental will post or fax the purchase order shown below, which will have been typed out in the office, or produced on a computer accounting program. The details of the laser paper will have been obtained from Stourford Office Supplies' catalogue, or possibly by means of a written or telephoned enquiry.

PURCHASE ORDER
MARTLEY MACHINE RENTAL LTD
67 Broadgreen Road
Martley MR6 7TR
Tel 090655 6576 Fax 090655 6342

Stourford Office Supplies
Unit 12
Avon Industrial Estate
Stourford SF5 6TD

No   47700
Date   13 March 19-5
Delivery   to above address

catalogue	quantity	description	price
3564749	15 reams	100gsm white Supalaser paper	£4.00 per ream

authorised   signature......C J Farmer.............................   date.13 March 19-5.............

Note the following details

- each purchase order has a specific reference number – this is useful for filing, and quotation on later documents such as delivery notes, invoices and statements – here it is 47700
- the heading 'Delivery' enables the buyer to indicate if the goods are to be delivered to an address other than the address on the letterhead, eg to a warehouse or to a different office
- the catalogue number of the goods required is stated – this number can be obtained from the supplier's trade catalogue
- the quantity of the goods required is stated – here it is supplied in reams (packs of 500 sheets)
- the description of the goods is set out in full
- the price will have been obtained from Stourford Office Supplies' catalogue or from an enquiry
- the purchase order is signed by the buyer in the purchasing department, and dated – without this authorisation the supplier is unlikely to supply the goods.

delivery note

The delivery note is prepared by the supplier of the goods, and is either typed in the supplier's office or produced on a computer printer if the supplier has a computer accounting program.

The delivery note travels with the goods, normally in the care of the van driver, in which case the person receiving the goods will be asked to sign the delivery note. If the goods are *posted*, the delivery note will be packed with the goods in the carton, or possibly in a transparent envelope on the ouside of the box containing the goods. If the goods are posted by letter post or parcel post, the signature of the recipient will not be needed, unless they are sent recorded delivery, registered post or datapost.

▬ DELIVERY NOTE ▬

Stourford Office Supplies
Unit 12, Avon Industrial Estate, Stourford SF5 6TD
Tel 0807 765434 Fax 0807 765123

Martley Machine Rental Ltd 67 Broadgreen Road Martley MR6 7TR	Delivery Note No 26754 Date 26 March 19-5 Your Order No 47700 Delivery Van Delivery

product code	quantity	description
3564749	15 reams	100 gsm white Supalaser paper

received
signature............ *G Hughes* ....name (capitals)............ *G HUGHES* ....
date............ *30 March 19-5* ....

Note the following details

- the delivery note has a numerical reference, useful for filing and later reference if there is a query
- the delivery note quotes the purchase order number – this enables the buyer to 'tie up' the delivery with the original order
- the method of delivery is stated – here the delivery is by van
- the delivery note quotes the supplier's catalogue reference, the quantity supplied and the description of the goods – these details will be checked against
  - the goods themselves
  - the invoice when it is received
- no price is quoted on the delivery note
- the delivery note will be signed and dated by the person receiving the goods
- the person receiving the goods will also print his or her name – this is to enable the person to be identified later if there should be a query about the goods
- if the person receiving the goods does not have time to check them there and then – as is often the case – the phrase 'Contents not inspected' can be written on the delivery note (not shown here)

invoice

The invoice is the trading document which is sent by the seller to the buyer to advise how much is owed by the buyer for a particular delivery of goods. The invoice, like the delivery note, is prepared in the supplier's office, and is either typed or produced on a computer printer by a computer accounting program. Invoices produced by different organisations will all vary to some extent in terms of detail, but their basic layout will always be the same. The invoice illustrated below is typical of a modern typed or computer printed document. Look at it carefully and then read the notes.

INVOICE

Stourford Office Supplies
Unit 12, Avon Industrial Estate, Stourford SF5 6TD
Tel 0807 765434 Fax 0807 765123
VAT Reg 0745 4672 76

Invoice to

Martley Machine Rental Ltd
67 Broadgreen Road
Martley
MR6 7TR

Invoice No	652771
Account	MAR435
Date/tax point	26 March 19-5
Your Reference	47700

deliver to

as above

product code	description	quantity	price	unit	total	disc %	net
3564749	100 gsm white Supalaser	15	4.00	ream	60.00	0	60.00

Terms
Net monthly
Carriage paid
E & OE

GOODS TOTAL	60.00
CASH DISCOUNT	00.00
SUBTOTAL	60.00
VAT (17.5%)	10.50
TOTAL	70.50

invoice details and terms

addresses   The invoice shows the address

- of the seller/supplier of the goods – Stourford Office Supplies
- where the invoice should be sent – to Martley Machine Rental Ltd
- where the goods were sent – if different from the invoice address

references   There are a number of important references on the invoice:
- the numerical reference of the invoice itself – 652771
- the account number allocated to Martley Machine Rental Ltd by the seller – MAR435 – possibly for use in the seller's computer accounting program
- the original reference number on the purchase order sent by Martley Machine Rental Ltd – 47700 – which will enable the buyer to 'tie up' the invoice with the original order

date   The date on the invoice is important because the payment date (here one month) is calculated from it. The date is often described as the 'tax point' because it is the transaction date as far as VAT calculations are concerned, ie it is when the sale took place and the VAT was charged. Note: VAT (Value Added Tax) is a tax on the supply of goods and services; at the time of writing the rate is 17.5%.

the goods   As the invoice is a statement of the amount owing, it must specify accurately the goods supplied. The details – set out in columns in the body of the invoice – include
- *product code* – this is the catalogue number which appeared on the original purchase order and on the delivery note
- *description* – the goods must be precisely specified
- *quantity* – this should agree with the quantity ordered
- *price* – this is the price of each unit shown in the next column
- *unit* is the way in which the unit is counted and charged for, eg
  – reams of paper (packs of 500 sheets)
  – boxes of ballpoint pens (100 in a box, for instance)
  – items of furniture (eg individual desks and chairs)
- *total* is the unit price multiplied by the number of units
- *discount %* is the percentage allowance (known as trade discount) given to customers who regularly deal with the supplier i.e. they receive a certain percentage (eg 20%) deducted from their bill
- *net* is the amount due to the seller after deduction of trade discount, and before VAT is added on

cash discount and VAT   Further calculations are made in the box at the bottom of the invoice
- *Goods* is the net amount due to the seller (the total of the net column)
- *Cash Discount* is a percentage of the Goods total (often a 2.5% discount) which the buyer can deduct if he or she pays straightaway rather than waiting the month allowed on the invoice – there is no cash discount in this example
- *Value Added Tax* (VAT), calculated as 17.5% of the total after deduction of any cash discount is added to produce the invoice total

terms   The terms for payment are stated on the invoice. In this case these include
- *Net monthly* – this means that full payment of the invoice (without cash discount) should be made within a month of the invoice date
- *Carriage paid* means that the price of the goods includes delivery
- *E & OE* stands for 'errors and omissions excepted' which means that if there is a error or something left off the invoice by mistake, resulting in an incorrect final price, the supplier has the right to rectify the mistake and demand the correct amount

credit note

A credit note is a document issed by the supplier which reduces the amount owed by the buyer. The document is prepared by the supplier and sent to the buyer. This could happen when

- the goods have been damaged, lost in transit or are faulty
- not all the goods have been sent – a situation referred to as 'shortages'
- the unit price on the invoice may be too high
- the buyer may not want some or all of the goods, and the supplier agrees to accept them back

A credit note is often prepared following the recipt by the seller of a *returns note* (sent with returned goods) or a *debit note* (issued, for example, when the buyer has been overcharged)

In the case of the credit note below, Martley Machine Rental have only received 10 reams of paper instead of 15; they are short by 5 reams and are therefore receiving a credit for £23.50.

━ CREDIT NOTE ━

Stourford Office Supplies
Unit 12, Avon Industrial Estate, Stourford SF5 6TD
Tel 0807 765434 Fax 0807 765123
VAT Reg 0745 4672 76

to

Martley Machine Rental Ltd
67 Broadgreen Road
Martley
MR6 7TR

Credit Note No	552793
Account	MAR435
Date/tax point	2 April 19–5
Your Reference	D/N 8974
Our invoice	652771

product code	description	quantity	price	unit	total	disc %	net
3564749	100 gsm white Supalaser	5	4.00	ream	20.00	0	20.00

Reason for credit
shortages –
only 10 reams of paper delivered, 15 ordered

GOODS TOTAL	20.00
CASH DISCOUNT	00.00
SUBTOTAL	20.00
VAT (17.5%)	3.50
TOTAL	23.50

Note the following details

- the invoice number of the original consignment is quoted
- the reason for the issue of the credit note is stated at the bottom of the credit note – here 'shortages'
- the details are otherwise exactly the same as on an invoice

statement and remittance advice

A supplier will not normally expect a buyer to pay each individual invoice as soon as it is received: this could result in the buyer having to write a number of cheques during the month. Instead, a *statement of account* is sent by the supplier to the buyer at the end of the month. This statement, which can be typed out, or printed by the seller's computer accounting program, will show exactly what is owed by the buyer to the seller. It contains details of

- invoices issued for goods supplied – the full amount due, including VAT
- refunds made on *credit notes*
- payments received from the buyer

The statement issued by Stourford Office Supplies to Martley Machine Rental Ltd for the transactions described on the previous pages is illustrated below. It lists

- the date of each transaction
- the invoice (abbreviated to 'inv') for the 15 reams of paper
- the credit note (abbreviated to 'CN') for the 5 reams that were short
- the outstanding amounts – ie what is actually owed on each invoice – here £70.50 less the £23.50 refund = £47.00

You will see that the statement has a tear-off slip attached on the right. This is known as a *remittance advice*. The buyer can detach this, tick the invoice(s) being paid in the far right-hand column, and send it with the cheque to the supplier. Some organisations will prepare their own remittance advice to send with the cheque (see next page). If the organisation has a computer accounting program the computer will probably print out the remittance advice, and in some cases the cheque as well.

statement					**remittance advice**		
Stourford Office Supplies Unit 12, Avon Industrial Estate, Stourford SF5 6TD Tel 0807 765434 Fax 0807 765123 VAT Reg 0745 4672 76					**Stourford Office Supplies** Unit 12, Avon Industrial Estate, Stourford SF5 6TD		
Account MAR435 Date 31 March 19-5					Account MAR 435		
Martley Machine Rental Ltd 67 Broadgreen Road Martley MR6 7TR					*please indicate items you are paying (✔) and return this advice with your remittance*		
date	type	reference	value	outstanding	ref	outstanding	✔
26/03/-5 02/04/-5	inv CN	652771 552793	70.50 23.50	47.00	652771	47.00	
			TOTAL	47.00	TOTAL	47.00	

REMITTANCE ADVICE
MARTLEY MACHINE RENTAL LTD
67 Broadgreen Road Martley MR6 7TR

Stourford Office Supplies
Unit 12
Avon Industrial Estate
Stourford SF5 6TD

Cheque No   000427
Date   20 April 19-5
Account   ST0006

date	our ref .	your ref.	amount	payment
20/04/-5	47700	652771	47.00	47.00

cheque value   £ 47.00

a separate remittance advice sent with the payment

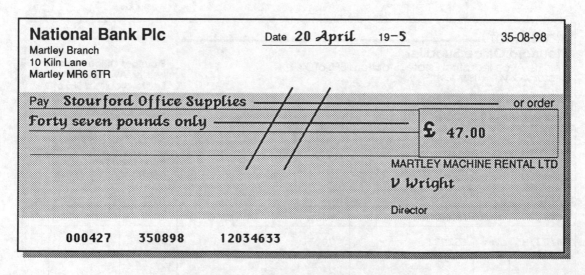

National Bank Plc
Martley Branch
10 Kiln Lane
Martley MR6 6TR

Date **20 April** 19-5

35-08-98

Pay **Stourford Office Supplies**   or order

Forty seven pounds only

£ **47.00**

MARTLEY MACHINE RENTAL LTD

V Wright

Director

000427   350898   12034633

the cheque sent with the remittance advice

business documents and computers

Many organisations now use computers to produce the business documents described in this chapter. Later in this book (Chapter 30) we will examine in detail how a typical accounting package is used to process financial transactions. If an organisation does not have a large mainframe computer, it can use a PC (personal computer) to print purchase orders, delivery notes, invoices, credit notes, statements and remittance advices, and in some cases, cheques. Once all the preliminary information is input into the computer (names and addresses of customers, product details, prices etc), the transaction details are input according to instructions given on the screen. All that is required is an inexpensive computer program and the necessary hardware. In Chapter 30 of this book we use the popular Sage™ software as an illustration of how a computer accounting package works.

There are many advantages of using computers to produce financial documents:

* *accuracy* – as long as the information input is correct, all the calculations, including the VAT, are performed automatically and accurately
* *speed* – the typist is spared the lengthy and repetitive production of individual documents
* *efficiency* – all statements can be sent out to customers on time: the computer will print them automatically at a given command
* *availability of information* – as all the information about sales and purchases is stored on computer file, it is a simple matter to call up on screen how much is owed by customers and how much is owed to suppliers

The type of computer accounting program described above is fast and efficient, but it relies on a paper-based system: the documents are posted (or faxed) to their destination and are checked manually. A recent development, Electronic Data Interchange, commonly known as EDI and described in detail below, does away with the paper documents.

Electronic Data Interchange (EDI)

As you will have found in your study of business systems, computers in different organisations can 'talk' to each other. Telephone links can be set up and computer data – word-processed files, databases and other types of data – can be transmitted, often at night when the telephone rates are cheaper. If you bought this book at a bookshop, the order may have been processed on a computer behind the counter, and the order data sent off that evening to Osborne Books via a computer link.

Systems now exist whereby all the business documents described in this chapter are generated on computer file and the data sent between the computers of the buyer and the seller. This system, known as *Electronic Data Interchange (EDI)*, is extensively used in the UK, particularly by large retailing organisations which need to renew stock frequently. You will have seen how the tills in large chains of shops operate by scanning bar codes with a laser. Each branch is linked to a central computer, so that each time an item is sold, the data is recorded by the laser, transmitted to the main computer, updating the stock records of the shop. When a certain minimum stock level is reached, an order for new stock is automatically triggered by the computer and sent to the computer of the supplier. The supplier then delivers new stock. No paper documents have been involved.

How does EDI work in practical terms?

definition   EDI is a system which transfers commercial and administrative instructions between computers using agreed formats for the messages

EDI standards   The two parties involved agree a format for the electronic messages which take the place of purchase orders, delivery instructions, invoices, credit notes and statements.   In the UK the standard retail transfer system is *Tradacoms*, and internationally the United Nations is sponsoring a worldwide EDI standard known as *UN-EDIFACT*.

EDI transfers

The transfer is normally sent from one computer to another via a third party known as a VAN (value added network). A VAN operates like an electronic post office: you deposit your information electronically in your 'post box' and the VAN transfers it to the 'postbox' of your trading partner.

EDI benefits

The benefits of EDI include
- reduced handling costs
- reduced postage costs
- reduced paper storage costs
- fewer errors (there is less re-keying of existing computer data)
- faster payment

'just in time' retailing

Holding stock costs organisations money and therefore the larger retailers – Tesco and Marks & Spencer for example – operate a 'just-in-time' ordering policy whereby stock is ordered as late as possible. Some food chains order from only two to five days before the goods are needed. This is useful for the retailers, but can cause headaches for the suppliers. One of the advantages of EDI is that *estimates* of future orders can be sent to suppliers so that they can produce approximately the correct quantity of goods in time for the expected orders.

EDI payments

In the normal course of paper-based trading (ie using paper invoices and other business documents), settlement is usually made by cheque which is posted to the supplier or by BACS (an inter-bank computer transfer system). The banks are now introducing a system – NatWest's BankLine for example – whereby the buyer can use the EDI system for authorising his bank to make payment to the supplier's bank. As the buyer's computer system already has details of each trade transaction – the parties involved and the amounts – it is a simple matter to add the banking details of the supplier, so that settlement can be made on the due date.

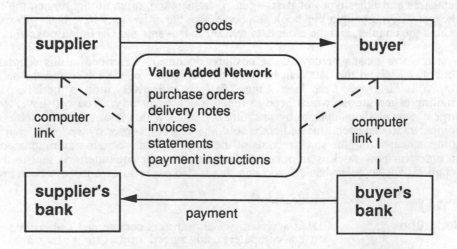

Fig. 24.2 The EDI system

credit control

So far in this chapter we have taken for granted that a supplier will supply on credit (i.e. allow the buyer to pay later), and also that the buyer will pay up on receipt of the statement. Unfortunately these are assumptions which in reality cannot be taken for granted. When selling on credit you must

* investigate a new buyer to ensure that he or she is creditworthy – ie has the financial resources to pay on the due date
* monitor existing buyers to ensure that they do pay up on time
* chase up debts which are overdue

This overall process is known as *credit control*. It is a sign of a well-run organisation that credit control is tight, and buyers who owe money, known as *debtors*, are chased up, and even taken to court for non-payment if the amount and the circumstances are appropriate.

We will now look at credit control through two Case Studies: the first looks at a person 'vetting' the creditworthiness of a potential buyer; the second looks at a supplier chasing up overdue debts.

Case Study 1: selling on credit

Situation

Matthew has recently started up in business with a fruit and vegetable stall in the local market. Up until now all his sales have been paid for by his customers in cash or by cheque (collectively known as 'cash sales'). He has today been approached by Goodfood, a firm of caterers who operate a number of works' canteens in the locality, to quote for all their fruit and vegetable supplies. The value of this potential contract is sales of about £300 each week; Goodfood require an invoice at the end of each week listing Matthew's sales to them for the week, and they agree to make payment not later than 30 days after the date of the invoice. What should Matthew do?

Solution

The steps that need to be taken by Matthew are:

* When approached by a previously unknown organisation wishing to buy goods on credit, the seller should ask for two references. One of these should be the buyer's bank, and the other a trader with whom the buyer has previously done business.

* The seller, Matthew, must, before supplying goods on credit, take up both references, and obtain satisfactory replies. (Note that it is not possible to approach a bank direct for a reference on one of their customers. It can only be done bank-to-bank, and so the seller must ask his or her own bank to approach the buyer's bank.)

* Once satisfactory replies have been received, a credit limit for the customer should be established. (This is similar to the way in which credit limits are established by credit card companies.) The actual amount of the credit limit will depend very much on the expected amount of future business – perhaps £1,000 in this example. The credit limit should not normally be exceeded.

* Matthew should ensure that invoices and monthly statements are sent out promptly.

* If a customer does not pay within a reasonable time, procedures should be followed to chase up the debt promptly; these include letters, telephone calls and even court action.

Case Study 2: chasing debts

Situation

Matthew has found that Goodfood, despite the good references received, are not paying up, and he is owed a total of £450 which should have been paid three months ago. What should he do? He has various courses of action available to him; what he does will depend on how reluctant Goodfood are to pay.

Solution

A typical procedure used by an organisation chasing up debts, which Matthew could adopt, would be

- Write a letter along the lines of

    "Dear Sir,
    Overdue Account
    We do not appear to have received settlement of your account with us, the balance of which is £450. We enclose an up-to-date statement and shall be grateful if you settle this overdue amount by return of post."

- If nothing is heard within seven days, then telephone and ask to speak to their Accounts Department, Purchases Ledger. Ask about the overdue payment. You may be told *"the cheque is in the post"* (it rarely is!) or *"can we have a copy of the last invoice –we don't seem to have received it?"*
    These replies can be stalling tactics to buy time; on the other hand, the telephone call may produce results and a payment in the post.

- If payment is not received as a result of the telephone call, Matthew has a number of options open to him:

    - to employ a solicitor to send Goodfood a formal demand for the money and possibly to take Goodfood to court (this is an expensive option)
    - to employ the services of a debt-collecting agency
    - to take Goodfood to the Small Claims Court (used for claims under £500) – a time-consuming process with no guarantee of success.

Matthew should realise that taking Goodfood to court and obtaining judgement against them still does not mean he will get his money back. It is often thought that going to court will solve all problems; it often results in a large solicitor's bill and nothing from the debtor. Goodfood may not *have* the money, and may even be bankrupt, which means that their liabilities exceed their assets. An unsecured creditor like Matthew is unlikely to be repaid anything at all. At a time like this Matthew will probably want to cut his losses and write off the £450 as a 'bad debt', an expense to his business. This procedure is explained more fully in Chapter 10.

computerised credit control – aged debtors schedule

Good credit control is an important ingredient for successful trading. Traders with computer accounting programs will be able to print out an 'aged debtors schedule', a list of individual debtors (buyers), the amounts they owe, and the period of time the debts have been outstanding. This will enable them to follow up overdue amounts, and recover money which might otherwise be lost. An example of an aged debtors schedule is illustrated in Fig 24.3 on the next page.

```
JR CATERING LTD            SALES LEDGER - AGED DEBTORS SCHEDULE


A/C   Account   Name      Turnover Credit Limit  Balance  Current  30 Days  60 Days  Older
----  --------------      --------  -----------  --------  --------  -------  -------  ------
201   Merrion & Co          370.00     1000.00    164.50   164.50     0.00     0.00    0.00
202   Kingfisher  Ltd       320.00      750.00    376.00   376.00     0.00     0.00    0.00
204   I Marcos          *  1730.00     1000.00   1632.75   799.00     0.00   833.75    0.00
205   Compusoft Ltd        2025.00     2000.00   1926.88  1880.00    46.88     0.00    0.00
208   R Weinberger          425.00      750.00    499.38   499.38     0.00     0.00    0.00

                          --------  -----------  --------  --------  -------  -------  ------
              Totals :     4870.00     5500.00   4599.51  3718.88    46.88   833.75    0.00
```

*Fig. 24.3 An aged debtors schedule for amounts owed to JR Catering Ltd
note: the asterisk marks an out-of-order account, ie one that is over its credit limit*

Chapter Summary

❑ All organisations use commercially accepted business documents to carry out trading transactions. The most commonly used business documents are
  • purchase order
  • delivery note
  • invoice
  • credit note
  • statement
  • remittance advice

❑ Organisations will either prepare business documents manually, or use a computer program; the standard format and terminology remaining the same whichever method is used.

❑ Some organisations are now using a paperless system known as EDI (Electronic Data Interchange) whereby the details normally found on paper business documents are sent as electronic messages beteeen the computers of the buyer and the seller.

❑ Suppliers of goods and services should take references on any new buyers - a bank reference and a trader's reference.

❑ Debts not received on time should be chased by letter and telephone; if payment is still not received, legal action can be considered, or alternatively the writing off of the debt.

❑ Organisations with computer accounting programs obtain information about overdue debts by means of an 'aged debtors schedule' which lists the accounts, amounts and the periods the debts have been outstanding.

In the next chapter we look at how the documents are recorded in the daybooks of the organisation.

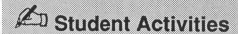 **Student Activities**

Some of the activities set out below involve the use of a number of different business documents. You can either use the specimen photcopiable blank forms available from Osborne Books, or you can design your own documents, using as a guide business documents encountered in your work or work experience. If you have access to a suitable computer accounting package, this can be used to produce the documents involved.

24.1 Look at the invoice shown below and explain what is meant by

    (a) deliver to   (b) account   (c) date/tax point (d) your reference (e) product code

    (f) unit   (g) carriage paid (h)net   (i) net monthly   (j) E & OE

24.2. A new accounts clerk at Martley Machine Rental Limited telephones querying the invoice shown below, saying that he does not understand why 'discount' appears twice – in a vertical column and also as 'cash discount' further down on the document. He asks how his organisation can qualify for each type of discount. What would you tell him?

INVOICE

Stourford Office Supplies
Unit 12, Avon Industrial Estate, Stourford SF5 6TD
Tel 0807 765434 Fax 0807 765123
VAT Reg 0745 4672 76

Invoice to

Martley Machine Rental Ltd 67 Broadgreen Road Martley MR6 7TR	Invoice No	652771
	Account	MAR435
	Date/tax point	30 March 19-5
	Your Reference	47700

deliver to

as above

product code	description	quantity	price	unit	total	disc %	net
3564749	100 gsm white Supalaser	15	4.00	ream	60.00	0	60.00

Terms
Net monthly
Carriage paid
E & OE

GOODS TOTAL	60.00
CASH DISCOUNT	00.00
SUBTOTAL	60.00
VAT	10.50
TOTAL	70.50

24.3 If you are studying in a group you should divide into pairs and play the roles of buyer and seller. The buyer is a clothes shop and the seller a clothes wholesaler.   You will need copies of two blank business documents: purchase order and invoice. You can use the current date and VAT rate but will need to make up the following details:

- the names and addresses of buyer and seller as appropriate to your locality
- catalogue numbers
- order numbers and invoice numbers

The buyer is to complete two separate purchase orders and the seller is to complete a separate invoice for each order. The orders are as follows:

(a) 100 pairs of tights (black) at £1.25
25 woollen jumpers (green) at £15 each
50 nighties (pink) at £8.50 each

(b) 25 dresses (red) at £15 each
30 pairs of denim jeans (black) at £17.50 each
50 pairs of tights (fishnet black) at £1.30 each

Assume that there is no trade discount available to the buyer. Add VAT at the current rate.

24.4 The student paying the role of the buyer in Activity 24.3 discovers that a 10% trade discount should have been applied to the two orders in Activity 24.3. He/she should write a letter to the supplier (Manager, Accounts Department) pointing out this fact. The date of the letter should be two weeks after the first invoice date. The person playing the role of the supplier should prepare a credit note refunding the 10% credit due. The date of the credit note should be three weeks after the first invoice date. The supplier should then prepare a statement dated one month after the first invoice date showing all the transactions and the amount due.

24.5 You work in the Accounts Departments of Mercia Building Supplies, Unit 3 Severnside Industrial Estate, Stourminster WR4 3TH. Your financial records show the following details about your customer N Patel:

1 Mar.	Balance due, £145
3 Mar.	Goods sold to N Patel, £210 (including VAT), invoice number 8119
10 Mar.	Cheque received from N Patel, £145
23 Mar.	Goods returned by N Patel, £50 (including VAT), credit note number 7345 issued.
28 Mar.	Goods sold to N Patel, £180 (including VAT), invoice number 8245

You are to prepare the statement of account to be sent to the customer at his address at 45 Archway Avenue, Stourminster WR2 5RT on 31 March. This should show clearly the balance due at the month-end.

24.6 You work for Deansway Trading Company, a wholesaler of office stationery, which trades from The Modern Office, 79 Deansway, Stourminster WR1 2EJ. A customer, The Card Shop of 126 The Crescent, Marshall Green, WR4 5TX, orders the following on order number 9516:

5 boxes of assorted rubbers at £5 per box, catalogue no 26537
100 shorthand notebooks at £4 for a pack of 10, catalogue no 72625
250 ring binders at 50p each, catalogue no 72698

Value Added Tax is to be charged at the current rate on all items, and a 2.5 per cent cash discount is offered for full settlement within 14 days. Prepare invoice number 8234, under today's date, to be sent to the customer.

24.7   You are in business as a sole trader who instals electronic alarm systems. You trade under the name of Electralarm. You are registered for VAT, registered number 454 7106 51. Your address is 67 Larches Avenue, West Roxton, WR6 6YP. Three months ago you installed a domestic alarm system for Mr Tom Gunsmith, at 8 Tresham Close, West Roxton, WR3 5FG. You sent him

- an invoice for £785.00 three months ago
- a statement at the end of month one
- a statement at the end of month two

You have received no money from Mr Gunsmith.

(a)   Using today's date and assuming that the item for £785 was the only one on the statement, draw up an appropriate letter to Mr Gunsmith chasing up this debt.

(b)   If you do not receive a reply to your letter, what courses of action are open to you? What would you chose to do?

24.8   You work as an assistant in the Accounts Department of JR Catering Limited, a contract caterer. Your supervisor has asked you to obtain an aged debtors schedule from the computer. The printout shown below is the first page of the schedule. The asterisk shows an account that is over its credit limit. J R Catering allows up to 30 days credit to all its customers.

Write a memorandum (using your own name and the current date) to the Supervisor (N Lamont) setting out

(a)   the accounts that may be a source of trouble, and why

(b)   corrective action that the business might take

```
JR CATERING LTD          SALES LEDGER - AGED DEBTORS SCHEDULE


A/C   Account   Name      Turnover Credit Limit  Balance  Current  30 Days  60 Days  Older
----  -------------       -------- ------------ -------- -------- ------- ------- ------

201   Merrion & Co         370.00    1000.00    164.50   164.50    0.00    0.00   0.00
202   Kingfisher Ltd       320.00     750.00    376.00   376.00    0.00    0.00   0.00
204   I Marcos        *   1730.00    1000.00   1632.75   799.00    0.00  833.75   0.00
205   Compusoft Ltd       2025.00    2000.00   1926.88  1880.00   46.88    0.00   0.00
208   R Weinberger         425.00     750.00    499.38   499.38    0.00    0.00   0.00

                         --------  ----------  -------- -------- ------- ------- ------
             Totals :    4870.00    5500.00   4599.51  3718.88   46.88  833.75   0.00
```

25 Financial records – day books

introduction

In the previous chapter we have seen how documents are used by organisations for the purchase and sale of goods. These documents are then used as a means of recording transactions in the accounting system.

The two most common types of accounting transactions recorded are:

- *the purchase of goods* with the intention that they should be resold at a profit, eg a plumbers' merchant buying bath taps from the manufacturer
- the *sale of goods* in which the business trades, eg a plumbers' merchant selling bath taps to plumbers and other customers

In this chapter we will examine how these transactions are recorded in the accounting system of the business in *day books*. As these books are the first books in which the transactions are recorded, they are also known as *books of prime entry* or *books of original entry*.

purchases day book

The purchases day book is a collection point for accounting information on the credit purchases of a business and it takes the following form (with sample entries shown):

Purchases Day Book

Date	Details	Invoice No	Folio	Net	VAT*	Gross
19-1				£	£	£
2 Jan.	P Bond Ltd	1234	PL 125	80.00	14.00	94.00
11 Jan.	D Webster	A373	PL 730	120.00	21.00	141.00
16 Jan.	P Bond Ltd	1247	PL 125	40.00	7.00	47.00
20 Jan.	Sanders & Sons	5691	PL 495	160.00	28.00	188.00
31 Jan.	Totals for month			400.00	70.00	470.00

* VAT = 17½ per cent

Notes:

- The purchases day book is prepared from invoices received from suppliers.
- It is totalled at intervals – daily, weekly or monthly, to suit the needs of the business – and the total (of the *net* column) will tell the business the amount of purchases for the period.
- The *gross* column records the full amount of each invoice, ie after VAT has been included.
- We will see in Chapter 26 how the amounts from the day book are recorded in the business' book-keeping system.
- The *folio* column is used for cross-referencing transactions to the book-keeping system: it will be explained in Chapter 26.

sales day book

The sales day book works in the same way as the purchases day book but, as its name suggests, it lists the sales made by a business. In its simplest form the total sales recorded by a shop till for the day, week or month acts as a sales day 'book'. For a business that sells on credit terms, with the issue of an invoice for each transaction, the sales day book, which is prepared from the invoices, takes the following form (with sample entries shown):

Sales Day Book

Date	Details	Invoice No	Folio	Net	VAT	Gross
19-1				£	£	£
3 Jan.	Doyle & Co Ltd	901	SL 58	120.00	21.00	141.00
8 Jan.	Sparkes & Sons Ltd	902	SL 127	160.00	28.00	188.00
12 Jan.	T Young	903	SL 179	80.00	14.00	94.00
15 Jan.	A-Z Supplies Ltd	904	SL 3	200.00	35.00	235.00
18 Jan.	Sparkes & Sons	905	SL 127	120.00	21.00	141.00
31 Jan.	Totals for month			680.00	119.00	799.00

Notes:

- The sales day book is prepared from invoices issued to customers.
- The total of the net column of the day book tells the business the amount of sales for the period.
- The gross column includes VAT.
- In Chapter 26 we will see how the amounts from the day book are recorded in the book-keeping system; the use of the folio column will also be explained.

Case Study: Mr I Lewis

Situation

Mr I Lewis runs an engineering business, which is registered for VAT. All his purchases and sales are on credit terms. He employs a clerk on a part-time basis to keep his accounting data up-to-date. Unfortunately the clerk was taken ill last week and Mr Lewis, knowing nothing about finance, asks if you can help. On investigation you find an 'in-tray' with last week's invoices received from suppliers of goods, together with copies of invoices sent out to customers by Mr Lewis' typist. The list is as follows:

19-1

8 Dec. Invoice no 1234 received from MPF Metals for £108.75 + VAT* of £19.03

8 Dec. Invoice no A 340 sent to Johnson Bros for £220.00 + VAT of £38.50

9 Dec. Invoice no X 678 received from A Osborne for £85.50 +VAT of £14.96

9 Dec. Invoice no A 341 sent to McGee's Metals for £180.25 + VAT of £31.54

10 Dec. Invoice no A 342 sent to Wilson Trading Co for £112.40 + VAT of £19.67

10 Dec. Invoice no P 41 received from Murray Ltd for £115.00 + VAT of £20.12

11 Dec. Invoice no 1256 received from MPF Metals for £111.50 + VAT of £19.51

12 Dec. Invoice no A 343 sent to Johnson Bros for £121.00 + VAT of £21.17

* VAT = 17½ per cent (note that fractions of a penny are ignored, ie VAT is rounded down to the nearest penny)

You are asked to enter these transactions in the appropriate day books (leave the folio column blank).

Solution

Purchases Day Book

Date	Details	Invoice No	Folio	Net	VAT	Gross
19-1				£	£	£
8 Dec.	MPF Metals Ltd	1234		108.75	19.03	127.78
9 Dec.	A Osborne	X678		85.50	14.96	100.46
10 Dec.	Murray Ltd	P41		115.00	20.12	135.12
11 Dec.	MFP Metals Ltd	1256		111.50	19.51	131.01
12 Dec.	Totals for week			420.75	73.62	494.37

Sales Day Book

Date	Details	Invoice No	Folio	Net	VAT	Gross
19-1				£	£	£
8 Dec.	Johnson Bros Ltd	A340		220.00	38.50	258.50
9 Dec.	McGee's Metals	A341		180.25	31.54	211.79
10 Dec.	Wilson Trading Co Ltd	A342		112.40	19.67	132.07
12 Dec.	Johnson Bros Ltd	A343		121.00	21.17	142.17
12 Dec.	Totals for week			633.65	110.88	744.53

day books and Value Added Tax

Many businesses and other organisations are registered for Value Added Tax (VAT). This means that:

- VAT is charged on invoices issued to customers
- VAT charged on invoices received from VAT-registered suppliers can be either reclaimed from HM Customs and Excise (the VAT authority), or set off against VAT charged on invoices issued

When writing up day books you should always check to see if VAT should be charged on invoices issued to suppliers, or has been charged on invoices received from suppliers; if so, the amount is entered in the VAT column of the day book, with the total amount of the invoice in the gross column, and the amount of the invoice before VAT in the net column.

When a business is not registered for VAT, it cannot charge VAT on invoices issued and it cannot reclaim VAT charged on invoices received from suppliers. In such circumstances the total amount of the invoice is recorded in both the net and gross columns; a dash may be inserted in the VAT column. In Chapter 26 we shall see how the VAT columns from the day books are entered into the book-keeping system.

returns day books

Whenever goods are bought and sold there are, inevitably, a number of occasions when they have to be returned. It might be that the wrong goods have been supplied, the wrong size or colour, or perhaps the goods are faulty. There are two aspects of returned goods to consider:

- *purchases returns* (also known as returns outwards) – goods which have been bought by the business are returned *by* the business to the supplier
- *sales returns* (also known as returns inwards) – here goods which have been sold by the business to a customer are returned *to* the business

Those businesses or organisations that have a reasonable number of returns transactions will use *returns day books,* one to record purchases returns and the other to record sales returns:

- *purchases returns day book* is prepared from credit notes received
- *sales returns day book* is prepared from credit notes issued

Returns books use the same layout as purchases day book and sales day book – the only difference is that the appropriate credit note number is recorded instead of the invoice number.

Chapter Summary

❑   Day books are used as listing devices for the credit transactions of purchases, sales, purchases returns and sales returns.

❑   Day books are books of prime entry because transactions are recorded in them first before being recorded in the book-keeping system.

In the next two chapters we shall look at the principles of double-entry book-keeping and see how the information collected by the day books is used in the book-keeping system.

Student Activities

- *In these Activities the rate of Value Added Tax is to be calculated at the current rate (17½% at the time of writing). When calculating VAT amounts, you should ignore fractions of a penny, ie round down to a whole penny.*
- *Leave the folio column blank.*

25.1   You are working for Wyvern Wholesalers and are required to enter up the purchases day book from the following details:

19-1
  2 Apr. Bought goods from Severn Supplies £250 + VAT, their invoice no. 6789
  4 Apr. Bought goods from I. Johnstone £210 + VAT, her invoice no. A241
10 Apr. Bought goods from L. Murphy £185 + VAT, his invoice no. 2456
12 Apr. Bought goods from Mercia Manufacturing £180 + VAT, their invoice no. X457
18 Apr. Bought goods from AMC Enterprises £345 + VAT, their invoice no. AMC 456
24 Apr. Bought goods from S. Green £395 + VAT, her invoice no. 2846

After entering the above, total the purchases day book at 30 April.

25.2   The following details are to be entered in the sales day book of Wyvern Wholesalers:

19-1
  2 Apr.   Sold goods to Malvern Stores £55 + VAT, invoice no. 4578
  4 Apr.   Sold goods to Pershore Retailers £65 + VAT, invoice no. 4579
  7 Apr.   Sold goods to E. Grainger £28 + VAT, invoice no. 4580
10 Apr.   Sold goods to P. Wilson £58 + VAT, invoice no. 4581
12 Apr.   Sold goods to M. Kershaw £76 + VAT, invoice no. 4582
14 Apr.   Sold goods to D. Lloyd £66 + VAT, invoice no. 4583
18 Apr.   Sold goods to A. Cox £33 + VAT, invoice no. 4584
22 Apr.   Sold goods to Dines Stores £102 + VAT, invoice no. 4585
24 Apr.   Sold goods to Malvern Stores £47 + VAT, invoice no. 4586
27 Apr.   Sold goods to P. Wilson £35 + VAT, invoice no. 4587
29 Apr.   Sold goods to A. Cox £82 + VAT, invoice no. 4588

After entering the above, total the sales day book at 30 April.

25.3   The following transactions are to be entered in the *appropriate* day books of Wyvern Wholesalers for the month of May; total the day books at the month-end:

19-1
  2 May   Bought goods from S. Green £180 + VAT, her invoice no. 2901
  3 May   Sold goods to P. Wilson £48 + VAT, invoice no. 4589
  6 May   Bought goods from Mercia Manufacturing £211 + VAT, their invoice no. X495
  8 May   Sold goods to Dines Stores £105 + VAT, invoice no. 4590
10 May   Some of the goods, value £50 + VAT, bought from S. Green are unsatisfactory and are returned to her; she issues credit note no. 221
12 May   Sold goods to D. Lloyd £105 + VAT, invoice no. 4591
14 May   P. Wilson returns goods £18 + VAT, we issue credit note no. CN989
17 May   Sold goods to M. Kershaw £85 + VAT, invoice no. 4592
20 May   We return goods £35 + VAT to Mercia Manufacturing; credit note no. 811 received
22 May   Bought goods from AMC Enterprises £55 + VAT, their invoice no. AMC 612
24 May   D. Lloyd returns goods £22 + VAT, we issue credit note no. CN990
26 May   Sold goods to Pershore Retailers £75 + VAT, invoice no. 4593

26 Double-entry book-keeping – an introduction

introduction

Having looked at the different financial documents (Chapter 24) and the way in which these documents are recorded in day books (Chapter 25), we now turn our attention to the further recording of financial transactions in the accounting system by means of *double-entry book-keeping*. Firstly, though, we will take an overview of the accounting system to see how the various parts fit together.

the accounting system

The accounting system can be summarised as follows:

documents
processing of prime documents relating to financial transactions

initial recording of transactions: books of prime entry
recording of financial transactions in summary books (books of prime entry – including day books)

double-entry accounts system
transfer from books of prime entry into the double-entry book-keeping system of accounts contained in 'the ledger'

trial balance
extraction of figures from all the double-entry accounts to check their accuracy in the form of the trial balance

financial statements
production of a profit statement, and a balance sheet – collectively known as the financial statements or final accounts.

We have already looked at the first two areas (in Chapters 24 and 25), and at financial statements (Chapters 7-17). The remaining two areas – double-entry accounts and the trial balance – are looked at in this and the next chapter.

the use of accounts

The accounting system is organised on the basis of a number of *accounts* which record the money amounts of financial transactions: collectively these accounts are known as 'the ledger'.

Accounts are maintained in the names of customers and of suppliers of the organisation, and also for other transactions such as the receipt and payment of money for various purposes. Accounts can be kept in the form of:

* handwritten records
* computer records

In a handwritten system, accounts are maintained either in a bound book or a series of separate sheets of paper – each account occupying a separate page. The organisation can set up its own manual system, or can buy one ready-made from a business supplies shop.

In a computerised system each account is held as data in a computer file. Whether a handwritten or computerised system is being used, the principles remain the same. We shall see how a business can use a computer to keep its accounts up-to-date in Chapter 30. The theory of keeping accounts is the same whether a handwritten system or a computer system is in use. For the time being we will concentrate on handwritten accounts.

A handwritten system can either use specially ruled accounting paper – known as ledger paper – which can be purchased from a business supplies shop, or a suitable layout can be ruled as follows:

Debit			**Name of Account, eg Purchases Account**		Credit	
Date	Details	£ p	Date	Details	£ p	
↑ of trans-action	↑ name of other account	↑ amount of trans-action				

Note the following points about the layout of this account:

* the name of the account is written at the top
* the account is divided into two identical halves, separated by a central double vertical line
* the left-hand side is called the 'debit' side ('debit' is abbreviated to 'Dr.' – short for <u>D</u>ebito<u>R</u>)
* the right-hand side is called the 'credit' (or 'Cr.') side
* the date, details and amount of the transaction are entered in the account
* in the 'details' column is entered the name of the other account involved in the book-keeping transaction

In practice, each account would occupy a whole page in a handwritten book-keeping system but, to save space when doing exercises, it is usual to put several accounts on a page. In future, in this book, the account layout will be simplified to give more clarity as follows:

Dr.		**Purchases Account**		Cr.
19-1	£	19-1		£

This layout is often known in accounting jargon as a 'T' account; it is used to illustrate accounts because it separates in a simple way the two sides – debit and credit – of the account. An alternative style of account has three money columns: debit, credit and balance. This type of account is commonly used for bank statements, building society passbooks and computer accounting statements. Because the balance of the account is calculated after every transaction, it is known as a *running balance account*.

debits and credits

The principle of double-entry book-keeping is that for every financial transaction:

• one account is debited, and
• one account is credited

The principle is often known as the *dual aspect* of book-keeping, ie each transaction has a dual effect on the accounts – one account gains while another account gives value by recording a payment or a liability.

Debit entries are on the left-hand side of the appropriate account, while credit entries are on the right. The rules for debits and credits are:

• *debit entry* – the account which gains value, or records an asset, or an expense
• *credit entry* – the account which gives value, or records a liability, or an income item

This is illustrated as follows:

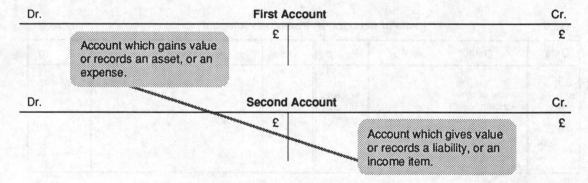

When one entry has been identified as a debit or credit, the other entry will be on the *opposite* side of the other account.

division of the ledger

Accounts, as mentioned above, are normally written on separate pages of a book known as 'the ledger'. In practice, several separate ledgers are kept, each containing different classes of accounts:

• *sales ledger*, containing the accounts of a firm's debtors (customers)
• *purchases ledger*, containing the accounts of a firm's creditors (suppliers)
• *cash book*, containing the bank account and cash account records of the business
• *general ledger* (often known as *nominal ledger*) containing all other accounts, such as income, expenses, fixed assets, owner's capital, etc.

When computers are used for accounting, the physical ledger books do not exist. However, the theory of manual and computerised accounting is the same and the term 'ledgers' is used in computer accounting systems. Accounting software is available for each of the ledgers mentioned above, as we will see in Chapter 30.

purchases and sales

In finance the terms purchases and sales have specific meanings:

* *purchases* – the purchase of goods with the intention that they should be resold at a profit
* *sales* – the sale of goods in which the business or organisation trades

Thus an office stationery supplies business buying goods from a manufacturer records the transaction in *purchases account*. When office supplies are sold to customers, the transactions are recorded in *sales account*. Other items purchased in connection with the running of the busines – eg buildings, equipment, vehicles – are recorded in suitably named accounts, ie buildings account, equipment account, vehicles account, etc.

The following accounts are used in connection with purchases and sales:

* *purchases account* – to record the purchase of goods, whether bought on credit or for cash
* *sales account* – to record the sale of goods, whether sold on credit or for cash
* *purchases returns account* – to record the return of goods to the supplier
* *sales returns account* – to record the return of goods by the customer
* *Value Added Tax account* – to record the VAT amount of purchases, sales and returns

double-entry book-keeping for purchases

Invoices received from suppliers form the prime documents for the preparation of the purchases day book (see Chapter 25). After the day book, the double-entry book-keeping accounts are written up.

The example purchases day book (already seen on page 279) is reproduced for reference:

Purchases Day Book

Date	Details	Invoice No	Folio	Net	VAT*	Gross
19-1				£	£	£
2 Jan.	P Bond Ltd	1234	PL 125	80.00	14.00	94.00
11 Jan.	D Webster	A373	PL 730	120.00	21.00	141.00
16 Jan.	P Bond Ltd	1247	PL 125	40.00	7.00	47.00
20 Jan.	Sanders & Sons	5691	PL 495	160.00	28.00	188.00
31 Jan.	Totals for month			400.00	70.00	470.00

* VAT = 17½ per cent

The accounts in the purchases ledger and general ledger to record the above transactions are:

PURCHASES LEDGER

Dr.			P Bond (account no 125)			Cr.
19-1		£	19-1			£
			2 Jan.	Purchases		94
			16 Jan.	Purchases		47

Dr.			Sanders & Sons (account no 495)			Cr.
19-1		£	19-1			£
			20 Jan.	Purchases		188

Dr.			D Webster (account no 730)			Cr.
19-1		£	19-1			£
			11 Jan.	Purchases		141

GENERAL LEDGER

Dr.		Purchases Account		Cr.
19-1		£	19-1	£
31 Jan.	Purchases Day Book	400		

Dr.		Value Added Tax Account		Cr.
19-1		£	19-1	£
31 Jan.	Purchases Day Book	70		

Note that from the purchases day book:

- the total of the net column, £400, has been debited to purchases account (ie the account which has gained value)
- the total of the VAT column, £70, has been debited to VAT account (which has gained value)
- the amounts from the gross column *for each separate purchase* have been credited to the accounts of the suppliers, ie the business owes to each creditor the amounts shown
- the purchases day book incorporates a folio column which cross-references each transaction to the personal account of each creditor in the purchases ledger (PL); this enables a particular transaction to be traced from prime document (invoice received), through the book of prime entry (purchases day book), to the creditor's ledger account

double-entry book-keeping for sales

Invoices issued by a business form the prime documents used in the preparation of the sales day book (see Chapter 25). After the day book, the double-entry book-keeping accounts are written up.

The example sales day book (see also page 280) is shown below:

Sales Day Book

Date	Details	Invoice No	Folio	Net	VAT	Gross
19-1				£	£	£
3 Jan.	Doyle & Co Ltd	901	SL 58	120.00	21.00	141.00
8 Jan.	Sparkes & Sons Ltd	902	SL 127	160.00	28.00	188.00
12 Jan.	T Young	903	SL 179	80.00	14.00	94.00
15 Jan.	A-Z Supplies Ltd	904	SL 3	200.00	35.00	235.00
18 Jan.	Sparkes & Sons	905	SL 127	120.00	21.00	141.00
31 Jan.	Totals for month			680.00	119.00	799.00

The accounts in the sales ledger and general ledger to record the above transactions are:

SALES LEDGER

Dr.		**A-Z Supplies Ltd** (account no 3)		Cr.
19-1		£	19-1	£
15 Jan.	Sales	235		

Dr.		**Doyle & Co Ltd** (account no 58)		Cr.
19-1		£	19-1	£
3 Jan.	Sales	141		

Dr.		**Sparkes & Sons Ltd** (account no 127)		Cr.
19-1		£	19-1	£
8 Jan.	Sales	188		
18 Jan.	Sales	141		

Dr.		**T Young** (account no 179)		Cr.
19-1		£	19-1	£
12 Jan.	Sales	94		

GENERAL LEDGER

Dr.			Sales Account		Cr.
19-1		£	19-1		£
			31 Jan. Sales Day Book		680

Dr.			Value Added Tax Account		Cr.
19-1		£	19-1		£
31 Jan. Purchases Day Book		70*	31 Jan. Sales Day Book		119

* Amount already entered from purchases day book.

Note that from the sales day book:
- the total of the net column, £680, has been credited to sales account (ie the account which has given value)
- the total of the VAT column, £119, has been credited to VAT account (which has given value)
- the amounts from the gross column *for each separate sale* have been debited to the accounts of the customers, ie the business has a debtor for the amounts shown
- the folio column gives a cross-reference to the debtors' accounts in the sales ledger (SL)

double-entry book-keeping for returned goods

Returns transactions make use of two accounts:
- *purchases returns account* – to record the return of goods to the supplier
- *sales returns account* – to record the return of goods by the customer.

The double-entry book-keeping transactions to record returns are:

- Sales returns: credit note issued to customer
  - *debit* sales returns account, with amount of credit note before VAT is added
  - *debit* VAT account, with amount of VAT on credit note
  - *credit* debtor's account, with total amount of credit note, including VAT

- Purchases returns: credit note received from supplier
  - *debit* creditor's account, with total amount of credit note, including VAT
  - *credit* purchases returns account, with amount of credit note before VAT is added
  - *credit* VAT account, with amount of VAT on credit note

recording credit transactions and returns: a summary

The diagram (Fig. 26.1) on the next page summarises the procedures for recording the transactions in the accounting system
- for purchases and purchases returns
- for sales and sales returns

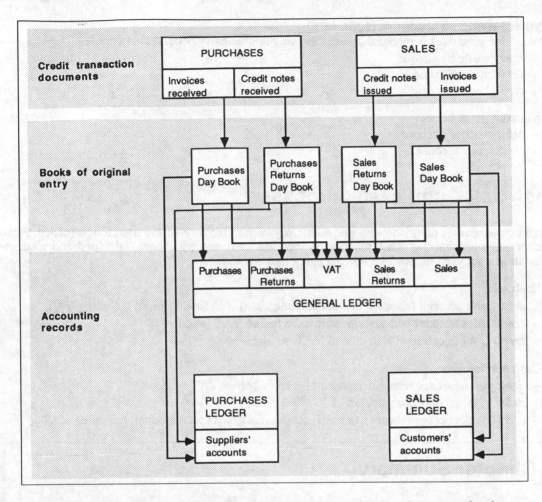

Fig. 26.1 Recording transactions in the accounting system of an organisation

recording payments

When payment is received from customers or made to suppliers, the method of payment is usually either by cheque or in cash. While separate accounts are kept for bank (ie cheque) transactions and for cash transactions, most organisations bring these two accounts together in a division of the ledger called *cash book*. We shall be looking at the use of cash book in detail in Chapter 28.

payment received from debtors (customers)
When debtors pay for goods that have been sold to them, the double-entry book-keeping entries are:

- payment received by cheque
  - *debit* bank account
  - *credit* debtor's account

- payment received in cash
  - *debit* cash account
  - *credit* debtor's account

payment made to creditors (suppliers)

Payment for purchases is recorded by the following double-entry book-keeping entries:

* payment made by cheque
  - *debit* creditor's account
  - *credit* bank account

* payment made in cash
  - *debit* creditor's account
  - *credit* cash account

cash sales and cash purchases

If sales or purchases are made with immediate payment at the time of the transaction (called a 'cash sale' or 'cash purchase' – when payment is made in cash *and* by cheque), debtors' and creditors' accounts are not used. Instead the book-keeping transactions are:

* Cash sales
  - *debit* bank account (cheque), or cash account (cash) with total amount, including VAT
  - *credit* sales account with amount of invoice before VAT is added
  - *credit* VAT account with amount of VAT on invoice

* Cash purchases
  - *debit* purchases account with amount of invoice before VAT is added
  - *debit* VAT account with amount of VAT on invoice
  - *credit* bank account (cheque), or cash account (cash) with total amount, including VAT

Chapter Summary

❏ The accounting system comprises a number of specific stages of recording and presenting financial transactions:
  * documents
  * books of prime entry
  * double-entry book-keeping
  * trial balance
  * final accounts

❏ Financial transactions are recorded in accounts using double-entry principles.

❏ The rules for debit and credit entries in accounts are:
  * *debit entries* – the account which gains value
  * *credit entries* – the account which gives value

❏ Division of the ledger divides the accounts contained in the accounting system between four sections:
  * *sales ledger* – containing the accounts of debtors
  * *purchases ledger* – containing the accounts of creditors
  * *cash book* – containing the bank account and cash account
  * *general (or nominal) ledger* – containing all other accounts

In the next chapter we see how 'T' accounts are balanced at the end of each month, and a trial balance is extracted.

✍ Student Activities

26.1 James Scriven started in business as a furniture wholesaler on 1 February 19-2. He has registered for Value Added Tax. During the first month of business, the following credit transactions took place.

19-2
1 Feb. Bought furniture for resale and received invoice no 961 from Softseat Ltd, £320 + VAT*
2 Feb. Bought furniture for resale and received invoice no 068 from PRK Ltd, £80 + VAT
8 Feb. Sold furniture and issued invoice no 001 to High Street Stores, £440 + VAT
14 Feb. Sold furniture and issued invoice no 002 to Peter Lounds Ltd, £120 + VAT
15 Feb. Bought furniture for resale and received invoice no 529 from Quality Furnishings, £160 + VAT
18 Feb. Sold furniture and issued invoice no 003 to Carpminster College, £320 + VAT
19 Feb. Bought furniture for resale and received invoice no 984 from Softseat Ltd, £160 + VAT
25 Feb. Sold furniture and issued invoice no 004 to High Street Stores, £200 + VAT

* VAT = 17½%

You are to:

(a)   enter the above transactions in James Scriven's purchases day book and sales day book

(b)   record the accounting entries in James Scriven's purchases ledger, sales ledger and general ledger

26.2 Anne Green owns a shop selling paint and decorating materials; she is registered for Value Added Tax. She has two suppliers, Wyper Ltd (account no 301) and M Roper & Sons (account no 302). During the month of May 19-2 Anne received the following business documents from her suppliers:

19-2
2 May Invoice no 562 from M Roper & Sons for £190 + VAT*
4 May Invoice no 82 from Wyper Ltd for £200 + VAT
10 May Invoice no 86 from Wyper Ltd for £210 + VAT
18 May Invoice no 580 from M Roper & Sons for £180 + VAT
18 May Credit note no 82 from M Roper & Sons for £30 + VAT
21 May Invoice no 91 from Wyper Ltd for £240 + VAT
23 May Credit note no 6 from Wyper Ltd for £40 + VAT
25 May Invoice no 589 from M Roper & Sons for £98 + VAT
28 May Credit note no 84 from M Roper & Sons for £38 + VAT

* VAT = 17½% (ignore fractions of a penny, ie round down to a whole penny)

You are to:

(a)   enter the above transactions in the appropriate day books which are to be totalled at the end of May

(b)   enter the transactions in the appropriate accounts in Anne Green's ledgers. (The credit balances of M Roper & Sons and Wyper Ltd at the beginning of the month were £85 and £100 respectively.)

26.3 A local company, Sidbury Trading Co Ltd, has asked your advice about computerising their accounts. At present, the company operates a manual double-entry book-keeping system.

Using professional computer magazines, investigate hardware and software suitable for accounting from reviews and advertisements; send away for details if necessary. Prepare a report for the company, listing a suitable machine (or machines) and appropriate software. Bear in mind the considerations of value for money and reliability. Present your findings in a report addressed to Sid Bury, Managing Director, Sidbury Trading Co Ltd, 55 Newtown Road, Rowcester RW5 2JA.

27 Balancing accounts; the trial balance

introduction

With the 'traditional' form of account (the 'T' account) that we have used to record business transactions, it is necessary to calculate the balance of each account from time-to-time – often at the end of each month – and at the end of the financial year. The balance of an account is the total of that account to date, eg the amount of sales made, the amount of wages paid. In this chapter we shall see how this *balancing of accounts* is carried out.

We shall then use the balances from each account in order to check the double-entry book-keeping by extracting a *trial balance,* which is a list of the balances of every account in the accounting system.

balancing the accounts

The balance of an account is the money amount of transactions on the account to date. Accounts are balanced at regular intervals – often at the end of each month – in order to show the amount:
* owing to each creditor
* owing by each debtor
* of sales
* of purchases
* of sales returns (returns in)
* of purchases returns (returns out)
* of money – in the bank (or a bank overdraft) and in cash
* of expenses incurred by the business
* of fixed assets, eg premises, machinery, etc owned by the business
* of capital and drawings of the owner of the business
* of other liabilities, eg loans

Where running balance accounts are used, there is no need to balance each account, because the balance is already calculated – either manually or by computer – after each transaction.

method of balancing accounts

The following is an example of a 'T' account, taken from the sales ledger, which has been balanced at the month-end (the balancing figure is shown with a shaded background for illustrative purposes):

Dr.			J Smith	Cr.		
19-1		£		19-1		£
5 Sep.	Sales	250		12 Sep.	Sales returns	50
25 Sep.	Sales	140		18 Sep.	Bank	200
				30 Sep.	Balance c/d	140
		390				390
1 Oct.	Balance b/d	140				

The steps involved in balancing accounts are:

Step 1
The entries in the debit and credit money columns are totalled; these totals are not recorded in ink on the account at this stage, but can be recorded either as sub-totals in pencil on the account, or noted on a separate piece of paper. In the example above, the debit side totals £390, while the credit side is £250.

Step 2
The difference between the two totals is the balance of the account and this is entered on the account:
- on the side of the smaller total
- on the next available line
- with the date of balancing (often the last day of the month)
- with the description 'balance c/d', or 'balance carried down'

In the account above, the balance carried down is £390 – £250 = £140, entered in the credit column.

Step 3
Both sides of the account are now totalled, including the balance which has just been entered, and the totals (the same on both sides) are entered *on the same line* in the appropriate column, and double underlined. The double underline indicates that the account has been balanced at this point using the figures above the total: the figures above the underline should not be added in to anything below the underline.

In the account above, the totals on each side of the account are £390.

Step 4
As we are using double-entry book-keeping, there must be an opposite entry to the 'balance c/d' calculated in Step 2. The same money amount is entered on the *other side of the account* below the double-underlined totals entered in Step 3. We have now completed both the debit and credit entry. The date is usually recorded as the next day after 'balance c/d', ie often the first day of the following month, and the description can be 'balance b/d' or 'balance brought down'.

In the example above, the balance brought down on J Smith's account on 1 October 19-1 is £140 debit; this means that J Smith owes the business £140.

A practical point

When balancing accounts, use a pen and not a pencil. If any errors are made, cross them through neatly with a single line, and write the corrected version on the line below. Do *not* use correcting fluid: at best it conceals errors, at worst it conceals fraudulent transactions.

extracting a trial balance

The book-keeper uses the balances from accounts to extract a trial balance in order to check the arithmetical accuracy of the double-entry book-keeping, ie that the debit entries equal the credit entries.

A trial balance is a list of the balances of every account in the accounting system, distinguishing between those accounts which have debit balances and those which have credit balances.

A trial balance is extracted at regular intervals – often at the end of each month.

example of a trial balance

Trial balance of A-Z Suppliers as at 31 January 19-1

Name of account	Dr. £	Cr. £
Purchases	750	
Sales		1,600
Sales returns	25	
Purchases returns		50
J Brown (debtor)	155	
T Sweet (creditor)		110
Rent paid	100	
Wages	150	
Heating and lighting	125	
Office equipment	500	
Machinery	1,000	
Cash	50	
Bank	455	
J Williams – loan		800
Capital		1,000
Drawings	250	
	3,560	3,560

Notes:

- The debit and credit columns have been totalled and are the same amount. Thus the trial balance proves that the accounts are arithmetically correct. (A trial balance does *not* prove the *complete* accuracy of the accounting records.

- The heading for a trial balance gives the name of the business or organisation whose accounts have been listed and the date it was extracted, ie the end of the accounting period.

- The balance for each account transferred to the trial balance is the figure brought down after the accounts have been balanced.

- As well as the name of each account, it is quite usual to show in the trial balance the account number. Most accounting systems give numbers to accounts – see the computer trial balances in Chapter 30 – and these can be listed in a separate 'folio' or 'reference' column.

debit and credit balances – guidelines

Certain accounts always have a debit balance, while others always have a credit balance. You will probably already know these, but the lists set out below will act as a guide, and will also help in your understanding of trial balances.

Debit balances include:
- cash account
- purchases account
- sales returns account (returns in)
- fixed asset accounts, eg premises, motor vehicles, machinery, office equipment, etc
- expenses accounts, eg wages, telephone, rent paid, carriage outwards, carriage inwards
- drawings account
- debtors' accounts (often, for the purposes of a trial balance, the balances of individual debtors' accounts are totalled, and the total is entered in the trial balance as 'debtors')

Credit balances include:
- sales account
- purchases returns account (returns out)
- income accounts, eg rent received, commission received, fees received
- capital account
- loan account
- creditors' accounts (often a total is entered in the trial balance, rather than the individual balances of each account)

Note: bank account can be either debit or credit – it will be debit when the business has money in the bank, and credit when it is overdrawn.

importance of the trial balance

A business or organisation will extract a trial balance on a regular basis to check the arithmetic accuracy of the book-keeping. However, the trial balance is also used as the starting point in the production of the *final accounts*. These final accounts, which are produced once a year (and sometimes more frequently), comprise:
- trading and profit and loss account
- balance sheet

Chapter Summary

❑ Traditional 'T' accounts need to be balanced at regular intervals – often at the end of each month.

❑ When each account has been balanced, a trial balance can be extracted.

❑ A trial balance is a list of the balances of every account in the accounting system, distinguishing between those accounts which have debit balances and those which have credit balances.

❑ The trial balance is used as the starting point for the preparation of the year-end or final accounts.

In the next chapter we look how a business keeps control of its cash and bank balances through the use of a cash book and a petty cash book.

Student Activities

27.1 The following balances have been extracted from the book-keeping system of James Green.

	£
Purchases	11,925
Sales	20,515
Sales returns	210
Purchases returns	85
Bank overdraft	695
Cash	50
Debtors	3,240
Creditors	2,935
Motor vehicle	5,500
Office equipment	1,220
Wages	4,620
Sundry expenses	2,840
Capital	?

You are to produce the trial balance of James Green and to insert capital as the balancing figure.

27.2 Lorna Pratt runs a computer software business, specialising in supplies to educational establishments. The business is registered for Value Added Tax. At the beginning of January 19-2 the balances in her ledgers were as follows:

Purchases ledger	Macstrad plc (account no 101)	£1,050.75 credit
	Amtosh plc (account no 102)	£2,750.83 credit
Sales ledger	Mereford College (account no 201)	£705.35 debit
	Carpminster College (account no 202)	£801.97 debit

During the month the following documents are issued and received (all plus VAT at 17½%):

19-2		
2 Jan.	Invoice from Macstrad plc, M1529	£2,900.00
3 Jan.	Invoice from Amtosh plc, A7095	£7,500.00
5 Jan.	Invoice to Mereford College, 1093	£3,900.00
7 Jan.	Invoice to Carpminster College, 1094	£8,500.00
10 Jan.	Credit note from Macstrad plc, MC105	£319.75
12 Jan.	Credit note from Amtosh plc, AC730	£750.18
13 Jan.	Credit note to Mereford College, CN109	£850.73
14 Jan.	Invoice to Carpminster College, 1095	£1,800.50
14 Jan.	Invoice to Mereford College, 1096	£2,950.75
18 Jan.	Invoice from Macstrad plc, M2070	£1,750.00
19 Jan.	Invoice from Amtosh plc, A7519	£5,500.00
20 Jan.	Invoice to Carpminster College, 1097	£3,900.75
22 Jan.	Invoice to Mereford College, 1098	£1,597.85
23 Jan.	Credit note from Macstrad plc, MC120	£953.07
27 Jan.	Credit note to Mereford College, CN110	£593.81

Note: when calculating VAT amounts, ignore fractions of a penny, ie round down to a whole penny.

You are to:
(a) enter the above transactions in the appropriate day books which are to be totalled at the end of January
(b) record the accounting entries in Lorna Pratt's purchases ledger, sales ledger and general ledger
(c) balance the accounts at 31 January 19-2

28 Financial records – control of cash

introduction

Cash and money in the bank is the lifeblood of any business or any other organisation. For example, a firm can have an excellent product or service and be making good sales, but a shortage of cash may mean that wages and other day-to-day running expenses cannot be paid as they fall due: this could lead to the rapid failure of the business.

For most organisations, the financial records for the control of cash – including bank and cash transactions – comprise:

- cash book
- petty cash book

These are the books of original entry for cash transactions, and we will examine them in detail in this chapter.

cash book

The cash book brings together the separate cash and bank transactions of an organisation into one book. The cash book is used to record the money side of book-keeping transactions and is part of the double-entry system. The cash book is used for:

- *cash transactions*
  - all receipts in cash
  - most payments for cash, except for low-value expense payments (which are paid through *petty cash book*: see later in this chapter)
- *bank transactions*
  - all receipts by cheque (or payment of cash into the bank)
  - all payments by cheque (or withdrawal of cash from the bank)

The cash book is usually controlled by a cashier who:

- records receipts and payments by cheque and in cash
- makes cash payments, and prepares cheques for signature by those authorised to sign
- pays cash and cheques received into the bank
- has control over the firm's cash, either in a cash till or cash box
- issues cash to the petty cashier, as and when required

layout of the cash book

Although a cash book can be set out in many forms to suit the requirements of a particular business, a common format is the *two-column cash book*. This has two money columns on the left-hand side, and two on the right-hand side, as shown below.

Dr.   **Cash Book**   Cr.

Date	Details	Folio	Cash	Bank	Date	Details	Folio	Cash	Bank
			£	£				£	£

The debit (left-hand) side is used for receipts, with one column for cash receipts and the other for bank receipts. The credit (right-hand) side is used for payments, with one column for cash payments and the other for bank (cheque) payments. Both the receipts and the payments sides have spaces for the date and details of each transaction. The folio column is used for cross-referencing transactions.

Case Study: a new business

Situation

You have been appointed the cashier of a new business. The first month's transactions to be entered in the two-column cash book are:

1 Jan.   Started in business with capital of £1,250: £250 in cash and £1,000 in the bank
3 Jan.   Bought a typewriter for £300, paying by cheque
7 Jan.   Paid office rent of £150 in cash
10 Jan. Bought office stationery for £75, paying in cash
12 Jan. Withdrew £300 from the bank for business use
16 Jan. Purchased goods for resale £200, paying by cheque
19 Jan. Sold goods £125, receiving a cheque
23 Jan. Sold goods £55, cash received
27 Jan. Paid £100 of cash into the bank

All cheques received are banked on the day of receipt.

Solution

The cash book (shown on the next page) will record these transactions. After they have been entered the cash book is balanced on 31 January.

Dr.						Cash Book				Cr.
Date	Details	Folio	Cash	Bank	Date	Details	Folio	Cash	Bank
19-1			£	£	19-1			£	£
1 Jan	Capital		250	1,000	3 Jan	Typewriter			300
12 Jan	Bank	C	300		7 Jan	Rent		150	
19 Jan	Sales			125	10 Jan	Stationery		75	
23 Jan	Sales		55		12 Jan	Cash	C		300
27 Jan	Cash	C		100	16 Jan	Purchases			200
					27 Jan	Bank	C	100	
					31 Jan	Balances c/d		280	425
			605	1,225				605	1,225
1 Feb	Balances b/d		280	425					

note the following points:

The transactions on 12 and 27 January involved a transfer of funds between cash and bank. As each transaction is both a receipt and a payment within the cash book, it is usual to indicate both of them with a 'C' - this stands for *contra* and shows that both parts of the transaction are in the *same* book.

A cash book is balanced as follows:

- add the two cash columns and subtotal in pencil (ie £605 in the debit column, and £325 in the credit column); remember to erase the subtotals afterwards

- deduct the lower total from the higher (payments from receipts) to give the balance of cash remaining (£605 – £325 = £280)

- the higher total is recorded at the bottom of both columns in a totals 'box' (£605)

- the balance of cash remaining (£280) is entered as a balancing item above the totals box (on the credit side), and is brought down underneath the total on the debit side as the opening balance for next month (£280)

- the two bank columns are dealt with in the same way (£1,225 – £800 = £425)

Notice that, in this example, the cash and bank balances have been brought down on the debit side. It might happen that the balance of the bank columns is brought down on the credit side: this happens where payments have exceeded receipts and indicates a bank overdraft.

It is very important to appreciate that the bank columns of the cash book represent the organization's own records of bank transactions and the balance at bank – the bank statement may well show different figures (see Chapter 29).

checking the cash book

In business there is little point in keeping records of cash and bank transactions if we cannot, from time-to-time, prove that the records are accurate. How can we check the cash book?

cash columns

To check the cash columns is easy. It is simply a matter of counting the cash in the cash till or box, and agreeing it with the balance shown by the cash book. In the example from the case study (above), there should be £280 in the firm's cash till at 31 January 19-1. If the cash cannot be agreed in this way, the discrepancy needs to be investigated urgently.

bank columns

How are these to be checked? We could, perhaps, enquire at the bank and ask for the balance at the month-end, or we could arrange for a bank statement to be sent to us at the end of each month. However, the balance of the account at the bank may well not agree with that shown by the bank columns of the cash book. There are several reasons why there may be a difference: for example, a cheque that has been written out recently to pay a bill may not yet have been recorded on the bank statement, ie it has been entered in the cash book, but is not yet on the bank statement. To agree the bank columns of the cash book and the bank statement, it is usually necessary to prepare a *bank reconciliation statement*, and this topic is dealt with fully in the next chapter.

cash discount columns

Often an additional column is introduced on each side of the cash book to incorporate cash *discount allowed* on the debit side and cash *discount received* on the credit side. Such a *three-column cash book* (with three money columns on each side) takes the following form (with example figures):

Dr.   **Cash Book**   Cr.

Date	Details	Folio	Discount allowed	Cash	Bank	Date	Details	Folio	Discount received	Cash	Bank
19-1			£	£	£	19-1			£	£	£
1 Apr.	Balances b/d			300	550	7 Apr.	J Crane		5		145
4 Apr.	S Wright		2		98	12 Apr.	Wages			275	
17 Apr.	J Jones		4	76		14 Apr.	T Lewis		3		117
20 Apr.	Bank	C		100		20 Apr.	Cash	C			100
23 Apr.	D Whiteman		3		45	28 Apr.	S Ford		5	70	
						30 Apr.	Balances c/d			131	331
			9	476	693				13	476	693
1 May	Balances b/d			131	331						

To explain the use of the discount columns in the cash book above, on the debit side, S Wright, for example, owed us a total of £100 but, in order to encourage prompt settlement, we have allowed him to deduct a *cash discount* of £2 and so he sends us a cheque for £98 in full settlement. On the credit side, we owe J Crane £150 but, provided we pay promptly, we are allowed to deduct a cash discount of £5, and so the cheque sent is for £145.

note the following points:

- The discount columns are used only to record the amount of *cash discount* for early settlement and *not* trade discount.

- The discount amount is entered in the appropriate discount column, while the net amount (ie actual amount received or paid) is entered in the cash or bank columns.

- At the end of the month each discount column is totalled separately – no attempt should be made to balance them. The two totals are transferred to the double-entry system as follows:

  - the total on the debit side (£9 in the example above) is debited to *discount allowed account* in the general (or nominal) ledger

  - the total on the credit side (£13 in the example) is credited to *discount received account,* also in the general (or nominal) ledger

- In debtors' accounts, eg S Wright (above), the cash discount allowed and the amount of the payment received are entered on the credit side as two separate amounts.

- In creditors' accounts eg J Crane (above), the cash discount received and the amount of the payment made are entered on the debit side as two separate amounts.

- The two discount accounts appear as follows:

Dr.	Discount Allowed Account			Cr.
19-1	£	19-1		£
30 Apr. Cash Book	9			

Dr.	Discount Received Account			Cr.
19-1	£	19-1		£
		30 Apr. Cash Book		13

The discount accounts represent an expense and an income respectively and, at the end of the firm's financial year, the totals of the two accounts will be used in the calculation of profit.

- The cash and bank columns are balanced in the usual way and the balances carried down to next month.

petty cash book

A petty cash book is used to record low-value cash payments for various small purchases by a business or organisation, eg small items of stationery, postages, etc. It would not be appropriate for such expenses to be entered in the main cash book, as a large number of payments would clutter it up. Instead, an amount of cash is handed by the main cashier to a member of staff, the *petty cashier,* who will be responsible for security of the money, and will make payments as appropriate.

In order to operate a petty cash system, the petty cashier needs the following:
- a *petty cash book* in which to record transactions
- a lockable *petty cash box* in which to keep the money
- a stock of blank *petty cash vouchers* (see page 305) for claims on petty cash to be made
- a *lockable desk drawer* in which to keep these items

what items can be passed through petty cash book?

Petty cash is used to make small cash payments for expenses incurred by the business or organisation. Examples of the type of payments made from petty cash include:
- stationery items
- casual wages
- window cleaning
- bus, rail and taxi fares (incurred on behalf of the business)
- meals (incurred on behalf of the business)
- postages
- tips and donations

For example, an employee might be asked to buy an item of stationery for the business or organisation: he or she will be reimbursed from petty cash. However, petty cash should not be used to pay for private expenses of employees, eg tea, coffee, and milk, unless these have been agreed in advance. Usually the petty cashier will have a list of approved expenses which can be reimbursed.

An organisation will also decide on the maximum value of each transaction that can be paid out of petty cash; for example, £20 is a common maximum.

the imprest system

Most petty cash books operate on the *imprest system*. With this method the petty cashier starts each week (or month) with a certain amount of money – the imprest amount. As payments are made during the week (or month) the amount of money will reduce and, at the end of the period, the cash will be made up by the main cashier to the imprest amount. For example:

Started week with imprest amount	£100.00
Total of petty cash amounts paid out during week	£80.50
Cash held at end of week	£19.50
Amount drawn from cashier to restore imprest amount	£80.50
Cash at start of next week, ie imprest amount	£100.00

If, at any time, the imprest amount proves to be insufficient, further amounts of cash can be drawn from the cashier. Also, from time-to-time, it may be necessary to increase the imprest amount so that regular shortfalls are avoided.

petty cash voucher

The petty cashier, who is likely also to have other tasks within the organisation, is responsible for control of the petty cash, making cash payments when appropriate, keeping records of payments made, and balancing the petty cash book at regular intervals.

Payments out of petty cash are made only against correct documentation – usually a petty cash voucher (see Fig. 28.1). Petty cash vouchers are completed as follows:
- details and amount of expenditure
- signature of the person making the claim and receiving the money
- signature of the person authorising the payment to be made
- additionally, most petty cash vouchers are numbered, so that they can be controlled, the number being entered in the petty cash book
- any relevant documentation, eg invoice or receipt, should be attached to the petty cash voucher

Petty Cash Voucher

No 807

Date *11 May 19-1*

For what required	AMOUNT	
	£	p
Envelopes	1	55
10 Floppy disks	6	10
	7	65

Signature *T. Harris*

Passed by *D. Adams*

Fig. 28.1 An example of a petty cash voucher

layout of a petty cash book

Receipts	Date	Details	Voucher No.	Total Payment	Analysis columns				
					VAT	Postages	Stationery	Travel	Ledger
£				£	£	£	£	£	£

The layout shows that:

* receipts from the main cashier are entered in the column on the extreme left
* there are columns for the date and details of all receipts and payments
* there is a column for the petty cash voucher number
* the total payment (ie the amount paid out on each petty cash voucher) is in the next column
* then follow the analysis columns which analyse each transaction entered in the 'total payment' column (note that VAT may need to be calculated – see below)

A business or organisation will use whatever analysis columns are most suitable for it and, indeed, there may be more than the columns shown.

petty cash and VAT

Value Added Tax is charged by VAT-registered businesses on their taxable supplies. Therefore, there will often be VAT included as part of the expense paid out of petty cash. However, not all expenses will have been subject to VAT. There are four possible circumstances:

* VAT has been charged at the standard rate
* VAT has not been charged because the supplier is not VAT-registered
* the zero rate of VAT applies, eg food and drink (but not meals, which are standard-rated), books, newspapers, transport (but not taxis and hire cars)
* the supplies are exempt (eg financial services, postal services)

Often the indication of the supplier's VAT registration number on a receipt or invoice will tell you that VAT has been charged at the standard rate.

Where VAT has been charged, the amount of tax might be indicated separately on the receipt or invoice. However, for small money amounts it is quite usual for a total to be shown without indicating the amount of VAT. To calculate the VAT amount, with VAT at a rate of $17\frac{1}{2}\%$, the full amount of the receipt or invoice is multiplied by 17.5 and divided by 117.5. For example:

Amount of receipt	£4.70
Therefore VAT is $17.5/117.5$ of £2.30	= £0.70
Amount, net of VAT	= £4.00

Here £0.70 will be entered in the VAT column in the petty cash book, £4.00 in the appropriate expense column, and the full £4.70 in the total payment column.

Remember that, when calculating VAT amounts, fractions of a penny are ignored, ie the tax is rounded down to a whole penny.

Case Study: petty cash book

Situation

A business keeps a petty cash book, which is operated on the imprest system. There are a number of transactions (all of which, unless otherwise indicated, include VAT at $17\frac{1}{2}\%$) to be entered for the week in the petty cash book:

19-1

10 Apr.   Started the week with an imprest amount of £50.00

10 Apr.   Paid stationery £3.76 on voucher no. 47

10 Apr.   Paid taxi fare £2.82 on voucher no. 48

11 Apr.   Paid postages £0.75 (no VAT) on voucher no. 49

12 Apr.   Paid taxi fare £4.70 on voucher no. 50

12 Apr.   Paid J Jones, a creditor, £6.00 (no VAT shown in petty cash book – amount will be on VAT account already) on voucher no. 51

13 Apr.   Paid stationery £3.76 on voucher no. 52

13 Apr.   Paid postages £2.85 (no VAT) on voucher no. 53

14 Apr.   Paid taxi fare £6.11 on voucher no. 54

14 Apr.   Cash received to restore imprest amount, and petty cash book balanced at the end of the week

Solution

The petty cash book is written up as follows:

Receipts	Date	Details	Voucher No.	Total Payment	Analysis columns				
					VAT	Postages	Stationery	Travel	Ledger
£	19-1			£	£	£	£	£	£
50.00	10 Apr.	Balance b/d							
	10 Apr.	Stationery	47	3.76	0.56		3.20		
	10 Apr.	Taxi fare	48	2.82	0.42			2.40	
	11 Apr.	Postages	49	0.75		0.75			
	12 Apr.	Taxi fare	50	4.70	0.70			4.00	
	12 Apr.	J Jones	51	6.00					6.00
	13 Apr.	Stationery	52	3.76	0.56		3.20		
	13 Apr.	Postages	53	2.85		2.85			
	14 Apr.	Taxi fare	54	6.11	0.91			5.20	
				30.75	3.15	3.60	6.40	11.60	6.00
30.75	14 Apr.	Cash received							
	14 Apr.	Balance c/d		50.00					
80.75				80.75					
50.00	14 Apr.	Balance b/d							

note the following points:

• The totals of the analysis columns add up to the total payment
• the amount of cash received from the main cashier to restore the imprest amount is the same as the total paid out during the week
• The petty cashier will give the book-keeper details of the total of each analysis column so that the amounts can be recorded in the double-entry book-keeping system

Chapter Summary

❑   The cash book records receipts (debits) and payments (credits) both in cash (except for low-value expense payments) and by cheque.

❑   A basic layout for a cash book has money columns for cash transactions and bank transactions on both the debit and credit sides, together with a further column on each side for discounts.

❑   In the discount columns are recorded cash discounts: discounts allowed (to customers) on the debit side, and discounts received (from suppliers) on the payments side.

❑   The petty cash book records payments for a variety of low-value business expenses, and most operate on what is known as the *imprest* system.

❑   Payment can only be made from the petty cash book against correct documentation – usually a petty cash voucher, which must be signed by the person authorising payment.

❑   Where a business is registered for Value Added Tax, it must record VAT amounts paid on petty cash purchases in a separate column in the petty cash book.

❑   At regular intervals – weekly or monthly – the petty cash book will be balanced – the main cashier will restore the imprest amount of cash.

The bank columns of the cash book and the balance calculated are unlikely to agree exactly with the bank statement: in order to agree them it is necessary to prepare a *bank reconciliation statement* which we will look at in the next chapter.

 Student Activities

28.1   You are employed as an accounts clerk by Juliet Johnson, who operates a transport company. The cashier is on holiday and you are required to take on the task of keeping the two-column cash book. The following transactions take place (all cheques are banked on the day of receipt):

19-1
1 May	Balances: cash £72; bank £2,297
3 May	Received cash from L. Williams £50
3 May	Received a cheque from Status Superstores for £755
5 May	Issued a cheque for £150 for office cash
6 May	Paid cleaner's wages £84 in cash
7 May	Received a cheque from J. Lewis & Co. for £1,354
9 May	Paid telephone account £158 by cheque
12 May	Received cash from P. Hardy £120
13 May	Received a cheque from Iowa Transport for £862
13 May	Paid Westland Garage £487 by cheque
16 May	Paid cleaner's wages £80 in cash
17 May	Received cash from H. Smithson £75
20 May	Paid Lowland Tyre Co. £261 by cheque
23 May	Paid Office Equipment Ltd. £176 by cheque
24 May	Paid salaries by cheque £2,687
24 May	Received a cheque from L. Carol & Co. for £347

(continued on next page)

25 May	Paid Western Oils Ltd. £629 by cheque
27 May	Issued a cheque for £150 for office cash
31 May	Paid cash £64 to petty cashier
31 May	Balanced the cash book and carried the balances down to 1 June

28.2 Walter Harrison is a sole trader who records his cash and bank transactions in a *three-column* cash book. The following are the transactions for June:

19-2

1 June	Balances: cash £280; bank overdraft £2,240
3 June	Received a cheque from G. Wheaton for £195, in full settlement of a debt of £200
5 June	Received cash of £53 from T. Francis, in full settlement of a debt of £55
8 June	Paid the amount owing to F. Lloyd by cheque: the total amount due is £400 and you take advantage of a 2.5 per cent cash discount for prompt settlement
10 June	Paid wages in cash £165
12 June	Paid A. Morris in cash, £100 less 3 per cent cash discount
16 June	Issued a cheque for £200 for office cash
18 June	Received a cheque for £640 from H. Watson in full settlement of a debt of £670
20 June	Paid R. Marks £78 by cheque
24 June	Paid D. Farr £65 by cheque, in full settlement of a debt of £670
26 June	Paid telephone account £105 in cash
28 June	Received a cheque from M. Perry in settlement of his account of £240 – he has deducted 2½ per cent cash discount
30 June	Received cash £45 from K. Willis

You are required to:
- enter the above transactions in Harrison's three-column cash book, balance the cash and bank columns, and carry the balances down to 1 July

- total the two discount columns and transfer them to the appropriate accounts

28.3 On returning from holiday, you are told to take over the petty cash book. This is kept on the imprest system, the float being £75 at the beginning of each month. Analysis columns are used for VAT, Travelling Expenses, Postages, Stationery, and Miscellaneous.

Enter the following transactions for the month. The voucher amounts include VAT at 17½%, except that there is no VAT payable on postages, donations, and rail fares. (Remember to round VAT amounts down to the nearest penny.)

19-1

1 Aug	Balance of cash £75.00
2 Aug	Voucher no 39: taxi fare £3.80
4 Aug	Voucher no 40: parcel postage £2.35
7 Aug	Voucher no 41: pencils £1.26
10 Aug	Voucher no 42: travel expenses £5.46
12 Aug	Voucher no 43: window cleaner £8.50 (miscellaneous)
14 Aug	Voucher no 44: large envelopes £2.45
17 Aug	Voucher no 45: donation to charity £5 (miscellaneous)
18 Aug	Voucher no 46: rail fare £10.60
20 Aug	Voucher no 47: recorded delivery postage £0.75
23 Aug	Voucher no 48: roll of packing tape £1.50
25 Aug	Voucher no 49: exces postage paid £0.55
27 Aug	Voucher no 50: taxi fare £5.40
31 Aug	Cash received from cashier to restore imprest amount to £75.00

28.4 Prepare a petty cash book with five analysis columns for VAT, Postages, Travelling Expenses, Meals, and Sundry Office Expenses. Enter the following transactions for the week (VAT is not payable on postages or on rail fares). Remember to round VAT amounts down to the nearest penny.

19-1
1 June	Balance of cash £100.00
1 June	Postages £6.35, voucher no 123
2 June	Taxi fare £3.25, voucher no 124
2 June	Postages £1.28, voucher no 125
3 June	Envelopes £4.54, voucher no 126
3 June	Window cleaning £5.87, voucher no 127
4 June	Meal £10.85, voucher no 128
4 June	Postages £9.50, voucher no 129
4 June	Taxi fare £9.40, voucher no 130
5 June	Marker pens £6.34, voucher no 131
6 June	Cash received from cashier to restore imprest amount to £100.00

28.5 Draw up a petty cash book with appropriate analysis columns and a VAT column, and enter the following transactions for the month, (the voucher amounts include VAT at 17½% unless indicated):

19-1
1 May	Balance of cash £150.00
1 May	Postages £7.00, voucher no 455, travel £2.85, voucher no 456 (no VAT on postages and travel)
2 May	Meal allowance £6.11, voucher no 457
3 May	Taxi £4.70, voucher no 458
4 May	Stationery £3.76, voucher no 459
7 May	Postages £5.25, voucher no 460 (no VAT)
8 May	Travel £6.50, voucher no 461 (no VAT)
9 May	Meal allowance £6.11, voucher no 462
10 May	Stationery £8.46, voucher no 463
14 May	Taxi £5.17, voucher no 464
17 May	Stationery £4.70, voucher no 465
21 May	Travel £3.50, voucher no 466, postages £4.50, voucher no 467 (no VAT on travel and postages)
23 May	Bus fares £3.80, voucher no 468 (no VAT)
26 May	Catering expenses £10.81, voucher no 469
27 May	Postages £3.50, voucher no 470 (no VAT), stationery £7.52, voucher no 471
28 May	Travel expenses £6.45, voucher no 472 (no VAT)
31 May	Cash received from cashier to restore imprest amount to £150.00

29 Bank reconciliation statements

introduction

In the last chapter we saw that the bank columns of the cash book record the organisation's own internal record of the bank transactions, and the balance at the end of the week or month. However, the bank statement received from the bank may show a rather different balance. There are two main reasons for this:

- *timing differences* caused by unpresented cheques, ie the time delay between, for example, writing out (drawing) a cheque and recording it in the cash book, and the cheque being entered on the bank statement
- *the cash book has not been updated* with items which appear on the bank statement and should also appear in the cash book, eg bank charges

Assuming that there are no errors, both cash book and bank statement are correct, but need to be reconciled with each other, ie the closing balances need to be agreed. In this chapter we will examine this process in detail.

timing differences

The two main timing differences between the bank columns of the cash book and the bank statement are:
- cheques drawn, not yet recorded on the bank statement
- amounts paid into the bank, not yet recorded on the bank statement

The first of these – unpresented cheques – is caused because, when a cheque is written out, it is immediately entered on the payments side of the cash book, even though it may be some days before the cheque passes through the bank clearing system and is recorded on the bank statement. Therefore, for a few days at least, the cash book shows a lower balance than the bank statement in respect of this cheque. When the cheque is recorded on the bank statement, the difference will disappear. We have looked at only one cheque here, but a business will often be issuing many cheques each day, and the difference between the cash book balance and the bank statement balance may be considerable.

With the second timing difference – amounts paid in, not yet recorded on the bank statement – the firm's cashier will record a receipt in the cash book as he or she prepares the bank paying-in slip. However, the receipt may not be recorded by the bank on the bank statement for a day or so, particularly if it is paid in late in the day (when the bank will put it into the next day's work), or if it is paid in at a bank branch other than the one at which the account is maintained. Until the receipt is recorded by the bank the cash book will show a higher bank account balance than the bank statement. Once the receipt is entered on the bank statement, the difference will disappear.

These two timing differences are involved in the calculation known as the *bank reconciliation statement*. The organisation's cash book *must not be altered* for these because, as we have seen, they will correct themselves on the bank statement as time goes by.

updating the cash book

Besides the timing differences described above, there may be other differences between the bank columns of the cash book and the bank statement, and these *do* need to be entered in the cash book to bring it up-to-date. For example, the bank might make an automatic standing order payment on behalf of a business – such an item is correctly debited by the bank, and it might be that the bank statement acts as a reminder to the cashier of the payment: it should then be entered in the cash book. Examples of items that show in the bank statement and need to be entered in the cash book include:

receipts

- standing order and BACS (Bankers' Automated Clearing Services) receipts credited by the bank, eg payments from debtors (customers)
- bank giro credit (credit transfer) amounts received by the bank, eg payments from debtors (customers)
- dividend amounts received by the bank
- interest credited by the bank

payments

- standing order and direct debit payments
- bank charges and interest
- unpaid cheques debited by the bank (ie cheques from creditors paid in by the business which have 'bounced' and are returned by the bank marked 'refer to drawer')

For each of these items, the cashier needs to check to see if they have been entered in the cash book; if not, they need to be recorded (provided that the bank has not made an error). If the bank has made an error, it must be notified as soon as possible and the incorrect transactions reversed by the bank in its own accounting records.

the bank reconciliation statement

This forms the link between the balances shown in the cash book and the bank statement:

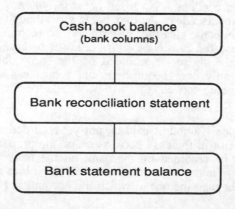

Upon receipt of a bank statement, reconciliation of the two balances is carried out in the following way:

- tick off the items that appear in *both* cash book and bank statement
- the unticked items on the bank statement are entered into the bank columns of the cash book to bring it up-to-date (provided none are errors made by the bank)
- the bank columns of the cash book are now balanced to find the revised figure
- the remaining unticked items from the cash book will be the timing differences
- the timing differences are used to prepare the bank reconciliation statement, which takes the following format (with example figures):

XYZ TRADING LTD
Bank Reconciliation Statement as at 31 October 19-1

		£	£
Balance at bank as per cash book			525
Add: cheques drawn, not yet recorded on the bank statement			
J Lewis	cheque no. 0012378	60	
ABC Ltd	cheque no. 0012392	100	
Eastern Oil Co	cheque no. 0012407	80	
			240
			765
Less: amounts paid in, not yet recorded on the bank statement		220	
		300	
			520
Balance at bank as per bank statement			245

Notes:

- The layout shown above starts from the cash book balance, and works towards the bank statement balance. A common variation of this layout is to start with the bank statement balance and to work towards the cash book balance.
- If a bank overdraft is involved, brackets should be used around the numbers to indicate this for the cash book or bank statement balance. The timing differences are still added or deducted, as appropriate.
- Once the bank reconciliation statement agrees, it should be filed because it proves that the cash book (bank columns) and bank statement were reconciled at a particular date. If, next time it is prepared, it fails to agree, the previous statement is proof that reconciliation was reached at that time.

Case Study: bank reconciliation

Situation

The cashier of Severn Trading Co has written up the firm's cash book for the month of February 19-2, as follows (the cheque number is shown against payments):

Cash Book

Dr.   Cr.

Date	Details	Cash	Bank	Date	Details	Cash	Bank
19-2		£	£	19-2		£	£
1 Feb.	Balances b/d	250.75	1,340.50	3 Feb.	Appleton Ltd 123456		675.25
7 Feb.	A. Abbott		208.50	5 Feb.	Wages	58.60	
9 Feb.	Sales	145.25		12 Feb.	Rent 123457		125.00
13 Feb.	Sales	278.30		14 Feb.	Transfer to bank c	500.00	
14 Feb.	Transfer from cash c		500.00	17 Feb.	D. Smith & Co 123458		421.80
20 Feb.	Sales	204.35		23 Feb.	Stationery	75.50	
21 Feb.	D. Richards Ltd.		162.30	24 Feb.	G. Christie 123459		797.55
26 Feb.	Sales	353.95		27 Feb.	Transfer to bank c	500.00	
27 Feb.	Transfer from cash c		500.00	28 Feb.	Balances c/d	98.50	954.00
28 Feb.	P. Paul Ltd.		262.30				
		1,232.60	2,973.60			1,232.60	2,973.60
1 Mar.	Balances b/d	98.50	954.00				

The cash balance of £98.50 shown by the cash columns on 1 March has been agreed with the cash held in the firm's cash box. The bank statement for February 19-2 has just been received:

National Bank plc

Branch ....Bartown............

TITLE OF ACCOUNT .....Severn Trading Co. .....

ACCOUNT NUMBER .....67812318 ....

STATEMENT NUMBER 45

DATE	PARTICULARS	PAYMENTS	RECEIPTS	BALANCE
19-2		£	£	£
1 Feb.	Balance brought forward			1,340.50 CR
9 Feb.	Credit		208.50	1,549.00 CR
10 Feb.	Cheque no. 123456	675.25		873.75 CR
16 Feb.	Credit		500.00	1,373.75 CR
17 Feb.	Cheque no. 123457	125.00		1,248.75 CR
23 Reb.	Credit		162.30	1,411.05 CR
24 Feb.	Bank Giro Credit: J Jarvis Ltd.		100.00	1,511.05 CR
26 Feb.	Cheque no. 123458	421.80		1,089.25 CR
26 Feb.	Direct Debit: A-Z Finance Co.	150.00		939.25 CR
28 Feb.	Credit		500.00	1,439.25 CR
28 Feb.	Bank Charges	10.00		1,429.25 CR

Note that the bank statement is prepared from the bank's viewpoint: thus a credit balance shows that the customer is a creditor of the bank, ie the bank owes the balance to the customer. In the customer's own cash book, the bank is shown as a debit balance, ie an asset.

Solution

As the month-end balance at bank shown by the cash book, £954.00, is not the same as that shown by the bank statement, £1,429.25, it is necessary to prepare a bank reconciliation statement. The steps are:

1. Tick off the items that appear in *both* cash book and bank statement.

2. The unticked items on the bank statement are entered into the bank columns of the cash book to bring it up-to-date. These are:
   * *receipt*   24 Feb. Bank Giro Credit; J Jarvis Ltd £100.00
   * *payments* 26 Feb. Direct Debit, A-Z Finance Co £150.00
                         28 Feb. Bank Charges, £10.00

   In double-entry book-keeping, the other part of the transaction will need to be recorded in the accounts, eg in J Jarvis Ltd's account in the sales ledger, etc.

3. The cash book is now balanced to find the revised balance:

Dr.			**Cash Book** (bank columns)			Cr.
19-2		£	19-2			£
	Balance b/d	954.00	26 Feb.	A-Z Finance Co		150.00
24 Feb	J Jarvis Ltd.	100.00	28 Feb.	Bank Charges		10.00
			28 Feb.	Balance c/d		894.00
		1,054.00				1,054.00
1 Mar.	Balance b/d	894.00				

4. The remaining unticked items from the cash book are used in the bank reconciliation statement:
   * *receipt*   28 Feb. P Paul Ltd £262.30
   * *payment* 24 Feb. G Christie (cheque no. 123459) £797.55

   These items are timing differences, which should appear on next month's bank statement.

5. The bank reconciliation statement is now prepared, starting with the re-calculated balance of £894.00.

SEVERN TRADING CO.
Bank Reconciliation Statement as at 28 February 19-2

	£
Balance at bank as per cash book	894.00
Add: cheque drawn, not yet recorded on the bank statement	797.55
	1,691.55
Less: amount paid in, not yet recorded on the bank statement	262.30
Balance at bank as per bank statement	1,429.25

In the above example, a statement has been produced which starts with the amended balance from the cash book, and finishes with the bank statement balance, ie the two figures are *reconciled*.

notes:

- *Cheque drawn, not yet recorded on the bank statement* is added back to the cash book balance because, until it is recorded by the bank, the cash book shows a lower balance than the bank statement.

- *Amounts paid in, not yet recorded on the bank statement* are deducted from the cash book balance because, until they are recorded by the bank, the cash book shows a higher balance than the bank statement.

The layout used above starts with the cash book balance and finishes with the bank statement balance. However, there is no reason why it should not commence with the bank statement balance and finish with the cash book balance: with this layout it is necessary to *deduct* cheques drawn, not yet recorded on the bank statement, and to *add* amounts paid in, not yet recorded.

importance of bank reconciliation statements

1. A bank reconciliation statement is important because, in its preparation, the transactions in the bank columns of the cash book are compared with those recorded on the bank statement. In this way, any errors in the cash book or bank statement will be found and can be corrected (or advised to the bank, if the bank statement is wrong).

2. The bank statement is an independent accounting record, therefore it will assist in deterring fraud by providing a means of verifying the cash book balance.

3. Unpresented cheques over six months old – 'stale' cheques – can be identified and written back in the cash book (any cheque dated more than six months' ago will not be paid by the bank).

Chapter Summary

❑ A bank reconciliation statement is used to agree the balance shown by the bank columns of the cash book with that shown by the bank statement.

❑ Certain differences between the two are timing differences. The two main timing differences are:
- cheques drawn, not yet recorded on the bank statement
- amounts paid into the bank, not yet recorded on the bank statement

These differences will be corrected by time and, most probably, will be recorded on the next bank statement.

❑ Certain differences appearing on the bank statement need to be entered in the cash book to bring it up-to-date. These include:

Receipts
- standing order and BACS receipts credited by the bank
- bank giro credit amounts received by the bank
- dividend amounts received by the bank
- interest credited by the bank

Payments
- standing order and direct debit payments
- bank charges and interest
- unpaid cheques debited by the bank

❑ Once prepared, a bank reconciliation statement is proof that the cash book (bank columns) and the bank statement were agreed at a particular date.

Student Activities

29.1 The bank columns of F. Jones' cash book for December 19-5 are as follows:

19-5	Receipts	£	19-5	Payments	£
1 Dec.	Balance	280	9 Dec.	W. Smith	40
12 Dec.	P. Jones	30	13 Dec.	Rent	50
18 Dec.	H. Homer	72	18 Dec.	Wages	85
27 Dec.	J. Hill	13	20 Dec.	B. Kay	20
			31 Dec.	Balance	200
		395			395

He received his bank statement which showed the following transactions for December 19-5:

BANK STATEMENT

19-5		Payments £	Receipts £	Balance £
1 Dec.	Balance			280
12 Dec.	P. Jones		30	310
15 Dec.	W. Smith	40		270
17 Dec.	Rent	50		220
20 Dec.	H. Homer		72	292
23 Dec.	Wages	85		207

You are required to prepare a bank reconciliation statement to agree the cash book figure with the bank statement.

29.2 The bank columns of J. Doyle's cash book for May 19-6 are as follows:

19-6	Receipts	£	19-6	Payments	£
1 May	Balance	300	2 May	P. Stone	28
7 May	Cash	162	14 May	Alpha Ltd.	50
16 May	C. Brewster	89	29 May	E. Deakin	110
24 May	Cash	60			
31 May	Cash	40			

She received her bank statement which showed the following transactions for May 19-6:

BANK STATEMENT

19-6		Payments £	Receipts £	Balance £
1 May	Balance			300
4 May	P. Stone	28		272
7 May	Cash		162	434
10 May	Dividend from investment		63	497
17 May	Standing order - insurance	25		472
17 May	Cheque		89	561
18 May	Alpha Ltd.	50		511
25 May	Cash		60	571
31 May	Bank Charges	10		561

You are required to:
- write the cash book up-to-date at 31 May 19-6
- prepare a bank reconciliation statement at 31 May 19-6

29.3 Malvern Wholesalers requires the bank statement and cash book balances (bank columns) to be reconciled. You are given the following information as at 30 April 19-3:

- the bank columns of the cash book show a balance of £500 in the bank
- a payment of £200 has been recorded as a receipt in the cash book by mistake
- cheques for £120, £150 and £40 have been sent out in payment to various suppliers but have not yet been paid into the bank by those suppliers; they are recorded in the cash book
- a direct debit payment of £45 has been recorded by the bank, but has not yet been entered in the cash book
- a cheque for £500 has been recorded as a receipt in the cash book, but has not yet been paid into the bank account
- bank charges amounting to £20 appear on the bank statement, but have not yet been entered in the cash book
- a bank giro credit from a customer for £150 appears on the bank statement, but has not yet been entered in the cash book
- a cheque for £125 has been returned by the bank marked 'refer to drawer' (i.e. unpaid), but has not been written back in the cash book
- the bank statement shows a closing overdrawn balance of £130

You are required to:

- write the cash book up-to-date at 30 April 19-3
- prepare a bank reconciliation statement at 30 April 19-3

29.4 According to the cash book (bank columns) of a business, the bank balance on 30 April 19-2 was £1,784.20, but the bank statement on that date showed a balance of £1,714.90.

An examination of the cash book and bank statement shows that:

- a bank giro credit of £28.50 received direct by the bank had not been entered in the cash book

- a cheque for £120 received and banked on 17 April 19-2 was unpaid (i.e. 'bounced'), but no entry recording that fact had been made in the cash book

- a standing order (in favour of H.P. Insurance Co.) for £10 paid by the bank had not been entered in the cash book

- £45 paid into the bank on 18 April 19-2 had been entered in the cash book as £54

- cheques totalling £212.60 sent to suppliers and entered in the cash book had not yet been presented for payment to the bank

- remittances from customers totalling £171.40 entered in the cash book and banked on 30 April 19-2 had not yet been credited by the bank

You are required to:

- write the cash book up-to-date at 30 April 19-2
- prepare a bank reconciliation statement at 30 April 19-2

29.5 Explain to a person who has recently joined the firm where you work the reasons why the bank balance, as shown in the cash book, may not agree with that shown by the bank statement. Give examples of each, and distinguish between those that are timing differences, and those that need to be entered in the cash book.

Assignment 8
Cash control: ABC Electrical

LEARNING OUTCOMES COVERED:
Petty cash book, cash book, bank reconciliation statements

SITUATION

You are working in the accounts department of ABC Electrical, a medium-sized electrical contracting firm that undertakes work for a range of private individuals, businesses, and local authorities. The cashier, who is responsible for both the firm's cash book and petty cash book, is away on holiday this week and you have been asked to carry out her work.

The following are the firm's cash/bank and petty cash transactions for the week:

19-1

8 May	Commenced the week with a bank balance of £420.50 and cash in hand of £125.25; the balance of petty cash is £50 (the imprest amount).
8 May	Sent cheque no. 123451 for £200 to Wiring Suppliers.
8 May	Paid £2.25 from petty cash for stationery: voucher no. 85.
8 May	Received a cheque for £138.50 from Bartown District Council.
9 May	Paid £2.80 from petty cash for travel expenses and £3.00 for postages: voucher no. 86.
9 May	Cash received from Mrs. Lewis for £27.50.
9 May	Withdrew £100 in cash from the bank (cheque no. 123452) for use in the business.
10 May	Received a cheque for £208.30 from J. Jones & Co.
10 May	Paid telephone account for £154.27 by cheque no. 123453.
10 May	Paid sundry expenses £1.82 and travel £2.50 from petty cash: voucher no. 87.
10 May	Paid stationery £1.60 and postages £2.00 from petty cash: voucher no. 88.
11 May	Paid wages £360.40 by cheque no. 123454.
11 May	Paid postages £2.68 from petty cash: voucher no. 89.
11 May	Paid Evans Ltd. £127.80 by cheque no. 123455.
11 May	Paid Building Supplies £54.50 in cash.
12 May	Paid £2.06 travel expenses and £1.50 sundry expenses from petty cash: voucher no. 90.
12 May	Received a cheque for £155.00 from Loamshire County Council.
12 May	Paid £1.66 for stationery from petty cash: voucher no. 91.
12 May	Restored petty cash imprest amount by transfer from the main cash book.

Notes:
- all cheques received are banked on the day of receipt
- Value Added Tax is to be ignored

At the end of the week the following bank statement is received:

IN ACCOUNT WITH

National Bank plc

Branch..Bartown................

TITLE OF ACCOUNT.....ABC Electrical........

ACCOUNT NUMBER.....12345678.....................

STATEMENT NUMBER 38

DATE	PARTICULARS	PAYMENTS £	RECEIPTS £	BALANCE £
19-6				
8 May	Balance brought forward			420.50
8 May	Cheque		138.50	559.00
9 May	123452	100.00		459.00
10 May	Cheque		208.30	667.30
11 May	123451	200.00		467.30
11 May	Standing order: Midland Hire Purchase Co.	90.50		376.80
11 May	123454	360.40		16.40
12 May	Bank giro credit: Johnson Bros.		54.20	70.60
12 May	Bank charges	25.00		45.60
12 May	Balance carried forward			45.60

STUDENT TASKS ——————————————————————

1.   Rule up columns for a two-column cash book, and for a petty cash book with analysis columns for stationery, postages, travel and sundries.

2.   Enter the above transactions for the week.

3.   Balance the petty cash book and, at the end of the week, restore the imprest amount to £50 by transfer of the appropriate amount from the cash book.

4.   Using the bank statement, write the cash book (bank columns) up-to-date.

5.   Balance the cash book, and prepare a bank reconciliation statement.

section six
applying information technology

In this section we look at how computer technology can be applied to solve financial problems and to process financial transactions in an organisation.

We look at two areas:
* *using computer accounting packages*
* *using computer spreadsheets*

There is a basic problem in dealing with computer applications in a general financial text of this nature: many different types of computer software are in current use. We have therefore adopted the following approach:

* *Chapter 30 – computer accounting – the use of the popular Sage™ computer software*

* *Chapter 31 – computer spreadsheets – in view of the many different and equally popular programs available, the text is not program specific; readers should therefore consult their training manuals for commands and formulas and not rely completely on the examples in this book*

30 Computer accounting in practice

introduction

This chapter looks at the application of computers to:
* sales ledger
* purchases ledger
* nominal (general) ledger

While the chapter follows the use of Sage™ Book-keeping and Accounting programs, most other accounting programs designed for use with personal computers operate in a similar way.

To work through this chapter you will need:
* a personal computer with either twin floppy disk drives, or a hard disk drive
* a printer
* a computer accounting program, such as Sage 'Book-keeper', 'Accountant', 'Accountant Plus', or 'Financial Controller'

In order to demonstrate the use of computer accounting, we will use the book-keeping transactions of a new business called Computer Shop Ltd.

After each set of transactions, the trial balance is given so that you can check the accuracy of your work as you make progress.

getting started

Firstly you will need to have configured the accounting program to suit the type of computer being used, following the instructions in the manual. When this has been done, the procedures are as follows:

Twin floppy disk drive
* switch on the computer and printer
* insert the operating system disk in the 'A' drive (usually on the left-hand side); press any key
* if necessary, key in the date and time
* the A prompt (A>) will now be showing
* remove the operating system disk and insert the program disk in the 'A' drive, and your own data disk (configured to suit your computer) in the 'B' drive
* key in SAGE (in upper or lower case) and press return

Hard disk drive
- switch on the computer and printer
- at the C prompt (C >) key in SAGE (in upper or lower case) and press return

The business name and address (or College name and address) will appear on the screen. Press return. The date will now appear and can be altered now if you wish. Press return and key in the password: this is set initially as LETMEIN. Press return to take you to the main menu, (other choices may appear, depending on the program you are running).

```
SALES LEDGER
PURCHASE LEDGER
NOMINAL LEDGER
UTILITIES
QUIT
```

Important note: To quit the program, always return to this menu and select [Quit]: by doing this the data files will be correctly updated. Never quit by just switching off or resetting the computer.

situation

Computer Shop Ltd is a new business which has just been set up by its owner, Richard Brown. The business operates from premises in St Nicholas Street, Mereford, where Richard sells computer hardware and software. He buys his stocks of hardware and software on credit terms from a number of suppliers. The business is registered for Value Added Tax.

Richard Brown intends that his main customers are to be the business community in Mereford. To these he must offer credit terms. In order to seek business, he has recently visited a number of firms and schools in the area offering the services of his company on credit terms of a 30 day payment period. A number of these have asked him to open an account for them.

You have just been appointed as an assistant in the shop and Richard Brown has asked you to set up an accounting system using the computer hardware and accounting software available to you.

purchases ledger

Details of suppliers
Richard Brown has arranged to purchase hardware and software on credit from the following:

Supplier's name and address	For your use – account number or short name*
Axis Supplies Ltd Unit 21 Ringway Trading Estate Barchester BR2 9JT	101 or AXIS
Bell Computers Ltd The Old Foundry Clapton-on-Sea CL9 8AJ	102 or BELL

* Note: With the Sage programs, any combination of up to six numbers and/or letters – selected by the user – identify each purchases ledger (and sales ledger) account.

Computer Supplies Ltd 35-40 Granbury Road Leeton LT1 8RZ	103 or COMP
Granta Trading Co Ltd Unit 6 Camside Industrial Estate Cambury CB5 2AQ	104 or GRANTA
Kingsway Technical Ltd 126 The Parade Kingsway Denham DM3 9PQ	105 or KINGS
Pratt and Co Ltd 28 Avon Lane Eveshore MR10 9HP	106 or PRATT

opening accounts in the purchases ledger

- From the main menu, select [Purchase Ledger]; press return.

- From the purchase ledger menu, select [Supplier Details], press return.

- The program will ask you for an account reference – for the first account, key in either the account number, 101, or the short name, AXIS, and press return. (If the account reference has already been used, details of the account will show on the screen.) Press return.

- The program will ask "Is this a new account: No Yes". The cursor will be positioned over the word No; move the cursor to the word Yes by pressing the [→] key, and then press return.

- Now enter the name and address of the supplier. If you make any errors use the arrow keys to move up or down the screen, and make the corrections.

- Ignore other details that could be completed.

- When all the details of the first account have been entered on screen, press [ESC]. The program now asks "Do you want to: Post Edit Abandon" – notice that the cursor is already positioned over Post, which is the default, ie the answer the computer expects. If the details are correct, simply press return and the data files will be updated.

- Repeat the process for the other supplier accounts.

- Return to the main menu by pressing [ESC] twice.

purchases account in the nominal ledger

As Richard Brown's business buys computer hardware and software, it is appropriate to open separate purchases accounts in the nominal ledger for each of these aspects of his business.

Your data disk will already include a standard layout for nominal ledger, with accounts already numbered. The purchases accounts are 5000, 5001, 5002, 5003: we will use the first two numbers for hardware purchases and software purchases respectively. However, we need to name them as such.

- From the main menu, select [Nominal Ledger].

- From the nominal ledger menu, select [Nominal Account Structure], press return; then, select [Account Names] from the sub-menu.

- You are now asked for an account reference: key in 5000.

- Change the account name by keying in Hardware Purchases and press return.

- Press [ESC] and, at the prompt, select Post and press return.
- Repeat the process for account reference 5001, which is to be called Software Purchases.
- To return to the main menu, press [ESC] three times.

using the purchases ledger
Richard Brown's business, Computer Shop Ltd, has the following credit purchases transactions for his first month in business:

Note: All purchases are subject to Value Added Tax. The amounts shown below need the addition of VAT: the program will calculate the amounts and will post them to the VAT account. (This chapter has been worked using aVAT rate of 17½ per cent.)

January
2	Bought software £500 from Axis Supplies Ltd, their invoice no 1341
3	Bought hardware £600 from Bell Computers Ltd, invoice no 1005
5	Bought software £350 from Granta Trading Co Ltd, invoice no T7648
7	Bought software £200 from Pratt and Co Ltd, invoice no A81721
8	Bought hardware £425 from Kingsway Technical Ltd, invoice no 900817
12	Bought software £200 from Axis Supplies Ltd, invoice no 1397
18	Bought hardware £365 from Granta Trading Co Ltd, invoice no T7721
22	Bought software £85 from Computer Supplies Ltd, invoice no 9987
27	Bought software £125 from Pratt & Co Ltd, invoice no A81795

Starting from the main menu, the purchases ledger transactions are entered as follows:
- Select [Purchase Ledger]; press return.
- Select [Batched Data Entry]; press return.
- Select [Purchase Invoices]; press return, and the data entry screen now appears.

data entry screen
- The cursor is in the 'A/C' column; enter the account number or short name of the first account you need. As this is Axis Supplies Ltd, key in 101 or AXIS (depending on how you opened the accounts earlier); press return. Note that the supplier's account name appears at the top of the screen. (Pressing function key F4 – the Search Key – will show on screen a list of the suppliers' accounts.)
- The cursor will have moved automatically to the 'Date' column. Key in the required date, eg 020192 (2 January 1992), or press function key F5 to display the system date.
- The cursor will have moved to the 'Inv' column; key in the supplier's invoice number 1341 (up to six numbers/letters can be entered); press return.
- The cursor will now be under the column 'N/C' – this stands for nominal code and here we must enter the nominal account number involved in the other half of the book-keeping transaction. As it is software that has been bought from Axis Supplies Ltd, the nominal code is 5001; enter this and press return. (Pressing function key F4 will show on screen a list of nominal account codes. The up and down arrow keys – or 'Pg Up' and 'Pg Dn' keys – can be used to move the highlight to the correct account. Return is pressed to accept the selected account.) Note that the name of the nominal account used shows at the top of the screen below the name of the supplier.
- The next column is 'Dep' (department); press return to miss this out.
- In the 'Details' column can be entered Software (in this first transaction), or Hardware. Alternatively, the items on the invoice can be described (in up to 19 characters). Press return.
- In the 'Nett Amt' column enter the amount before VAT: for this first transaction it is £500. Press return.

- In the 'Tc' (tax code) column, key in T1 and press return. VAT will be calculated and displayed at the standard rate – currently 17½ per cent. (Other tax codes available are T0 for zero-rated and T2 for exempt goods.) Function key F9 can also be used to input the T1 tax code. Press return.

- Note that the batch total (top right-hand side of the screen) shows the total (value of goods, plus VAT) of the screen transactions.

- The cursor will now be at the start of the next line and you should enter the other credit purchases of Richard Brown's business.

- When all the other transactions have been entered, ensure that the cursor is on a blank line, and press [ESC]. The prompt "Do you want to: Post Edit Abandon" appears. If all the details are correct, select Post and press return. The data files will now be updated. (If any items need to be edited, move the cursor by using the arrow keys, amend the details, press return, and then move the cursor back to a clear line before pressing [ESC].)

- Press [ESC] to return to the purchase ledger sub-menu

reports

The following reports can be displayed on screen, printed or filed on disk:

- Day book, showing purchases invoices
- Transaction history (for each account) – an asterisk against a money amount indicates that it has not yet been paid
- Account balances (aged) – after the first screen use the [→] key to display the aged balances

Select each in turn and follow the screen prompts. Where the prompt asks for account references or dates, press return. (If the data files were larger than those created so far, we would need to be more selective to avoid being inundated with information.) At the prompt "Display, Print or File" press return for the information to be shown on screen, or enter P for the information to be printed, and press return. (The computer will remind you to switch on the printer).

Do ensure that you print out the day book. When you have finished with reports, press [ESC] twice to return to the main menu.

trial balance

Choose [Nominal Ledger] from the main menu, and then [Trial Balance] which can be displayed on screen, or printed (key in 'P') as follows:

Ref	Account Name	Debit	Credit
2100	CREDITORS CONTROL ACCOUNT		3348.77
2200	TAX CONTROL ACCOUNT	498.77	
5000	HARDWARE PURCHASES	1390.00	
5001	SOFTWARE PURCHASES	1460.00	
		3348.77	3348.77

Note that, instead of showing the balance of the account of each creditor, a total of all suppliers' accounts is shown under the heading *Creditors Control Account*. Control accounts are used where there is a need to show a total for a ledger section. *Tax Control Account* shows the balance of Value Added Tax – the amount of VAT is recorded automatically as each transaction is entered. In the trial balance above, the tax authorities currently owe £498.77 to Richard Brown's company.

sales ledger

details of credit customers

The following customers have asked Richard Brown, the owner of Computer Shop Ltd, to open credit accounts for them:

Customer's name and address and credit limit (decided by Richard Brown)	*For your use – account number or short name**
Able, Baker & Clark Orchard House The Green St Peters Mereford MR3 8AK Credit limit £1000	201 or ABLE
Hitech Trading Co Unit 16 Factory Estate Eveshore MR10 8PW Credit limit £750	202 or HITECH
Jones & Co Ltd 123 High Street Mereford MR1 2DB Credit limit £500	203 or JONES
Sixth Form College Whittington Avenue Mereford MR2 7QH Credit limit £1000	204 or SIXTH
Teleservice 78 Bruton Road Mereford MR2 4PT Credit limit £500	205 or TELE
Wyvern County Council County Hall Eveshore Road Mereford MR4 8AP Credit limit £2500	206 or WCC

* Note: With the Sage programs, any combination of up to six numbers and/or letters – selected by the user – identify each sales ledger (and purchases ledger) account.

opening accounts in the sales ledger

- From the main menu, select [Sales Ledger]; press return.
- From the sales ledger menu, select [Customer Details]; press return.
- Key in the first account number, 201, or the short name, ABLE. Follow the same procedure as with purchase ledger. Remember to key in the credit limit for each customer.
- After the customer details have been entered, return to the main menu by pressing [ESC] twice.

sales account in the nominal ledger

Two separate sales accounts are to be opened in the nominal ledger, one for hardware sales, the other for software sales. Follow the same procedure as for opening purchases accounts. The sales accounts to be opened are numbered:

    4000   Hardware sales

    4001   Software sales

Return to the main menu by pressing [ESC] three times.

using the sales ledger

Richard Brown's business, Computer Shop Ltd, has the following credit sales transactions for his first month in business (all sales are subject to VAT):

January
6	Sold software £100 to Able, Baker & Clark, invoice no 1001
10	Sold software £300 to Teleservice, invoice no 1002
13	Sold hardware £600 to Sixth Form College, invoice no 1003
15	Sold software £125 to Jones & Co Ltd, invoice no 1004
17	Sold hardware £700 to Wyvern County Council, invoice no 1005
20	Sold software £50 to Hitech Trading Co, invoice no 1006
23	Sold software £125 to Teleservice, invoice no 1007
24	Sold hardware £450 to Sixth Form College, invoice no 1008
27	Sold software £130 to Able, Baker & Clark, invoice no 1009

These transactions are entered to the sales ledger in a similar way as purchases are entered in the purchases ledger:

• Select [Sales Ledger] from the main menu; press return.

• Select [Batched Data Entry]; press return.

• Select [Sales Invoices]; press return, and the data entry screen now appears.

• Enter the transactions in a similar way as purchases are entered in the purchases ledger.

• When all transactions have been entered, press [ESC] and, at the prompt, select Post and press return: the data files will now be updated.

• Press [ESC] to return to the sales ledger sub-menu.

reports

The following reports can be displayed on screen, printed or filed on disk:

• Day book, showing sales invoices

• Transaction history (for each account) – an asterisk indicates items that have not yet been paid

• Account balances (aged) – after the first screen use the [→] key to display the aged balances

• Statements

Ensure that you print out the day book.

For sales ledger, an aged analysis of debtor balances is particularly useful as a management report in order to see the amounts owing analysed in terms of 'current, 30 days, 60 days, 90 days, older'. Overdue debts can be identified and action taken to chase for payment.

Statements can be printed on commercially available forms: they can then be dispatched to the customers.

Press [ESC] twice to return to the main menu.

trial balance

Choose [Nominal Ledger] from the main menu, and display or print the trial balance which now appears as:

Ref	Account Name	Debit	Credit
1100	DEBTORS CONTROL ACCOUNT	3031.51	
2100	CREDITORS CONTROL ACCOUNT		3348.77
2200	TAX CONTROL ACCOUNT	47.26	
4000	HARDWARE SALES		1750.00
4001	SOFTWARE SALES		830.00
5000	HARDWARE PURCHASES	1390.00	
5001	SOFTWARE PURCHASES	1460.00	
		5928.77	5928.77

Note that the *Debtors Control Account* totals the individual debtor balances; *Tax Control Account* shows the net balance of Value Added Tax – in the trial balance above, the tax authorities currently owe £47.26 to Richard Brown's company.

recording receipts and payments

All receipts and payments pass through nominal account no 1200 'Bank Account': this is already open in the nominal ledger.

receipts

Richard Brown's business has the following receipts from customers in the first month:

January

15	Received a cheque for £117.50 from Able, Baker & Clark
20	Received a cheque for £352.50 from Teleservice
24	Received a cheque for £400.00 from Sixth Form College
30	Received a cheque for £146.88 from Jones & Co Ltd

These receipts are entered as follows:

- Choose [Sales Ledger] from the main menu, and then [Receipts].

- Press return to accept the nominal code of Bank (account no 1200).

- The data entry screen requires the account reference of the debtor, date of payment, cheque number (press return if not giving a number), and the amount of the cheque.

- The screen now displays the outstanding transactions on the debtors account (or the first ten transactions, if there are more). At the bottom of the screen is asked "Method of Payment: Automatic Manual" with the cursor positioned over the default of Automatic.

automatic allocation

This goes through the transactions in numerical order and pays off outstanding invoices until either the amount of the receipt reaches zero or there are no more invoices to pay off. If there is insufficient money to pay off an invoice in full, the remaining money will be used to partially pay the invoice. Press [ESC] if you are satisfied with the allocations made, and then press return at the prompt "Do you want to: Post Edit Abandon" to post the receipts.

manual allocation

This is selected in order to allocate payment to a particular invoice, either in full or partially. Simply move the cursor up or down by using the arrow keys. Now select one of the four payment options: 'Full, Part, Discount, or Cancel'. If part payment is selected, the amount needs to be keyed in. Once the allocations have been made, press [ESC], and then press return at the prompt "Do you want to: Post Edit Abandon" to post the receipts.

- After posting receipts, return to the main menu by pressing [ESC] twice.

payments

Richard Brown makes the following payments to suppliers in the first month:

January
22	Paid Pratt & Co Ltd a cheque for £235.00, cheque no 860005
27	Paid Axis Supplies Ltd a cheque for £587.50, cheque no 860006
31	Paid Bell Computers Ltd a cheque for £705.00, cheque no 860009

These payments are entered as follows:

- Select [Purchase Ledger] from the main menu, and then [Payments].
- Press return to accept the nominal code of 'Bank'.
- At the data entry screen, follow the same procedure as for receipts (enter the cheque number).
- Choose between either automatic or manual allocation, and post the payments.
- Return to the main menu by pressing [ESC] twice.

trial balance

Choose [Nominal Ledger] from the main menu, and display or print the trial balance which now appears as:

Ref	Account Name	Debit	Credit
1100	DEBTORS CONTROL ACCOUNT	2014.63	
1200	BANK CURRENT ACCOUNT		510.62
2100	CREDITORS CONTROL ACCOUNT		1821.27
2200	TAX CONTROL ACCOUNT	47.26	
4000	HARDWARE SALES		1750.00
4001	SOFTWARE SALES		830.00
5000	HARDWARE PURCHASES	1390.00	
5001	SOFTWARE PURCHASES	1460.00	
		4911.89	4911.89

Note that the bank is overdrawn.

recording returned goods

Most computer accounting systems do not use separate purchases returns and sales returns accounts to record returned goods. Instead, they credit purchases account with purchases returns, and debit sales with sales returns.

purchases returns
Richard Brown's business has the following purchases returns in the first month:

January
20 Returned software to Axis Supplies Ltd for £50, plus VAT, and received a credit note reference CN251
31 Returned hardware to Granta Trading Co Ltd for £120, plus VAT, and received a credit note reference 8524

These are entered as follows:
* Choose [Purchases Ledger] from the main menu, then [Batched Data Entry].
* From the sub-menu, select [Purchase Credit Notes].
* The data entry screen is similar to that for purchases invoices.
* When the entries have been recorded, press [ESC] and post the transactions.
* Press [ESC] three times to return to the main menu.

sales returns
Richard Brown's business has the following sales returns in the first month:

January
24 Wyvern County Council returns hardware £300, plus VAT; credit note no. CN101
27 Hitech Trading Co returns software £50, plus VAT; credit note no. CN102

These are entered as follows:
* Choose [Sales Ledger] from the main menu, then [Batched Data Entry].
* From the sub-menu, select [Sales Credit Notes].
* The data entry screen is similar to that for sales invoices.
* When the entries have been recorded, press [ESC] and post the transactions.
* Press [ESC] twice to return to the main menu.

trial balance
Choose [Nominal Ledger] from the main menu, and display or print the trial balance which now appears as:

Ref	Account Name	Debit	Credit
1100	DEBTORS CONTROL ACCOUNT	1603.38	
1200	BANK CURRENT ACCOUNT		510.62
2100	CREDITORS CONTROL ACCOUNT		1621.52
2200	TAX CONTROL ACCOUNT	78.76	
4000	HARDWARE SALES		1450.00
4001	SOFTWARE SALES		780.00
5000	HARDWARE PURCHASES	1270.00	
5001	SOFTWARE PURCHASES	1410.00	
		4362.14	4362.14

other nominal account transactions

The standard default layout for nominal ledger comprises many accounts which are already numbered. In this section we will enter transactions to expenses accounts, capital and loans, and fixed assets.

expenses

Richard Brown pays the following business expenses by cheque in his first month:

January

10   Paid travelling expenses (nominal account no 7400) £25.00, cheque no 860003

19   Paid staff salaries (account no 7003) £645.00, cheque no 860004

20   Paid stationery (account no 7504) £70.50 *including* VAT (see below), cheque no 860007

31   Paid shop rent (account no 7100) £176.25 *including* VAT (see below), cheque no 860008

The various expenses of the business, eg salaries, rent, electricity, etc do not usually pass through the purchase ledger. They are paid direct by cheque, and so the double-entry book-keeping is:

– *debit* appropriate expense account (with amount excluding VAT, if any)

– *debit* VAT account (with amount of VAT, if any)

– *credit* bank account

To see the nominal ledger accounts which are already open on your data disk:

• From the main menu select [Nominal Ledger], then [Nominal Account Structure], then [Account Names].

• Press function key F4 to see the existing accounts: use the arrow keys – or 'Pg Up' and 'Pg Dn' keys – to move up or down the list.

• Press [ESC] to remove the display.

• Press [ESC] twice to return to the main menu.

Where expenses are paid by cheque, transactions are entered by using the bank payments routine, as follows:

• From the main menu choose [Nominal Ledger], then [Bank Transactions], then [Bank Payments].

• At the data entry screen, press return to accept the nominal account no 1200 for Bank. Enter the nominal account number for the expense and check that the correct account name shows towards the top of the screen.

• Enter the other details: note that the VAT tax code for travelling expenses will be T0 (zero-rated), while that for salaries will be T9 (outside the scope of VAT). With stationery and rent, which are subject to VAT at 17½ per cent, the amount paid *includes* VAT. The program can calculate the VAT amount:

   – enter the amount of the cheque (eg £70.50 for stationery) in the 'Nett Amnt' column

   – enter the tax code in the 'Tc' column, as T1 (or use function key F9)

   – in the 'Tax Amnt' column, press the shift *and* [<] keys (later versions of the program use function key F10 to deduct VAT at the standard rate)

   – the program will deduct tax from the figure in the net column and show the changed net value and amount of VAT

• When the entries have been recorded, press [ESC] and post the transactions.

• Press [ESC] three times to return to the main menu.

Note: Some business expenses may be made through purchase ledger if a creditor's account is opened. For example, a business may have an account open in the name of the local garage to which petrol, servicing and repair costs are credited, with settlement being made at the end of each month.

capital and loans

Richard Brown's business, Computer Shop Ltd, has the following capital and loans transactions:

January

1   Started in business with ordinary share capital (nominal account no 3000) of £10,000, received by cheque

10   Received a loan (account no 2300) of £5,000, by cheque

These are entered through the bank receipts routine, as follows:

* From the main menu choose [Nominal Ledger], then [Bank Transactions], then [Bank Receipts]; press return.

* At the data entry screen, enter the transactions: use the tax code T9 for both ordinary share capital and the loan (both transactions are outside the scope of VAT).

* When the entries have been recorded, press [ESC] and post the transactions.

* Press [ESC] three times to return to the main menu.

fixed assets

Richard Brown's business buys the following fixed assets:

January

4   Bought office equipment (nominal account no 0030) for £2,350 *including* VAT, paying by cheque no 860001

8   Bought a delivery van (nominal account no 0050) for £9,400 *including* VAT, paying by cheque no 860002

These are entered in a similar way to expenses (see previous page) using the bank payments routine. Note that both of these purchases *include* VAT at the standard rate (tax code T1), so use the automatic tax calculation method described in the expenses section above.

trial balance

Choose [Nominal Ledger] from the main menu, and display or print the trial balance which now appears as:

Ref	Account Name	Debit	Credit
0030	OFFICE EQUIPMENT	2000.00	
0050	MOTOR VEHICLES	8000.00	
1100	DEBTORS CONTROL ACCOUNT	1603.38	
1200	BANK CURRENT ACCOUNT	1822.63	
2100	CREDITORS CONTROL ACCOUNT		1621.52
2200	TAX CONTROL ACCOUNT	1865.51	
2300	LOANS		5000.00
3000	ORDINARY SHARES		10000.00
4000	HARDWARE SALES		1450.00
4001	SOFTWARE SALES		780.00
5000	HARDWARE PURCHASES	1270.00	
5001	SOFTWARE PURCHASES	1410.00	
7003	STAFF SALARIES	645.00	
7100	RENT	150.00	
7400	TRAVELLING	25.00	
7504	OFFICE STATIONERY	60.00	
		18851.52	18851.52

If your trial balance fails to agree with that shown on the previous page, choose [Utilities] from the main menu, and then [Audit Trail]. Print out all the transactions for January and 'tick' them off against the transactions in this chapter. Errors can be corrected, as described below.

saving data files to disk

As you worked through the chapter, each time you posted transactions the data files were updated, either on the floppy disk in drive 'B' or on the hard disk. There is no requirement to save data at regular intervals during the processing. However, in a business, it makes good sense to save data at regular intervals throughout the day to a back-up disk. With accounting data, we cannot consider to be correctly posted until it is backed-up on a separate disk.

correction of errors

The audit trail (from the Utilities sub-menu) lists all of the transactions and gives each a reference number. When an error is located from the audit trail, the Utilities sub-menu Data File Utilities provides a Posting Error Corrections routine. Selecting this offers two choices:

• Reverse Posting
• Correct Posting

Reverse posting cancels out an incorrect posting, ie it deletes the effect of the transaction from the book-keeping records. The number of the wrong transaction from the audit trail is entered; the program will then indicate the accounts affected and will ask "Proceed with Correction?: No Yes". If the error correction is proceeded with, a transaction will be recorded on the audit trail. As reverse posting only cancels an incorrect transaction; it will then be necessary to post the correct transaction (which adds another transaction to the audit trail).

Correct posting allows certain details of a previously-posted transaction to be altered, eg account code, date, reference, tax code. The audit trail number of the transaction is entered and, if the transaction exists, the details are displayed on screen. The arrow keys are used to move the cursor to the information that is to be changed. The cursor can only be placed on information which may be changed. Press return. After details have been changed, press [ESC] and return. The program will state the corrective posting to be made and will then ask "Proceed with Correction?: No Yes". This error correction routine will usually add two transactions to the audit trail, depending on the correction carried out. Press [ESC] to return to the main menu.

allocation of credit notes

Credit notes posted to accounts need to be allocated against invoices – at present in the chapter outstanding invoices and credit notes on debtors' and creditors' accounts are indicated with an asterisk.

allocating sales credit notes
• From Sales ledger, choose [Receipts]. Accept the nominal code for Bank by pressing return.
• Enter the debtor's account reference and the date.
• Press return to enter the cheque amount as zero. Transactions on the debtor's account will now be showing on the screen.
• Select Manual allocation of receipts, and press return.
• Select the credit note first and pay it off in full by pressing return; this will cause the cheque balance to increase by the amount of the credit note.

- Now pay off the invoice – either in full or in part – by moving the cursor to it, and pressing return.
- Press [ESC], and then press return at the prompt "Do you want to: Post Edit Abandon" to allocate the credit note.
- Return to the main menu by pressing [ESC] twice.

allocating purchases credit notes
- From Purchases ledger choose [Payments]. Accept the nominal code for Bank by pressing return.
- Enter the creditor's account reference and the date.
- Press return to enter the cheque amount as zero. Transactions on the creditor's account will now be showing on the screen.
- Select Manual allocation of payments and press return.
- Select the credit note first and pay it off in full by pressing return; this will cause the cheque balance to increase by the amount of the credit note.
- Now pay off the invoice – either in full or in part – by moving the cursor to it, and pressing return.
- Press [ESC], and then press return at the prompt "Do you want to: Post Edit Abandon" to allocate the credit note.
- Return to the main menu by pressing [ESC] twice.

Chapter Summary

❏   We have used a computer accounting program to:
- open debtors' accounts in the sales ledger
- open creditors' accounts in the purchases ledger
- enter business transactions in the sales ledger, purchases ledger and nominal ledger

❏   We have seen some of the reports that can be produced:
- day books
- transaction history for each account
- statements of account for debtors
- aged account balances
- trial balance
- audit trail

❏   It has only been possible to look at the main features of computer accounting. It may be that you will wish to investigate other aspects of the program. In addition you may have the opportunity to use other computer accounting programs, eg
- invoicing
- stock control
- payroll

In the next chapter we look at the use of computer spreadsheets in finance.

Assignment 9
Computer accounting: Computer Shop limited

LEARNING OUTCOMES COVERED:
Applying information technology: computer accounting packages

SITUATION

You are the assistant to Richard Brown, the owner of Computer Shop Ltd. You are required to enter the transactions for February into a computer accounting system. Before commencing you must ensure that you have worked through Chapter 30, recording the transactions for January, and ensure that your trial balance agrees with that shown on page 333.

STUDENT TASKS

Starting with your data disk with January's transactions, you are to enter the following transactions of Richard Brown's business for the month of February:

1. Open new accounts in the purchases ledger for:

    • Software Supplies
    Unit 10
    Newtown Trading Estate
    Newtown NT1 7AJ
    Account no 107 or SOFT

    • Trade Tech Ltd
    45-50 The High Road
    Dunton DT4 7AL
    Account no 108 or TRADE

2. • Enter the following credit purchases transactions for the month (all subject to VAT at 17½ per cent):
    February

4	Bought software £150 from Software Supplies, invoice no. AB452
5	Bought hardware £220 from Trade Tech Ltd, invoice no. H3974
7	Bought hardware £550 from Granta Trading Co Ltd, invoice no. T7849
10	Bought software £200 from Axis Supplies Ltd, invoice no. 1529
15	Bought hardware £320 from Kingsway Technical Ltd, invoice no. 901072
18	Bought hardware £525 from Bell Computers Ltd, invoice no. 1149
20	Bought software £110 from Computer Supplies Ltd, invoice no. 10105
23	Bought hardware £610 from Granta Trading Co Ltd, invoice no. T7927
25	Bought software £500 from Software Supplies, invoice no. AB641

    • Print the day book for February, showing purchases invoices (transaction numbers† 38 to 46)
    • Print the trial balance
    † *Note:* transaction numbers referred to assume that no errors/corrections have occurred.

3. Open new accounts in the sales ledger for:

    • Adams & Co
    The Old Rectory
    Church Street
    Eveshore MR8 7PP
    Account no 207 or ADAMS; credit limit £500

    • Stone, Wall Ltd
    Builders Merchants
    Station Yard
    Mereford MR2 1BT
    Account no 208 or STONE; credit limit £750

4. • Enter the following credit sales transactions for the month (all subject to VAT at 17½ per cent):
    February

2	Sold software £350 to Adams & Co, invoice no. 1010
4	Sold hardware £1,100 to Wyvern County Council, invoice no. 1011
5	Sold software £425 to Stone, Wall Ltd, invoice no. 1012
8	Sold hardware £750 to Teleservice, invoice no. 1013

10	Sold hardware £630 to Sixth Form College, invoice no. 1014
12	Sold software £320 to Hitech Trading Co, invoice no. 1015
16	Sold hardware £450 to Sixth Form College, invoice no. 1016
20	Sold software £250 to Able, Baker & Clark, invoice no. 1017
24	Sold hardware £850 to Teleservice, invoice no. 1018

- Print the day book for February, showing sales invoices (transaction numbers† 47 to 55)
- Print the trial balance

† *Note*: transaction numbers referred to assume that no errors have occurred and been corrected.

5. • Enter the following returns for the month (all subject to VAT at 17½ per cent):

February

Purchases returns

18	Returned software to Software Supplies for £50, and received a credit note reference 3219
27	Returned hardware to Kingsway Technical Ltd for £220, and received a credit note reference CN681

Sales returns

20	Sixth Form College returns hardware £400; credit note no. CN103 issued
26	Able, Baker & Clark return software £110; credit note no. CN104 issued

- Print the trial balance

6. • Enter the following receipts and payments for the month of February

Receipts

4	Received a cheque for £152.75 from Able, Baker & Clark
19	Received a cheque for £411.25 from Adams & Co
20	Received a cheque for £100.00 from Teleservice
28	Received a cheque for £1,762.50 from Wyvern County Council

Payments

5	Paid Axis Supplies Ltd a cheque for £176.25, cheque no 860010
10	Paid Kingsway Technical Ltd a cheque for £499.38, cheque no 860013
18	Paid Pratt & Co Ltd a cheque for £146.88, cheque no 860015
28	Paid Computer Supplies Ltd a cheque for £229.13, cheque no 860016

- Print the trial balance

7. • Enter the following nominal account transactions for the month of February

Payments

6	Paid stationery £152.75 *including* VAT, cheque no 860011
10	Paid advertising £293.75 *including* VAT, cheque no 860012
15	Paid travelling expenses £30.00 (zero-rated – use tax code T0), cheque no 860014
28	Paid staff salaries £650.00 (outside the scope of VAT – use tax code T9), cheque no 860017
28	Bought office equipment £587.50 *including* VAT, cheque no 860018

Receipts

15	Received a loan £1,500 (outside the scope of VAT – use tax code T9)

- Print the trial balance. What is the significance of the balance of VAT account?

8. Print out the aged account balances from the sales ledger at 1 March. Which account should be brought to the attention of Richard Brown, the owner of Computer Shop Ltd? What action would you advise him to take?

31 Using computer spreadsheets

introduction

In this chapter we turn to the use of computer spreadsheets which are used to store, manipulate and calculate numerical information. A full explanation of what a spreadsheet *is* can be found in the section which follows.

Because there is a wide variety of different spreadsheet programs currently available, this chapter does not refer to specific computer commands and conventions. The aim is to provide material which can be used with the most popular programs. Readers should refer to the computer training manuals for specific instructions and commands, and should not rely solely on the sample commands given in the text of the chapter.

computer spreadsheets – how they work

what spreadsheets do

If you wanted to carry out a budget calculation – for example working out how much money you have available to spend in a week after you have met all your expenses – you could set it out in column form on a sheet of paper – a *worksheet* – and use a calculator or your brain for the calculations. The budget would look something like this:

Wages		£150
less expenses:		
food and housekeeping	£45	
rent	£50	
petrol	£15	
clothes	£15	
entertainment	£10	
total of expenses		£135
Money left for spending		£15

All you have done is to perform a simple budget: you have added up the expenses (total £135) and have deducted them from your wages (£150) to give the spending money total of £15. Suppose that you then discover that your rent is to be increased. You will have to cross out some of the original figures and do all the calculations again. Suppose you wanted to do the same calculation the following week, but decide that you are not going to spend any money on entertainment – you will have to draw up the figures again and recalculate the totals. In short the process involving paper and calculator takes time and involves much crossing out and recalculation.

A computer spreadsheet is specifically designed to speed up tasks of this type, and can be used by the individual for personal finance, or by organisations. *A spreadsheet is a calculation worksheet displayed on the computer screen.* Once you have input the figures and given the instructions for the calculations, the spreadsheet carries them out on the screen. You can change the figures and the totals will be re-calculated automatically. Spreadsheets are used for a wide variety of tasks by organisations: projecting budgets (estimating income and expenditure), maintaining financial records, and keeping track of the bank account.

Before we examine how to enter the figures in a spreadsheet to carry out calculations we will first look at how a spreadsheet is set out on the computer screen.

the spreadsheet on the screen

If you want to access a spreadsheet on your computer screen you will either load a specific program (from hard or floppy disk) or load a spreadsheet option from an integrated package. You will then access a spreadsheet file; this may either be a new file (the equivalent of a blank piece of paper ready for calculations) or it may be an existing file set up to perform a specific calculation. Whatever the case, the format of the screen will always be the same. Look at the example below.

	A	B	C	D	E	F
1						
2						
3						
4						
5						
6						
7						
8						
9						
10						
11						
12						

a new spreadsheet file as it appears on the screen

A new spreadsheet file is set out as a series of blank boxes in rows and columns into which data can be entered. The terms used in this 'grid' layout are as follows:

rows   each horizontal *row* is given a *number* (shown in the left margin)

columns   each vertical *column* is given a *letter* (shown at the top of the screen)

cells   each box is known as a *cell* and is used for entering data; the location or 'reference' of each cell is determined by its column (letter) and row (number), for example A1, B2, C3 and so on . . .

The screen shows only a limited number of cells, often 20 rows and 8 columns. In fact a typical spreadsheet file can provide over 4,000 rows and over 250 columns. As there are only 26 letters in the alphabet, columns after the letter Z are given a two letter reference: AA, AB, AC, AD, AE, and so on. You can move around the spreadsheet file by using the 'cursor' keys or by inputting a specific command indicating the reference (eg F6) of the cell to which you wish to move the cursor.

The illustration below shows a spreadsheet file into which data has been entered. The calculation is the expected sales income and expenses (budget) for Electra Limited, a business. The principle behind the calculation is exactly the same as that of the personal budget on page 338.

	A	B	C	D	E
1	ELECTRA LTD				
2	Budget for Jan-March				
3		January	February	March	Totals
4	Sales	10000	10000	10000	30000
5					
6	Expenses:				
7	Purchases	5000	7500	2500	15000
8	Wages	1000	1000	1000	3000
9	Overheads	750	500	750	2000
10	Total expenses	6750	9000	4250	20000
11	Profit	3250	1000	5750	10000
12					

a completed spreadsheet file as it appears on the screen

entering data into the cells - labels values and formulas

The cells of the completed spreadsheet contain different types of data – labels, values and formulas. We will deal with each of these in turn by looking at columns A and B. Later we will deal in a worked example with the technicalities of input, ie which keys and commands to use. In the descriptions below we concentrate on what labels, values and formulas actually *are* and *do*.

labels

A *label* is a piece of *text* input into a spreadsheet cell, ie a word or a phrase. A label does not *normally* contain any numerical information, except where it is used for the purposes of illustration, eg a year '1992' or '1993'. A label is used to explain what appears in the row or column to which it applies. Your computer program may enable you to print a label in **bold type** or <u>underlined type</u> for emphasis. Column A is made up entirely of labels:

cell A1　　　　　the title **ELECTRA LTD**
cell A2　　　　　the subtitle **Budget for Jan-March**
cell A3　　　　　the descriptions of the figures in each row, eg Sales

Column B has one label – the name of the month in question: January (B3)

values

A *value* is a *number* which is input into a spreadsheet cell. Column B contains the following values which will have been input (note the column/row reference used for each cell):

cell B4　　　　　10000 (money received from Sales for the month)
cell B7　　　　　5000 (money spent on Purchases for the month)
cell B8　　　　　1000 (wages for the month)
cell B9　　　　　　750 (other standard expenses for the month)

Note that B10 and B11 are *not* values, but are totals calculated from the values by means of formulas, which we will examine next.

formulas

A *formula* is an equation input on the computer keyboard into a spreadsheet cell. It automatically performs a calculation on the value cells which you specify in the equation, and displays the result in the formula cell.

The cell B10 on the previous page is the total of B7+B8+B9. The equation input on the computer keyboard at cell B10 is

$=B7+B8+B9$.

The cell B11 is B4 *less* B10. The equation input at cell B11 is

$=B4-B10$

Note that:
- the formula starts with the 'equals' sign: = (see the note below)
- the formula specifies the cells which are to be used in the calculation
- most programs include other useful arithmetic functions which can be entered into a formula, eg multiplication, division, percentages and averages of value cells
- if the figures in the value cells are changed, the result shown in the formula cell will automatically change

In the worked example which follows we look in detail at the way in which a spreadsheet is set up.

> NOTE: BEFORE READING ANY FURTHER, CHECK THE FORMULA COMMANDS FOR YOUR OWN PROGRAM – THEY MAY DIFFER FROM THOSE SHOWN IN THE WORKED EXAMPLE BELOW.

setting up the spreadsheet - a worked example

In the following pages we will

- plan a spreadsheet
- set up a spreadsheet
- input data into a spreadsheet
- save and back up the data
- print the spreadsheet
- produce a chart from the spreadsheet

the task

You work for Western Audio Limited, a small hi-fi company which concentrates on selling British audio equipment. The owner, Mike Hendry, has been asked by the bank (whom he is approaching for a loan) to prepare some profit projections for the first three months of the year. He gives you some figures on a rough piece of paper and asks you to enter them into a computer spreadsheet so that they can be printed out in presentable form for the bank. The calculation will be

Sales for the month less all expenses for the month equals profit for the month

The piece of paper is shown on the next page.

> *Projected sales for January £35,000, Feb £35,000, March £45,000.*
> *Purchases £20,000 (Jan), £20,000 (Feb), £30,000 (March)*
> *Wages £3,000 per month, rent and rates £1,000 per month, other*
> *expenses £4,000 (Jan), £5,000 (Feb), £6,000 (March).*
> *Please work out the profit per month (i.e. sales less all expenses) and*
> *also the totals for the three month period*

step 1 – work out a plan on paper

It is useful first to plan out the format in rough on paper – ie the headings and columns – before keying any data into the computer. In this case the descriptions, the monthly figures and the totals can be entered in separate columns. A suggested plan is set out below.

WESTERN AUDIO LIMITED
Profit Projections for January - March 199-

	Jan	Feb	Mar	Totals
Sales	35,000	35,000	45,000	
Purchases	20,000	20,000	30,000	
Wages	3,000	3,000	3,000	
Rent & rates	1,000	1,000	1,000	
Other expenses	4,000	5,000	6,000	____
Total expenses	____	____	____	____
Profit	____	____	____	____

Note from this worksheet plan that
- you have given the worksheet a *title* – the name of the organisation
- you have given the worksheet a *subtitle* – 'Profit projections for January – March 199-'
- no calculations have been carried out – this will be the job of the computer

step 2 – open a new file

Load the spreadsheet program, either from a hard disk or from a floppy disk, and open a 'New' file and name it according to the organisation's convention. You might call this file 'Profit Forecast'. You will see on the screen a blank set of cells similar to that shown on page 339.

step 3 – entering text: title and subtitle

entering text

To enter text into the spreadsheet you will need to select the cell where you want the entry to appear. You will do this by using the keyboard cursor keys or by using a mouse to point to the cell.

As you type the text on the keyboard, the letters appear in a display box at the top (or the bottom) of the screen. When you have finished typing the text for the cell, check your text and correct any errors (as you would on a word processor). If you are happy with the result, you press the ENTER key; this will then transfer the text from the display box permanently into the cell, and you are now ready to move to another cell.

Note: we will abbreviate the ENTER key to [E]

enter the title
• select cell A1 and type in WESTERN AUDIO LIMITED [E]

enter the subtitle
• select cell A2 and type: Profit Projections for January-March 199- [E]

step 4 – enter column and row headings
column headings
The column headings are the names of the months and the word 'Totals'. Row 3 is best left blank so that the title and subtitle are shown as being separate from the rest of the input. The input is therefore in Row 4:
• select cell B4 and type: January [E]
• select cell C4 and type: February [E]
• select cell D4 and type: March [E]
• select cell E4 and type: Totals [E]

row headings
The row headings are the income and expense items, and are all in column A
• select cell A5 and type: Sales [E]
• select cell A7 and type: Purchases [E] (row 6 will be kept blank)
• select cell A8 and type: Wages [E]
• select cell A9 and type: Rent & rates [E]
• select cell A10 and type: Other expenses [E]
• select cell A11 and type: Total expenses [E]
• select cell A13 and type: Profit [E] (row 12 is left blank)

You now have all the headings (labels) entered into the spreadsheet. One problem which immediately occurs is the *width* of the columns. The cells are not wide enough for some of the text. We will deal with how to widen columns in the next step.

step 5 – adjusting column widths
All columns in a most spreadsheet programs are nine or ten characters wide, unless you change their width. If you exceed this number, as in the title of the spreadsheet WESTERN AUDIO LIMITED, the text will continue in the next cell to the right of the selected cell if it is empty.

In rows 1 and 2 of the example there is no problem because there is no other text apart from the title and subtitle input in column A. There will however be a problem with some of the other labels in column A (eg 'Other expenses') because column B is needed for numbers.

How do you widen a column? Enter the appropriate command (known as Column Width Set on most programs) and enter the number of characters you require for the width - in this case 15 characters.

step 6 – entering the numbers

To enter numbers (values) into a spreadsheet you should select the required cell, type the numbers required (they will appear in the display box and the cell) and press ENTER to confirm the entry in each case. It is recommended that you input the numbers by proceeding along a row at a time. If the number is the same each month (as it is for Wages) most programs will have the facility for selecting a range of cells – here B8 to D8 for example – and 'filling' them with the same number. Check your computer manual.

You now have all the numerical information ready for the input of the *formulas* for performing the calculations.

step 7 – entering the formulas

To input a formula you should move to the cell where the result is to be shown and type the appropriate command (check your manual) which will tell the program that a formula will follow. We will use the equals sign (=) here for illustrative purposes. The equals sign and the formula will be shown in the display box. When the ENTER key is pressed the formula will activate and *the result of the calculation will be displayed in the selected cell*. A formula will perform a calculation on specified value cells. For example, the following formula adds together all the value cells from B7 to B10

=B7+B8+B9+B10

Most programs will offer the facility of adding a range of cells by the use of a command such as SUM followed by the range of cells in brackets, eg SUM (B7.B10). Check your computer manual for the appropriate command to use.

The formulas for the Western Audio Limited spreadsheet are shown below in the appropriate cells. The spreadsheet will not normally show the formulas in this way, although they can be shown when an appropriate command is given. They are shown here so that you can use them as a guide for input.

	A	B	C	D	E
1	WESTERN AUDIO LIMITED				
2	Profit Projections for January-March 199-				
3					
4		January	February	March	Totals
5	Sales	35000	35000	45000	=B5+C5+D5
6					
7	Purchases	20000	20000	30000	=B7+C7+D7
8	Wages	3000	3000	3000	=B8+C8+D8
9	Rent & rates	1000	1000	1000	=B9+C9+D9
10	Other expenses	4000	5000	6000	=B10+C10+D10
11	Total expenses	=B7+B8+B9+B10	=C7+C8+C9+C10	=D7+D8+D9+D10	=E7+E8+E9+E10
12					
13	Profit	=B5-B11	=C5-C11	=D5-D11	=E5-E11

formulas to be input into the spreadsheet

copying formulas

When you are inputting the formulas set out above you will see that the formulas on row 11 are identical except for the column reference letter. Most programs will allow you to copy a formula in a cell (usually a simple command) and then transfer the formula to other cells.

step 8 – the finishing touches

Look at the finished spreadsheet set out below and check your figures. You will also see that lines have been inserted, figures justified (lined up) to the right hand side of the columns, and some text printed in bold type. Check your manual to see if your program enables you to carry out these finishing touches.

	A	B	C	D	E
1	WESTERN AUDIO LIMITED				
2	Profit Projections for January-March 199-				
3					
4		January	February	March	Totals
5	Sales	35000	35000	45000	115000
6					
7	Purchases	20000	20000	30000	70000
8	Wages	3000	3000	3000	9000
9	Rent & rates	1000	1000	1000	3000
10	Other expenses	4000	5000	6000	15000
11	Total expenses	28000	29000	40000	97000
12					
13	Profit	7000	6000	5000	18000

step 9 – saving the spreadsheet

You will need to save the spreadsheet. If you are working in a business and have a hard disk the file should be saved to the hard disk and backed up on a floppy disk. If you are working in a College network you should save onto a floppy.

step 10 – printing the spreadsheet

You will want the finished spreadsheet to look presentable when printed. The Western Audio Limited spreadsheet is a simple single sheet printout. Other spreadsheets may be more complex and cover a number of pages. Whatever type of printer you use, take care with page breaks and margins.

step 11 – charting the spreadsheet

Most spreadsheet programs have a *charting* option which enables you to select numeric data from the spreadsheet and display them in graph or chart form. The bar chart shown on the next page was produced from the Western Audio Limited spreadsheet, and shows the projected sales (Row 5) and projected profit (Row 13). The chart shows clearly that sales should increase, but the profit will decline. Consult your computer manual to see how your spreadsheet program produces charts.

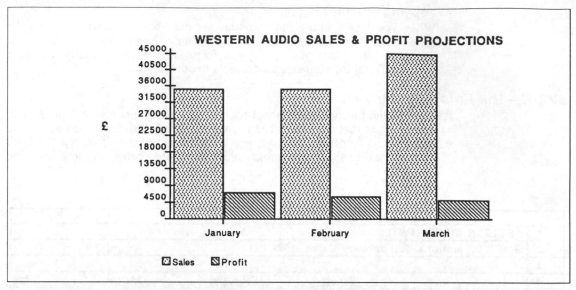

a bar chart produced by the spreadsheet charting function

Chapter Summary

❑ A spreadsheet is a calculation worksheet set out on the computer screen

❑ The worksheet is composed of cells set out in rows (given numbers) and columns (given letters)

❑ Each cell can be used for
   • a label (text)
   • a value (a number)
   • a formula (an instruction to carry out calculations on given cells)

❑ The major advantages of spreadsheets include
   • speed of recalculation if a figure is changed
   • complete accuracy – provided the input is accurate
   • job satisfaction – spreadsheets take the hard work out of complex calculations
   • presentation – the finished product looks neat, and the charting facilities are helpful

❑ Common uses for spreadsheets include
   • profit projections and budgets (including cash flow forecasts)
   • sales analyses
   • Net Present Value calculations

---

a note on student activities

no specific Student Activities are included here as they are integrated into the Activities and Assignments set throughout the book

index